CREATIVE GLUT

CREATIVE GLUT

Selected Essays of

KARL SHAPIRO

EDITED WITH AN INTRODUCTION BY

Robert Phillips

IVAN R. DEE

Chicago

To the memory of

Sophie Wilkins Shapiro

Library of Congress Cataloging-in-Publication Data:
Shapiro, Karl Jay, 1913–2000
    Creative glut : selected essays of Karl Shapiro / edited with an introduction
  by Robert Phillips.
       p. cm.
    Includes bibliographical references and index.
    ISBN 1-56663-556-X (cloth : alk. paper) — ISBN 1-56663-557-8 (pbk. :
  alk. paper)
     1. Poetry. I. Phillips, Robert, 1938– II. Title.

PS3537.H27A6 2004
811'.52—dc22   2003061924

CONTENTS

INTRODUCTION

℟ ONCE UPON A TIME there was an entire generation of American poet-critics: Jarrell, Berryman, Schwartz, Blackmur, Warren, Winters, Ransom, Tate, Bogan, Deutsch, Eliot, Auden, Zaturenska, Gregory, and more. Today most professional criticism is done, instead, by professors (Helen Vendler) and by journalists (Michiko Kakutani and Janet Maslin, to name two of the better known). There are of course some exceptions, including Robert Hass, Richard Howard, Robert Pinsky, and the redoubtable William Logan.

Among the earlier generation of poet-critics, Karl Shapiro thought Jarrell the most brilliant, but I could argue Shapiro himself was. He was recognized at an early age. Born in Baltimore in 1913, he was educated at the University of Virginia and Johns Hopkins University, though he never took a degree. His first substantial group of poems appeared in *Five Young American Poets*, published by New Directions in 1941, when he was twenty-eight. His first full-length collection, *Person, Place and Thing*, appeared the next year while he was serving in the U.S. army in New Guinea. He wrote three books of poems while in the service, sending the typescripts to his fiancée in the States, including *V-Letter and Other Poems*, which won the 1945 Pulitzer Prize, and *Essay on Rime* (1945), a treatise on verse in 2,072 decasyllabic lines which he composed in three months. It has since influenced such diverse poets as Czeslaw Milosz and John Updike.

Released from the service in 1946, Shapiro returned to the States and found himself a celebrity as the poet-soldier. He was named consultant in poetry to the Library of Congress (the post now called poet laureate). He won the Shelley Memorial Award and honorary membership to Phi Beta Kappa at Harvard University. In 1950 he was appointed editor of *Poetry* magazine in Chicago. He won two

Guggenheim Fellowships and in 1956 became editor of *Prairie Schooner* at the University of Nebraska. In 1959 he was elected to membership in the National Institute of Arts and Letters.

In addition to the Pulitzer, his other awards included the Bollingen Prize for Poetry (1969). He published fourteen books of poetry, four books of essays, a novel, two books of autobiography, four books on prosody, and several plays. Shapiro died in New York City in 2000 at the age of eighty-six.

Certainly Shapiro was original and outspoken. In an age when T. S. Eliot was the leading poet and the leading arbiter of poetic taste, Shapiro alone said that the emperor had no clothes, that Eliot was not only a failed theologian but also a failed poet. Shapiro even went so far as to declare *The Waste Land*, that *vade mecum* of modern literature, "a jumble of sacred and profane myths, adding up to nothing." When Shapiro delivered his Eliot essay as a talk at the University of Cincinnati in 1959, he later reported that half the audience walked out. Such was the tenor of the times, or, as Shapiro might have quipped, the tenure of the times. He was always eager to criticize academia, though he himself taught at Johns Hopkins, Nebraska, and the University of California at Davis.

He was equally outspoken about Ezra Pound, that other poetry kingpin of the 1930s and '40s. Shapiro was part of the committee responsible for awarding the first Bollingen Prize for Poetry. Originally it was to go to Pound for his *Pisan Cantos* (1948). Shapiro had acquiesced, arguing that giving the prize to Pound was a statement that poetry should be above considerations of politics. A day later Shapiro changed his mind, declaring that, as a Jew, he could not agree to award the prize to an anti-Semite. In his *Paris Review* interview (1986), Shapiro called that decision the turning point of his life. "It was a great blow to me, the publicity and the scandal. I was suddenly forced into a conscious decision to stand up and be counted as a Jew." Afterward, in 1958, he collected all his poems on Jewish themes and titled it *Poems of a Jew*. In his Introduction he wrote, "The poems here were written over a long period of time and are extracted from volumes which have nothing to do with the present theme. But the undercurrent of most of my poems is the theme of the Jew, and for this reason I collected these examples now as a separate presentation." In my copy of the book he inscribed, "This strange book is in many ways my most characteristic."

It makes sense to read Shapiro's essays on Eliot and Pound in tandem, because it was Eliot who created Pound. Further, both Eliot and Pound wrote unpleasantly about Jews. In the Pound essay Shapiro continues to flail away at Eliot, calling him a more dangerous element in society than Pound, and declaring that Eliot knew nothing about versification. On the subject of Pound he is equally withering: "The *Cantos* are a series of experiments that failed"; "The poems in *Personae* (1909) are nearly all bad ...."; "Pound uses more archaisms than the Poet Laureate of Florida." This is not only fresh criticism, it is fun to read. Shapiro continued to hold Whitman as the only American poet worthy of the term *greatness*.

The British generally fare better with Shapiro. Though he is dismissive of Donne, he calls Yeats "a poet of true genius and not a mere opportunist" [like Pound and Eliot], "but he's off to make a sociological ass of himself all the same." Shapiro approved of Wilfred Owen's ingenious slant-rhymes, while Auden he found lacking for a failure to find a personal form or poetic direction. He accuses the latter of overintellectualizing his poems at the expense of narrative. On the other hand, Shapiro admires Auden's poems for their charm and for their modernization of diction, "the enlarging of dictional language to permit a more contemporary-sounding speech." Shapiro could have gone beyond diction to point to Auden's subject matter. Auden brought the age of mechanization into English-language poetry, writing on business managers and airports and even bathrooms. He was acutely aware of science, as in the famous chorus from his "In Memory of W. B. Yeats,"

> What instruments we have agree
> the day of his death was a dark cold day.

Shapiro learned a lot from Auden's poetry. As Louis D. Rubin, Jr., wrote recently in the *Sewanee Review*, Shapiro's strength as a poet "had come from his ability to invest the objects and emotions of middle-class American experience with the language and dignity of poetry." Clearly Shapiro took note of Auden's subject matter. His poems "Auto Wreck," "Drug Store," "Air Liner," "Manhole Covers," and the like might not have been conceived without Auden's examples of the commonplace. He also seems to have learned from Auden's impeccable prosody. No twentieth-century American poet came to know more about prosody than Shapiro. He attributes this, in his *Paris Review* interview, to working in a large Baltimore library: "Nobody ever read prosody books except me." He published three prose books on the subject, plus his *Essay on Rime* in verse.

Little has been noted about Shapiro's indebtedness to Dylan Thomas. In these essays Thomas comes off less scathed than other modernists, and certain of Shapiro's works, like Poem 69 of *The Bourgeois Poet* ("They held a celebration for you, Charles, in Iowa"), moving between "sexual revulsion and sexual ecstasy," can be read as Thomasian. Even more so is an early Shapiro poem like "Buick." The subject matter might be linked to Auden, but the language seems written in the delirium of Thomas, with an excited richness of language and regular metrical beat. Notice especially Shapiro's assonance and alliteration:

> As a sloop with a sweep of immaculate wing on her delicate spine
> And a keel as sleek as a root that holds in the sea as she leans,
> Leaning and laughing, my warm-hearted beauty, you ride, you
> ride . . .

Shapiro published that in 1942. Thomas's first book appeared in 1934.

Compare the energy of Shapiro's lines with the following, chosen at random, from Thomas:

> If I were tickled by the rub of love,
> a rooking girl who stole me for her side,
> Broke through her straws, breaking my bandaged string.
> If the red tickle as the cattle calve . . .

Shapiro admired Thomas's distinctive idiom, his lyricism, and his total independence from the school of Eliot and Pound. Perhaps that independence is why Shapiro is so effective in his Thomas essay. He calls Thomas a genius and praises him for restoring poetry to an audience that had been deprived of real poetry for fifty years. He claims that at least thirty of Thomas's poems will stand with the best of our time, and he tells us which they are. This is a rare act of literary generosity on Shapiro's part.

William Carlos Williams was a different story. What Shapiro admired in Williams was the spontaneity and immediacy of experience. It was the opposite of the poetry of "culture" as in Eliot and Pound (those two whipping boys again). Dr. Williams, a pediatrician in New Jersey, he saw as "an authority and a savior and a cop, a force in the little town." The single work of Williams's of which Shapiro disapproved was *Paterson*, his one attempt at a culture poem, which Shapiro calls "his large bad poem." Shapiro felt that, in a way, Williams was "our first American poet since Whitman." Here Shapiro's admiration is more difficult to explain than his admiration for Thomas. Shapiro was dedicated to formal poetry (except when he wrote the poems of *The Bourgeois Poet* and a few early prose poems) whereas Williams's poetry is always seemingly offhand, almost tossed off. (Making fun of Gertrude Stein, Delmore Schwartz proclaimed, "You are all a tossed generation.") Shapiro's extended discussion of Williams's versification is valuable, as is his perception of Williams's evocation of American poetry out of nothing. And of course both Williams and Shapiro thought Eliot a disastrous influence on American poetry, as did Horace Gregory.

Another free-verse and spontaneous poet of the people who Shapiro finally approved was Carl Sandburg. In his long essay "A *Malebolge* of Fourteen Hundred Books" (not included here), he even forgave Sandburg's apostasy to showbiz, which is at war with Shapiro's hatred of pretension. (Sandburg had taken to appearing on the "Johnny Carson Show" with his banjo.) I remember one evening Sandburg shuffling onstage with his white bangs and Carson saying, "What do you want to talk about, Mr. Sandburg?" The poet replied, "Let's talk about semen. I understand they're doing marvelous things with it these days." For once Carson seemed nonplussed.

It is not my intention to march through all twenty of these essays. I want to save many discoveries for the reader. Shapiro does appear to have preferred poets and writers with what he called "the cosmic individualism" of Whitman, Rimbaud, Rilke, and Henry Miller to that of intellectuals. In his essay on Miller, he amusingly calls the writer "Gandhi with a penis." By this he means he regards Miller as a holy man and not a pornographer. Shapiro's defense of *Tropic of Cancer* helped lift the ban on that book in this country and has been reprinted in every edition since.

There are also some general cultural essays included here, notably "To Abolish Children" and "To Revive Anarchism." The former includes a seven-step program "to slow down or stop the strangulation of American life by children"; the latter concludes that "modern competitive society is incapable of keeping the peace." These might have been written by Jonathan Swift or the later Mark Twain. In his note "To the Reader" in his first essay collection, Shapiro wrote, "I make no apologies for the excesses of style and the extreme opinion in this book. Against the hollow, impersonal voices of the official literati we must raise the sound of the living human voice. Only in this way can we restore the prerogatives of judgment to the reader and the right to create as he will to the poet." This echoes the strains of moral judgment, social revolution, contempt for pretense, and satire found in some of Shapiro's strongest poems, such as the celebrated "University," which begins,

> To hurt the Negro and avoid the Jew
> Is the curriculum . . .

Or this, Poem 79 from *The Bourgeois Poet*:

> The term *generation* is a deadly weapon. When a poet says, "my generation," move off a few feet. He probably has a switch-blade knife up his sleeve, and it's for "my" generation. . . .

A word about Shapiro's stands in this book. When he wrote most of these essays, English departments and critics paid obeisance to *the* tradition of Modern Poetry, meaning Pound, Eliot, and Yeats. Since then we have moved into postmodernism, a label generally given to literature since the 1960s, which usually means work in free verse and free of classical and historical allusion. Shapiro himself made the leap into postmodernism with *The Bourgeois Poet* (1964), writing confessional poems without rhyme or versification. (But he retreated back into modernism with his next book, *White-Haired Lover* (1968), in which he generally returned to the traditional verse forms he had abandoned.)

Historically, next came theorism, including deconstruction, post-structuralism, the new historicism, queer theory, and God knows what all. Because Shapiro published his final book of essays in 1975, we don't have his fulminations on these developments in the academy. But we have his epigraph to *In Defense of Ignorance*: "Everything we are taught is false." I'm sure he would stand by that even today.

Not all the critics were in love with all of Shapiro's ideas in his essays. The poet Hayden Carruth, writing of *In Defense of Ignorance* in *The New Republic*, was of two minds: "Karl Shapiro has written an animated, corrupt, repetitious, illogical, necessary, and dangerous book. He has written it in defense of the indefensible—ignorance—and he has given it a shrill and ranting tone which will affront a good many readers. But perhaps this is necessary, because what Shapiro has done, very courageously, is to throw open the whole plight of American poetry at the present time; and although there has been a good deal of sniping and bitching among coterie poets in recent years, he is the first prominent poet to have attempted it."

The critic Alfred Kazin, writing in *The Reporter*, also had reservations about the book, but concluded, "There is no better critic than a professional judging in his own field. Much of what Shapiro has to say about particular works by Eliot and Pound seems to me absolutely first-rate. His criticisms of Auden are cruelly shrewd."

Here then, for a new generation to judge, are Shapiro's most important essays. As the estimable Joseph Epstein has put it, "Karl Shapiro wrote the best poems he could, and his best were extraordinarily good; and in prose he never wrote anything he didn't believe, a practice not many poets have been able, or appear even to try, to maintain. He plied his craft with the honor that only complete integrity brings."

—ROBERT PHILLIPS

ACKNOWLEDGMENTS

Thanks to Adam Muhlig for the index. These essays appeared originally in *Beyond Criticism* (Lincoln: University of Nebraska Press, 1953); *In Defense of Ignorance* (New York: Random House, 1960); *To Abolish Children* (Chicago:

Quadrangle Books, 1968); and *The Poetry Wreck* (New York: Random House, 1975).

REFERENCES

Hayden Carruth, "In Defense of Karl Shapiro," *The New Republic*, 142 (June 20, 1960), 19–20. Reprinted in *Working Papers: Selected Essays and Reviews by Hayden Carruth*, ed. by Judith Weissman (Athens: University of Georgia Press, 1982), 33–36.

Babette Deutsch, *Poetry in Our Time*, revised and enlarged edition (New York: Doubleday, 1963), 416–419.

Joseph Epstein, "The Return of Karl Shapiro: The Library of America Freshens Old Laurels," *The Weekly Standard*, May 12, 2003.

Alfred Kazin, "The Poet Against the English Department," *The Reporter*, June 9, 1960. Reprinted in *Contemporaries* (Boston: Little, Brown, 1962), 489–493.

Ralph J. Mills, Jr., *Contemporary American Poetry* (New York: Random House, 1965), 101–121.

Robert Phillips, "Karl Shapiro: The Art of Poetry, XXXVI," *Paris Review*, 99 (Spring 1986), 182–216. Reprinted in *The Madness of Art: Interviews with Poets and Writers* (Syracuse: Syracuse University Press, 2003), 49–74.

Louis D. Rubin, Jr., "Karl Shapiro, 1913–2000: He Took His Stands," *Sewanee Review*, CIX, 1 (Winter 2001), 108–119.

Stephen Stepanchev, *American Poetry Since 1945: A Critical Study* (New York: Harper & Row, 1967), 53–68.

John Updike, "Introduction," *Karl Shapiro: Selected Poems* (New York: Library of America, 2003), xvii–xxxi.

CREATIVE GLUT

I

POETS AND WRITERS

T. S. ELIOT:
THE DEATH OF
LITERARY JUDGMENT

¶ THERE IS NO passable essay on Eliot at this time (about A.D. 1960) and little chance of there being one. As far as the literary situation goes, nothing could be more useful today, but the literary situation has seen to it that this essay does not exist. The very idea of a summary of Eliot's writings seems a kind of blasphemy, or an act of unpardonable rudeness. For the Literary Situation (whatever that ecclesiastical expression is supposed to mean) is largely Eliot's invention, and for that reason it is all but impossible to discuss. Eliot is untouchable; he is Modern Literature incarnate and an institution unto himself. One is permitted to disagree with him on a point here or a doctrine there, but no more. The enemy at Eliot's gate—practically everybody—searches his citadel for an opening and cannot find one. Eliot has long since anticipated every move; he and his men can prevent ingress or exit. Eliot resembles one of those mighty castles in Bavaria which are remarkably visible, famed for their unsightliness, and too expensive to tear down. Life goes on at the bottom; but *it* is always up there.

The question of Eliot as the chief obstacle to poetry today may not be a real question; it may be precisely the kind of imaginary question which Eliot himself brings up in his writing. Insofar as one tries to deal with it, he is simply playing Eliot's game, with all the odds against him. I do not myself consider the question real, but I know of no way to discuss the ultimate value of Eliot's work without first discussing the exploits of his straw men. Eliot's reputation and the antagonism to it may both be false. I propose in this essay to show both

5

the reputation and the opposition to it in another light. That there is
something of value in Eliot's poetry and Eliot's criticism is quite possible, even from my pessimistic point of view; though the valuable
portion is miniscule and is much different from what has been supposed.

Eliot is both the hero and the victim of a historical predicament.
And he himself is as much the author of that predicament as "history"
itself. Eliot created a literary situation deliberately; he and his "situation" are fabrications, and very plausible fabrications at that. In other
words, Eliot invented a Modern World which exists only in his version of it; this world is populated by Eliot's followers and is not a reality. The Eliot population consists of a handful of critics and
professors and a few writers of Eliot's generation, though one would
think, reading modern criticism and teaching from modern literary
textbooks, that there really is a kingdom of Modern Poetry in which
T. S. Eliot is the absolute monarch and Archbishop of Canterbury in
one.

You will be thinking that I am using metaphorical language and
am attempting to work up a nice critical discussion, the subject of
which is the overestimation of T. S. Eliot. I am saying something
quite different, namely, that Eliot exists only on paper, only in the
minds of a few critics. No poet with so great a name has ever had less
influence on poetry. At no point in the career of Eliot has there been
the slightest indication of a literary following. For example, W. H.
Auden, for a decade or so, set patterns for poetry which were followed by thousands of new poets all over the world. Dylan Thomas
did the same, as did Wallace Stevens. Neither Eliot nor Pound ever
had any such effect on their readers or on young writers. Eliot's "influence" is confined purely to criticism. Insofar as Eliot has enjoyed a
poetic influence, it lies outside literature entirely and is what can only
be called a "spiritual" influence. This spiritual influence is itself calculated and synthetic; and insofar as it fails as a true influence, it re-
moves Eliot's one and only claim to literary power. But here he does
not entirely fail.

To deal with Eliot outside the literary situation which he has invented, means to deal with his poetry head-on. It means passing judgment upon it as good or bad poetry or, in some cases, as not poetry at

all. But how is one to look at Eliot, if not from his own viewpoint? There is the rub. Eliot has arranged matters in such a way that criticism of his own poetry is impossible.

Eliot has written a small body of poetry which is sacrosanct; he has written his most favorable criticism about poetry which is like his (namely Pound's); and has surrounded both with a full-scale esthetic-social doctrine. What I would like to do is to draw attention to Eliot's poetry—for that is the heart of the matter. For those who do not instinctively and spontaneously reject this poetry, I suppose some form of argument is required. Perhaps this essay will be of some assistance to them. I have in mind students primarily, those who are given Modern Poetry as gospel; I also have the young critic in mind, and also teachers and scholars. Poets do not need these remarks. I have met hundreds of poets in my life but not more than one or two who entertained the reverence for Eliot which they find in the textbooks. As most poets are not intellectuals and are the opposite, they are always stunned by the intellectual pretensions of Eliot and are at a loss to deal with them.

Eliot's preparation of the historical ground upon which he would found his position was the territory of all literature—excluding the Chinese, which was the preserve of Pound. He did not, evidently, intend a personal seizure of intellectual power; Eliot's famous humility testifies to his uneasiness in the face of overwhelming success. His irrational and subservient association with Pound also points to a genuine desire to refuse intellectual leadership, or at least to share it with others.

There was, it appears, a need for an Eliot about 1910. Eliot arrived on the literary scene at the point of vacuum; and he filled this vacuum which literary Nature abhors. Such at least is the accepted view. What is probably nearer the truth is that Eliot appeared at a time when the vitality of the audience was low; and when this is the case, criticism pours into the void. It is the critic in the guise of poet that we have to deal with, not a new kind of poet. For it is criticism which is the twentieth-century substitute for poetry.

The Historical Situation which Eliot exploits under the banner of Tradition was in the beginning the Educational Situation. It was local and Anglo-American, a defense of the Gentleman's Education. I put it vulgarly because that is the way it was. Too many writers have commented on Eliot's fears of being taken for a provincial for me to add my comment. These fears, however, are part of the New England heritage—the worst part—which leads the New Englander to become the Old Englander. Eliot's early life and work follow an almost hypnotic pattern; one might call him that pseudo-American, the type which finally won New England from the immigrant and gave it back to "history." The cultural dryness of New England was a by-product of this attitude which Eliot exemplifies even better than Henry James: that of relating America to New England, New England to England. Eliot was simply retracing the path back to Europe, exactly as Pound did, and as so many of our nineteenth-century writers tended to do, all but those specifically American.

The criticism of Eliot and Pound has blighted enormous literary areas, as far as we can tell.

The critics who helped establish Eliot were no less instrumental than Eliot himself in opening the frontiers of the cultural territory. Eliot with his palaver about the Tradition could gather in the entire Indo-European world, leaving North Asia and Africa to his senior. I do not want to go into the story of Eliot's critical rise to fame, but to illustrate what I mean I want to point to two literary critics who from every indication should have become his strongest foes; instead of becoming foes they were easily engaged to take his part in the high venture of Modern Poetic Culture. They are Edmund Wilson and F. O. Matthiessen.

Edmund Wilson may be fairly described as a critic in every way the natural opposite of Eliot. In his early estimate of Eliot in *Axel's Castle*, probably the first work to install Eliot in a high position in the literary mind, he pointed out almost every serious defect of the poet: his "fear of vulgarity," his intention to "depersonalize" literature, his overintellectuality, his obsessive imitativeness, and so forth. Wilson described Eliot as the Puritan-turned-artist and expressed the fear that the extravagant praise of Eliot on all sides would perhaps unbalance literary judgment, as of course it did. What then attracted Wilson to Eliot? *It was Eliot's influence on literary criticism.* Wilson walked straight into the trap which Eliot had baited for all humanists and run-of-the-mill men of letters. Eliot had written so high-mindedly about the literary past and so dolefully about the present that Wilson was taken in. He even began to praise Eliot's prose style—probably the worst prose style in the history of the English essay, as well as the most personal. What attracted the budding critic Wilson was, of course, the keenness of intelligence, the range of ideas, the feel of authority, and the sense of History. Also, a hopeful critic like Wilson was on the search for a poet to praise, and Wilson thought he had found him. Meanwhile Wilson was popped into the Eliot oven to be turned into a nice little, right little gingerbread man. Fortunately, he escaped, but that chapter does not belong to our chronicle.

F. O. Matthiessen's relationship to Eliot is even more extraordinary than that of the humanist critic who gazes in fascination at the Puritan-turned-artist. Matthiessen, I think, felt the same attraction for New England that Eliot did, the one coming from the West Coast, the other from the Midwest. To the critical and historical mind of Matthiessen, Eliot must have seemed an incarnation of American history. But Matthiessen had some adjusting to do in his own thinking in order to place Eliot in the same high position that Wilson had. He acknowledged his indebtedness to Wilson and also to I. A. Richards, the man who tried, and almost succeeded, in driving the poetic mind into the test tube. Matthiessen could not agree with Eliot's philosophy, his religion, or his politics, and yet he felt he must adulate Eliot! The result was his book on Eliot in which Matthiessen disdains the kind of criticism that deals with the poet's "ideas" and praises the kind of criticism that deals with the "forms." This book, *The Achievement of T. S. Eliot*, was published during the height of the Depression and at a time when Marxism was strong in the United States. Matthiessen was perhaps the most intensely engaged political mind among the English professors of his day, and a leftist; *yet he chose to cut himself off from the politics of Eliot's poetry and criticism to talk about the "forms."* This was a split that Eliot had invented for himself and which Eliot evidently kept from being fatal in his own life by various makeshifts of criticism. The false dualisms set up by Eliot between art and social action are symptomatic of the insanity of much modern criticism. In any case, it was Eliot's attractive formulation of these dualisms that neutralized so many critics and led Criticism itself into a squirrel cage where it still performs so brilliantly for its own amusement. Even Eliot's most favorable critics have never been able to resolve his major contradictions, which are central and irreducible conflicts rising from a false view of art as a function of history and culture, and a twisted attitude toward human nature.

Eliot's criticism is not "one thing" and his poetry another. They are one and the same. Herein lies the only unity of his work and of his "sensibility." This unity has been achieved coldly and ruthlessly, on paper. It has only as much relation to life as books can have: experience in Eliot is always and necessarily literary experience. All other experience is vulgar, with the possible exception of the religious experience, which is Eliot's escape hatch. His poems are therefore illustrations of the various stages of his "position," just as Pound's poems are illustrations of Pound's politick. Pound is not interested in poetry as poetry but in demonstrating what poetry is for. Eliot is above pedagogy, being closer to philosophy than to history. But the unifying element in Eliot is theology: and it is not inaccurate to describe Eliot as a theologian gone astray. The difference between Eliot's respectability and Pound's notoriety lies here as well. The frequent violence of Eliot's feelings is overlooked because of the "religious" context. Both his verse and his prose are held together by the main strength of certain theological abstractions. Eliot shows a positive hatred for originality and in fact condemns it in every manifestation; originality is irresponsible freedom to him. It is for this reason that he consigns Blake to limbo while hanging on to Pascal for dear life. Blake, says Eliot, is homemade religion. Eliot stays within the shadow of his theological law, which shelters his politics, his religion, and his esthetics.

How then is one to deal with his poetry without bringing in such terms as "mythic form," the "objective correlative," the "auditory imagination," the "dissociation of sensibility," the "Tradition," and fifty or sixty other concepts which are supposed to explain his poetry to us? The answer is by dealing with the poetry as poetry, as if Eliot had never published a single line of critical theory or laid down a single law or set up a single guidepost to "correct" taste. Ignore the criticism, if possible. Eliot's criticism, like all literary criticism, has a place in the seminar room in the philosophy department; let's keep it there. How it ever got out is a biographical question which we will leave to anyone daring enough to violate Eliot's fiat against biography. I take it that Eliot is mainly responsible for the modern taboo against literary biography, one of his less publicized fields of propaganda.

In another section of these notes I have made a distinction between criticism and judgment. The strategic purpose of Eliot's criticism was to prevent judgment; that is the purpose of the criticism which he gave birth to (called the New Criticism), to replace judgment by theory. Eliot's own judgment is seldom shown, governed as it is by precept. His intellectualization of feeling and taste led him to such twisted judgments as the praise of Kipling and the execration of Whitman, the approval of Donne and the disparagement of Milton, and to pronouncements such as "the novel died" on such and such a date. One of Eliot's followers, taking a suggestion from the master, writes a long, seemingly "objective" account of the weaknesses of the poetry of D. H. Lawrence. Lawrence had committed the horrible sin of expressing his own feelings in poetry. Instead of following "the discipline of a rationally constructed imagination," Lawrence *expresses*. If only, this critic complains, Lawrence had learned to use "controlled hysteria" like Eliot. And so forth. ("Controlled hysteria" strikes me as an accurate description of Eliot's poetry from an amateur psychology point of view, but the critic in question, R. P. Blackmur, egregiously takes Eliot's tightly buttoned-up pathology to be the normal state of affairs for poetry.)

To Eliot and Pound, with their provincial and educated horror of the unlettered and the spontaneous, the idea of a large or mixed audience was unspeakable. Throughout the criticism of these two leaders of modern taste the audience is constantly defined as a danger to the *status quo*. Pound, for example, in making up his booklist for converts to his criticism is even suspicious of the ballad. He cannot explain to himself that the ballad may be and probably is the product of the "unliterary" mind; he distrusts Shakespeare for the same reason. Eliot's own plays, of course, are addressed to a good sound upper-middle-class audience, British preferably, even though a couple of his dramatic works have a popular appeal. Eliot must get quite a chuckle out of that.

In discussing Eliot's or Pound's idea of the audience (or what they would call the *function* of literature, in their strangely mechanistic language) one runs into the old danger of bogging down in points of doctrine and definition. It is no exaggeration to say that Eliot's criticism contains a definite plan of action, leading from a theory of poetics to political philosophy and covering all the intermediate stages. I will come back to this matter in my remarks on Yeats and Pound and their part in the religion of modern poetry. As far as the audience is concerned it is enough to say Eliot and Pound have not really had one—Eliot not until a few years ago, Pound never. The public has consistently rejected all of the poetry of 1915–25 from the beginning and has ignored both the poetry and its scales of values. In the voluntary withdrawal of the audience, the critics have created an academic audience, that is, a captive audience. The true audience, when it is allowed to grow, may of course reach all levels of appreciation from the lowest to the highest; it is ever the job of the poet to address himself to the present *condition* of the audience and to the language of that audience. Eliot and Pound have both attempted to find the language of their time: both have failed miserably and have succeeded only in constructing parodistic copies of the language. (This is the cogent argument of William Carlos Williams against both poets.) Eliot's style of deliberate plagiarism is the first symptom of failure to locate the language—in his case a lifelong admission of defeat. Modern poetry is macaronic because, in fact, it is not linguistically modern at all. It is high time we related the Pound-Eliot antiquarianism in ideas to the antiquarianism of their styles. Pound uses more archaisms than the Poet Laureate of Florida.

I am going to deal with only a sample of the most typical and celebrated poems of Eliot's, from "Prufrock" through the *Quartets*, trying to *judge* these poems as if Eliot had never written any criticism. I judge them from the point of view of writing, on the assumption, which is to me a certainty, that all English-speaking people can appraise their worth as English poetry. This is the way poetry has always been read—without criticism or in spite of it. I disregard, as far as possible, Eliot's talk about the form of this and the form of that. I am confident that my judgments of these poems as poetry, not as sociology or esthetics, are extremely close to the judgments of nearly all readers of modern poetry who have not been conditioned by the criticism.

"The Love Song of J. Alfred Prufrock"—this is probably Eliot's best poem and is a little masterpiece of its kind. It is highly unoriginal in content and in style, based as it is on the rhythms, the attitudes, and sometimes the very lines of minor Symbolist poets like Corbière and Laforgue. Rhythmically it is the most successful of Eliot's poems, possibly because it was conceived as a dramatic unit. The meter is varied within the conventional English line, and the rhyming is superb. There is every indication that at the time of composition (age twenty-three) Eliot still took seriously the customs of English prosody and was trying in earnest (i.e., without irony) to develop this technical side of our poetry. The general tone of the poem is that of polite sophisticated ennui, an essay in self-mockery. The literary allusions in the poem, not counting the epigraph, are of the most obvious nature. This poem does not offend on the side of Culture. The epigraph from Dante purportedly throws a special light on the meaning of the poem; it is the epigraph which critics talk about most and which teachers teach. This quotation is gratuitous, a meaningless decoration; later it becomes the actual method of the Eliot poem. The difficulties of the poem, which are intentional, are not insurmountable, say, to a reader quite conversant with poetry tending toward the baroque or self-conscious. "Prufrock" is a poem *about* self-consciousness. The split personality of Prufrock creates the chief obstacle to a first understanding of the poem. The other primary difficulty is imagistic, but this is also the main virtue of the poem. The famous opening image of the evening prostrate "like a patient etherized upon a table" is one of the most brilliant examples of the poetry of exhaustion; very possibly it is a variation of Baudelaire's statement that the sexual act is like a surgical operation. Eliot's poem, however, is humorous rather than vicious and develops a kindly pathos to the very end. The imagery of the poem is all related to suggestion, a watering-down of the extreme suggestiveness of "effect" of poets like Mallarmé and Poe, and is, in fact, a retreat from official Symbolism. (Eliot would already be conscious of all the "historical" possibilities of his "position.") "Prufrock" is a masterpiece of a "period," the high point of Eliot's poetry. It is a true poem and also an experiment in criticism. It is a true poem by virtue of a personal content, which we can only guess at, for Eliot is always more sensitive about the autobi-

ographical than any other writer I know of. But many things in the
poem point to the so-called objectification of experience; even after
Eliot airs to the public his problem of the personal and the impersonal, Life versus Art. The figure of Hamlet in "Prufrock" he finds
particularly expressive of his own dilemma, even though Prufrock
disclaims a true identity with the Prince. But Hamlet is the figure
who makes an art of indecision. Indecision leads to thinking things
over, soliloquizing, becoming an intellectual. Eliot's poetry all turns
to talk. As it goes on through the years it becomes nothing but talk,
and talk about the kind of poetry that comes closer and closer to talk.
Technically, the poem prefigures all the criticism, with its debates
about the personal and the impersonal, the more and more "objective," the great struggle toward "unified sensibility" and what not.

Eliot's failure as a poet is his success as a critic. Prufrock as a character is of no intrinsic interest but he is of high *literary* interest to all.
In this poem Eliot has remained close enough to a human footing to
make poetry out of a personal complex of crises, private, social, and
intellectual. Had he written nothing else he would be remembered
for this masterly little poem.

The "Portrait of a Lady" is also a young poem, written apparently
at the time of "Prufrock." The "Portrait," however, is not a textbook
piece; it is too much of a love poem. It is not as good a poem as
"Prufrock," actually, because it has the tone of adolescence rather
than the tone of a prefigured worldliness, as in "Prufrock." In the
"Portrait" the woman is made fun of; she is wiser but inferior to the
young Eliot; the poem leaves the reader nothing much to dwell upon
except its excellence of execution. It appears to be one of Eliot's many
exercises in tone. The epigraph in this case is a falsification. Eliot
takes three lines from Marlowe's *The Jew of Malta*, the meaning of
which he distorts for his own purpose. The lines are these:

> Thou hast committed—
> Fornication: but that was in another country,
> And besides, the wench is dead.

These three lines are actually part of a long involved dialogue; two
people are speaking, not one. Eliot does not mean to convey that only
one person is speaking, but he must for convenience gloze over the

sense of the play. Eliot exegetes can retrace the quotation and explain that a friar is accusing the traitorous Jew, Barabas, of a series of crimes and that the Jew is evading answering; in the same way the Eliot in the poem is evading answering the questions of the woman. Psychologically this kind of thing can become so involved that everything reverts back to the meaning of the *quotation*. This is the crux of the Eliot poem, as we all know: how does the quotation fit the poem? Very shortly the matter is reversed and the question becomes: how does the poem fit the *quotation?* The beauty of the "Portrait" testifies to Eliot's residual interest in the poem, not in its possible intellectual overtones; the quotation (virtually a misquotation) also indicates the poet's concern about what he writes rather than what he quotes. But the quote is also a loophole for the meaning of the poem, permitting Eliot to evade his meaning or permitting critics to elaborate it.

In both of these poems Eliot displays a mastery of sound and rhythm which marks the poet of genius. The rhyming is dazzling, a mixture of shock (the use of near-comic pairs such as Pole-soul) and the much more subtle effect of nonrhyme, such as we find in "Lycidas." It is almost, but not quite, apparent that Eliot at the beginning of his career is playing the weary virtuoso. But this is not sufficient, either for Eliot or for the literary scene. There is not much to be gained by becoming another Anglo-American Laforgue.

The remaining poems of this early style are even more "French" than the longer ones, but more satisfying evidently to Eliot. "Preludes" introduces the typical sordid furniture of the Eliot world, a Baudelairean rather than Laforguean world. The poem is a series of images evoking despair and disgust. The popularity of the poem comes from its seriousness, the transference from youthful, well-educated ennui to a genuine, if not very thoughtful, revulsion for all those people "raising dingy shades in a thousand furnished rooms." Eliot here imports the clichés of nineteenth-century French poetry about the wickedness (i.e., mediocrity) of the modern city. "Rhapsody on a Windy Night," a much more convincing poem, dramatizes and symbolizes the horror of the city. Eliot has already found the Culture of the modern city; by simply recording its images (a broken spring in a factory yard, a morsel of rancid butter, the toothbrush hanging on the wall) he evokes a cultured response—the response of the *avant-*

garde reader to society. It is assumed, without having to say so, that the modern city is a degeneration of the Past. *Now he knows what to say:* the housemaids have "damp" souls; people await the evening paper for want of something better, the old order changeth and Cousin Nancy has taken to smoking; the poet is quietly rejecting both the present and the immediate past—the American past.

The first really literary poem comes in this phase also. (I use the term "literary" opprobriously.) "Mr. Apollinax" marks the new Eliot; the Greek epigraph becomes an integral part of the poem, an explanation of it; and there is no attempt to provide links from the reader's experience to the cultural cues. The meter begins to break and the rhymes are now artfully coarsened (afternoon-macaroon). Mr. Apollinax is something of a pagan oracle to Eliot and a Priapic figure, but not to the Boston professors who entertain him. The poem is inferior to the "Rhapsody" in every way; it is already a culture poem and an exercise in footnoting.

Eliot's reputation to a large extent is based upon the poems of this early period, and rightly so. "Prufrock," "Portrait of a Lady," "Preludes," and the "Rhapsody" are among his best works. Of these "Prufrock" is head and shoulders above the rest and is sufficient to justify Eliot's claim as one of the most gifted twentieth-century poets. At the same time it is extremely close to *vers de société*, as the first reviewers were aware (and first impressions are generally valuable in literary criticism), while the other poems mentioned are almost mannerist in their attention to theory and precedent. These are true weaknesses and Eliot is evidently conscious of their defects, the proof being that he deserts these forms for new ones.

In the next phase we find the majority of the poems in pedantic and ironic quatrains. There is one attempt at a "major" form, as the critics say, in the poem "Gerontion," and there are several poems in French, which certainly cannot be judged as English poems. The quatrain poems introduce Sweeney and various minor characters in Eliot's pantheon. In this group there is also the extraordinarily crude anti-church poem named "The Hippopotamus," one of those surprising lapses of Eliot's which almost equal his good poems in number. Equally crude is the embarrassing anti-Jewish poem "Burbank with a Baedeker," a typical utterance of the modern "classical" school.

Eliot's anti-Semitism, which I am not going to discuss, is connected with his view of American commercial wealth: Bleistein is "Chicago Semite Viennese" and he is described in disgusting physical detail. It is interesting to note that as Eliot's feelings become more violent and shocking the epigraphic matter becomes more talky and deranged. The quotation affixed to this poem is a hodgepodge of a French poem, a Latin motto, something from Henry James, something from Shakespeare, something from Browning, and something from Marston. It is as obscure as the quatrains are clear. The Chicago Shylock and the British baronet with a Jewish name have taken back Venice, according to this culture lyric. Stylistically and otherwise there is little virtue in the piece.

Stylistically there is little or nothing of value in all the quatrain poems, "Sweeney Erect," "A Cooking Egg," "Whispers of Immortality," "Mr. Eliot's Sunday Morning Service," and the famous "Sweeney Among the Nightingales." In these poems Eliot is exploring the possibilities of character symbols; most turn out to be mere caricatures and do not appear again. Sweeney survives as a representation of Eliot's dim view of modern man. Eliot tries humor in the poems, if humor is the proper word (a highly polysyllabic bumbling kind of pseudo-British joking); and this he alternates with scenes of horror and disorder made ironical by the propriety of the meters. The close of the "Nightingale" poem is said by critics to mark a high point of nobility, why I am not sure, unless it is that Eliot leaves off "Rachel *née* Rabinovitch" and switches to Agamemnon and the Convent of the Sacred Heart. These closing lines, if indeed they are serious, are cheap rather than noble and so poorly articulated that they can barely be pronounced. These poems show a drastic falling-off from the poet's earlier work. (I have said nothing of the complexities of cultural allusion in these poems; most people know them and accept them as part of the rocky road to modern poetry.)

"Gerontion" is usually placed high among Eliot's works; but it is not much better than "Mr. Apollinax" and is in fact an extension of that poem in its manner. In order to escape a derivative Symbolism, Eliot has settled on the borrowing of quotations. Without a knowledge of the sources the poems sound more or less unified; the quotations themselves remove some of the author's responsibility for what the poems say. Eliot was here working out a method for a kind of poem which would implant certain ideas and images in the reader's mind, almost as if Eliot himself had nothing to do with the poem. The use of quotation without reference has a further advantage: it creates a specialized class of readers; I am quite serious when I say that Eliot is here providing texts for a new academic faculty. In the same way as Pound he is trying to solve an educational problem. But "Gerontion" is also a personal catechism of the poet's religious hopes and doubts and is part of his spiritual autobiography. Its best feature is the rhetorical accretion of the same grammatical form and the use of meaningless but suggestive names. The theme of the youthless-ageless man, which is Eliot's one contribution to symbology, is advanced again, as in all his earlier poems. There is in "Gerontion" a careful propaganda for Eliot as a symbolic figure, the poet deep in thought, seated among the ruins of the ages, longing for a salvation which will suit his intellect as well as his desires for spiritual comfort.

The Waste Land is the most important poem of the twentieth century, that is, the one that has caused the most discussion and is said by critics to be the culmination of the modern "mythic" style. The poem, by Eliot's own admission, is a collaboration with Pound. Pound edited it and removed a third or two thirds of it. The "continuity," we can assume, is therefore the work of Pound, who abhorred continuity in his own more ambitious poetry. As everyone knows how to read the poem or can find out by visiting the nearest library, I will say nothing about its meaning. I will speak rather of the success and the failure of the poem. That it is lacking in unity is obvious (assuming, as I do, that unity is a literary virtue). Any part of The Waste Land can be switched with any other part without changing the sense of the poem. Aside from the so-called "mythic" form, which is worthless and not even true—for Eliot misread James Joyce's Ulysses when he saw it as a parallel to Homer—the underlying unity of the poem is tonal and dramatic, exactly as a Victorian narrative poem would be. Eliot tries to conceal this indispensable literary method by mixing languages, breaking off dramatic passages, and by dividing the poem into sections with titles. But what really keeps the poem moving is its rhetoric, its switches from description to exclamation to interrogation to expletive, sometimes very beautifully, as in the passages beginning "Unreal City." The straight descriptive passages are weak: "A Game of Chess" is one of the dullest and most meretricious of Eliot's writings, indicating his own dissatisfaction with that kind of verse. The dialogue, on the other hand, is generally good. The best moments of all are the image passages, where the images are set in dramatic tonalities: "What the Thunder Said" is the finest of these. The very worst passages are those which are merely quotes; even Eliot's most abject admirers can find no justification of the last lines of the poem, with its half-dozen languages and more than half a dozen quotations in a space of about ten lines.

The Waste Land, because of its great critical reputation, not because of any inherent worth it might have, is one of the curiosities of English literature. Its critical success was, I dare say, carefully planned and executed, and it was not beyond the realm of possibility that the poem was originally a hoax, as some of the first readers insisted. But hoax or not, it was very shortly made the sacred cow of modern poetry and the object of more pious literary nonsense than any modern work save the Cantos of Pound. The proof of the failure of the "form" of this poem is that no one has ever been able to proceed from it, including Eliot himself. It is, in fact, not a form at all but a negative version of form. It is interesting to notice that in the conventional stanzas of the quatrain poems Eliot is more personally violent and ugly about his own beliefs; in his unconventional style the voice of the poet all but disappears and is replaced by characters from his reading.

The emergence of Eliot's piety in "The Hollow Men" and in Ash Wednesday takes the form of self-disgust in the one and self-pity in the other. "The Hollow Men" is in every way a better poem than The Waste Land, though the parodistic style again enforces a poverty of statement and language which become the marks of self-imitation in Eliot. Ash Wednesday is probably even more laden with gratuitous quotation than The Waste Land, but its ecclesiastical imagery and richness of music give the poem a beauty which the poet can finally accept as beauty. Eliot here luxuriates in the emotions of piety and surrender which seemed shameful to his Puritan soul in a purely human situation. The Eliot-God equation, once he has made the daring step, gives him an intellectual-emotional balance for the first time in his career. After the publication of this poem, Eliot's former work seems more of a piece and his future work is all laid out for him, everything from church pageants to Christmas-card poems. The *Ariel Poems* are relatively simple and almost narrative. The rest of the poems are shelved under "fragments," minor pieces, and unfinished experiments. Eliot's career as a poet virtually comes to a close with *Ash Wednesday*. After that there is criticism, theology, and drama. The *Four Quartets* is the only attempt at what modern criticism calls a major poem—meaning a poem that deals with Culture wholesale. The *Quartets* were hailed by the Eliot critics as his crowning achievement; actually they are evidence of the total dissolution of poetic skill and even a confession of poetic bankruptcy. Eliot is quite open about this in the *Quartets*.

The *Quartets* are Eliot's bid to fame as a "philosophical poet." In it he expounds his metaphysics, his poetics, and his own place in the scheme of things. All of this is quite legitimate and not at all surprising; what is disturbing about the poems is their commonplaceness, their drabness of expression, their conventionality, and, worst of all, their reliance on the schoolbook language of the philosophy class. Eliot has traded poetry for the metaphysical abstraction, as in *The Waste Land* he had traded narrative for "myth." This development is psychologically consistent, a descent from French Symbolism to Metaphysical complexity-for-the-sake-of-complexity, to pastiche, to the myth-science of *The Golden Bough*, to philosophical abstraction without poetic content. It all ends in the complete abandonment of poetry. When he comes to the drama in earnest he knows, of course, that he must use human language and he begins a new ascent into literature and the voices of poetry. But the *Quartets* lie at the bottom of the literary heap. All the so-called lyric sections, with one or two exceptions, are written with such disregard for the ear that one cannot associate them with the Eliot of "Prufrock" or the "Rhapsody." "Garlic and sapphires in the mud! Clot the bedded axle-tree" is typical of this diction devoid of both image and music. Eliot, who used to condemn poets like Tennyson for what he called crudeness of feeling, here shows an insensitivity toward language which is marvelous. The more prosy passages are even voided of that kind of poetry which rises from the use of imagery or sound. As for the philosophical development, it fails to reach a state of poetry, and it may fail as philosophy—of this I am no judge. The much-quoted third section of "East Coker" about everyone going into the darkness, even people in the Almanach de Gotha and the Stock Exchange Gazette, is possibly the best passage of a long, very bad piece of writing; one feels that here there is an acceptance of the badness of the writing, as if good writing no longer held any meaning for the poet. The "lyric" section that follows contains a stanza ("The whole earth is our hospital! Endowed by the ruined millionaire . . .") which in its vulgarity of thought and expression is hardly superior to "Only God can make a tree." For the rest there is a kind of narcissistic figure of the aging Eliot lolling through the poem, the climactic Dante imitation in "Little Gidding," and finally the magnificent passage "Sin is Behovely, but/ All shall be well . . ." Unfortunately these glorious lines are not Eliot's but are one of his borrowings. In general, the *Four Quartets* appears to be a deliberately bad book, one written as if to convince the reader that poetry is dead and done with. We should remember Eliot's lifelong interest in the final this and the final that, and at least entertain the possibility that the *Four Quartets* was intended to stand as the last poem in the Great Tradition. Eliot and Pound have both shown themselves capable of such arrogance.

I have now said all the wicked things I can think of about Eliot and it remains at last to say something favorable. At the beginning of these remarks I mentioned one phase of Eliot's work in which I regard him as a true poet and a man of rich spiritual insight. While I cannot feel that Eliot has contributed anything to the spiritual advancement of our age, I am convinced that he tried. But why is it that his own poems are rubrics rather than works of art? What are they for? What are they trying to say? Is it really all just sociology, reactionary politics, bitterness, spite and despair? I think not. I have spoken of the apparently deliberate erosion of his great gifts, leading to the final desertion of poetry. And I have touched on Eliot's lapse into religion. Here is a capital puzzle for the critic.

My solution to the puzzle is this. The motivating force in Eliot's work is the search for the mystical center of experience. This search in his case has been fruitless and increasingly frustrating. Eliot's entire career is a history of his failure to penetrate the mystical consciousness. He begins as a youth with Symbolism when it is already a dying religious-esthetic *mystique*. He moves from Symbolism to the Metaphysical poets of the seventeenth century. (Neither the dictionary nor modern criticism explains what it is that interested Eliot in these poets, for it certainly was not extreme metaphorical technique or what the textbook calls the conceit.) Eliot was fascinated by the Metaphysical poem because it is virtually a demonstration of prayer. Nearly all the Metaphysical poets were Divines, men deeply troubled by the new scientific knowledge. What Eliot studied in their poetry was the possibility of fusing sacred with secular knowledge in poetry. Metaphysical poetry lies close to absurdity because it is premised on this peculiar dualism. We recall also that Eliot associated the fairly recent French poet Laforgue with the English Metaphysicals, for at one time it seemed to Eliot that a keen enough wit might serve as a key to the door that refused to open. But neither Symbolism nor Metaphysical sacred poetry offered a way to Eliot, even when he tried a fusion of the two. Third, he attempted secular mythology as a way to penetrate the mystical consciousness. It was in this phase that he wrote *The Waste Land*, a poem which is a jumble of sacred and "profane" myths, adding up to nothing.

Meanwhile, both Eliot and Pound had discovered T. E. Hulme, whose essays provided written authority for them both, in different ways. Every major doctrine of Eliot's can be found in Hulme's *Speculations*, the most basic the one that relates fundamental Christian doctrine to a theory of society and a theory of poetics. Hulme formulated for Eliot the attack on Romanticism and the attack on mysticism (for the Romantic and the mystical are always related, while the Classical and the orthodox are related in their ways, at least in the critical mind). Hulme pointed the way for Eliot to orthodoxy in letters and to ritual and dogma in the spiritual realm. I consider Hulme's book as the *Mein Kampf* of modern criticism and a thoroughly evil work; and it was Eliot's undoing. For after the assimilation of Hulme, the rest is elaboration. Except for one thing: the search for the mystical center of experience goes on. Eliot worries it in Dante, in the Hindu scriptures, in St. John of the Cross, and in Julianne of Norwich. But poets of more recent vintage who come closer to mysticism infuriate Eliot, and he pours out his scorn on Blake, Lawrence, Whitman and our own Transcendentalists. Yet it is eternally to Eliot's credit that he does not fake the mystical (as he seems to accuse Blake of doing) and it is also to his credit that he does not relapse into magic and spiritualism, as Yeats did. It appears that Eliot is not even acquainted with esotericism; at least he does not even seem to be conscious of the esoteric meaning of the Tarot, which he uses in *The Waste Land* for "fortunetelling."

The failure to achieve mystical consciousness (which indeed is one of the rarest achievements in mankind) drove Eliot back to metaphysics proper and to religion proper. This in my view is the great failure of Eliot. Eliot ends up as a poet of religion in the conventional sense of that term. And once having made the religious commitment he tried to visualize a religion-directed society; he thus becomes an official of the most conservative elements of society and a figurehead for all that is formalized and ritualized. Yeats' fascination for the Byzantine betrays the same spiritual conservatism, as does Pound's fascination for the corporate state and the leadership principle. And Eliot ends his quest with his caricature of the modern poet-priest or psychiatrist-priest who alone has power to allay the Eumenides. Witch-hunting runs through Eliot from beginning to end.

Eliot is a poet of religion, hence a poet of the second or third rank; he is a thoroughgoing anachronism in the modern world, a poet of genius crippled by lack of faith and want of joy. I believe in Blake's proverb that "the road of excess leads to the palace of wisdom." Had Eliot ever set foot on that road he might have been as great a seer as Whitman or Rimbaud or even Dylan Thomas.

EZRA POUND:
THE SCAPEGOAT OF
MODERN POETRY

*". . . the goat shall bear upon him all their
iniquities unto a land which is cut off; and
he shall let go the goat in the wilderness."*

IN ANY WAY you look at it, writing about Ezra Pound and his poetry is an unpleasant business. It is unpleasant for his friends and fellow travelers, who must either by-pass or explain away the various
Pound scandals; just as unpleasant for his ill-wishers and critics; and
unpleasant as well for the scholars, book reviewers, and historians of
the age who find him looming up menacingly from the card catalogue. Pound is not the kind of writer who once did something
wrong and can now be forgiven in the mellowness of time. It is hard
to forgive him because everything he did wrong he insists was right.
He is righteous about his wrongness; he forces his worst upon us
wherever we meet him, and there is no escaping it.

People who try to minimize Pound's sins, errors, and crimes are
simply playing a game that Pound himself refuses to play. Critics who
would like to shelve the ugly side of Pound's poetry for its virtues are
also playing a game that Pound refuses to have a hand in. Of all the
modern didactic poets there is none more didactic than this one,
none more "topical," whether the topic is religion, politics, war, or
money and banking. Eliot hopes that his readers will distinguish between his poetry and criticism, but Pound demands a thorough iden-

tification of his prose with his poetry. They are one and the same, all a single immense prose-poem supposedly covering in time all the known civilizations in all their main ramifications. The size, scope, and style of this prose-poem raises the most embarrassing question of all about Pound, which I am going to express my opinion about. This question is whether Pound is insane.

The question of whether Pound is insane is, properly speaking, none of our business. Many poets and artists have been, or have been adjudged, insane and have spent terrible years in asylums. But we who are readers and lovers of poetry are not doctors and it is not within our scope, except out of human sympathy or curiosity, to dwell upon an artist's worst moments or periods of life. What does concern us is whether the poet's *poetry* is insane. If it is, and we as readers should be able to tell that, then we must treat it as such, as the work of a sick mind, or, sometimes, a dangerous one. I have read Pound's poetry all my life, carefully, with pain and with pleasure, and I know that his poetry is anything but insane. People who have termed it so may know a good deal about insanity but they know little about poetry. One of the chief defects of Pound's poetry, in fact, is that it is too *rational*, forced, and wanting in imagination. Insofar as we can reconstruct the character and intellect of a man from his writings, we can get a fairly whole portrait of Pound. I will be sketching that portrait for you, and you will see that he is a perfectly normal, though badly frustrated, fellow American. He is, in fact, a well-known American type, the provincial overexposed to the guidebook.

But leaving the question of insanity aside, there is also the question of the social dangerousness of Pound. Pound is, or rather wants to be, thought dangerous, but it appears that the danger is now a thing of the past. Eliot, if anything, is a much more dangerous element in society than Pound. He is more persuasive, highly respectable, a better strategist, a theologian, a modernist, and a gentleman saint. No one that I ever heard of has been seriously influenced by the theories of Pound—except Eliot! But Eliot's danger period has also passed; in any case, his job has been done; he has put literature back in the Reference Room and has apologized for his youthful indiscretions about the lower races and popular governments. Eliot today is the kindly Greco-Judaic-Christian gentleman who made

good. There is an almost touchingly comic element in the Pound-
Eliot team, their spats and undying loyalties to one another, their di-
vision of the empires of literature into East and West; but there is a
good bit of pathos as well.

The chief difference between Pound and Eliot is one of intelligence. As far as poetic talent goes, Pound sometimes seems the superior poet; but as far as the I.Q. goes, Eliot is head and shoulders
above his teacher. In the case of writers like these two, we must speak
of intelligence because they make us consider their minds, their ideas,
and their opinions, and not simply their poetry. They make a cult of
Intelligence. Dylan Thomas, for example, makes no pretenses about
his intelligence, and it is hard to tell whether he was or was not a man
with a good thinking apparatus. That Eliot has a fine intellect we all
somehow agree; it is his chief claim on our attention. Eliot even talks
about the importance of the intelligence in such a way that it seems
an attribute comparable with poetic artistry. It is one of his tricks of
strategy. Following this mode of criticism, W. H. Auden writes an introduction to the poems of Tennyson warning the reader that he
must not make the mistake of considering Tennyson intelligent.
Auden (mimicking the tone and manner of Eliot) says: "He had the
finest ear, perhaps, of any English poet; he was also undoubtedly the
stupidest." According to "modern" criticism, Tennyson is unintelli-
gent or stupid because he did not develop a fine critical sensibility.
Those are Auden's words. One could wish that a fine critical sensibility (whatever that is) would prevent a critic from calling a poet like
Tennyson stupid, if only for the sake of common decency. On the
other hand, I am tempted to call Ezra Pound stupid, but in this case I
think even Pound's best friends might agree.

The question of the intelligence of the artist is one of those phony
questions which have been brought to the fore in our time by critics
like Eliot, Valéry, and Auden. Once we begin to debate this question
we are in the Dismal Swamp of criticism. It is an endless and irrelevant question, like art and homosexuality, or art and science—questions which belong anywhere but in literature. Was Mozart
intelligent or "stupid"? Critics sometimes point out the "stupidity" of
Beethoven, based on the laborious evidence of his notebooks.
Beethoven was slow, Mozart quick as a flash, but "stupidity" some-

how seems the improper term for so great a genius as either. I think we should consider the intelligence of the artist within the framework of art. It is meaningless to call Tennyson stupid while complimenting him on his excellent ear. Ear *is* to a great extent what poetic intelligence means; not "critical sensibility" or a sense of history, and so on. What annoys Auden about Tennyson is that Tennyson had not read sociology or thought deeply enough about Original Sin. (I will deal with this quirk in Auden's thinking in another place.)

But when the poet makes a boast of intelligence like Pound and is defended at the last ditch on the grounds of his *ideas*, and is elevated by T. S. Eliot as the most important critic of the age—what are we to do? For Pound has chosen to be the "poet of ideas" (grotesque and unbeautiful phrase), and it is as a poet of ideas that we have to accept him. The ideas in Pound are not only explicit, they are magnified, repeated and spelled out in block letters. No poet in history has boasted so loudly of what he believes; none has tried harder to convince, without trying to please. So, discussing Pound's intelligence is something one would almost rather not do: it is like taking candy away from the baby.

I have called Pound the scapegoat of modern poetry. This is true in a very real sense. Pound is famed for being the teacher of modern writers: of Eliot, of Joyce, and of Yeats. This reputation, while it is the kind of exaggeration that approaches falsehood, is true in the legendary sense. Yeats must have used Pound in order to avoid certain mistakes which Pound insisted upon making. And to Yeats, Pound must have seemed a voice of the future. Joyce could have learned nothing of consequence from Pound; and Eliot, who evidently learned a very great deal from him, still developed in a direction that seemed to Pound seditious. What all three got from Pound was not so much inspiration as the sanction to use the "poetry of ideas." In return, and possibly out of a sense of guilt, Pound was overpraised, especially by Eliot, without whom Pound's reputation would probably be no greater today than that of, say, Richard Aldington. Eliot's defense of Pound and his wild encomiums are also a self-defense. Eliot has had to bear the brunt of all of Pound's mistakes, poetic, esthetic, and cultural. There is a kind of haggard nobility in Eliot's support of his mentor and friend. But it bears looking into.

There are two large classes of "ideas" in Pound's work; one has to do with works of poetry (his esthetic), and the other with social ideas. The second category comprises whatever he has to say about philosophy, science, history, ethics, and economics. All of the ideas in the second class are exposed, in the worst sense of the word. They are vulnerable. They are vulnerable because they all relate back to source works, other books. This throws Pound into an arena where readers of any description can have a go at him. Purportedly Pound makes connections between his various interests, such as economic theory and esthetics, and this becomes one of the worst burlesques of poetry we know of in modern literature: in Eliot's case, we have a different, more sophisticated element at work. But we cannot understand Pound without Eliot, or Eliot without Pound. One is the wide-awake, cautious scholastic; the other is the wild, noisy, system-crazy Yankee who demands to be a prophet, at any expense. My own sympathies are much more with Pound than with Eliot; and this is the case with William Carlos Williams also, who is revolted by Pound but who is always ready to go bail for him. Eliot uses Pound, not for his own advantage but for the advantage of the intellectual position. There is in Pound something which appeals to every American writer—it is the super-European drive and the blundering arrogance that goes with it—and there is also the provincial snobbery. It is the snobbery that appeals to Eliot, the bluster that makes him cling to Pound as an American-in-exile and a displaced European at once. In speaking of Pound's career we should keep in mind that this man was almost a contemporary of Henry James and Mark Twain—that he was born in the twilight of American literature. Pound has been busy in literature for half a century.

Pound started out as a young poet and scholar who was not appreciated in the America of about 1905. Having behind him a tradition of cultural expatriation and discontent, he thought he would assail England. But Pound was not really for England—he was a Romance-language scholar, not an "Anglo-Saxon man." In England he was the type of belligerent European-American we know so well through our literature. He married an Englishwoman named Shakespear and left for the Continent. Pound became European editor of Harriet Monroe's *Poetry* until he could no longer stomach her Americanism. He then became a one-man literary movement—but there is no point in recapitulating all this. The only fact of interest about Pound's *biographia literaria* is that he managed to capture the esteem of such poets as Eliot and Yeats, though almost no others.

Pound's ideas are neither very complex nor very extensive. In the first place he is without religion and practically without a *mystique* of any kind. He is a rational poet, a humanist *manqué*, if one needs a name for him (though not many humanists would claim him). Pound's humanism is, of course, a bookish variety and derives from the periods of art and poetry he admires. The eighteenth century is about as far as he wishes to go in time, Jefferson and Adams being the main political figures he admires from our own past. The Italian Renaissance and similar periods in China are his two main focal points. In the twentieth century he tries with miserable results to equate Jefferson with Mussolini; and Mussolini he even compares with Christ. His worship of "the Boss" of course is partly born of spite, but it contains rational elements also. Mussolini's paternalism and economic program somehow recall Jefferson in Pound's mind. That Pound could not recognize the Chicago-gangster quality of his hero is typical of the humorlessness and childishness of Pound's political ideas. This is the poet who will spend his life writing an epic of world history and culture and who is claimed by Eliot as his peer. As far as a social order goes, Pound has a vestigial idea of a kind of hierarchy based upon the good-ruler-art-patron equation; very likely it is this simple notion which led him to a study of Oriental history. Confucius provides what basis for an ethical-social order there is in Pound's world; Chinese calligraphy and the imagistic character of Chinese writing help convince Pound that an interest in clear definitions leads directly to good government. Finally there is Pound's own economic system, which according to his view could stop war, balance all national economies and bring about something like a terrestrial paradise. His precedents for this belief are a few non-usurious banks tried out here and there in history. Evidently the greatest crime Pound can invent in his world ideology is the crime of Usury; and it is because of Usury that he devotes a good deal of his prose and poetry to imprecations against capitalism and the Jews, whom he associates historically with *Usura*.

Pound's lifelong problem has been to establish an equation between poetry and society, between the esthetic and the politick. The
nexus is economics. Good economic system and good ruler equal civilization. That is the whole story. His solution is not convincing even
to his adherents, and the best of it is based partly on the sayings of
Confucius. Pound acts out the pathetic drama of Modern Poetry, that
of trying to make a place for the poet in the modern world by remak-
ing the world. It is in this phase that Pound's so-called insanity has
been brought to the attention of nonliterary folk. It is his air of conviction rather than any series of acts or writings which has struck the
bystander as lunacy.

This brings us to the most unaccountable paradox of all in
Pound's writing, that of his own style as the exemplum of precision in
language and in ideas. If it is the high responsibility of the poet to
clarify the language, as the good ruler clarifies economic life, then
certainly we should expect the poetry of Pound to execute this service. But instead of clarity and precision we get an epic poem which
not even scholars can read without long study. Recently the University of California published an index to the *Cantos* with seventeen
thousand references to names, dates and other factual information in
the poem. Certain references could not be solved even by the editors;
nor would the author lend a helping hand! Clarity, evidently, is not as
simple a matter as telling someone what you mean. But the *Cantos* are
supposed to be case studies of the economic-esthetic failures of all
civilizations, and the quantity of data available is, of course, sizable.
The style of the poem represents the brave and hopeless attempt to
carry over into poetry all the sad prose of History. These case studies
are documented by the use of large image groups. For instance,
Ovid's *Metamorphoses* is used to denote change, Dante to denote pun-
ishment, Homer to denote the brave exile, etc. This is pretty much
what Pound means by the ideogram method—giving one image or
anecdote or document after another to build up the total ideogram.

In looking at the vagaries of Pound's various styles we must not
lose sight of the fact that he is a Modern, that he is one of the poets
who flourished around 1915–25. We must remember his proximity to
the James Joyce of *Ulysses*, Eliot of *The Waste Land*, the heyday of the
little magazine, and so on. The *Cantos* are an anachronism, or rather a

historical phenomenon of a certain decade of long ago. While Eliot abandoned the fads of the twenties, Pound did not. The method of the *Cantos* is precisely the method of *The Waste Land*. Had the so-called mythic method, with all its artificiality, proved successful, we may be sure Eliot would have hung on to it. No other poet has profited by this "form," and only Pound would not give it up. The reason he did not give it up is that he was still searching for the meaning of the form. The *Cantos* are a series of experiments that failed; they are almost scientific in their exhaustive persistence. But this hysterical search for "form" is the chief characteristic of modernism.

If anyone needs proof that there is no form to the *Cantos* he can take Pound's word for it. When the poem was three-fourths finished (1939) Pound wrote to an American poet: "As to the *form* of the *Cantos*: All I can say or pray is, wait till it's there. I mean wait till I get 'em written and then if it don't show, I will start exegesis . . ."

As with the poetry of Eliot, we must look closely before we can find a point of departure to discuss the poetry of Pound. Pound is even more permeated with his own criticism than Eliot, though fortunately almost nobody reads Pound's prose. But Eliot is also intertwined with Pound's poetry and in fact has misled the entire literary world as to the worth of this and that poem and in the total assessment of Pound's work. Looking, for instance, at Eliot's introduction to Pound's *Selected Poems*, a book which every twentieth-century poet will have a copy of, I can see how all of my own early ideas about Pound's work derive from Eliot. I am sorry to revert to Eliot this way, but that is where all the arrows point in modern criticism. And this is Eliot on his favorite subject—Pound. Here Eliot is making some mysterious remarks about Pound and Whitman which are supposed to show why Pound is the better poet. Eliot says that Whitman's originality is spurious as well as genuine. Whitman, says Eliot, speaking of Whitman's poetry, was a great prose writer," and his originality "is spurious insofar as Whitman wrote in a way that asserted that his great prose was a new form of verse." But Pound, he goes on to say, is original (Eliot slyly changes the subject while he seems to be talking about versification). "Now Pound is often most 'original' in the right sense, when he is most 'archeological' in the ordinary sense." . . . "One of Pound's most indubitable claims to genuine orig-

inality is . . . his revivification of the Provençal . . ." Anyhow, in this
typical shell game of Eliot's, the pea under the shells is the word
"original."

The poems in *Personae* (1909) are nearly all bad, full of the worst
"romantic" and sentimental affectations and the most archaic English. Pound has never really stopped being archaic—it is another of
his inherent weaknesses—and even in the late *Cantos* when he becomes moved he drops back into the *thee's* and *thou's* and *hadst's* of
old. This becomes painfully ludicrous when he is *theeing* and *thouing*
about money, as in the much-quoted Usury *Canto*:

> Usura slayeth the child in the womb
> It stayeth the young man's courting
> It hath brought palsey to bed . . .

Pound sentimentalizing over usury in Quakerish English is almost
too painful to read. Many of the *Personae* poems are translations or
adaptations, nearly all in the pre-Raphaelite manner and different
from late Victorian verse only in their reliance on the erudition of the
student of Romance culture. A few of the poems are still repeated in
anthologies, for instance the "Sestina: Altaforte," which is appealing
in its loudness—"May God damn for ever all who cry 'Peace!'"
Pound's good effects are frequently based on volume of sound. The
theeing and *thouing* are also forms of loudness, as in the translation
of Leopardi, where he also uses "ye" as a half-colloquialism, half-
archaism for the second person singular. These may be details but
they spoil any quality of the poetic Pound. Pound so far fails to
achieve a style and covers up its absence with a mixture of noise and
gimcrackery. Even the pretense of a rich tradition underlying the
poems is dissipated by all the flailing around on the surface.

Ripostes (1912) and *Lustra* (1916) are different and contain the best
of Pound's poetry, the best of his experiments and the best of his
"translations." Except for a few passages in the *Cantos*, all that is good
in Pound as a poet is represented in these collections. Significantly,
one of the books is dedicated to William Carlos Williams. It is in
these poems that Pound produces his best epigrammatic verse; the
translations and adaptations are still uneven, as they will remain, not
so much in their incorrectness but in their failure to convey the qual-

ity of the originals. His chief defect is trying to invent a diction which he cannot achieve; throughout his life Pound plays with dialects in all languages. His use of dialects in English is poor and one can assume they are not much better in Old French, Latin, Greek, or Chinese. Sometimes Pound claims to write in what he calls the American language, with results that few Americans can recognize. His translation of Confucius' *Ta Hio, The Great Learning*, is subtitled "Newly Rendered into the American Language." In this work he renders the Chinese for "make it over" into

"Renovate, dod gast you, renovate!"

Great chunks of the *Cantos* are composed in this pidgin. But in *Lustra* Pound reaches his best style, possibly because he begins to write about himself (this is also true of the *Cantos*; the *Pisan Cantos* are the best because they are so personal). Many of these poems are on the subject of Pound's "exile" and the sorrows of the artist. They are not very important and they are badly dated but they are honest and dear and to a degree dramatic. If one compares them with poems of the same period by Lawrence, Sandburg, John Gould Fletcher and especially Williams, one will see that Pound is doing the same thing as these poets, almost as well. As for the epigrams and translations from the *Greek Anthology* and such sources, Pound is about on a par with Horace Gregory's *Catullus*, which is saying a great deal. Gregory has done *Catullus* better in English than anyone else in our time. Pound, however, is not content to be a mere translator, because he is always teaching some lesson about history or civilization. Consequently, even his translations have a queer evangelistic ring. His haiku are neither better nor worse than all such Japanese forms in English. English being what it is and Japanese being what it is, the haiku seems destined to sound silly in our language. The general tone of all these poems is that of the world-weary college instructor who writes tweedy poems about the burden of being so horribly well educated. "O God, O Venus, O Mercury, patron of thieves,/ Give me in due time, I beseech you, a little tobacco-shop, . . ." [anything] "save this damn'd profession of writing, where one needs one's brains all the time." One feels for Pound, trying so desperately to justify his existence with such verses. The fact is that Pound has not yet found anything to be heroic about except Romance languages; he is still innocent, still a poet, though the most bookish one we hear about.

The *Cathay* poems (1915) are also at his best level and form the only group of complete poems Pound ever wrote. Chinese was the making of Pound, not in the misleading sense that Eliot means when he says *ex cathedra* that Pound is the "inventor" of Chinese poetry for our time. This is not it at all. Pound's discovery of Chinese poetry was good for Pound but for no one else. As Eliot says, the poems are paraphrases. They lead not to China but to Pound, and that is valid for Pound and for us. Pound can here write complete paraphrases because he is out of Europe, out of America, out of a literature which presumably nobody knows except a few functionaries at the British Museum. It was about this time that Pound wrote conspiratorially to a young lady that it was good for a writer to know a certain large body of knowledge which nobody else did. Any large body of knowledge would do as long as it was more or less unknown, even to experts. China was to be that knowledge for Pound. Parenthetically, I must make mention of the *Letters* of Pound, which like his poetry are almost devoid of human substance, character, and relationship. Pound is a littérateur, even in his letters; the letters are meticulously offhand, each one a specimen for future publication. There is no question about it. Poor James Joyce's letters are human, all too human, with his broken glasses and failing eyesight and poor wages; Joyce poured all his artistry into his novels and stories; but a letter to him was a letter. Not so with Pound. A letter to Pound is a document for the ages, even if it refers to having his shoes half-soled or varnishing his floor.

Let us glance now at the poem *Hugh Selwyn Mauberley*, which Eliot has nominated as a great poem, "genuine tragedy and comedy," etc. Eliot introduces *Mauberley* as a great poem in his typical manner: his opinion worms its way into a discussion of versification, of all things, in which Eliot guffaws that "I only pretend to know as much about versifying as my carpenter knows about woodwork..." He does and he doesn't; you can never quite pin Eliot down. Anyhow, *Mauberley* is a great poem, according to Eliot.

Mauberley is a miniature of the *Cantos*; it has all the defects and only a couple of suggestions of the virtues. No one but T. S. Eliot, and that for his own reasons, would ever call it a good, much less a great poem. It has the kind of skill which we associate with putting a full-rigged four-masted schooner, with people on deck, inside a bottle. But there is nothing to be gained by making fun of a very bad poem and the only reason for mentioning it at all is that it has been called a great poem by the critic who has the greatest authority in the twentieth century. There is no question that the poem would never have reached publication, much less "greatness," had it not been for the critical hoodwinking of the Eliot-Pound team. In addition to calling the poem great (as if that weren't enough) he calls it the most advanced portion of what is a textbook of modern versification. Eliot's snide references to versification lead one in two directions: (a) that there is really no such thing as versification for Serious Poets (this is the meaning of his remark that he knows only as much about versification as his carpenter knows about woodwork), and (b) that versification is the real key to the esotericism of poetry. Actually, Eliot is right on both counts: he knows nothing about versification, even though like all good natural poets, it comes naturally to him. He is also right that successful rhythms lie at the bottom of any successful poem. And he is wrong about *Mauberley*, which is a childish work of versification, as well as being a childish work of intellect. In charity to Eliot, one must say that his loyalty to Pound is magnificent.

Hugh Selwyn Mauberley does have some sections which are good poetry: Part IV about the World War, Part V, and the envoi to Part VI. The rest is student poetry which every teacher of Creative Writing sees at least once in a semester, the weighty and deliberate display of what and how much the author knows, put into "poetry." This is not meant as a joke: it is an exact description of *Mauberley*, which is such a poor little poem that one turns away from it with a blush. Everyone, that is, except T. S. Eliot. The poem is a literary critique and an autobiography, very cryptic supposedly, but in reality a ponderous summation of the literary mistakes of the author. It contains such juvenilities as the rhyming of Τροίη with *lee-way* and the pun of the Greek τίν' with the English *tin;* it contains all the Baudelairean platitudes about modern commercialism and the failure of the Esthetes, all decorated with Pound's linguistic cartouches and pseudo-

British harumphing ("Dowson found harlots cheaper than hotels"), all dedicated to a farewell to Style. There are even little provoking pseudonyms in epigraphs, a variation on the more grim headnotes of Eliot's poems. Nowhere is there the faintest note of Versification or Style or anything that would hold the attention of anyone but a close friend. In a very biographical sense the poem is, among other things, a confession of hopelessness. The cry is against "the faint susurrus of his subjective hosannah" of whatever Dowsons and Lionel Johnsons that Pound was plowing under. He himself would not succumb to that. But my sole point here is to remind the reader that this is a poem which Eliot has made a standard of form and content (evidently) of the modern canon. There is little proof that anyone, even Eliot followers, has been convinced by this pronouncement of Eliot's; and yet the record is there, one of the larger stumbling blocks of modern criticism and modern poetry.

The big poem of the "Age," however, is the *Cantos*, the modern poem *par excellence*, and I want to relate this big poem to the shorter ones and to the criticism by Pound.

First, there is no form, plan, or subject matter of the *Cantos* except the reading matter of the poet. There is a very simple proof that Pound himself did not know what "form" he was using when he began the epic. The first versions of the *Cantos* which appeared in *Poetry* magazine are quite intelligible and almost confessedly written in the manner of Robert Browning. Immediately after these attempts he began the final version which we know. There are ponderous books written about the form of the *Cantos* and it is of interest to note that the obscurity of the criticism is in a direct ratio to the difficulties of the poems. The difficulties of the *Cantos* are, as I have said, entirely encyclopedic and linguistic, and not structural. With a good reference work at hand one can piece together the main names and dates; with a half-dozen foreign dictionaries one can make real headway; with the Pound Index all difficulties evaporate, except those having to do with the relationships in the poet's ideas. Even these are not insurmountable; as all of the poet's ideas are derivative, based upon other books, one has only to compare him with the originals. The only really deep water Pound ever enters is Confucianism; but Confucianism, compared with, say, the Hermetic philosophy of Yeats or the religious symbolism of Eliot, is child's play. The so-called obscurities are then the obscurities of the pedant and the obscurities of pedantic rhetoric, plus certain profundities inherent in the quoted works. The most original canto is the one which is a malediction against Usury; it is, sadly, the high point of the whole poem. As for the form, Pound is still looking for it; he says so himself.

Critics of Pound, pro and con, have paid him the highest compliments as adaptor and translator. Here lies his strength. As the *Cantos* begin with a translation of a translation, the entire work is a rewriting from language to language of the documents, literary and historical, which the poet tries to organize into a pattern. The use of bits and pieces of other languages is often of great beauty; and the method itself offers possibilities for originality, although the limitations are obvious. Pound also develops a prosody for the poems, which more than anything else suggests a unity. The prosody is an approximation of the Greek heroic dactyl: the most common rhythmic figure through the poem appears in a line like

And then went down to the ship,
Set keel to breakers, forth on the godly sea . . .

This is an excellent device, lending itself to some of the properties of modern speech. But it fails to achieve a standard for all the levels of diction and foreign languages the poet uses. Eliot's versification is nearly always a variation of standard iambic, and it is no surprise to see his later dramatic verse falling back into a weak iambic line. Pound's verse is stronger because he reverses the iambic from the beginning, thus opening the way for new forms such as Whitman invented. But Pound is more conservative than Whitman or Williams and falls back on "Greek" rhythms, where Whitman took as his model the English of the King James Bible and the idiom of America. Whitman's free verse is therefore more natural because it is English, not Greek.

But the fatal weakness of Pound's *Canto* style is his inability to relate one passage or "ideogram" or "image cluster" with another. His usual device is simply to use a conjunction at the beginning of the line (there are passages of great length which rely on this weakest of all English structures of grammar. The weakness, however, is inherent in the material; there is no way to relate it because the relations are arbitrary, chaotic, and without design). There is no vision or ideal central to the *Cantos*, only a tangle of data, prejudices and galvanic twitches of emotion. One would think a poem of this kind would plunge into the universe of philosophies, theories, and systems of knowledge which fill most libraries; but Pound has very little of even this kind of intellectual interest. American that he is, he is so bowled over by facts and statistics that he hardly ever pauses to consider the relevance of his data.

Let us keep in mind the place of Eliot in the appreciation of these poems of Pound. It is impossible to separate Eliot from Pound just as, according to Eliot, it is impossible to divide Pound's criticism from his poetry. "His criticism and his poetry, his precept and his practice, compose a single *oeuvre*," says Eliot. They are the least dispensable body of critical writing in our time, he continues, underlining *least dispensable*. Let us glance hurriedly at this least dispensable body of criticism. Incidentally, Eliot warns against quoting Pound out of context, but it is hard to find the context in these jottings. Pound's criticism is no more than a series of maxims repeated over and over again and illustrated with threats and imprecations—all designed to show that poets are the most important people in history. For example: "A civilization was founded on Homer, civilization not a mere bloated empire." This saying supplies the rationale for the poetry of Pound.

"It is as important for the purpose of thought to keep language efficient as it is in surgery to keep tetanus bacilli out of one's bandages." "Efficient language" of course is Pound's way of trying to make poetry as respectable as science.

Or again: "Great literature is simply language charged with meaning to the utmost possible degree." This is a good definition of poetry as far as it goes. Pound makes his definition in order to talk about those who are inventors and those who are masters and those who are "diluters" of language. The only point of interest here is that Pound is trying to invent categories of poetry which can then be applied to a curriculum of books. The language of poetry is also broken down into categories; the three divisions of lyric, image, and idea-poetry imply a theory of psychology which Pound never states.

Pound's simplification of literature and history is convenient for him. Poetry, he tells us, is a science, just as chemistry is a science. Bad art is inaccurate (unscientific) and is therefore immoral. I am not sure how he makes the jump from "inaccurate" to "immoral," but he does. On this basis he can relate a civilization which he dislikes with the art he dislikes. Thus democracy, a form of government which went to pot after the death of Jefferson or thereabouts, would give rise to such degenerate poetry as *Leaves of Grass*.

"Most important poetry has been written by men over thirty," he announces as he approaches his thirtieth birthday. The Eliot-Pound war against the poetry of youth and what they call Romanticism is an attempt to show people that poets can sit at conference tables as well as the next man.

"The disease of the last century and a half has been 'abstraction.' " This is one of Pound's better directives, and makes him, in practice, a better poet than Eliot.

"There is no use talking to the ignorant about lies, for they have no criteria," says Pound, speaking of the hideous "lie" that poetry is made to entertain.

"The twenty-three students of Provençal and the seven people seriously interested in the technique and aesthetic of verse may communicate with me in person." No comment.

"I do not think the rhyme-aesthetic, *any* rhyme-aesthetic, can ever do as much damage to English as that done by latinization in Milton's time and before." Pound rails against Milton's style but he himself invents a whole new polyglot on the analogy of the Chinese written character!

"A sound poetic training is nothing more than the science of being discontented."(!)

"Democracies have . . . always fallen, because humanity craves the outstanding personality." ". . . there should be definite subsidy of individual artists." These are platitudes, of interest only because of the connections Pound makes between the effect of art on history, the basic premise of his work, unprovable and in any case unexplored by Pound.

"The British public liked, has liked, likes and always will like all art, music, poetry, literature, glass engraving, sculpture, etc., in just such measure as it approaches the Tennysonian tone. It likes Shake-

speare, or at least accepts him in just so far as he is 'Tennysonian.'"
While intended to be a cute remark, this denotes Pound's contempt
for nearly all things British. Speaking of America and her view of the
artist he says: "America has not yet realized that never in history had
one of her great men abandoned his citizenship out of shame." This
is in praise of Henry James and is also an explanation of Eliot's contempt for his native land, as well as Pound's.

These few quotations I have taken from Eliot's edition of Pound's
essays, the introduction to which announces Pound's critical supremacy in our time. I have not combed the essays for their worst but
for their typical ideas, the ones that appear over and over again in the
Cantos. On what ground Eliot considers his colleague a great critic it
is hard to say. One of the most curious facts of modern poetry is that
Pound has had followers such as Archibald MacLeish, men who are
in direct opposition to Pound's atrophied political and social views
but who use Pound as a symbol of their own literary plight. In looking at such poets we must come to the dismal conclusion that they
have been infected by the belief that the poet is the handmaid of History. It was this self-important attitude that led to the infamous
Bollingen Prize award to Pound in 1948, when under the leadership
of Eliot, a group of his followers presented a prize to Pound (at that
time under indictment for treason) in the name of the Library of
Congress. I was myself a member of that group and narrowly escaped
being pressured into voting the prize to the *Pisan Cantos*, which
among other things, contained Pound's wildest anti-American and
racial outbursts (by that time fused into the same thing). Eliot's criticism had by 1948 so far penetrated the critical mentality of his followers that they dared ignore the plain English in the poems for what
they called their magnificent artistry. The insults in the *Cantos*, curiously, are quite clear English, so clear that much of it is given in dots
and dashes, which every schoolboy would delight to fill in. One of the
judges even informed me sanctimoniously that the award to Pound
was a great act of piety, a remark which I am still puzzling about after
all these years.

Everything I have thus far written about Pound I have written
with a feeling of lassitude and distaste. I do not want to write about
Pound; I do not think he is worth my time or yours, but as you can

see, there is no escaping him even now. I hope that this essay will help remove Pound from the position of prominence in which Eliot has placed him. I am also aware that all Pound adherents will immediately discount everything I have said about Pound on the grounds that I am a Jew. This is not the place to deny such a motive: I am dealing with the poetry and prose of Pound and not with Pound's ethnological prejudices. It happens that these prejudices occupy a large place in all of Pound's writings and that they are inescapable.

Everything about Pound seems to sum itself up in the photograph that appeared in the papers a few months after his release from the prison asylum. There was Pound back at his home in Rapallo, arm outstretched in the Mussolini salute! Charlie Chaplin couldn't have been more true to life.

I would like to close with an apology and a summary.

The apology is for continuing to hammer away at Eliot. This is tiring, I know, but it is the crux of the matter. I will continue to deal with Eliot wherever he rears his critical influence, and that unfortunately is practically everywhere. I have no apologies for my remarks about Pound himself because I consider him an effect rather than a cause. Actually, I have been gentle with Pound; if you don't believe me, pick up one of his books of criticism, or his pamphlets on economics, or his broadcasts for the Axis, or the *Cantos* themselves: you will see how criticism works with no holds barred and with flowing introductions by the Possum himself, as Pound calls Eliot.

By way of summary: Pound and Eliot meet on the grounds of Education, if that is the right term. They begin as students, one of philosophy, the other of Romance literature. Both are poets and expatriates, anti-American and antidemocratic. The one becomes a monarchist, the other a Fascist. Both gravitate toward orthodoxy, the one toward a national church freighted with tradition; the other toward a ritualism of culture without religious sanction. Both construct theories of literature out of opposition to individualism, "freethinking" and what they label Romanticism. Both center their attention throughout their careers not on poetry nor on belles-lettres nor on literature proper, but on the function of these things in a controlled society. As late as 1940 Pound and Eliot are worrying about the Ideal Curriculum to save civilization via the American university student.

They even try to enlist George Santayana, aged about eighty at the time, to lend respectability to their project. What project is this? Is it only Pound's poor old booklist of Homer, Dante, Ovid, and Confucius, which he thinks will save the world because it leaves out Virgil and Milton? Very likely it is no more than that.

But to Pound the great curriculum is the *Cantos*, a manual for princes, as it were, a compendium of history and culture morphology, as well as guidebook and a bibliography, as well as an exposé of Judaism and Christianity, the New Deal and the vocabulary of the American Army.

Eliot's part in these schemes has been more frivolous and irresponsible than Pound's, for Eliot knows better. With Pound the scheme to save civilization with a poem is true-blue evangelism and rather poetic to boot. Pound at bottom shares that American optimism which, when it goes bad, attempts to destroy itelf in a wholesale negation of everything that can be tagged American. We recognize in Pound that peculiar buffoonery of the frontier American, the intellectual dandyism of the tourist abroad, and the enormous wasted energy of the crank.

How much of Pound's worst can we attribute to the solemn encouragement of T. S. Eliot? How much to reckless journalism? How much to criticism itself, which disdains so haughtily to talk about anything except the poem *in vacuo?*

And yet under it all one feels a flow of sympathy, a kindliness, and a sorrow for Pound. He is such a storybook American, a stereotype, and a scapegoat certainly. And when you come right down to it, there is something lovable about the old man.

W. B. YEATS:
TRIAL BY CULTURE

I

A CLEVER FRENCH CRITIC once said the nineteenth century began with the poetry of religion and ended with the religion of poetry. This saying sticks in my mind; it is one of those epigrams which would be fascinating for somebody to document and even write a book about. One can see the plan of strategy at once: the nineteenth century begins in France with the Romantic Catholicism of Chateaubriand and ends with the poet-priests Mallarmé and Valéry. It begins in England with the religious mysticism of Blake and Wordsworth and ends with the poetic high seriousness of Arnold, Pater, and Yeats. Even in America the equation works, with the poetic mysticism of Emerson and Whitman turning into the cultural priestliness of T. S. Eliot. Anywhere you look, in fact, it appears that "poetry of religion" resolves into the "religion of poetry."

The trouble with epigrams like the one I mentioned is not that they are false but that they are misleadingly true. And when we analyze such a saying, which is made in good faith certainly, we find that it is not an answer after all but only a new question to be solved. It is an elegant question, and it is hard to resist answering.

The question is whether modern poetry has metamorphosed into a religion. And the answer is: Yes. But then one must define both "modern poetry" and "religion," a tedious business. But like most poets, I have thought about this matter a great deal, and have what I think is a passable answer.

In the first place, "modern" poetry is not synonymous with contemporary poetry. Modern Poetry to my mind refers to a group of

43

writings of about one decade, say 1915–25, and comprises all the
works which we refer to mentally when we use the term Modern.

"Modern" poetry is a school, a literary philosophy, with definite
and precise aims, all of which have been enunciated boldly by Pound,
Eliot, Yeats, and their associates and followers. This philosophy,
called "Classicism" in the textbooks, has its own poetics, its own esthetic, and its own world-view. That it has fathered a new pedagogy
and a new criticism every sophomore is dismally aware. Modern Poetry is the official poetry of the twentieth century in all English-
speaking countries. But properly speaking, it is not a religion; *it is a
surrogate for religion.* If we could digest this extraordinary fact, we
would have the key to Modern Poetry as a "religion."

Let us look at three or four of the chief Moderns ("Classicists") in
relation to religion: Pound, Eliot, Yeats, and Stevens. Stevens sets poetry apart from and above religion. Yeats gingerly dissociates himself
from religion, while pursuing occult and mystical studies. Pound
comes no closer to religion than an Oriental ethics permits; Christianity he X's out. Eliot alone makes a specific religious commitment.
But at the same time, all four poets observe one or another version of
the central religious doctrine of Original Sin. It is at this point that
Modern Poetry differentiates itself from "Romantic" poetry, whether
by Whitman, Blake, Lawrence, or Williams. It is also at this point
that Modern Poetry becomes anti-American and anti-twentieth century. All four poets adulate the Tradition, accepting the "fall" of man
from Civilization, and an esthetic Ideal which is capable of reinstat-
ing the artist as the carrier of Civilization. All four are anti-Humanist
(therefore politically pessimistic). All are anti-"Rationalist" (that is,
anti-Science).

Modern Poetry (still using the famous decade as the point of reference) recognized the failure of Symbolism, the poetry-religion of
the late nineteenth century. It is for this reason that Symbolism is
used sparingly, if at all, by our quartet. We note that Eliot takes off
not from Mallarmé but from Laforgue, for Symbolism is already
bankrupt when Eliot picks it up. Pound denigrates the great Symbolists for the same reason. Yeats remains closer to Symbolism, as
Stevens does in a more superficial manner, but neither is a "purist" in
the Mallarméan sense. (It is curious to see Eliot use the line from

Mallarmé about Poe in which it is said that Poe purified "the dialect of the tribe." Eliot has no admiration for Poe but pays his respects to dead Symbolism in that manner.)

Symbolism in the hands of the French lay close to a proper religion. The Symbolists believed that poetry through symbols apprehended the secret meanings of the world. Symbolism failed as a religion because of its divorce from the commonplace. A bona-fide religion must have a pyramidal base and not merely an apex. Symbolism finally led to its own defeat through its own idealism; it virtually parodied itself out of existence in such works as *A Rebours, Un Coup de Dés*, and even in the tragicomic life of Oscar Wilde. When the movement collapsed, poetry found itself once again on the street.

It has always struck me that Eliot's use of Laforgue is somewhat counterfeit. Laforgue did not mean what Eliot meant by Banality, for instance. To Laforgue banality was a phase of the landscape. To Eliot it is a religious miasma of some kind, related to spleen, accidia, and so forth. Nevertheless, our four poets all recognized the new attraction of the commonplace, the "antipoetic." Their object was not to exalt the commonplace but to explore it as a cultural site. Eliot's empty lots and sputtering lamps all point to the "fall" from civilization. Yeats has it in a perfect epigram in which God takes (not Eve) the spinning jenny out of the side of—Locke. No French Symbolist would have come that close to the history book. Yet Symbolism was a profitable failure for the Moderns. Pound knew that poetry must, according to his lights, descend to history and even politics, and he taught Yeats this message. Eliot's religion is, in fact, a *descent* from Symbolism to a lower plane of poetic endeavor; for religion in Eliot is just another name for Civilization.

Modern poetry claims a moral prerogative which is in effect a religious prerogative; but it does not claim it in the name of religion. Modern poetry claims a moral prerogative in the name of Culture. It is this Culture which is the substitute for religion and which is the cement of Modern Poetry.

There is, of course, no secret about the aims of the culture religion instituted by Modern Poetry. This poetry began, to be sure, as a poetic movement, or a series of poetic movements, such as a new "Classicism," Imagism and so on; it then became a theoretical educational revolt, the more conservative motto of which was to "correct taste." The correction of taste led to a full-scale re-examination of history. It is very important to remember that with Pound, Yeats, and Eliot it is not the history of poetry or of literature that matters, but history itself. Poetry is actually secondary to anthropology and sociology in the writings of Eliot and Pound. Yeats alone tried to escape from this culture revolution with his head; but his own later poetry is much contaminated with cultural theorizing and historical prophecy.

In what seems an innocuous statement in *Notes Toward a Definition of Culture* Eliot says: "The dominant force in creating a common culture between people each of which has its distinct culture is religion." Even so, he spreads his definition of this culture to include the "legacy of Greece, Rome, and Israel." In other words, it is not simply Christianity which the poet must transmit, according to Eliot, but the whole cultural complex of the Western past. This Culture, supposedly derived from religion, is larger than the religion and subsumes it. Culture is therefore the chief business of the poet, his religion in fact.

It is my opinion that Eliot scamps the relationship between Culture and religion, despite his own churchly affiliations. It would be unfair and pointless to accuse Eliot of exploiting religion for the purposes of literary ambition, but even a casual look at Eliot's religious view reveals that it is much more eclectic than the European tradition calls for. The chief object seems to be not religion for its own sake, or even for Eliot's sake, but for the sake of civilization, for Culture. Eliot approaches mysticism from time to time but retreats hurriedly into metaphysics. He quotes the mystics but is not on good terms with them. The mystics are too original, unmanageable, and "homemade," as he says of Blake. Yeats, however, is a better example of the Modernist withdrawal from religion into some cultural substitute. In Yeats' case it is magic and occultism which are the cultural substitutes for mysticism.

Yeats begins an essay on magic with these words: "I believe in the practice and philosophy of what we have agreed to call magic, in what I must call the evocation of spirits, though I do not know what they are; in the power of creating magical illusions, in the visions of truth in the depths of the mind when the eyes are closed . . ." And in three doctrines, he adds: that many minds can flow into one another and reveal a single mind; that our memories are part of the Great Memory of Nature herself; and that this great mind and great memory can be evoked by symbols.

This credo represents only one of the phases of Yeats' occultism, but it is one which he never rose above. Yeats' use of magic is closer to primitive science than it is to mysticism. There is in all spiritualist and theosophical activity an element of spite, based on the envy of modern science and its triumphs. Even Blake's cry that "Sir Francis Bacon is a Liar" partakes of this bitterness against rational science. Blake, however, appears to be more of a true mystic or gnostic than Yeats. Mysticism and magic are two different things, and it is on the latter inferior level that Yeats rested.

We should remember that in the great decade of Modernism, magic in such forms as spiritualism and theosophy reached its greatest popularity among artists and intellectuals; and that it was in fact an acceptable convention of the poet. Eliot's use of the fortuneteller in *The Waste Land* is a very *topical* allusion. Rilke himself indulged in spiritualism, even though he was aware that greater powers lay in himself than outside him. ("... my greatest, my most passionate wonderment lies with my own achievement ... and with certain movements in Nature rather than with any mediumistic occurrences, however much they have stirred me on occasion.") But Rilke knew enough as an artist not to enter the lists against Science or to fight battles for Culture. Neither Blake nor Yeats made a distinction between mysticism proper and magic. We gather from this fact that both poets were exploring the possibilities of a cultural *mystique*, a *mystique* lying outside religion and outside modern rationalist science.

I take it that the failure to distinguish between mysticism and magic in Modern Poetry is deliberate and strategic. Religion is not a primary force in modern civilization and some substitute for religion must be found. So reasoned the Pounds and Eliots and Yeatses and Stevenses. Mysticism proper was therefore suspect; it lay at the very heart of religions. The mystical must therefore be intellectualized in some manner. Stevens took the most tentative path, that of the minor techniques of Symbolism and doodling with a theory of the Imagina-

tion. Imagination is the Providence in this version of the culture religion of the Moderns. It is probably because of Stevens' relatively Per-
functory view of a total Culture poetry that he was not "recognized"
by Eliot, Pound, and Yeats. "The poet is the priest of the invisible,"
says Stevens in his notebook, but he goes no further. To do so would
be to encourage the Sweeping Romantic outlook of, say, Shelley. We
cannot understand the anti-Romantic bitterness of Stevens without
taking into account his fear of mysticism proper.

Yeats' scrambling of mystics, alchemists, theosophists, neo-
Platonists, and so forth, is his attempt to steer clear of both religion
and philosophy. "Science" of course is his avowed enemy, but so are
clericalism and orderly philosophical speculation. Occultism was to
Yeats what anthropology was to Eliot—an instrument for fashioning
the culture religion. It is commonly said about Yeats' interest in the
magical that it helped him perceive his poetic images, or something
equally silly. Yeats himself is responsible for that interpretation of *A
Vision* and of most of his culture poetry. In reality, *A Vision*, like the
notes to *The Waste Land*, the *Notes Toward a Definition of Culture*, or
Pound's book on *Kulchur*, is a highly programmatic, even political
work. The occultism suddenly jells into a practical psychology and
ethics, providing not "metaphors for poetry" as the spirits whispered
to Yeats, but a full-scale commentary on socialism, democracy, famous periods of history, and great men. The object of the book is to
help create the cultural climate in which the poet can again take up
the robes of authority, dethroning rationalism and clericalism. Everyone who loves poetry forgives Yeats this book, although it would be
foolhardy to overlook its dangers.

All Modernists, including Eliot, agree unanimously that Pound is
the father of the Culture religion of Modern Poetry. And Pound certainly makes no bones about it. He proposes to lay down a "system"
and does. It is a way of life, an *Anschauung* dealing with man and with
nature. God, significantly, does not come into the system. Pound's
anti-Semitism and anti-Christianity, by the way, are his version of the
poetic liberation from religion. (I should think that Catholics would
complain more about the *Cantos* than the Jews.) Pound is almost
charming in his arrogance about the founding of the culture religion—"these are notes for a totalitarian treatise and I am in fact con-

sidering the New Learning or the New Paideuma . . ." What this New Learning is everyone knows by now: a full-scale culture revolution in which the end justifies any means at hand, "ideas in action," and the rest. But in the long run Pound turns out to be the weakest link in the cultural chain. Eliot's commitment to him, Yeats' acknowledgments and the tacit approval of the New Critics (students of the New Paideuma) all throw a strong light on their own motivations as culture religionists. It does no good to brush Pound off as old Assen Poop, as Williams calls him; he remains the figurehead of the religion. Eliot does not miss an opportunity to defend him in every phase.

Eliot, however, is the key to the religion of culture. Eliot is the only Modern of any consequence who decided to take the risk of religion. Pound was furious; it was almost as much of a betrayal as Jung's branching away from Freud. I do not pretend to know the ins and outs of Eliot's spiritual biography, for it is a labyrinth. But the most interesting thing about it is that it appears to be a highly suspect commitment and may be no more than an intellectual stratagem to capture confidence. When Pound calls him the Reverend Eliot he is very nearly letting the cat out of the bag; evidently Pound refuses to believe that his prize pupil has really turned respectable.

Eliot's sanction of religion is a parallel to Pound's cultural sanction of Fascism. Religion to Eliot is primarily a social question, and not a *mystique*. It is a dismal crutch for a society he detests. In Eliot's words: "As political philosophy derives its sanction from ethics, and ethics from the truth of religion, it is only by returning to the eternal source of truth that we can hope for any social organization which will not, to its ultimate destruction, ignore some essential aspect of reality." The term *democracy* (says Eliot) "does not contain enough positive content to stand alone against the forces that you dislike . . ." Notice how easily democracy becomes almost incompatible with God in this little recital.

Eliot's cultural development may be sketched in this manner. He begins as an uneasy Symbolist; he knows something is wrong with Symbolism, and that it has not worked. He approaches religion in the typical manner, by negating it (at a time when negating religion is an anachronism). The negation is also typical in its dual anti-

Catholicism and anti-Semitism. He then explores the possibility of a relativistic mythology, thus flattering the more rationalistic of the mythologists and anthropologists, such as Sir James Frazer. This is the famous "mythic method" and it is so overwhelmingly a *succès d'estime* that Eliot is suddenly elevated over and above Yeats and Pound and becomes the living incarnation of Modernism. He has now earned the authority to proceed on his own, and it is at this juncture that he makes his extraordinary conversion to the Church of England. It is extraordinary in every respect: the last decision anyone would expect from a twentieth-century American intellectual and poet. Now, with religious authority behind him, and with historical tradition at his side, he begins the elaboration, not of his poetry but of his criticism. He even seems to defend Humanism, though it is a brand which Eliot calls *pure* Humanism.

By fixing his spiritual authorities and antecedents, his literary references and forebears, he manages to rewrite English poetic history, resurrecting the forgotten Metaphysical poets, burying the Romantics and Victorians, removing Walt Whitman to a footnote, and so forth. Finally, departing from Church of England orthodoxy, he scans the mystics. Any suspicion of parochialism is therewith removed, and he is now free to take up his real job of pronouncing about world culture. He becomes in his own lifetime a culture god. This is not the place to delve into the school of literary criticism of which Eliot is godfather. The New Criticism is one of the more noxious byproducts of the culture religion and it is too large a subject for me.

Before the coup d'état of the culture religion, readers of poetry tended to think of it as a "secular" art, or a refined amusement, an expression of the national or of the individual psyche. That is, there was at the beginning of the twentieth century very little doctrinaire agreement about the nature and the uses of poetry. Eliot began by explaining the uses of poetry and the uses of criticism, as Pound had begun with his great blast about a total cultural upset. But by 1925, poetry was no longer "secular"; neither was it "religious," nor philosophical, nor rationalist. It had found a way to compete with every other form of intellectual activity: by pronouncing a curse on the century and everything it stood for; by plunging back into the past and "making it new"; by removing the arts from the people and returning them to the classroom; by promulgating new theories of the Imagination, of the State, of the "sensibilities," and of the *Spiritus Mundi*. Systematically this culture faction eradicated as best it could any influence by D. H. Lawrence, William Carlos Williams, Blake, Walt Whitman, and all other "Romantics" and humanists. It ignored the great poetry being written on the Continent by Lorca, by Rilke, by Cavafy (a much finer "traditionalist" than either Eliot or Pound).

It would be interesting to speculate upon the narrowly "Anglo-Saxon" character of this religion of culture, but I had best not go into that. Suffice it to say that this religion has all the earmarks of puritanism at its worst. Its bitterness, its sense of exile from one or another homeland or paradise, its strong theocratic flavor, its sanctimoniousness, its hatred of spontaneity, originality, and freedom, its insistence on orthodoxy—these are all symptoms of the puritanical hatred of poetry and its cynical abuse for purposes of power.

II

Only a few years before his death Yeats paid a visit to Ezra Pound at his home for the purpose of seeking advice about a play he was writing. Yeats had been troubled by loss of creative power and he thought he would see what Ezra would have to offer as an oracle. The anecdote has been repeated now and then for its anecdote value, but no one seems to have taken it more seriously. But the fact that Yeats went to the trouble to print the story as a note to one of his books signifies, to me at least, that Yeats was finally washing his hands of the American panjandrum. Here are Yeats' own words:

> A year ago I found that I had written no verse for two years; I had never been so long barren; I had nothing in my head, and there used to be more than I could write. Perhaps Coole Park where I had escaped from politics, from all that Dublin talked of, when it was shut, shut me out from my theme; or did the subconscious drama that was my imaginative life end with its owner? but it was more likely that I had grown too old for poetry. I decided to force myself to write, then take advice. In 'At Parnell's Funeral' I

rhymed passages from a lecture I had given in America; a poem
upon Mount Meru came spontaneously, but philosophy is a dangerous theme; then I was barren again. I wrote the prose dialogue
of *The King of the Great Clock Tower*, that I might be forced to
make lyrics for its imaginary people. When I had written all but
the last lyric I went a considerable journey, partly to get the advice of a poet not of my school who would, as he did some years
ago, say what he thought. I asked him to dine, tried to get his attention. 'I am in my sixty-ninth year,' I said, 'probably I should
stop writing verse. I want your opinion upon some verse I have
written lately.' I had hoped he would ask me to read it but he
would not speak of art, or of literature, or of anything related to
them. I had, however, been talking to his latest disciple and knew
that his opinions had not changed: Phidias had corrupted sculpture, we had nothing of true Greece but Nike dug up from the
foundations of the Parthenon, and that corruption ran through all
our art: Shakespeare and Dante had corrupted literature, Shakespeare by his too abounding sentiment, Dante by his compromise
with the Church.

He said, apropos of nothing 'Arthur Balfour was a scoundrel,'
and from that on would talk of nothing but politics. All the other
modern statesmen were more or less scoundrels except 'Mussolini
and that hysterical imitator of his, Hitler.' . . . He urged me to
read the works of Captain Douglas who alone knew what caused
our suffering. He took my manuscript and went away denouncing
Dublin as 'a reactionary hole' because I had said that I was re-
reading Shakespeare, would go on to Chaucer, and found all that
I wanted of modern life in 'detection and the wild west.' Next day
his judgment came and that in a single word 'Putrid.'

Then I took my verses to a friend of my own school and this
friend said, 'Go on just like that. Plays like *The Great Clock Tower*
always seem unfinished but that is no matter. Begin plays without
knowing how to end them for the sake of the lyrics. I once wrote
a play and after I had filled it with lyrics abolished the play.' Then
I brought my work to two painters and a poet until I was like Panurge consulting oracles as to whether he should get married and
rejecting all that did not confirm his own desire.

Now this seems a lengthy and uncalled-for footnote from the poet who in 1935, when this was penned, was probably the most revered living poet in the world. We notice the graciousness of Yeats' manner even in this footnote and his sly Swiftian style ("Then I brought my work to two painters and a poet until I was like Panurge . . .") but underneath the story and the style we are aware that Yeats' blood is boiling. Because of the little insult or because of the long, slightly unsavory association with Pound? It is hard to tell. But the fact that Yeats ever wandered into the Pound orbit at all is one of the more disturbing facts of modernism.

Yeats takes his place along with Eliot and Pound as the third of the triumvirate of Modern Poets who have made the Modern canon respectable. But Yeats was never happy in the company of either. He had a barely concealed contempt for Eliot and he used Pound as a kind of antithesis of his own being. But the fact remains that Yeats is part of the club.

People generally agree that there are several Yeatses: the youthful romantic poet of love and the Celtic twilight, the Yeats of Ireland reborn, the Yeats of the Hermetic societies, and finally the Yeats of world culture. These appellations are grotesquely crude but in effect they give the well-known departments of Yeats' writings. And they are somewhat related. The love poems are also folklore poems to a degree; the patriotic poems of the Irish revolution are also part of the folklore idealism and part of the esoteric explorations simultaneously; and the Culture poems are the final effort to project the subjective personal Yeats, the national Yeats, and the magus or alchemist Yeats into the figure of the seer of history. It is in this final phase that Yeats writes his occult book *A Vision*, in which he contends that he will adapt the symbolic and mythological techniques of Swedenborg and Blake to an interpretation of history, "historical movements and actual men and women." So here is Yeats acting precisely like Pound and Eliot. Yeats is a poet of true genius and not a mere opportunist, but he's off to make a sociological ass of himself all the same. And with much the same results as we have already seen.

I would like to run through one poem of each of Yeats' main phases as a way of seeing him as a whole. If my observations are right, this bird's-eye view of Yeats should lead us to a complete sketch of him. In any case, Yeats cannot suffer from critical myopia on my part; he is too good a poet; he even escaped the condemnations of Ezra Pound. But did he escape the blandishments of the culture religion? That is the question.

Here is the young poet nostalgically in love with the old Celtic Ireland before he knows much about the mysteries of the Irish past. He takes a song he has heard a few lines of from a peasant woman, and he rewrites it. The poem is the famous and pretty song "Down by the Salley Gardens" and was printed as long ago as 1889. The book it appeared in contained several pieces of the same exquisite lyric quality which were to make Yeats famous long before the intellectuals arrived on the scene. What Yeats did with the poem was typical of his gift for changing the sense of a line by using an unusual sense of a word. The original song read "Down by my Sally's garden my love and I did meet"—this version evidently being something of a bawdy song. Yeats changes the proper name Sally to the word *salley*, meaning willow.

> Down by the salley gardens my love and I did meet;
> She passed the salley gardens with little snow-white feet.
> She bid me take life easy, as the leaves grow on the tree;
> But I, being young and foolish, with her would not agree.
> In a field by the river my love and I did stand,
> And on my leaning shoulder she laid her snow-white hand.
> She bid me take life easy, as the grass grows on the weirs;
> But I was young and foolish, and now am full of tears.

What Yeats was doing here besides writing a lovely song was to find and modernize some of that poetry of the past of his country which had evidently died out. This was Yeats' first concern as a poet and a true one: to discover his poetic identity. Forty years later he was using the identical technique to write the modern poem " 'I Am of Ireland,' " which is one of the best of all Yeats' poems. Now here, too, Yeats has had his material given to him, he says, by someone else. He himself never went to the trouble to immerse himself in the old languages, or that is my understanding. And I dare say there is a clue here to all of Yeats' later difficulties, obscurities, and pretenses, namely, that he never gave himself to that Ireland at all and was afraid

of it. The Irish poets take their pride in Yeats but they know after all
that he is Anglo-Irish in letters. Yeats virtually exiled himself to England off and on throughout his life. When we remember that Yeats'
life spans the high moments of the struggle for independence and
that Yeats wished to be the spokesman for Ireland, we have the making of a rich conflict. The biographers have handled these questions
well; but I see in Yeats' English-Irish ambivalence the thing that
made him a prey for the Pounds and the Eliots, men without a country. Most important of all, Yeats never developed completely away
from his early Irish "Celtic" romanticism. It was still the Holy Ireland, not of St. Patrick but of the pre-Christian religions. Yeats, of
course, spent almost as much time combating the official religions of
Ireland as he did writing poetry. This is the poem "'I Am of Ireland'":

> *'I am of Ireland,*
> *And the Holy Land of Ireland,*
> *And time runs on,' cried she.*
> *'Come out of charity,*
> *Come dance with me in Ireland.'*

> One man, one man alone
> In that outlandish gear,
> One solitary man
> Of all that rambled there
> Had turned his stately head.
> 'That is a long way off,
> And time runs,' he said,
> 'And the night grows rough.'

> *'I am of Ireland,*
> *And the Holy Land of Ireland,*
> *And time runs on,' cried she.*
> *'Come out of charity,*
> *And dance with me in Ireland.'*

> 'The fiddlers are all thumbs,
> Or the fiddle-string accursed,

The drums and the kettledrums
And the trumpets all are burst,
And the trombone,' cried he,
'The trumpet and trombone,'
And cocked a malicious eye,
'But time runs on, runs on.'

'I am of Ireland,
And the Holy Land of Ireland,
And time runs on,' cried she,
'Come out of charity,
And dance with me in Ireland.'

Yeats puts a note on this poem telling that he heard a bit of it from
someone who told him it was from a fourteenth-century Irish dance
song. One would assume as a certainty that Yeats would have at some
time made a mad dash for all that old Irish literature which, we are
told, is still unexplored, still untranslated, and which only the post-
Yeats poets are beginning to get at. Why did Yeats avoid it and yet
saturate himself in spiritualism, theosophy, neo-Platonic cabalism,
and finally cyclical theories of history? I think the answer is apparent.
Ireland wasn't big enough for Yeats, even mythologically. But in " 'I
Am of Ireland' " he is beckoned to come "out of charity," too late, and
can do no more than cock a malicious eye. The voice of pagan Ireland never held Yeats the way the poetry and mysticism of Bengal
held his friend Tagore. The difference between them is the most vital
one possible between two such similar poets: Tagore accepted the
mystical content of the folk poetry of Bengal; Yeats rejected the mystical content of the Irish tradition while hanging on to the superficies
of the "supernatural" (ghosts on the stair, the wee folk, ectoplasm,
etc). There is a lifelong silliness about Yeats' preoccupation with
magic which he himself contributed to by not ever quite believing in
it; and in the end it weakened his whole structure of thought. Not
that the esotericism is inherently weak—it is not; it is one of the most
powerful elements of literature, though we are seldom led to literature via the occult. But Yeats dallied with it; he was hangdog about it,
or "literary" or affected, as the case might be. He was expelled from
one Hermetic society for breaking the discipline; he was rather cava-

lier about the leaders of magic of his day, though he was in it up to his ears.

I seem to be getting ahead of the early Yeats in mentioning the Yeats of " 'I Am of Ireland,' " but these phases of Yeats do overlap and recur. Here next is Yeats of the Irish revolution, which is his best phase of all. Possibly a fourth of all Yeats' poems deal with modern Irish history and nearly all of them are of the highest caliber of that type of topical verse which almost invariably defeats itself in time. What is it about Yeats' patriotic poems that keeps them readable long after so much other "political" poetry has died? The best answer is that Yeats wrote them; second, that they are not patriotic but that they deal with a more or less imaginary Ireland, Yeats' Ireland. This is an Ireland compounded of Irish mythological heroes, national heroes, literary and political, and personal acquaintances; Yeats' Irish poems all have a closely personal quality; an intimacy which is born of a common cause. And Yeats always managed to extract the dramatic and the heroic from the scene; he was a dramatist and a hero in his Irish political poems, inside and outside the scene at once. Yeats sees the poetry of the rebirth of all Ireland through the firing of a few shots. The most trivial and meaningless persons have become transformed through the Easter Rebellion and the Civil War; Ireland itself becomes a symbol of tragic and noble power in the modern world. Here is a piece of the stirring poem "Easter 1916":

> Too long a sacrifice
> Can make a stone of the heart.
> O when may it suffice?
> That is Heaven's part, our part
> To murmur name upon name,
> As a mother names her child
> When sleep at last has come
> On limbs that had run wild.
> What is it but nightfall?
> No, no, not night but death;
> Was it needless death after all?
> For England may keep faith
> For all that is done and said.

We know their dream; enough
To know they dreamed and are dead;
And what if excess of love
Bewildered them till they died?
I write it out in a verse—
MacDonagh and MacBride
And Connolly and Pearse
Now and in time to be,
Wherever green is worn,
Are changed, changed utterly:
A terrible beauty is born.

I doubt whether any other poet of the English tongue in the twentieth century could have pulled out all those stops without making a
mockery of the poem: everything is in it, from mother and childhood
to God, England, Ireland, and the names of four of the revolutionaries who were shot by the English, including MacBride who took
Yeats' beloved Maud Gonne away from him. But instead of a sham-
bles we get a ringing elegy and something like a battlecry. Yeats has
managed to put together a vision of the old listless Ireland and the
new, with the sixteen dead men as the metamorphosis and himself as
the seer; a wonderful performance.

So far so good. But when Ireland has become a contemporary reality and even a national literature has been brought into being,
largely through the efforts of Yeats, when the cause is won (or as
much won as it can be), what then? Was Yeats ever really concerned
about the political Ireland as much as he was about the "magical"
symbolic Ireland?

There is something indeterminate about Yeats' interest in magic
and the occult. That he belonged to various Hermetic and spiritualist
and theosophical societies off and on from early youth we know.
What we are not sure of is whether Yeats was a believer or an experimenter. I am inclined to think the latter. His entire performance as a
magus from beginning to end smacks of the literary. The interest itself seems to have grown from the reaction against the modern commonplace world, and is a plunge back into that age when science and
alchemy were still undifferentiated. Yeats' distaste for modern scien-

tific progress was another thing that drew him toward Pound. Yeats also shares with Pound a distaste for religions of any description, but he takes religion seriously enough to want to be heretical about it. In the poem "The Magi," Yeats shows the Wise Men slipping away from the revelation of Christ and the "turbulence" of the crucifixion to the pre-Christian vision of some Dionysian mystery. In this poem, too, one can see the rather violent sexual preoccupation of Yeats.

> Now as at all times I can see in the mind's eye,
> In their stiff, painted clothes, the pale unsatisfied ones
> Appear and disappear in the blue depth of the sky
> With all their ancient faces like rain-beaten stones,
> And all their helms of silver hovering side by side,
> And all their eyes still fixed, hoping to find once more,
> Being by Calvary's turbulence unsatisfied,
> The uncontrollable mystery on the bestial floor.

So with all Yeats' poems that touch the religions: he will preserve the symbol, if he can, but not the form of a belief. It is really striking the way he skims over the surface of religion:

> I asked if I should pray,
> But the Brahmin said,
> 'Pray for nothing, say
> Every night in bed,
> "I have been a king,
> I have been a slave,
> Nor is there anything,
> Fool, rascal, knave,
> That I have not been . . .

For an oversimplification of Hindu homiletics this goes pretty far, unless we keep in mind that Yeats is probably not even thinking about religion but about the kind of reincarnation which can be used to explain historical data. Everything in Yeats' esoteric activities points to a search for a plan of history. As a religious agnostic and poet he must gravitate toward one or another system of symbols to explain cause and fate, personality, great events, creativity, himself in the cosmos, and so on. I find Yeats' solutions always charming and brilliant and disappointing; he seems unnecessarily driven to patent a system; his system after all is not much more convincing than Pound's view of history.

Yeats is a modern "Classicist" by virtue of his emphasis on the civilized and the aristocratic. Civilization is the touchstone. He defines it: "A civilization is a struggle to keep self-control, and in this it is like some great tragic person, some Niobe who must display an almost superhuman will or the cry will not touch our sympathy. The loss of control over thought comes towards the end; first a sinking in upon the moral being, then the last surrender, the irrational cry, revelation—the scream of Juno's peacock." Yeats' fear of the mystical revelation weakens him as a poet; and the irrational and the popular become identified in his mind, as in the mind of Pound, with demagoguery, the decline of the West and what not. What he has to say about his extraordinary sonnet "Leda and the Swan," though it may be one of those critical irrelevancies which we are accustomed to nowadays, signifies that Yeats had very little inspiration for poetry outside his historical speculations. These are his words: "I wrote 'Leda and the Swan' because the editor of a political review asked me for a poem. I thought, 'After the individualist, demagogic movement, founded by Hobbes and popularized by the Encyclopedists and the French Revolution, we have a soil so exhausted that it cannot grow that crop again for centuries.' Then I thought, 'Nothing is now possible but some movement from above preceded by some violent annunciation.' My fancy began to play with Leda and the Swan for metaphor, and I began this poem; but as I wrote, bird and lady took such possession of the scene that all politics went out of it . . ." The rape of Leda by Zeus in the guise of a swan resulted in the birth of Helen, the symbol of perfected female beauty and the cause of war. Yeats seems to be asking for some violent annunciation or rape, "from above," as he puts it.

> A sudden blow: the great wings beating still
> Above the staggering girl, her thighs caressed
> By the dark webs, her nape caught in his bill,
> He holds her helpless breast upon his breast.

How can those terrified vague fingers push
The feathered glory from her loosening thighs?
And how can body, laid in that white rush,
But feel the strange heart beating where it lies?

A shudder in the loins engenders there
The broken wall, the burning roof and tower
And Agamemnon dead.
                          Being so caught up,
So mastered by the brute blood of the air,
Did she put on his knowledge with his power
Before the indifferent beak could let her drop?

Lucky for this poem, Hobbes and the Encyclopedists and the French
Revolution are nowhere to be seen. But Yeats uses the poem as the
frontispiece to one of the sections of *A Vision*, the work said to have
been dictated to his wife by spirits and taken down by her in a species
of automatic writing. *A Vision* is a "system of thought," in Yeats'
words, that would leave his imagination free to create as it chose and
yet make all that it created part of the universal history. All history is
fixed upon a lunar wheel; the individual human personality as well as
historic and cosmic events can be plotted according to the twenty-
eight phases of the moon. The wheel, its phases, and the gyrations of
great and small events make an understanding of past civilizations
and their mythologies possible; more important, in the case of Yeats,
they make prophecy possible. Yeats took a dim view of the chances of
our scientific civilization to survive; he envisioned a new terror
abroad in the world which he likened to the Antichrist. He wrote
poems to that effect but his prose from *A Vision* is even more explicit;
this was written in 1925:

> It is possible that the ever-increasing separation from the
> community as a whole of the cultivated classes, their increasing
> certainty, and that falling-in-two of the human mind which I have
> seen in certain works of art is preparation. During the period said
> to commence in 1927, with the 11th gyre, must arise a form of
> philosophy, which will become religious and ethical in the 12th

gyre and be in all things opposite of that vast plaster Herculean image, final *primary* thought. It will be concrete in expression, establish itself by immediate experience, seek no general agreement, make little of God or any exterior unity . . . Men will no longer separate the idea of God from that of human genius, human productivity in all its forms.

Unlike Christianity which had for its first Roman teachers cobblers and weavers, this thought must find expression among those that are most subtle, most rich in memory; that Gainsborough face floats up; among the learned—every sort of learned—among the rich—every sort of rich—among men of rank—every sort of rank—and the best of those that express it will be given power, less because of that they promise than of that they seem and are. This much can be thought because it is the reversal of what we know, but those kindreds once formed must obey irrational force and so create hitherto unknown experience, or that which is incredible . . . it may grow a fanaticism and a terror, and at its first outsetting oppress the ignorant—even the innocent—as Christianity oppressed the wise . . .

This passage is laden with obscurities, of course, but it is clear that Yeats envisions a turn of the wheel of history which will mean the end of our era. "A decadence will descend" he says; and the new era will bring its stream of irrational force. "I imagine new races . . . each with its own Daimon or ancestral hero . . . history grown symbolic, the biography changed into a myth . . ."

In all of which I detect overtones from T. E. Hulme, Eliot, and especially Pound. But primarily the theme is Yeats' own and goes back to his earliest years when he dreamed romantically of a world made perfect for love. As Yeats matures, this passion for the earthly paradise expresses itself in the extreme symbol of Byzantium. Yeats looked upon Byzantium as next to Heaven. "I think if I could be given a month of Antiquity and leave to spend it where I chose, I would spend it in Byzantium a little before Justinian opened St. Sophia and closed the Academy of Plato . . . I think that in early Byzantium and maybe never before or since in recorded history, religious, aesthetic, and practical life were one . . ." This then is the ideal, that absolute stylization and depersonalization of experience which we associate with the Byzantine mosaic but of which Yeats sang so fervently:

O sages standing in God's holy fire . . .

To the aged Yeats, the cold fire of the impersonal mosaic was an answer to the unquenchable passions of the flesh. In fact, what keeps Yeats lively and interesting to the very end of his poetic life is this intensity of conflict between body and soul which he could never resolve. The jaunty Crazy Jane poems are a record of that conflict also. Yeats was a Puritan as much as Eliot and Pound; in the Irish Senate he once made a speech defending the divorce laws. Later he felt guilty about it—it was hardly the kind of thing to come from the leading poet of the land—but there you have it. In Byzantium everything is fused together, in Yeats' fine phrase, "into the artifice of eternity."

Altogether, Yeats poses one of the central questions of the modern Classical poet, of which he is one of the gods. That question is also Eliot's question and Pound's question, namely, what is the position of the poet vis-à-vis history? From my point of view, I consider the question unreal and not worth the asking. If the self-consciousness of this attitude and the pompousness of it did not utterly defeat Yeats, that can only be because his genius never completely deserted him even throughout his intellectual soul-searchings. But it is my opinion that Yeats will always remain pretty much a poet of his time, because of his commitment to the historical role. The burlesque magus and spiritualist do not add to his stature; they detract from it; all the pronouncements about history and historical types are so much doodling in the margins of his mind. The poetry itself becomes affected; while the idiom steadily increases in subtlety and beauty, the feeling becomes more violent, turning against himself. Yeats could not make peace with age in any aspect; his central image becomes that of "this caricature," decrepit age tied to him "as to a dog's tail." Even that simple wisdom of reconciliation with age is denied him. That Byzantium symbol is a desperate remedy, no remedy at all. That vision of history is hardly a great vision after all but more of a travesty of the great cosmic systems of emanation which he had borrowed from the

Hindus and the Neo-Platonists. The flaw in Yeats is his narrowly conceived idea of civilization; Yeats is quite eighteenth century in the long run. He loved Blake, but did he really learn anything from Blake? It appears not. There is no marriage of heaven and hell in William Butler Yeats—save in Byzantium. Think of the Byzantine mosaic and then try to set beside it the flowing angelography of Blake's pen. There is a complete divergence of imaginations.

The key with Yeats is the word "civilization," the alpha and omega of his culture philosophy. And civilization apparently is—Byzantium. Little wonder that Yeats, a scant generation after his death, is considered a master craftsman of the poem, and nothing else.

THE RETREAT OF
W. H. AUDEN

I DOUBT WHETHER any man living has read everything published by W. H. Auden, probably the most prolific poet-critic of the twentieth century. Not only the quantity but the range of Auden's writing is the most extensive of any contemporary poet's; what is more remarkable, everything he writes is readable. The luxuriance of the Auden bibliography, even in his mid-years, recalls the Victorians, who provided not only the high literature of their time but the popular literature as well. Auden, however, is not popular, any more than T. S. Eliot is popular. Like all Moderns he has eschewed popularity.

The Victorian analogy is a fair one. There is in the quantitative Auden as in the ideal Auden a comfortable paternalism and a sense of cultural responsibility which dates back to the days of Herbert Spencer, Thomas Huxley, and the great novelists who wrote—who must have written—eight hours a day for decades. There is a pervasive and convincing pastness about Auden's writing which always leaves me wondering whether he really is a twentieth-century man or one of those creatures flung over the time barrier by a nineteenth-century time machine.

Auden is probably the most *English* poet since Thomas Hardy died in 1928, the year Auden published his first book. Internationalism has never sat on him well; nor has Americanism (Auden has camped out in America for many years); he is indeed the chief ornament of English letters in the twentieth century. But English poetry is to this day largely "nineteenth century" compared with American or French or Spanish poetry.

In calling these remarks the *retreat* of W. H. Auden I am not referring to the fact that Auden was in his early days a Marxist and is

65

today a poet more involved with theology than with anything else. The fact is that Auden was never as much interested in the social revolution or in religion as he was in psychology; it is Auden's fascination with psychological behavior that makes him readable, charming, and, it may be, lasting. The retreat of Auden is the retreat from poetry to psychology, an almost total sacrifice of the poetic motive to the rational motive. We shall see that Auden is as great a schoolmaster as Pound, though a much more kindly one. Auden is truly a civilized, rational poet (if these are not contradictions in terms), the last of a long line of illustrious "new-classicists" and the father of contemporary poetic style. There is in him nothing of the visionary or the seer, everything of the conversationalist and the classroom wit. Auden, moreover, is an intellectual through and through, and poetry to him is a species of talk. The retreat of poetry into talk, which Auden has made a respectable poetics, is part of the canon of Modernism.

There is no point, in a brief essay of this kind, in trying to sort Auden out into phases, styles, genres, categories of ideas, allegiances, and what not. My aim rather is to determine to what extent Auden takes poetry seriously; and if he does not, what view of it he does hold.

There is one minor matter I would like to dispose of first, namely, the relationship between Auden's earlier social revolutionary poetry and his present-day theological poetry. Readers of Auden have been greatly disturbed (*a*) by the conversion of Auden from humanism to religion, and (*b*) by the fact that Auden has tried to rewrite much of his early humanistic verse to make it conform with his later views. The question of rewriting one's early poems to make them sound ideologically like the later ones is such a curious question of literary morals that we had better not try to deal with it at all. This "police" question has been dealt with in J. W. Beach's book, *The Making of the Auden Canon*. The question of Auden's religious conversion from a youthful revolutionary fervor, on the other hand, is a common literary question, one we meet in poets who live through more than one phase of history. I do not find this question very important, however; a poet's politics and his religion are pretty much his own affair, unless they actually do run afoul of the law, as Pound's did. Auden, as far as this reader knows, has never broken any laws and is not likely to; he is thoroughly law-abiding and is in fact a great respecter of the law, in poetry and elsewhere. A poet's religious and political attitudes are of no concern to the reader unless they become part of the poetry.

From the beginning Auden adopted a position about religion and about history; and this meant a personal encounter with Eliot. Auden was too much the scholar and the gentleman ever to be other than respectful to Eliot, but he presented himself as the chief member of the loyal opposition. By the time Auden began to publish, in the early thirties, Eliot was so deeply entrenched in his self-styled Classical revetment that it had become heroic for the young to adopt the pose of the Romantic poet. One could not be a simple Romantic like Rupert Brooke or Shelley (whom Auden always goes out of his way to tell how much he detests); one must be a Romantic and an intellectual to boot. The construction of a Romantic program was a simple matter of drawing a diagram of the Eliot-Pound-Hulme platform and then writing in the opposite terms. Instead of Classicist there would be Romantic; instead of Monarchist there would be Socialist; instead of Anglican there would be Agnostic. Not that Auden was ever so unsophisticated as to write a manifesto, but he saw the literary opportunity quite clearly. And he had organizational ability. Social revolution was thick in the air when he began; clinical psychology and "depth" psychologies were all over the place; and textbooks of every description were as much "experience" to Auden as fields of daffodils to Wordsworth. While Eliot is a learned poet, one who adjusts his poetry to his education, Auden adjusts all knowledge to the poem. It is interesting to note about Auden that he never espouses an extreme cause; his opinions are extensive in range and thorough in their digestion of the material, but never radical. In this he differs from his early associates like Spender and Day Lewis, both of whom were willing to take Causes literally. Auden has always been too detached from people, one gathers from his poetry, and too excited by theories about people (psychology) to ever become more than a paper Romantic. A more horrendous way of putting it would be to term him a Cultural Romantic. Even his religious poems give the impression that he is concerned with the idea of religion, rather than with the religious experience.

Auden's disinterest in unseating Eliot and the things which Eliot symbolizes is one of the chief factors in the continued pre-eminence of Eliot as a critic. Either Auden failed to see the profoundly reactionary quality of Eliot's poetics, or he was content to compromise with them. The latter is probably the case. In the long run, as we all know, Auden became completely magnetized to the Eliot position and is today only a satellite spinning around him. The fact is that Auden never did develop a poetics of his own, as one would expect the author of so much criticism to do. Auden's poetics are inclusive: they comprise the sum total of poetry in the English tongue, from Beowulf through the young poets he chose to appear in the Yale Younger Poets series. This is quite a different thing from Eliot's "Tradition" which excludes practically everybody in English poetry— and includes almost no living poets. Auden's rejections are dislikes rather than principles. When Eliot points his finger at John Milton and says, "Go!" Milton must be gone. When Auden, on the other hand, tells us that Shelley is loathsome, we feel that this is more of a personal than a literary matter. Auden is the editor of the best general anthology in English poetry, among his other numerous anthologies, and he knows the tradition in a true sense, and loves it. He is part of it; he is heir to it. In fact, one can understand Auden best by seeing him in the role of curator of the tradition of English poetry. One of the reasons Auden fled England must have been his fear of being recognized as a traditional English poet to the manner born. He has Poet Laureate written all over him.

But the career of Auden is curiously without center; it is uninteresting. It consists of a series of reports on the goodness and the badness of English poets and their ideas. These reports are sometimes in prose, just as frequently in verse. He arranges and classifies, he is meticulously neat, tireless, painstaking, accurate, patient, polite (except on rare occasions of schoolroom outburst), thoughtful, intelligent, sensitive, and more knowledgeable "in his field" than any other poet of the time. For all of this the world is immeasurably in his debt. Eliot once made the remark, which was quite far from the truth, that Pound's poetry is a kind of textbook of modern versification. But such a remark would be true of Auden; Auden is the teacher of prosody.

There is a consistent ambiguity about Auden's position at whatever point we observe it. We must give him the benefit of the doubt and hope that his uncertainties are not fatal. While Auden has a somewhat ferocious capacity for belief, we can never be sure whether it is belief or love of argument that moves him. Auden is a highly argumentative poet and he is always trying to convince the reader of something; one begins to wonder if he isn't trying to convince himself as well. From the standpoint of poetry this constant debating is foreboding; a poet's beliefs, after all, should be taken for granted in his poetry. A tremendous quantity of Auden's poetry fades quickly; very seldom does it rise above the argument, whatever the argument happens to be at the moment. In Auden one is constantly thrown back on the "content" because the content is never purely taken for granted. He is forever washing his intellectual linen in public. His most interesting poems are those in which he generalizes the troubled "I," into "we"; Auden's preoccupation with pronouns is famous.

In his work we see an enormous mass of unrelated poems and verses covering every possible category of the poem, as the textbook and anthology classify the English poem. The poet's hallmark is always evident; the turn of phrase, the vocabulary, the rhythms themselves are always distinctively his, so characteristic that one can spot them in a second. And these forms run from the smallest to the largest, from the minutest epigram to the oratorio, libretto, verse play, prose-poem; everything, in fact, except the modern "epic" like the *Cantos* or the straight narrative, like "Roan Stallion." Yet we cannot find a particular form which we identify as Auden's, one he has invented.

As a guide in this essay I will use Auden's *Collected Poetry*, published over a decade ago, with mention of his later works at random. This is not a study of Auden's totality of production but only of his significant books, the most significant being the *Collected Poetry* published in 1945. The book is the first great landmark in his career, his first plateau of achievement. It is in many respects a peculiar book, not so much a collection as a final rewriting of all the nonrejected poetry—an attempt, in other words, at a unity which Auden covets and seems unable to accomplish.

The book, close on to five hundred pages, has as an epigraph a tellingly ambiguous quatrain. It reads:

Whether conditioned by God, or their neural structure, still
All men have this common creed, account for it as you will;—
The Truth is one and incapable of contradiction;
All knowledge that conflicts with itself is Poetic Fiction.

In this dedication, as in so many of Auden's poems, it is hard to tell
where he stands. There is an antithesis as follows: The Truth (with a
capital T) is one. But all knowledge that conflicts with itself (that is,
which is not one) is Poetic Fiction. What the reader has to dope out
is whether Auden is being serious about the meaning of Truth and serious about Poetic Fiction (also capitalized). Or whether he is being
serious about one and not the other. Or finally, whether he is being
serious at all. Even his initial statement is open to question—that all
men have this common creed. It is Auden's typical way of saying that
what he believes at the moment, all men believe. The epigram is
therefore a subjective statement around a typical dualism. It is at once
a justification for his poetry and a kind of poetics. It gives him an aim
(Truth) and it rationalizes "conflicting knowledge" as poetry. In what
sense of irony Auden uses Poetic Fiction is hard to tell. Evidently he
both accepts and rejects the idea of Poetic Fiction. In one of his recent poems Auden writes about wanting to live in a cave "with two
exits." The epigram I have cited has more than two exits. Notice that
Auden does not say that all knowledge that conflicts with itself is Poetry, as Yeats would have it, but Poetic Fiction. Perhaps Poetry is
Truth and near-poetry is poetic fiction; it is hard to tell. We rather
expect Auden to say something startling like Truth is Beauty, but in a
more Modern manner, more subtly. This poem is not important except that it is the frontispiece to the *Collected Poetry* and is a web of
dualisms.

The poems themselves are arranged in a manner which every
critic has noticed and been annoyed at. Many of the poems did not
have titles originally, but are given offhand titles and put in a sequence depending on the spelling of the first word of the first line.
The purpose here, aside from the obvious one of scrambling the
chronology, is to suggest a unity and spontaneity which lie beyond
any preconceived plan. There is a kind of waggery and even tomfool-
ery about the arrangement which is supposed to bear out the poet's

notion of poetry as "play." The notion that it is play is paired with the
somewhat desperate hope that this play, this Poetic Fiction, will
somehow lead to the Truth.

But a chronological view of Auden's poems will not yield much insight anyway; at any one time Auden can be found practicing a
goodly number of "forms." In every case they are retrospective and
can be related to a model from the past or the present. He makes no
effort to invent in the sense that, say, Hopkins invents or Pound
strives to invent; there is a different "prosody" operating in Auden
and it is the prosody in the old-fashioned sense of line, stanza, and
rhyme. Auden's great achievement, on the other hand, is the modernization of diction, the enlarging of dictional language to permit a
more contemporary-sounding speech. In this endeavor he has created a revolution in English poetic speech for our time *which is in effect part of the counterrevolution of T. S. Eliot.* In Auden's case this was
an honest and perhaps inevitable development, not a scheme to rule
the poetic roost. The Eliot-Pound "form" is, as we know, barren, and
nothing new has grown out of it. Its failure permitted Auden to return to the standard forms. English poetry, as I mentioned, has been
singularly weak in the aspect of invention for a hundred years in comparison to French or American poetry of the same period. The fact
that an inventive poet like Gerard Manley Hopkins went unnoticed
in his lifetime is evidence of this. Even Yeats, a basically conventional
writer, thought Hopkins a bit queer. While Auden has no part in the
polemics of the American Moderns about schools of poetry, his work
in bulk represents a slowing-up of the formal process, through a
broadening of the diction for the sake of inclusiveness. The Auden
poem is intelligible, with the logic of beginning, middle, and end, and
intelligible within the semantics of the dictionary.

Diction is that aspect of style which refers back to wording; its
final authority is the dictionary. The inventive poet uses the dictionary, if at all, as a point of departure, not as a resting place. The orthodox poet, or classical poet, or academic poet, or intellectual poet,
however you call him, always gravitates toward language in its accepted state. It is his authority. In this respect Auden is a dictionary
poet, one who refers to the authority of the lexicon and the authority
of the anthology. He is himself a scholar and superb editor, with a

tremendous grasp of his material. Even his theorizing is handsomely documented.

But Auden has no poetic direction; his theory as well as his practice of poetry reverts to play; he develops a kind of self-defeating technique which prevents even his followers from making him the center of a poetic cult. He would like to be as dogmatic as Blake, for instance, but cannot; as flamboyant as Byron (or Dylan Thomas); or as desperate as Rimbaud. But he is in fact too much a poet of debts and obligations, too happy with books, and too civilized a man to kick over the card catalogue and run howling to his Muse.

"About suffering they were never wrong, / The Old Masters:" begins his *Collected Poetry*. It is one of his best-known poems and a poem that has become the prototype for younger writers throughout the English-using world. Everything about it makes it a model poem, a poem for the album. The title is "Musée des Beaux Arts," signifying that the poem is and is not a museum piece. It suggests the poet magnetized to the museum, whose experience is limited to the big city where the masterpieces settle down after their hard careers in the outside world. The poet is not really looking at the picture of Brueghel's *Icarus* but thinking about it as he walks away. The poem is something like a twenty-one line sonnet. It has the grace and structure and smugness of the sonnet. But of course it is not a sonnet, any more than it is a poem about a picture. The theme of the poem is Icarus in relation to the landscape of man as seen in a famous painting and put into a poem. The whole tone of the poem is that of the man walking down the street after having been to the museum, explaining the significance of a certain famous work of art to a young friend. This is the peculiar intimacy of Auden and it is never without its charm. It is serious, accurate, and urbane with the authoritative urbanity of the city-cultivated man. The example of the work of art is indispensable to Auden as a center of value; for he can provide none without the examples of art. Thus Auden has led us back to the art-gallery poem, the poem suffused with the golden light of the museum and the library. It is Browning without the narration. It is what young people mean by "academic."

Auden regards his own book as an anthology, a museum, not out of conceit but because of a confidence that his poetry is part of the great flux of the past, as it is. His earliest poems are the most exciting as experiment, with their play on the rhythms of Skelton and Old English, the primitive movements of a great literature. In these poems the meaning is more approximate than precise and it appears that Auden will try for a breakthrough into new forms, like Williams. But it transpires quickly that Auden is not thinking of poetry in this aspect but of poetry as it has always been; he reverts to the forms, loosening them, making them generally available and comfortable to use. And meanwhile he uses the poem as a blackboard to chalk out his views. Voltaire, Freud, Yeats, places he has been, wars he has lived through, Utopias he has dreamed and which have or have not failed him, psychological types, the great artifacts like the Sphinx, and Oxford. At the same time there is never the poem bound wholly to a subject; the subject in Auden's poetry is always moving away from the subject, toward the psychological monologue. This monologue develops naturally from discussion of societal man to spiritual man, from social science to spiritual science, theology.

One finds it impossible to do more than to praise Auden for his extraordinary competence, and after that to talk about the significance of this competence. Each work of his achieves its own perfection; and there is probably no poet in English who has written so much whose successes are so many. In this excellence Auden is like a superb athlete, unaware of his own agility, and spectacularly lucky. I leave to others the discussion and analysis of Auden's scholasticism, his observations about society and about man's spiritual place in the modern world. The pageantry of Auden's poetry is the pageantry of ideologies; to the degree that Auden makes his poetry serve the ends of argument his poetry is in mortal danger of dying with the century. While *The Waste Land* and the *Cantos* may always be retained in the museum of literary knickknacks, Auden's poetry suggests the fate of period literature. It appears that Auden has already lost touch with a contemporary audience and that even his enormous influence over the diction has been assimilated and forgotten. But it is Auden more than any other poet who has stamped the modern poem with a style. To Auden belongs the honor of having brought to perfection what everyone nowadays calls the Academic Poem.

The academic poem is discursive poetry; it is versified thinking. I

am not speaking of Auden now but of Audenesque. Eliot and Pound
returned poetry, as William Carlos Williams never tires of saying, to
the university by making literary data the center of the poem. Auden
followed the cue and made all printed data of every description the
center of the poem. This was the revolution in diction that I mentioned earlier. If Pound quotes a saying by an American soldier it is to
demonstrate the degeneration of Americans in language. When
Auden studies and adopts American journalism, he is not trying to
demean it but to see its possibilities as poetic usage. Auden uses all
the jargons, from social science to advertising, accepting them as current languages of communication, allowing for just enough irony of
tone to save himself from being identified with these jargons. The
dictions border on the comic, sometimes even imitating Ogden Nash
or Edward Lear. They open the door to the old rhetorical devices like
the capitalized abstraction of allegory, which with Auden is an unseri-
ous way of being serious. By doing this with such apparent ease, he
has made the discursive poem casual and universal.

What distinguishes Auden from, say, the "Georgian" poets is the
intellectualizing of emotions. Yeats admired greatly a villanelle of
Ernest Dowson's with the refrain "Wine and women and song,
/Three things lighten our way." Auden writes "I sit in one of the
dives /On Fifty-second Street" and shortly begins to talk about the
"low dishonest decade." Dowson mourned in the bar about his fellow
artists and his own emotional griefs; Auden in the bar mourns about
politics, society, and war. This fusion of personal emotion with intellectual debate was something quite new. Eliot and Pound had rid the
poem of emotion completely and talked about "felt" ideas. Eliot advised poets to "feel their thought" like Dr. Donne. Auden reversed
the process and showed the poet how to "think his emotions" in poetry. Eliot and Pound failed to create a following because poets *are*
enormously emotional animals, and do not want to use thought as an
experience, as Eliot advises. Poets would much rather feel sorry for
themselves (if that is the only emotion available, as it seems to have
been for Ernest Dowson) or generalize their emotion into "universals," like Keats in his somber odes. They do not want to "feel their
thoughts" like the Wits and the Metaphysicals Eliot is so fond of. But
in a pinch they are quite willing to "think" their feelings, like Auden.

The Auden poem is intellectualized emotion. The academic poem is intellectualized emotion, when there is any emotion to intellectualize. Most often there is only a pretense of emotion and this pretended emotion is intellectualized and versified. Auden's emotion is usually vital and warm, even though he chews it over in the poem. The truly academic poem is cold and clammy; whatever feeling it had to begin with is filtered through the screen of wit until it is unrecognizable as feeling. In the academic poem the reader does not know what the emotional direction is; to this charge the academic critic replies that that is not important: if you want your emotions directed, go to the movies.

I suppose I should give an example of an academic poem, one in which the original feeling is lost through talk about it. For this purpose I might use almost any poem chosen at random from the big literary quarterlies or the small reviews, as this is the type of poem most in favor with editors today. But I do not feel that I should make fun of some other poet's work and I will use a poem of my own. The only thing I want to say in defense of the poem is that I rather like my version of the academic poem. Notice that there is a double meaning of some kind in almost every line of the poem, that some words are used simultaneously as nouns and verbs or adjectives and that there are so many instances of this kind of play in the poem that I find new ones every time I look at the poem. Such a remark would elicit a chuckle from the modern critic to the effect that "I told you so; there is even more to your poem than *you* think."

The poem is titled "A Calder," the title being a play on words for: Alexander Calder, the inventor of mobile art; the article "a," signifying a particular Calder mobile; and also his initial. Here is the poem:

To raise an iron tree
Is a wooden irony,
But to cause it to sail
In a clean perpetual way
Is to play
Upon the spaces of the scale.
Climbing the stairs we say,
Is it work or is it play?

Alexander Calder made it
Work and play:
Leaves that will never burn
But were fired to be born,
Twigs that are stiff with life
And bend as to the magnet's breath,
Each segment back to back,
The whole a hanging burst of flak.

Still the base metals,
Touched by autumnal paint
Fall through no autumn
But, turning, feint
In a fall beyond trees,
Where forests are not wooded,
There is no killing breeze,
And iron is blooded.

No one, I think, could tell from this poem that I am a fervent admirer of Calder. I am. The feeling is almost entirely obscured by paradoxes: an iron tree, a wooden irony, the use of work and play as both nouns and verbs, and so on. I call this an Audenesque poem, a poem in which the emotion is thought to pieces. Auden himself would never be this obvious in a poem; he would think the poem a good deal further along the line than I have. Or he might write one stanza with the mobile in it and then take off into a rarer atmosphere of speculation, as Yeats does in his schoolroom-visiting poem, another model of the age in which the human element is all but snuffed out by Yeats' talk about metaphysics.

To recapitulate what I have said: Eliot and Pound destroyed all emotion for poetry except emotion arising from ideas. (The formula is theirs, not mine, and I take no responsibility for the obscurity of it.) Observing their stigma against emotion, Auden used emotion in the poem as a subject for intellectual speculation. Auden's use of emotion-as-conversation was the model for what we call the academic poem. It was not only Auden's great skill in making this kind of poem readable that turned it into a genre; it was also the fact that people in the twentieth century tend to intellectualize emotion anyway. The curse laid upon emotion by the Moderns was inherited by Auden, who apologizes for his emotions by talking about them in the poem. To use the critical jargon, the academic poem can be recognized by its Objective Form, objective form being anything from jamming the text, the use of concealed metaphor, involved stanzaic form, "personae," to anything else that prevents direct expression of feeling. The modern critic considers the expression of personal or subjective emotion a "fallacy."

Auden is essentially a lyric poet but lyricism also was frowned on by the inventors of Modernism. Pound had expressed some interest in Robert Burns and Villon, it appears mostly for the dialect quality of their poems; but what he called in his terminology "Melopoeia" was not at the top of the poetic heap. At the top of the heap was the "poetry of ideas." People used to speak of Dylan Thomas as a great "lyric" poet, meaning that they liked his work but didn't think it would produce much intellectual aftermath. It didn't; but it produced the first spontaneous audience for good poetry since the moderns ruled out audiences as immaterial. Auden's own lyric talent has been subsumed under his own intellectual talent. Auden, in fact, has created a genre, the intellectual lyric: he says:

> O who can ever praise enough
> The world of his belief?

Every Auden lyric or ballad has an intellectual point to make—there is no story for the story's sake, no song for the song's sake.

The lyricism of Auden is almost always spoiled by self-conscious siftings and ruminations. Many of them are little parables, some are leftovers from plays, but very few are lyrics. Generally Auden treats the lyric too gingerly, like an archeological find which he has just dusted off. Here is an example, using the recently discovered American folk-song idiom, which our poet is a little uncertain about.

> "Gold in the North," came the blizzard to say,
> I left my sweetheart at the break of day,
> The gold ran out and my love turned grey.
> *You don't know all, sir, you don't know all.*

"The West," said the sun, "for enterprise,"
A bullet in Frisco put me wise,
My last words were "God damn your eyes."
You don't know all, sir, you don't know all.

In the streets of New York I was young and swell,
I rode the market, the market fell,
One morning I woke and found myself in hell,
You don't know all, sir, you don't know all.

In Alabama my heart was full,
Down by the river bank I stole,
The waters of grief went over my soul,
You don't know all, ma'am, you don't know all.

    In the saloons I heaved a sigh,
    Lost in deserts of alkali I lay down to die;
    There's always a sorrow can get you down,
    All the world's whiskey won't ever drown.

Some think they're strong, some think they're smart,
Like butterflies they're pulled apart,
America can break your heart.
You don't know all, sir, you don't know all.

Many of Auden's lyrics are all that endure of some of his plays. This may be as good a place as any to add a note about the use of drama among modern poets. What do we find is the state of the drama in the hands of modern poets whom we have been talking about?

In the first place, Pound puts a virtual ban on drama. To him the theatre is too public and all sorts of illiterate and noisy folk crowd into the playhouse. Pound turns his back on the Greek dramatists and on Shakespeare, and all other drama except perhaps the Japanese Noh. What Pound understood about the Noh was its subtlety as a spirit-play and dance-play; and it was this element that he recommended to Yeats. Pound's insight was excellent here. But Pound also recommended the "aristocratic" quality of the Noh, a typical Pound misinterpretation. The Noh had been killed off by the Western

opening of Japan in the nineteenth century, but it was not aristocratic; it began in fact as a public and even mystical art connected
with the sect of Zen Buddhism. Yeats followed up the Noh as best he
could and wrote dance plays and closet drama and other "aristocratic" forms, some of them quite beautiful, all of them far out of
reach of a living stage. Even the quality of the poetry in the Yeats play
is thinned out, and there are no characters in the sense that Synge
knew and used character. Yeats' dramatic defect was that of the Modern Poet who does not really recognize the existence of people at all,
but only voices and masks.

Eliot's place as dramatist is more interesting. In the absence of any
poetic drama in our language for centuries, Eliot approached the
problem cautiously and intelligently, experimenting with such simple
and traditional forms as the church pageant: *Murder in the Cathedral*
is not only his best play; it is one of the best "miracle" plays of the literature. Eliot uses only pre-Shakespearian dramatic forms and post-
Shakespearian dramatic forms. The high period of English drama he
does not try to duplicate. *Family Reunion* is an attempt to reproduce
tragedy in the old sense. The later drawing-room plays are evidently
modeled on Oscar Wilde. (Eliot's understanding of character is
Wildean and requires a static social atmosphere in which the characters can make epigrams.) The success of some of Eliot's drawing-
room plays is based not on any use of character or plot or poetry, for
the poetry grows less and less and finally disappears, but on the use
of the quasi-supernatural man, in reality a *deus ex machina*. Eliot's inability to deal with true character is similar to that of Yeats, neither
poet evidently having had sufficient knowledge of, or sympathy for,
people to know what to do with them. The chief virtue of Eliot's
plays is that for a moment they reversed the tendency of realism in
the theatre.

Auden is more attuned with dramatic literature than any of the
foregoing poets and from the very beginning of his career has stayed
close to the uses of dramatic poetry and theatre poetry. It is interesting to note that Auden has never had a stage success like Eliot or even
Yeats, while his use of dramatic forms *not* intended for the stage is
better than that of any other contemporary. He is a librettist, not a
dramatist; Auden's use of character is even weaker than Eliot's. There

are no characters proper in his plays, only literary voices, or rather radio voices, for Auden prefers not even to delineate the face and form of a character. By far the most brilliant of these voice-poems is *For the Time Being*, which is to date the best work of Auden's and one that promises to survive much of his other poetry. This oratorio, as Auden calls it, uses all the lyric forms in a burlesque mode, saucily and with all the voices of wit. Considering the subject, which is the "Christmas story," the whole poem is light and pleasant and enlivened by a great deal of sophisticated talk about society and community. There is no particular unity to the poem; Auden prefers the lyric plus recitative form which allows full use of the intellectual choric voice. *The Age of Anxiety* makes even less pretense of being playable; like *The Sea and the Mirror* and *New Year Letter*, it is discursive poetry in voices. Auden's inventiveness in this realm is another of his contributions to literary form; the basis of the form is again diction and the action is all verbal and psychological. One is reminded of the masque of Jonson or Milton.

Auden has moved drama even further from the stage than Yeats. Eliot has moved it closer to the stage than any other poet since the Jacobeans, but only in a technical sense. The Eliot play is a *tour de force* tending toward the kind of brittle stylization we get in Christopher Fry. A true poetic drama must begin from the theatre as it exists today, not from the poem as it exists today. We have the seeds of this drama in a playwright like Tennessee Williams, really a poet, not in Eliot or in Auden or Yeats. Williams' exaggeration of character and situation is poetic exaggeration; the characters are rooted in reality but are not realistic; Eliot's and Auden's are not rooted in reality but in "ideas." Tennessee Williams represents a beginning of a poetic view of character and circumstance. The lurid and baroque atmosphere of his plays should not distract us from the fact that Williams is dealing with recognizable realities. The popularity of his plays attests to the fact that his audiences see beneath the surface distortions, violences, and perversions of their situations. And in general, what is called "Southern" literature in America is more vital than any other literature, not because of its dark and catastrophic surface but because certain effects of American life are best seen through characters who live closer to the real nature of American violence and passion.

This is where the poet comes in. It is not a question of setting a play in New Orleans or Oxford, Mississippi, but of dealing with characters whose daily emotions are forced into overt behavior by the spirit of place. Synge could do this with the Aran islanders; Yeats could not do it because he could not see emotion on the streets; he could see it only in dreams. Some of Eliot's characters are convincing in scenes of domestic altercation but in nothing else. Eliot has to get rid of characters by pushing them off boats or sending them into the tropics to be eaten by ants. Auden's characters, on the other hand, have a kind of Gilbert and Sullivan charm, "real" enough, but only for *opéra bouffe*.

The career of Auden thus far has demonstrated one fact over all others, that he has advanced the "Classicism" of Eliot and Pound. With more than half the twentieth century gone it is now possible to see the pattern of poetry as it was established by the founders of Modern Classicism and to see the meaning of the discipleship of Auden.

In the face of the enormous productivity of Auden and the relative success of all his work, it is difficult at first to see his connection with Eliot. Where Eliot and Pound failed to effect a revolution in poetry they succeeded in providing cultural sanctions for poets and critics of the next generation. There is no indication that Pound approves of Auden; he would consider him one of the second category of poets, those who consolidate the "inventions" of their masters. Eliot, of course, would take a much more sympathetic view of Auden. Eliot abandoned the pretense of free verse after it had served his purpose; actually he never used it at all except in a few early "imagistic" poems. Eliot used modified French forms which he admittedly copied; by the time of the *Quartets* he no longer pretends any loyalty to new forms but relapses into a gauche lyricism, alternating with a slack line of prose. Pound has, on the other hand, stuck to his conception of a new form of verse, enough to impress William Carlos Williams, among others. Auden evidently saw through the "experimentation" of his elders to their real purpose, which lay beyond poetry. It may be that Auden took literally the Classicists' talk about Tradition, as later he seems to have taken seriously their talk about religion. In any case, Auden's service to Modernism, Classicism, or whatever you want to call it, is the determinant of the common style of poetry in English today.

All of Auden's talk about Romanticism, the romantic voyage, the quest, loneliness, the romantic artist as *poète maudit*, and so on—is all talk. It is well documented, handsome talk, but it comes from books and nothing but books. The sectarian battles between Romantic and Classic one would have thought bad died ages ago, but we find them revived by Eliot and his friends, with Auden providing a little fencing practice for the Romantic team. The great "Romantics"—Nietzsche, Whitman, Rimbaud, Lawrence—do not enter into the game, having been polished off by Eliot long since. The whole point of Auden's "Romanticism" seems to have been to accommodate that persuasion to the tenets of the Classicists. In any case, this most academic of struggles has simmered down in Auden to textbook discussion and no longer plays any serious role in poetry as a living art.

Ironically, Auden brings to our attention the fact that "modern" poetry still has not come into existence. What has passed for Modern Poetry is in no wise comparable to the painting and music of our time, but a weak imitation of those arts. The new poetry which Eliot and Pound bragged they were bringing into existence has its fruits in the stanzas, sestinas, oratorios, and libretti of Auden, the typical New-Classical and academic literature of our time. Nor has Auden profited from the true modern poetry outside of the English language. Except for one translation of Cavafy, which had already been done quite well, Auden shows little sign of interest in the poetry of modern Spain, Italy, Greece, France, Germany, or South America. Stephen Spender has done far more to introduce the European poets into English than Auden.

It is an astonishing fact about the twentieth century that it is without its poet. Auden set out to be the Poet of the Age: at least he was always inventing slogans which the literary journalists readily picked up. He had the air and authority of a Spokesman, but for whom did he speak? We remember that Auden began as the voice of English revolutionary youth and that the enemy was the entrenched bourgeoisie with its country-club ethics, its smug clericalism, and its imperialist bank account. This was the intellectual fashion in England until after the Spanish Civil War and the famous Moscow trials;

Auden was the first of the Marxist poets to slip quietly out of the meeting. By the time he was missed he was already ruminating in New York over the failure of Collective Love and the sad truth of the need for personal love. An extraordinary amount of Auden's poetry of this time is an anguished repetition of the cry that self-love is the only possible love. The recoil from the class-war morality was very severe for Auden; in exile he became an American citizen and a parishioner of the Church of England. Auden has always had to have his papers in order; an intellectual decision to him means signing on the dotted line. He shuffles his papers, or reshuffles them and is ready to begin again. But for whom is he the Spokesman this time? It becomes harder and harder to tell. The tone of conviction is as firm as ever; the generalizations as sweeping as before, but now they are couched in theology. As far as Auden's instinct for the public sensibility goes, he is probably right to switch from the language of anthropology and depth psychology to the language of Angst, Eros and Agape, for there is no question that the Dismal Science, Theology, is in the ascendency in the mid-century. And I have no doubt that Auden can hold his own among the best of the doctors of religion. But my interest in him stops there.

Auden's achievement is thus far that of the great stylist, not that of the primary poet, the actual creator of poetry like Hopkins or Rimbaud or, among his own contemporaries, Dylan Thomas. Auden is more than a literary movement: he is practically a period of literature all to himself. But his is a period of reexamination—of forms, of vocabularies, of ideologies. He is the great amateur of our time; he has taught us all how to improvise. But one would be hard put to find the small handful of poems which are the core of Auden, the man himself, the poet himself. Auden is already forgotten by the present generation, the poets who have begun to write since about 1940; he has been absorbed completely. This is sad for a poet of such rich talents and a man of such good will; but the reason is at hand: he calls his own integrity into question. I began with Auden's quatrain about Truth and Poetic Fiction and I must end with an example of his Poetic Fiction (or is it his Truth?) contradicting itself.

This is part of the passage from his play *The Dog Beneath the Skin*, which, among other things, is a bitter anticlerical diatribe. A hypocritical vicar is delivering a sermon and Auden is pulling out all the stops to show how revolting are the vicar and his message. The sermon is, in fact, a violent satire on religion at its worst. But note this: when Auden publishes his *Collected Poetry*, ten years after the play itself, he makes a separate place for this very sermon and calls it "Depravity," introducing it with a strange bit of Pecksniffiana:

> I can only hope that this piece will seem meaningless to those who are not professing Christians, and that those who are, and consequently know that it is precisely in the religious life that the worst effects of the Fall are manifested, will not misinterpret it as simple anticlericalism which always implies a flattery to the laity.
>
> It is concerned with two temptations: the constant tendency of the spiritual life to degenerate into an aesthetic performance; and the fatal ease with which Conscience, i.e., the voice of God, is replaced by "my conscience," i.e., the Super-Ego which . . . holds one variant or another of the Dualist heresy.

In this passage the vicar is attacking the idea of freedom and social revolution which Auden (at least when he wrote the play) was defending. (The stage directions have the vicar in an hysterical frenzy, crying and with saliva flowing from his mouth.)

> And so, today, we are here for a very good reason. His enemies have launched another offensive, on the grandest scale, perhaps, that this poor planet of ours has ever witnessed. As on the first awful occasion in Eden, so now; under the same deluding banner of Freedom. For their technique of propaganda has never varied . . . that thee-syllable whisper: "You are God," has been, is, and alas, will be sufficient to convert the chapped-handed but loyal ploughboy, the patient sufferer from incurable disease, the tired economical student or the beautiful juvenile mama into a very spiteful maniac indeed . . . [The vicar then draws a picture of what it would be like to live under the slave state in the name of Freedom. Then he exhorts his congregation:]
>
> But mind, God first! To God the glory and let Him reward! God is no summer tourist. We're more than scenery to Him. . . . Oh delight higher than Everest and deeper than the Challenger

Gulf! His commodores come into His council and His lieutenants know His love. Lord, I confess! I confess! I am all too weak and utterly unworthy. There is no other want. . . .

Oh Father, I am praising Thee, I have always praised Thee, I shall always praise Thee! Listen to the wooden sabots of Thy eager children running to Thy arms! Admit him to the fairs of that blessed country where Thy saints move happily about their neat, clean houses under the blue sky! O windmills, O cocks, O clouds and ponds! Mother is waving from the tiny door! The quilt is turned down in my beautiful blue and gold room! Father, I thank Thee in advance! Everything has been grand! I am coming home!

Here is Auden in a nutshell. A passage condemning an idea is used ten years later to defend the idea that the passage originally condemned. What was a burlesque of ecclesiastical rhetoric is now presented as a sober sermon. Which is the Truth, which the Poetic Fiction? You will have to decide for yourselves. For as Auden says in one of his poems:

This might happen any day;
So be careful what you say
    And do:
Be clean, be tidy, oil the lock,
Weed the garden, wind the clock;
    Remember the Two.

Thus the master of the Middle Style, the poet who will probably give his name to our age of moral expediency and intellectual retreat—the age of Auden.

WILLIAM CARLOS WILLIAMS:
THE TRUE CONTEMPORARY

ℝ WHEN I WAS twenty years old I published a little book of poems privately. It was a confused book, a mixture of Elizabethan and Modern. This volume I sent to several famous poets, only one of whom took the trouble to reply. He was William Carlos Williams. Williams did not praise my book, but his letter, the first I had ever received from a real writer, was full of sympathy and kindliness for a young man who wanted to be a poet. While he had nothing encouraging to say about my poems, he had a good deal to say about the month of March and his anger at T. S. Eliot. The month of March figures a great deal in Williams' poetry, a violent and beautiful season in Williams' New Jersey, as it was in Maryland, where I lived. The diatribe against Eliot disturbed me deeply. I was a worshiper of Eliot then and a devout reader of the *Partisan Review*, which, although a highbrow left-wing magazine, took Eliot to be the sovereign poet and critic of the twentieth century. I could not understand how any modern poet, especially Williams, who seemed of an extraordinary freshness and originality, could say unkind things about Eliot. If I had ever developed the habit of reading literary criticism I would have known what he meant. But my natural antipathy for criticism kept me away from it for many years. It was not until I began to teach in universities that I was forced to examine criticism; and it was not until I examined it carefully that I began to appreciate Williams' opinion of Eliot, the true significance of Eliot and everything he has promulgated under the name of criticism.

The radical difference between Williams and, say, Eliot, is that Williams divorces poetry from "culture," or tries to. Williams is fighting for the existence of poetry (while Eliot and Pound fought for the "uses" of poetry). Williams' entire literary career has been dedicated to the struggle to preserve spontaneity and immediacy of experience. His explanations of these aims are certainly not as impressive as Eliot's and in fact lead to such confusing theories as Objectivism. In defense of Williams one can say that his theorizing is innocent, while in the case of the Pounds and Eliots it is calculated and tricky. Williams does not stand or fall on theory; he is willing to void it at a moment's notice. But it is unfortunate for him that he must engage in theory at all. At bottom Williams is not an intellectual, and he is too human, too sympathetic, too natural to become a symbol of the anti-intellectual. Besides, as he says in his published letters, he is illogical. He would never be able to impress the quarterly reviews or the highbrows who consider him a kind of intellectual slob. The literary quarterly follows a party line of Culture, any Culture, but Culture is a *sine qua non* for the poet, according to them.

Williams is a guinea pig of modern poetry. He lends himself to the literature of the laboratory and a thousand trials and errors of criticism. He even writes a "mythic epic" like Pound and Eliot which all the culture critics seize on as proof that Williams is not a literary imbecile but one you can practically write books about. *Paterson* is a typical culture poem, the only full-dressed one Williams ever wrote but, according to the critics, the real thing, a kind of New Jersey *The Waste Land*. Williams is so innocent that he would even do that. In writing his large bad poem Williams was perhaps trying to test the validity of works like the *Cantos* and *The Waste Land*, even to compete with them. While he carried on a lifelong fight against Eliotism—a one-sided fight, for Eliot hardly deigned to notice this gadfly—he maintained a lifelong relationship with Pound. Williams' relationship to Pound is very much like Yeats': an antimagnetic relationship. Pound leaned on Williams in the same way that Eliot and Pound leaned on each other. And Williams remained loyal to Pound because Pound seems to remain American rather than English. Williams is faithful to Pound through thick and thin, always annoyed with him, and always attempting to understand his position. Williams can see the demagoguery of Eliot but not of Pound. Somehow he identifies himself with Pound. Williams a few years ago was unseated from the poetry consultantship of the Library of Congress, with no organized protest from writers and scarcely any mention of it in the press. Pound was awarded a prize from the Library of Congress which was backed up by all the self-styled Great Poets of the English-speaking countries. Pound got his prize, was feted in the editorials of the national magazines, and was eventually freed without a trial. Williams went home and had a series of strokes. My point is that because Williams abhors fixed positions in politics as in poetics he cannot impress officialdom.

Williams is the American poet who tries to fight off Europeanism. He fights it off, singlehanded, but he cannot impress the European with his cause. Neither can he impress the American. Lacking the arrogance of an Eliot or a Pound, lacking philosophy or religion or logic, he is battered back and forth by the literati, who are always armed to the teeth with Positions and who can make anything out of him they want, except a bad poet. Eliot tried to polish him off by remarking that he had a kind of "local interest." To Eliot anything that is not of world cultural interest is "local."

Williams belongs to the generation of Modern Poetry, those poets who suddenly organized literature in 1920 or thereabouts. He was not a high-powered Modern because he lacked the political instinct, but he was aggressive and fought the distortions of Modernism throughout his life. His letters and essays and even his poems are all "local" in the sense that they are contemporary. He wanted poetry to belong to the present, not the past. This is the clue to his involvements with Ezra Pound and his hatred of Eliot.

Williams has written a good deal of literary criticism himself, but he is not a critic in any accepted sense of that word. He is a poet even in his criticism; he refuses to use terminology and everything terminology stands for. He builds up no system; he abjures "style" in his prose, except when he is not sure of his ground. (In such cases he writes a jaunty, affected lingo reminiscent of Pound or Hemingway.) A good many of his judgments seem to be affected by personal loyalty mixed with an overpowering desire to be fair. One time, because of a letter from Robert Lowell, he seemed about to revise his opinion of Eliot. In Williams' world there are no hard and fast rules; the entire literary process is fluid; the governing principle is contemporaneity—immediacy.

There are basic contradictions of judgment in Williams' appraisals. For instance, he praises Marianne Moore excessively while he sees nothing of importance in Eliot. Williams also places Gertrude Stein with Pound as an important innovator. Pound he is inclined to favor from the start, even to a slight imitation of Pound's ideas of American history and banking. But the treatment of Pound is always anguished. One is inclined to feel that Williams does not look up to Pound but is pleased by Pound's interest in *him!* Williams has little use for Stevens, but this is consistent with Williams' objections to prettified language. At the bottom of Williams' specific poetic judgments lies a theory of language, which is practically a *mystique*. Usually it is referred to as a *prosody*, and in the widest meaning of that term it is.

Compared with Pound's prose, which has the tone of the Public Address System, Williams' critical style is weak and plaintive. At times it contains a note of hysteria, frequently its shrillness gets in the way of the clarity, but on the whole there is the pervading innocence and warmth of personality, heightened by genuine excitement. But when he intellectualizes he follows in the footsteps of the Eliot-Pound faction. He praises Joyce for his clarity and his great interest in form but his basic liking for Joyce has to do with Joyce's humanity. This is not a virtue that the Joyceans usually single out. And of course Williams is attracted by the banality of subject in *Ulysses*.

His allegiances are unstable and extreme. Williams reacts sharply to the immediate political or literary event. He is as prone to follow the Right (where the politics are not too obviously putrescent) as he is to follow the Left. Extremism seems to him worth a diagnosis. His detestation of Eliot seems to be a hatred for compromise; Williams does not compromise but he veers crazily from side to side. He writes about Lorca with a political passion while clinging with one hand to the coattails of Pound. He follows Pound's admiration of Jefferson while taking a "leftist" position on Jefferson. "Let's have a revolution every ten years," is Williams' view of Jefferson. Whereas Pound would say: a solid aristocracy without hereditary rights. At the end of a stirring, almost scholarly essay on Lorca he works in a little stab at Whitman, saying that Whitman was a romantic "in a bad sense." Williams is always looking over his shoulder at Pound; in himself he feels no critical authority. Here he mimics the Modern Classical view of Whitman.

Frequently he takes off into the realm of esthetic speculation, always with a certain desperate gaiety that characterizes his criticism. "The poem alone focuses the world," he says. This pleases the Pound side of Williams. Or in an essay about E. E. Cummings: "We are inclined to forget that cummings has come *from* english to another province having escaped across a well defended border . . ." This is about the difference between English and American, which Williams makes the center of his criticism. But he knows he is on the side of the Romantics, on the side of anyone who is opposed to "lapidary work," anyone who opposes a literary poem. Williams is always more or less on the right track, but he never comes to the point in his criticism. He does in the poems. Again he will buckle down to a first-rate piece of criticism in his bitter essay about the failure of Sandburg to continue as a poet. Here he is on safe ground. Williams is as close to Sandburg as twins but he can tell the difference between himself and the professional Americanism of Sandburg. He understands Sandburg because he has been through the same process of handling Americana. But Sandburg's soft-pedaling is to Williams the worst sort of propaganda verse. Sandburg follows the identical course Williams does in his own "formless" poetry; but Sandburg settles for a "form" and Williams still continues the search. When Williams talks about Auden he can say something as mixed-up and as *true* (reading Williams' criticism one begins to write like him, on both sides of the fence) as: "I wish I could enlist Auden in . . . a basic attack upon the whole realm of structure in the poem. . . . I am sure the attack must be concentrated on the *rigidity of the poetic foot.*" When Williams begins to underline something like the "rigidity of the poetic foot" he sounds even more sophomoric than his friend Ezra. It is as though Williams had reduced all the cultural viciousness of modernism to prosody—which in fact he has done. Marianne Moore seems to him to have taken recourse "to the mathematics of art." He adores her persnickety syllable snipping but he cannot abide Auden's much more fluid and graceful "feet." The point of argument seems to be British versus American. Puzzling over Dylan Thomas' poems after his death, Williams said that they smacked of the divine. But having fallen between the two stools of the "divine" Thomas and the agnostic Pound, one is not sure what *divine* is, except, as Williams says, "drunken." Clinging desperately to the only poetic he knows he cries at last: "Without measure we are lost." Measure is used prosodically and abstractly, as the rule, the law—one is not sure how it is used.

As a critic Williams has no credit whatever. Eliot puts up a full-scale esthetic which anticipates every question and answer. Pound bludgeons his opinions across to a few listeners. Yeats weaves over the crystal ball in a trance of culture sensibility. And poor Williams is haunted by the two specters of Whitman and Pound, the genius and the crank. All of which ends up as an unresolved internal monologue on *Prosody!* The prosody *mystique* in Williams is the center of all his prose and must be understood if the nature of Williams' poetry is to be vindicated. As my own opinion of Williams as a poet puts him over and above Pound and Eliot and Cummings and Marianne Moore, all the theorists and purveyors of sociological opinion, I will attempt to examine Williams' "prosody."

Williams has no critical reputation but he has somehow maintained the respect of the official literati. Simultaneously, he has maintained the loyalty of the literary "underground." (It was Williams who introduced Allen Ginsberg's *Howl,* and dozens of similar works which only poets have ever heard of.) He is the only modern poet who searches everywhere for new poetry.

Imagine any of the official critics, new critics, or editors of the highbrow quarterlies taking notice of a poem like Eli Siegel's *Hot Afternoons Have Been in Montana: Poems*—which Williams alone had the courage and honesty to reintroduce as one of the best twentieth-century poems. *Hot Afternoons* was one of the last authentically American poems, save Williams' own, before the final triumph of Eliot's culture poetry.

The new schools of criticism have always tried to give Williams the benefit of the doubt as a poet of their persuasion. Especially the poem *Paterson* appeals to them as a work comparable to *The Waste Land* and the *Cantos* or the *Anabase* of St. John Perse. *Paterson* to these critics seems an epic in modern style, a "mythic" poem. Controversy over *Paterson* has been considerable; but at least it is recognized by

these critics that Williams is as culturally ambitious as his contemporaries in such an undertaking.

It is a waste of time to discuss this kind of criticism, but it is necessary to set it aside if one is to get at a fair judgment of Williams' poetry. There is at least one full-scale intellectual probe of Williams. It
is a quibbling book, laden with minor points of pedantry and with a
dark knowledge of "structures." It is apparent in this work that the
author is not able to read poetry except as "comparative ideology."
For instance, in speaking of a character in Williams' *Paterson* named
Elsie, the critic says: "Elsie is a kind of Yeatsian 'Crazy Jane' presented without Yeats' idealization of the desecrated woman as the authentic guarantor of some superior wholeness, an authenticity with
which Yeats also endowed his fools and lunatics." This gibberish rises
from the critic's intense interest in "mythic" character rather than poetry. But one of the funniest examples of this kind of criticism is as
follows. A critic takes a delightful little poetic quip by Williams and
treats it to the following exposition. Here is the poem, "This Is Just
to Say":

> I have eaten
> the plums
> that were in
> the icebox
>
> and which
> you were probably
> saving
> for breakfast
>
> Forgive me
> they were delicious
> so sweet
> and so cold

The irony of this poem, the critic says, "was that precisely that which
preserved them (the plums) and increased the deliciousness of their
perfection (the refrigeration) contained in its essence the sensuous
quality most closely associated with death; coldness. So the plums'
death (or formal disappearance and disintegration) was symbolically

anticipated in the charm of their living flesh. This is, I believe, the exact pathos of this brief poem. . . ."

Whenever I quote something like this I feel constrained to add that this is a true quotation and not a parody I have made up. Most criticism about Williams is written in this patois: in a discussion of the poem "The Yachts" we are told that "suddenly the physical referents are expanded into universals more overtly than had been Williams' earlier custom when the reader had been given the responsibility for making the concrete particulars yield the universals . . ." etc. What the critic is trying to say is that in this poem Williams is using symbols; she cannot say anything so obvious; and she invents a way of saying the obvious to make it look profound.

A similar "explication" is published by the poetry editor of *The Nation* about the little wheelbarrow poem. This is the poem, "The Red Wheelbarrow":

so much depends
upon

a red wheel
barrow

glazed with rain
water

beside the white
chickens

Says the critic: "The poem's design is a striving for value, for significant realization, against the resistant drag of the merely habitual." This kind of highbrow marginalia is, funnily enough, *sanctioned* by Williams, who is always looking for someone to bestow critical respectability upon him.

Williams' poetry is bounded by *Kora in Hell* (1917) at the beginning of Williams' literary life and the epical *Paterson* at the other end. Pound wrote him about *Kora in Hell* and said, "The thing that saves your work is *opacity*, and don't forget it. Opacity is NOT an American quality." The opaque was something Pound might praise; and there is no telling how deeply influenced Williams might have been by this great literary law of Pound's. There are two books preceding *Kora* but the original preface to *Kora* is a mightily opaque and gossipy monologue in the Pound style. More important, Williams announces that the plan of *Kora* is "somewhat after the A.B.A. formula, that one may support the other, clarifying or enforcing perhaps the other's intention." This is the "form" of the *Cantos*, *The Waste Land*, and other "mythic structures" of the twenties. The real precedents for the book, however, are the so-called prose-poem, the *Illuminations* of Rimbaud, the poetic notes of Baudelaire, the abortive prose experiments of Eliot, etc. Probably the model of the poem was the pretty little French poem, for children perhaps, called *Aucassin et Nicolete*. Williams was charmed by this piece and evidently kept it in his mind as a form using both verse and prose. But the official precedent for *Kora*, we are told, is a book called *Varie Poesie* dell'Abate Pietro Metastasio, Venice, 1795, designedly dropped on Williams' desk by Pound.

Kora in Hell is a series of observations about poetry and the stance of the poet, full of little psychological asides about our civilization, not in the Poundian political way but in the Surrealist associational manner. Williams is concerned, like all the *avant-garde* writers of his time, with the feasibility of "associations"—the random use of intellectual and personal experience. Williams simply made it his business to jot down something every night, however nonsensical, and then make a comment on it. The chief and it may be the only fact of interest about *Kora* is that *Paterson*, coming at the apex of Williams' poetry, uses the identical method. The method consists of a free use of poetic languages in various states of excitement, alternating with a free use of prose languages. Eliot, Pound, and Joyce all attempted the same technique, with varying success.

But in between *Kora* and *Paterson* we have close to a thousand pages of some of the best or most interesting American poetry in our history. Almost all of this poetry is in a style which is immediately recognizable as Williams' own; further, it is a workable style, one which permits him to write a poem almost at random. At its best, which is a good bit of the time, it is not "experimental" poetry or crank technique. Naïve it certainly is, even what some writers call primitive; it is precisely Williams' innocence of forms that frees him to respond to daily experience as a poet. Williams went on writing, day after day, year after year, losing manuscripts, not finishing them, giving them away, but never letting up. Poetry to him was a daily function of life, a means of seeing. In a sense, he is our first American poet since Whitman. It hardly matters that his counselors poisoned his mind against Whitman; Whitman is his mentor after all.

Critics and journalists tend to heroize Williams for writing poems late at night after a hard day's work at the hospital. Williams has never felt heroic about being a physician. It is pointless to try to imagine Williams ensconced in some village on the Italian Riviera brooding over the effects of the 1905 nickel on the souls of little children. Williams was a New Jersey doctor and that is that. His poetry is the poetry of a very busy man, as busy, say, as Sir Walter Raleigh or Gerard Manley Hopkins. Not that one can generalize about busy poets and poets of leisure. Williams wanted to be a doctor, have a family, live near New York City, and write poetry. As far as anyone knows, he did all these things very admirably.

But the seeming offhandedness of Williams' poems is a condition of his life. Obviously the poems would be different had Williams not been a doctor. New Jersey, New York City, Ezra Pound, the delivery room, the back alleys of charity patients, home, the little magazine, the month of March, these are all the elements in which his poetry moves. Williams accommodates himself to the brutal round of modern professional life. It does not embitter him; it sweetens him. And the poems are "scrappy," as the critics note, but there is a method to their scrappiness. And they are not astrology or economics or theology. The element of speed in composing the poem is part of the technique of his poetry, just as speed is a factor in certain kinds of painting. There is, in fact, a definite "Oriental" tendency in his work, not cultural Orientalism like Pound's but an instinct for the work that is as natural as nature herself. And the daily life has a lot to do with it. He survives as a poet even better than his contemporaries, a consequence, perhaps, of his roots in a pedestrian world. Williams never became an "exile"; how can an obstetrician be an exile?

The earliest poems are marked by the ornate imprint of Pound (the use of foreign exclamations and translation-sounding rhetoric and even the "Browning" dramatics which Pound quickly switched

away from when he discovered that he could be opaque with im-
punity). The character of this style is that of a half-biblical, half-
Victorian tone which is the quality of all of Pound's early adaptations.
In Williams it sounds like:

> Eight days went by, eight days
> Comforted by no nights, until finally:
> "Would you behold yourself old, beloved?"

Actually Pound never rose above this style, either in the *Pisan Cantos*
or in the latest additions to his epic. Williams saw through it more
quickly. It goes on intermittently through "So art thou broken in
upon me, Apollo" and many such imitations of Style, but soon it
stops abruptly. One can see the sudden transition in:

> Your thighs are apple trees
> whose blossoms touch the sky.

which is more or less phony Pound, but is followed by:

> Which sky? . . .
> Which shore? . . .
> what/sort of man was Fragonard?

This is the beginning. Williams sheds figurative language as a snake
sheds its skin; henceforth he is naked, a poet without decoration,
without metaphor.

> March,
>   you remind me of
> the pyramids, our pyramids—

There is still a lot of mincing Italian, Spanish, Latin quotation, but
this falls away also.

> a green truck
> dragging a concrete mixer
> passes
> in the street—
> the clatter and true sound
> of verse—

•   •   •

Moral
        it looses me
Moral
        it supports me
Moral
        it has never ceased
        to flow

(through various series of data, menus, signs on walls and labels on bottles). Then a descent into pure spoken idiom, the rejection of all the devices of poetry for speech, always a sign of the poet's sincerity. Where Eliot ends up snipping philosophy from textbooks, Pound cutting whole chapters from history documents and statistics, Williams dives back into the spoken tongue.

It can never be said of Williams that he writes a well-rounded poem like "Ode on a Grecian Urn" or "The Love Song of J. Alfred Prufrock" or "even my father moved through dooms of love." He loathes the *fait accompli* in poetry or in painting. On the other hand, he does not worship the "fragment" for the fragment's sake. He tries to find the center of his experience in relation to the art of poetry; and he finds it over and over again. His "discoveries" are many more than "The Red Wheelbarrow" or "The Botticellian Trees"—good poems but two of many hundreds which are not repeated in the anthologies.

Williams puts his poetry in a direct relationship with daily experience. With Eliot there is no daily experience: there are "symbols" of the quotidian (empty lots, carbuncular young men, sandwich papers along the Thames, the silence in the subway) and with Pound there are stock-market reports, the struggles of artists and war communiqués. Williams tries to accommodate his poetry to what the day brings to a poet in a place like New Jersey, where there is no dazzle of the past or of the cultural present. Williams writes about an apple rotting on the porch rail.

He does not exploit his knowledge. It does not occur to him that what he happens to know as an expert might be turned to the uses of poetry. Yet he himself is the organizing center of the poem, bringing together around him the untold *disjecta membra* of the day. *Without metaphor.* This is the challenge. Hence the directness of all his poems and their somewhat shocking physical quality. Williams is like Catullus in his outspokenness and unthinking sensuality and amorality—for there is no bragging or sexual athleticism (or asceticism either) in the poems. Pound is sexless, Eliot ascetic, Yeats roaring with libidinal anguish and frustration. Williams includes the physical in the day's work; he meets it at every turn, being a doctor, and is not obsessed.

> The young doctor is dancing with happiness
> in the sparkling wind, alone
> at the prow of the ferry! He notices
> the curly barnacles and broken ice crusts . . .

or

> I bought a dishmop—
> having no daughter—

There is very little twentieth-century poetry like this except outside the English language. But Williams does not "translate" or "adapt" except infrequently. He refuses to improve upon the language—this is the whole secret of his flatness of style and the inconclusiveness of the forms. He writes in his speaking voice.

In his autobiography, Williams refers to the publication of *The Waste Land* as "the great catastrophe." Looked at from Williams' point of view and from that of all the *avant-garde* of his time, it was indeed the great catastrophe. "It wiped out our world," says Williams, "as if an atom bomb had been dropped upon it . . . I felt at once that it had set me back twenty years . . . Critically Eliot returned us to the classroom just at the moment when I felt that we were on the point of an escape . . . I knew at once that in certain ways I was most defeated." Williams' recognition of the true nature of *The Waste Land* marks him as first-rate prophet in criticism. And the effects of Eliot's poem were even more far-reaching than Williams said; not only was it the poem the academy needed as a pseudomodern example; it was a poem that made poetry and criticism one and the same thing, and that provided a justification for a new critical philosophy. Williams was also right in seeing that he was more damaged by this poem than anyone else. He was left high and dry: Pound, who was virtually the co-author of Eliot's poem, and Marianne Moore were now polarized to Eliot. Williams felt all this and would feel it for another twenty years. His own poetry would have to progress against the growing orthodoxy of Eliot criticism.

At first glance, Williams' remarks about poetic form seem superficial and even inane. One thinks, well, here is a nice man who is sick and tired of effeminate poeticizing and who would like American poets to display some gusto and originality. On second glance, one thinks, the old boy is becoming a bore with his din about prosody and "the line." All that shrieking about the "language" in *Paterson* is as bad as "the precise definition" in the *Cantos* or the "way of saying it" in the *Four Quartets*. And because Williams refuses to use the standard terminology of criticism, because he has a sincere interest in an American poetry, and because he is so suggestible, at least in his early years, to the literary politics of his fellow writers, he generally sounds half unintelligible. But there is a lot more to his "prosody" than that, much more, in fact, than exists in the new criticism.

Prosody is the science of verse. In English there is not and there has never been such a science. English scholars have long since given up prosody studies as a hopeless task. Because prosody and versification have such a justifiably bad name in English literature, no reader is apt to prick up his ears when William Carlos Williams or anyone else introduces the subject. Prosody is a mare's nest. Eliot and Pound took care not to identify themselves as prosodists, even while they were quietly laying down laws for it. In public they always guffawed at the mention of the word.

By prosody Williams does not mean versification. If you examine his own poems or his own remarks about what he calls mysteriously "the line," you will see the following things: He neither preaches nor practices "foot" prosody; he does not preach or practice meters; nor syllabic versification, such as Marianne Moore adopted; nor is his prosody accentual; nor is it "typographical" or what one critic calls grandly "spatial" form; nor does he base versification on rhyme nor on the internal figurations which rhyme may produce. The prosody of Pound is based on cadence which runs close to foot prosody—an imitation of Homeric and English trisyllabic. Eliot's prosody is extremely conservative, either a copy of Laforgue, at its most daring, or of Milton's *Samson Agonistes* (though I have never examined this closely) and it degenerates easily into modified "iambic." Williams' prosody is more advanced than any of these: it consciously departs from every intonation of the past. This is also its danger, as it is its advantage.

The thing to remember about Williams' "line" is that it is not a prosodic line at all. The word "prosody" for him is a metaphor for the whole meaning of the poem. Iambics to him mean cottages all in a row: sameness, standardization of things and of lives. His refusal to write iambic is therefore the same thing as Whitman's. It means that the iambic is not a language for the American poet. Pound and Eliot maintained the same doctrine, each in a less convincing way.

A good start for understanding the significance of Williams' belief about prosody and language (they are the same thing) is to consider his contempt for the modern sonnet. The virtue of the sonnet (which is the only "set" form in the English language) is that it prescribes a kind of syllogism. A sonnet in its simplest form makes a statement, develops or contradicts it, then resolves it. It is a game; hence its popularity with lovers. Eliot began by rejecting the sonnet; Pound rejected it after a few acrobatic flops. On the other hand, a poet like Cummings has advanced the sonnet to a new fame. With him it becomes the most ironical sonnet in English literature. What Williams resents about the sonnet form, even in the hands of Cummings, is the neatness of it. That is what the sonnet is for. The sonnet "line" can lead to nothing but a trick poem or exercise. A poem, according to Williams, should not be that closed, should not click like a box (which was Yeats' way of describing his own metrical poetry). The "closed" poem—the poem that clicks like a box—is the type of poem which has lately become a standard in the twentieth century; the most recent models were made by W. H. Auden.

All the appurtenances of the closed poem, especially the stanza, become anathema to Williams from the beginning. Rhyme itself seems to him meretricious; when he uses it (and he uses it as well as anybody), it is with a slur. The poem must not be governed by meters—any meters—nor by periods and paragraphs (stanzas), nor by the figures of speech. What is left? Nothing. The raw material of the poem is all. It is the same process that Whitman went through: a rebirth.

But Williams had even rejected Whitman's line. (We must try to remember that Williams uses the word "line" in the metrical sense, and in the linguistic sense at once.) The turning away from Whitman is all but fatal in Williams, but he manages to do pretty well in his own way. Williams grew up in the day when Whitman seemed incorrigibly nineteenth century and Emersonian. How Williams could have missed the lesson of Whitman is beyond me. But Williams started over, too. No ideas, no meters, no forms, no decorations; only the search for the raw poetry of experience.

"No ideas but in things," Williams said over and over, for a time. He became an "Objectivist," a man on the search for objects instead of thoughts. But this was just a variation of Pound's Imagism; for there could be no object-poetry that would lead anywhere; any more than Imagism could stand on its own legs. Williams dropped the Objectivist idea, just as he dropped the "antipoetic." These were harmful simplifications. Williams' larger conception of poetry is based on the understanding that a thing is neither poetic nor anti-poetic, neither prose nor poetry: there is something else which cannot be so bound. To write a poem about a rotten apple is not "antipoetic"; people laugh at such a poem and love it precisely because it is the poetry of the thing. The poetry of the rotten apple lies outside prosody, outside what is proper for apple-poetry, and outside what is called Symbolism (if you say *apple* to a modern critic you will be pelted with religion, mythology, and Freud before you can duck—but to Williams an apple is an apple).

As for Williams' versification, it goes entirely by ear, and luckily for him he has a good ear most of the time. It is not cadenced, not accentualized, not syllabified, not metered. It may or may not have a "typographical" form: sometimes it has, sometimes it hasn't. For certain periods Williams will print in "couplets"; at other times in tercets; he is not averse to the single word per line nor the long line. Generally (and this is the significant thing) he accommodates the "line"—that is, the typographic or verse line—to the sense of the whole poem. Thus he is doing approximately what Hopkins did in sprung rhythm, creating a total form rather than a unit form. It was a horror to Williams to see *The Waste Land,* partly because of Eliot's use of the old "unit" forms: an iambic passage here; a trochaic passage there; an image poem here; a long rhetorical build-up there and so on, with no organic principle anywhere.

But Williams himself in his desperate moments does the same thing. *Paterson* is just as artificial as *The Waste Land* when it comes to the "line."

Williams and his contemporaries had been schooled to despise "narrative poetry." To tell a tale in verse seemed to the early modern poets of our century the weakest excuse for writing a poem. They tried to get rid of tale-telling altogether and switch to Ideas, which are much more "masculine" than narratives. There is a large residue of narration in Williams' collected poetry which for years he did not know what to do with. The wonderful episode 17 in *Paterson*, one of the most powerful passages Williams ever wrote, was without a context until he stuck it in *Paterson*. But true to his Modernist upbringing, he could not even then *narrate* it, any more than he could narrate *Paterson*. Williams' "epic" poem is thus just another example of *The Waste Land* technique. He is better when he writes about Sacco and Vanzetti (a theme which could not move the great culture poets to even a single word) or about the death of D. H. Lawrence (which the culture poets also avoided like the plague). An interesting thing about Williams' poems is that they move from one to the next easily. The "secret of that form," as Williams calls it somewhere, is to make poetry natural, not literary. This is, in fact, the secret of his "prosody," the secret of his "antipoetic" line, the secret of his concentration upon objects as ideas. *The "secret of that form" is the eradication of the line between poetry and prose, between life and art.* Eliot speaks of an art emotion, an emotion reserved for the moments when one turns on the esthetic faucet. And it is precisely this attitude toward poetry that Williams condemns.

At the present, at the end of his long struggle with prosody, Williams turns to something very like a "form" but so loose that one can hardly call it a form. Perhaps it began with an admiration of a little quatrain by Byron Vazakas which resembled typographically a toy pistol or the State of Oklahoma. Vazakas managed this thing for speaking in his own voice. Williams hit upon a step-down kind of typography which he has used constantly in recent years. But it is not a be-all and end-all; he may drop it any time he likes. It is not a syllogistic sonnet or sestina at any rate. This style differs from Williams' earlier style only in that it appears to conform to a certain regularity. But there is none, except the regularity of thought as it progresses in the poem.

Had Williams been as good a theoretician as he was a poet he would probably be the most famous American poet today. But Williams cannot explain, fortunately for him, or he explains badly when he does. It is the poem he is after. His kind of poem may be the chief development of the American poem since *Leaves of Grass*. When it is successful, as it is an amazing number of times, it abolishes the dualism of form-content, expression-artistry, and all those other dualisms which get in the way of art. Williams' almost mystical repetitions about "the line" (and somewhat wildly in *Paterson* about the *Language*) are a decree against critical speculation about forms. He knows that forms are not predetermined, not inherited, not traditional. He knows, too, that forms do not matter for the honest artist, whether he uses them or not. It is when form becomes a fetish that he draws back and howls.

Speaking of howling, Williams has been the sole example in twentieth-century poetry, along with Lawrence, for hundreds upon hundreds of poets, the majority of whom are Americans who oppose the Eliot "line." Williams knows too much about poetry to set up a critical shop or lay out a curriculum like Pound. He is the godfather, all the same, of nearly all the existent *avant-garde* poetry, all the free poetry that exists in the English world today. This is recognized by the young poets who long ago branched away from the cultural highway and took to the backstreets and bohemias of the land. Williams is no bohemian; he is a serious man of letters (as the stuffy expression goes) but he is closer to the life of the poet than any of his contemporaries. By the life of the poet I mean the man to whom the daily life is the poetry itself, whatever his occupation. Williams may have been trying to do the impossible in taking for granted the unity of expression and artistry in the early years of the century, but he was one of the few who accepted this high premise of the poet. When the "great catastrophe" (the publication of *The Waste Land*) occurred, most of

Williams' friends dropped by the wayside or split into little groups or
went over to the enemy, as Williams put it. It is curious that through
all the ensuing years Williams remained loyal to Pound and could not
perceive that it was Pound who was the lever for the catastrophe and
would continue to be.

A newly published book by Williams serves better than anything I
have ever read about him to clarify and sum up his poetry and his poetics. It is a strange and charming work called *I Wanted to Write a
Poem*. The book is an informal bibliography which is also a kind of
autobiography. The editor (Edith Heal) lists the books chronologi-
cally, fifty of them, and gets the poet to discuss their inception. Mrs.
Williams, the poet's editor throughout his career, makes additional
comments. Throughout this running commentary one can follow the
fifty-year search for form which has been Williams' lifelong preoccupation. I would like to conclude by condensing and commenting
upon his own findings, after which I will give my evaluation of his
achievement.

His earliest influences, he says, are Keats and Whitman. He
would rather be a painter than a poet (his mother is an artist) but cannot because of the medical profession. He finds his contemporaries
quickly: Wallace Stevens, Marianne Moore, Hilda Doolittle, Ezra
Pound. Pound is the only one of these to whom he feels literary loyalty. Stevens tags him with the label "anti-poetic," which Williams
resents ever after. (Mrs. Williams, curiously enough, does not understand the poet's rage over this designation.) He abandons rhyme and
meter in his second book (1913). While he is writing *Kora*,
"Prufrock" appears; Williams says: "I had a violent feeling that Eliot
had betrayed what I believed in. He was looking backward; I was
looking forward. He was a conformist, with wit, learning which I did
not possess . . . But I felt he had rejected America and I refused to be
rejected . . . I realized the responsibility I must accept. I knew he
would influence all subsequent American poets and take them out of
my sphere. I had envisioned a new form of poetic composition, a
form for the future. It was a shock to me that he was so tremendously
successful; my contemporaries flocked to him—away from what I
wanted. It forced me to be successful . . ." He consciously rejects free
verse, simultaneously rejecting metered verse. "The greatest problem

[he says] was that I didn't know how to divide a poem into what perhaps my lyrical sense wanted." *Paterson* seems to him the answer: he
personifies a city and follows its river (the Passaic) and the river-of-
history from Paterson down to the sea. Documentary prose breaks
the flow of the poetry. Evidently it is the formless form that he has
been searching for. In *Paterson, II* he hits upon the step-down form in
which all his subsequent poems are written. The line he now refers to
as the "variable foot."

What then is the "prosody" of the Williams poem? If we can believe that every good poem ever written in form is good despite the
form, and that every formless (free verse) poem that succeeded has
succeeded despite its formlessness, then we will be getting close to
the idea of Williams' form. It is the purest theory of poetry I have
ever heard of and I take it to be the ideal of all poets, formalists or
vers librists. For meter has nothing to do with it; meter is an after-
effect. Metaphor and simile have nothing to do with it. "The coining
of similes is a pastime of very low order, depending as it does upon a
merely vegetable coincidence . . ." Structure has nothing to do with
it: you cannot remove the parts from the whole; or rather you cannot
find the structure. Beautiful language has nothing to do with it any
more than the antipoetic. And finally, poetry is a secular art "free
from the smears of mystery."

I am not sure I understand all this (assuming I've got it down accurately) but I know in my bones it is right. It is not theory; it is the
laborious explanation of an artist stammering out the reasons why his
poem came out the way it did. Each poem is its own form, as it must
be. The poem is unique and unrepeatable; it is when you repeat that
form arises, for form is imitation, as in Eliot, precedent heaped upon
precedent. With Williams the poem is raw, quivering, natural, an
objet trouvé, something you look at twice before you pick it up. It is
the extreme of the original, the condition of poetry which frightens
off most poets, a complete breakthrough to his own language. It is
the kind of poetry which it may take years to see but once seen remakes all other poetry and conceptions of poetry.

But I do not mean that Williams' works are perfection or even
that he has written a score or two of poems which will set him beside
Milton or Catullus or Marlowe. It is hard to judge such work com-

paratively; it is too new, too unlike anything else. But there is one sure sign of its value; it has already penetrated the poetry of a whole generation of American poets, not the ones we read month after month in the apple-pie-order journals of letters or the fat anthologies, but in the less-known, less-official magazines and pamphlets strewn over the countryside, which Williams has always lent his hand to. With D. H. Lawrence, Williams is the leader of what authentic American poetry is being written today. Little enough of it is up to his mark, yet the tendency is the right one. The example is there in Williams' poems, not in his criticism. And it is being followed. When I read his poems I feel I am reading a foreign language, my language. After all, there is practically no American poetry to speak of, and nearly all of it has come in the twentieth century, and a good portion of that has been written by William Carlos Williams.

I call him the true contemporary because be saw the challenge from the beginning and saw it whole: to create American poetry out of nothing, out of that which had never lent itself to poetry before. To do this without betraying the present to the past (like Eliot) and without exploiting the present (like Sandburg) and without trying to force the future (like Pound). I call him the true contemporary also because he could not resist trying to write the Great American Epic. But in Williams' case this can be overlooked: he has written enough true poetry to show the twentieth century that *American* and *poet* are not contradictions in terms.

DYLAN THOMAS

IN THE DEATH OF Dylan Thomas in 1953 was the cause of the most singular demonstration of suffering in modern literary history. One searches his memory in vain for any parallel to it. At thirty-nine Thomas had endeared himself to the literary youth of England and America, to most of the poets who were his contemporaries, and to many who were his elders; he was the master of a public which he himself had brought out of nothingness; he was the idol of writers of every description and the darling of the press. (The Press scented him early and nosed him to the grave.) Critics had already told how Thomas became the first poet who was both popular and obscure. In an age when poets are supposed to be born old, everyone looked upon Thomas as the last of the young poets. When he died, it was as if there would never be any more youth in the world. Or so it seemed in the frenzy of his year-long funeral, a funeral which, like one of Thomas' own poems, turned slowly into a satanic celebration and a literary institution.

When Yeats and Valéry died, old and wise and untouchable, there were held, so to speak, the grand state funerals. It was Civilization itself that mourned. When Thomas died, a poet wrote wildly how, to get him up in the morning, he plugged Thomas' mouth with a bottle of beer—"this wonderful baby." All the naughty stories were on everybody's lips; all the wrong things began to be said, and the right things in the wrong way. Someone quoted bitterly: Kill him, he's a poet! and this childishness was the signal for a verbal massacre of the bourgeoisie, reminiscent of the early decades of our century.

The death of a young poet inflicts a psychic wound upon the world and is the cause among poets themselves of frightening babbling and soothsaying. Such doings may be likened to a witches' Sabbath, and some have seen in these morbid celebrations the very coming-to-life of Thomas' poems. It is his death as an occasion for literary and psychological insurrection that must interest us today, if we are to understand the meaning of Thomas' poetry and the significance his contemporaries have given it. It is one thing to analyze and interpret poetry and keep it all in a book; it is another to watch that poetry enter an audience and melt it to a single mind. I want to speak about the second thing, the live thing, the thing that touched the raw nerve of the world and that keeps us singing with pain. The poetry of Thomas is full of the deepest pain; there are few moments of relief. What is the secret of his pain-filled audience? How are we to place Thomas among the famous impersonal poets of our time, when this one is so personal, so intimate and so profoundly grieved? Thomas was the first modern romantic you could put your finger on, the first whose journeys and itineraries became part of his own mythology, the first who offered himself up as a public, not a private, sacrifice. Hence the piercing sacrificial note in his poetry, the uncontainable voice, the drifting, almost ectoplasmic character of the man, the desperate clinging to a few drifting spars of literary convention. Hence, too, the universal acclaim for his lyricism, and the mistaken desire to make him an heir to Bohemia or to the high Symbolist tradition.

Writers said of Thomas that he was the greatest lyricist of our time. The saying became a platitude. It was unquestionably true, but what did the word mean? It meant that, in contrast to the epic pretensions of many of the leading modern poets, he was the only one who could be called a singer. To call him the best lyric poet of our time was to pay him the highest, the only compliment. Nearly everyone paid him this splendid compliment and everyone knew its implications. Few realized, however, that this compliment marked a turning point in poetry.

During his life there were also the armed camps who made him honorary revolutionary general; and we cannot be sure Thomas refused the homemade epaulets of these border patrols. I rather think he was proud to be taken in. Who were these people? First there was the remnant of Bohemia. These are people who exist in the belief that everyone is dead except themselves. I saw one of these poets lately; he had just come from England and he informed me casually

that everyone in England is dead. To change the subject I asked him
if he was glad to be home; but it turned out that everyone in America
is also dead. Among these poets there is a sincere belief in the death
of our world, and it is curious to speculate upon their adoption of
Thomas as a leader and a patron saint. In the same way nearly all of
Thomas' followers have spoken of him as a Symbolist. The Symbolists praise the love of death as the highest order of poetic knowledge.
"Bohemian" and Symbolist are never far apart.

All the same, this theory of posthumous vitality seems to make
sense when we speak of Thomas. How much did Thomas subscribe
to official Symbolism? Just enough to provide ammunition for those
people. How much did he love death as his major symbol? As much
as any poet in the English language. These factions have a claim on
Thomas which we cannot contradict.

Thomas is in somewhat the relation to modern poetry that Hopkins was to the Victorians—a lone wolf. Thomas resisted the literary
traditionalism of the Eliot school; he wanted no part of it. Poetry to
him was not a civilizing maneuver, a replanting of the gardens; it was
a holocaust, a sowing of the wind. And we cannot compare Thomas,
say, with Auden, because they are different in kind. Thomas' antithesis to Auden, as to Eliot, is significant. Thomas grew up in a generation which had lost every kind of cultural leadership. The poets who
began to write during the Depression, which was worse in Wales
than in America, were deprived of every traditional ideal. The favorite poem of this generation was Yeats' "The Second Coming."
Yeats' poems gave to a generation of prematurely wise young poets an
apocalypse, a vision of Antichrist and a vision of the downfall of civilization. The theatricality of the Yeats poem was a great convenience
to a poet like Thomas who, having nothing of true philosophical or
religious substance to fall back upon, could grasp this straw. The acknowledged precedence of Yeats in modern English literature—in
world literature perhaps—has been a makeshift consolation to all
modern poets. Yeats, with his cruel forcing of the imagination, his
jimmying of the spirit, is a heroic figure in modern poetry. Yet he belongs to the past, with all its claptrap of history and myth. Thomas'
poetry was born out of the bankruptcy of the Yeats-Pound-Eliot "tradition" and all it stood for. It was born out of the revulsion against the

book-poetry of Auden and the system-mongering of the social revolutionaries. Thomas' poetry was orphaned from the start.

Thomas suffers from the waifishness imposed upon his generation. The so-called Apocalyptic poets, which he was supposed to be a
member of, never existed. Nor is he one of the Metaphysical school.
One can see that he plays around with copying the superficies of
Vaughan and Herbert and Traherne and maybe David ap Gwilym
(who in English is not much better than James Whitcomb Riley) and
Yeats and Hopkins. But Thomas was outside the orbit of the English
poets and maybe the Welsh. He was antitradition by nature, by place,
by inclination. Certainly Thomas' grisly love for America can also be
seen in this light; America is the untraditional place, the Romantic
country *par excellence.*

Thomas' technique is deceptive. When you look at it casually you
think it is nothing. The meter is banal. It is no better and no worse
than that of dozens of other poets his age. There is no invention and
a great deal of imitation. There is no theory. But despite his lack of
originality, the impress of Thomas' idiom on present-day English poetry is incalculable. One critic said not many years ago that Thomas
had visited a major affliction on English poetry. This was an un-
friendly way of saying that Thomas had captured the young poets,
which he certainly had. How did he do this? He did it through the
force of emotion, with the personal idiom, a twist of the language,
bending the iron of English. Once he had bent this iron his way
everybody else tried it. Thomas has more imitators today than any
other poet in the literature. Whether this excitement will last a year
or a hundred years, no one can tell. But it is a real excitement.

Yet even when we examine the texture of his language we fail to
find anything original, although we find something completely distinctive. It is hard to locate the distinctiveness of Thomas' idiom.
There are a few tricks of word order, a way of using a sentence, a
characteristic vocabulary, an obsessive repetition of phrase, and so
on—things common to many lesser poets. Again, if we scrutinize his
images and metaphors, which are much more impressive than the
things I have mentioned, we frequently find overdevelopment,
blowziness, and euphemism, on the one hand, and brilliant crystal-
lization on the other. But no system, no poetic, no practice that adds

up to anything you can hold on to. The more you examine him as a stylist the less you find.

What does this mean? It means that Thomas is a quite derivative, unoriginal, *unintellectual* poet, the entire force of whose personality and vitality is jammed into his few difficult half-intelligible poems. To talk about Thomas as a Symbolist is dishonest. Not long ago in Hollywood Aldous Huxley introduced a Stravinsky composition based on a poem of Thomas'. Huxley quoted that line of Mallarmé's which says that poets purify the dialect of the tribe. This, said Huxley, was what Thomas did. Now anybody who has read Thomas knows that he did the exact opposite: Thomas did everything in his power to obscure the dialect of the tribe—whatever that high-and-mighty expression may mean. Thomas sometimes attempted to keep people from understanding his poems (which are frequently simple, once you know the dodges). He had a horror of simplicity—or what I consider to be a fear of it. He knew little except what a man knows who has lived about forty years, and there was little he wanted to know. There is a fatal pessimism in most of his poems, offset by a few bursts of joy and exuberance. The main symbol is masculine love, driven as hard as Freud drove it. In the background is God, hard to identify but always there, a kind of God who belongs to one's parents rather than to the children, who do not quite accept Him.

I went through the *Collected Poems* recently to decide which poems I would keep if I were editing the best poems of Dylan Thomas. Out of about ninety poems I chose more than thirty which I think stand with the best poems of our time. If this seems a small number, we should remember that there are not many more poems upon which the fame of Hopkins rests; of Rimbaud; or, for that matter, of John Donne. And yet we expect a greater volume of work from such an exuberant man. Thomas' sixty poems that I would exclude are short of his mark, but they are not failures. I would like to name by name those poems which I think belong to the permanent body of our poetry—or most of them anyway: "I see the boys of summer"; "A process in the weather of the heart"; "The force that through the green fuse drives the flower"; "Especially when the October wind"; "When, like a running grave"; "Light breaks where no sun shines"; "Do you not father me"; "A grief ago"; "And death shall have no dominion"; "Then was my neophyte"; "When all my five and country senses see"; "We lying by sea-sand"; "It is the sinners' dust-tongued bell"; "After the funeral"; "Not from this anger"; "How shall my animal"; "Twenty-four years"; "A Refusal to Mourn"; "Poem in October"; "The Hunchback in the Park"; "Into her Lying Down Head"; "Do not go gentle"; "A Winter's Tale"; "On the Marriage of a Virgin"; "When I woke"; "Among those Killed in the Dawn Raid"; "Fern Hill"; "In country sleep"; "Over Sir John's hill"; and "Poem on his birthday." I leave out the sonnets, which I think are forced, and the "Ballad of the Long-legged Bait," and the "Prologue," and many others. My list is probably off here and there, but I think it is the substantial list of works by which Thomas will be remembered.

The "major" poems, that is, the more pretentious poems, such as the ten sonnets (called "Altarwise by owl-light"), reveal most of what we know of Thomas' convictions and what we can call his philosophy. He believed in God and Christ; the Fall and death, the end of all things and the day of eternity. This is very conventional religion and Thomas was uncritical about it. Add to this the puritanism which runs through his whole work, and, finally, the forced optimism in the last poems such as "In country sleep," in which, although the whole sequence is unfinished, there is a recognizable affirmation of faith in life. But one feels that these matters are not of paramount importance in the poetry of Thomas. Thomas was not interested in philosophical answers. Religion, such as he knew it, was direct and natural; the symbolism of religion, as he uses it, is poetry, direct knowledge. Religion is not to be used: it is simply part of life, part of himself; it is like a tree; take it or leave it, it is there. In this sense, one might say that Thomas is more "religious" than Eliot, because Thomas has a natural religious approach to nature and to himself. The language of Thomas, not the style, is very close to that of Hopkins, not only in obvious ways, but in its very method, Hopkins, however, arrived at his method philosophically, abstractly, as well as through temperament and neurosis. Thomas, with no equipment for theorizing about the forms of nature, sought the "forms" that Hopkins did. The chief difference between the two poets in terms of their symbols is that Hopkins draws his symbology almost entirely from the God-symbol.

God, in various attributes, is the chief process in Hopkins' view of the world. Sex is the chief process in Thomas' view of the world.

Thomas' idea of process is important. The term itself is rather mechanistic, as he uses it. He always takes the machine of energy rather than some abstraction, such as spirit or essence. Hence the concreteness of his words and images; obscurity occurs also because of the "process" of mixing the imagery of the subconscious with biological imagery, as in Hopkins. But there is also a deliberate attempt to involve the subconscious as the main process: Thomas' imagination, which is sometimes fantastic, works hard to dredge up the images of fantasy and dreams. Very often the process fails and we are left with heaps of grotesque images that add up to nothing. I would equate the process in Thomas' poetics with his rather startling views of the sexual process. Aside from those poems in which sex is simply sung, much as poets used to write what are called love poems, there are those poems in which sex is used as the instrument of belief and knowledge. Using the cliché of modern literature that everyone is sick and the whole world is a hospital, Thomas wants to imply that sex will make us (or usually just him) healthy and whole again. And there are suggestions of Druidism (perhaps) and primitive fertility rites, apparently still extant in Wales, all mixed up with Henry Miller, Freud, and American street slang. But sex kills also, as Thomas says a thousand times, and he is not sure of the patient's recovery. In place of love, about which Thomas is almost always profoundly bitter, there is sex, the instrument and the physical process of love. The activity of sex, Thomas hopes in his poems, will somehow lead to love in life and in the cosmos. As he grows older, love recedes and sex becomes a nightmare, a Black Mass.

Thomas moves between sexual revulsion and sexual ecstasy, between puritanism and mysticism, between formalistic ritual (this accounts for his lack of invention) and vagueness. In his book one comes, on one page, upon a poem of comparative peace and lucidity, and on the next page upon a poem of absolute density and darkness. His dissatisfaction with his own lack of stability is reflected in his devices which tend to obscure even the simple poems; he leaves out all indications of explanation—quotation marks, punctuation, titles, connectives, whether logical or grammatical. In addition he uses every extreme device of ambiguity one can think of, from reversing the terms of a figure of speech to ellipsis to overelaboration of images. There is no poetic behind these practices—only catch-as-catch-can technique. One is always confused in Thomas by not knowing whether he is using the microscope or the telescope; he switches from one to the other with ease and without warning. It is significant that his joyous poems, which are few, though among his best, are nearly always his simplest. Where the dominant theme of despair obtrudes, the language dives down into the depths; some of these complex poems are among the most rewarding, the richest in feeling, and the most difficult to hold to. But, beyond question, there are two minds working in Thomas, the joyous, naturally religious mind, and the disturbed, almost pathological mind of the cultural fugitive or clown. On every level of Thomas' work one notices the lack of sophistication and the split in temperament. This is his strength as well as his weakness. But it is a grave weakness because it leaves him without defense, without a bridge between himself and the world.

Thomas begins in a blind alley with the obsessive statement that birth is the beginning of death, the basic poetic statement, but one which is meaningless unless the poet can build a world between. Thomas never really departs from this statement, and his obsession with sex is only the clinical restatement of the same theme. The idealization of love, the traditional solution with most poets, good and bad, is never arrived at in Thomas. He skips into the foreign land of love and skips out again. And he is too good a poet to fake love. He doesn't feel it; he distrusts it; he doesn't believe it. He falls back on the love-process, the assault, the defeat, the shame, the despair. Over and over again he repeats the ritualistic formulas for love, always doubting its success. The process is despised because it doesn't really work. The brief introduction to the *Collected Poems* sounds a note of bravado which asserts that his poems "are written for the love of Man and in praise of God." One wishes they were; one is grateful for, and slightly surprised by, the acknowledgment to God and Man, for in the poems we find neither faith nor humanism. What we find is something that fits Thomas into the age: the satanism, the vomitous horror, the self-elected crucifixion of the artist.

In the last few years of his life Thomas was beginning to find an audience. No one, I think, was more taken aback than he at this phenomenon, because most of the poems which the audience liked had been in books for five or ten years already. Thomas was the one modern poet who by his *presence* created an audience. His audience was the impossible one: a general audience for a barely understandable poet. His way of meeting this audience, at the end, was no solution for Thomas as a poet. He became a dramatist, a writer of scenarios, a producer. What he wrote in this phase was not negligible by any means; but it was probably not what he wanted and not what his audience wanted. His audience wanted the poetry; they wanted the agony of the process.

The frenzy that attended Dylan Thomas' death was a frenzy of frustration. Many times, in his stories and letters and his talk, Thomas tried to leap over this frustration into a Babelaisian faith; but it never rang true enough. After the gaiety came the hangover, the horrible fundamentalist remorse. Yet through the obscurity of the poetry everyone could feel the scream of desperation: not a cry of desire; on the contrary, it was the opposite; it was the cry of the trapped animal; the thing wanting to be man; the man wanting to be spirit.

He is a self-limiting poet and an exasperating one. He runs beyond your reach after he has beckoned you to follow; he arouses you and then slumps into a heap. He knows, more than his readers, that he has no bridge between life and death, between self and the world. His poetry is absolutely literal (as he himself insisted all the time). But its literalness is the challenge to literature which is always significant. He is too honest to rhapsodize or to intone over the great symbols; rather he growls or rages or more often hypnotizes himself by the minute object, which he is likely to crush in his anger. Unlike Hopkins, he has no vision of nature and cannot break open the forms of nature; he cannot break open words. He focuses madly on the object, but it will not yield. He calls a weathercock a bow-and-arrow bird. Metaphor won't come and he resorts to riddle, the opposite of metaphor. A good half of his poetry is the poetry of rage; not rage at the world of society or politics or art or anything except self. He is impatient for a method and the impatience early turns into desperation, the desperation into clowning. He is another naïf, like Rimbaud,

a countryman, who having left the country wanders over the face of
the earth seeking a vision. He is running away from his fame, which
he does not feel equal to. He is running away from the vision of self,
or keeping the integrity of self by fleeing from the foci of tradition. I
interpret the life and work of Thomas this way: the young poet of
natural genius and expansive personality who recoils from the ritual
of literary tradition and who feels himself drawn into it as into a den
of iniquity. This is both the puritanism and the wisdom of Thomas.
Such a man can never acquire the polish of the world which is called
worldliness, and he turns to the only form of behavior, literary and
otherwise, permissible both to society and to self. That is buffoonery.
All the literary world loves a buffoon: the French make a saint of the
clown. But folklore has it that the clown dies in the dressing room.

It is the most certain mark of Thomas' genius that he did not give
way to any vision but his own, the one authentic source of knowledge
he had—himself. And it is the most certain mark of his weakness that
he could not shield himself from the various literary preceptors who
buzzed around him. He became immobile, I think, out of pure fright.
He wrote personal letters (which are now being published) apparently meant for publication, in which he adopted the modern clichés
about modern life. He pretended to be horrified by the electric
toaster, or maybe he really was.

The doctrinaire impersonality of our poetry demands allegiance
to a Tradition, any tradition, even one you rig up for yourself.
Thomas represents the extreme narrowness of the individual genius,
the basic animal (one of his favorite symbols) in man. The animal to
Thomas is everything and we listen because he calls it animal, not
spirit or essence or potentiality or something else. It is the authentic
symbol for a poet who believes in the greatness of the individual and
the sacredness of the masses. It is Whitman's symbol when he says he
thinks he could turn and live with animals, because they are natural
and belong to nature and do not try to turn nature out of its course.
They do not try to believe anything contrary to their condition.

But Thomas is drawn away from his animal; he becomes brute.
And this he knows. In the brute phase of his poetry (which is the
phase loved by the modernists who picked up his scent) the poetry is
a relentless cuffing down to the quick—surgery, butchery, and worse.

And as Thomas is the one and only subject of his poems, we know what is being destroyed.

It is some of the saddest poetry we have. It leaves us finally with grief. The pathos of Thomas is that he is not diabolical, not mystical, not possessed; he has not the expansive imagination of Blake nor even the fanatical self-control of Yeats. He is the poet of genius unable to face life. Like D. H. Lawrence he is always hurling himself back into childhood and the childhood of the world. Everyone speaks of Thomas as a child. He became a child.

It is easy to dismiss him but he will not be dismissed. He was a tremendous talent who stung himself into insensibility because he could not face the obligations of intellectual life, which he mistakenly felt he must. He could not take the consequences of his own natural beliefs; and he could not temporize; there was no transition, no growth, only the two states of natural joy and intellectual despair, love of trees and fascination of the brute process. He said everything he had to say: it had little to do with wars and cities and art galleries. What he said was that man is a child thrust into the power of self, an animal becoming an angel. But becoming an angel he becomes more a beast. There is no peace, no rest, and death itself is only another kind of disgusting sex.

But something happened to his poems. Somehow the spark escaped; it leapt out of the hands of literature and set a fire. Thomas, I think, did the impossible in modern poetry. He made a jump to an audience which, we have been taught to believe, does not exist. It is an audience that understands him even when they cannot understand his poetry. It is probably the first nonfunereal poetry audience in fifty years, an audience that had been deprived of poetry by fiat. Thomas' audience bears certain characteristics of the mob—but that, under the circumstances, is also understandable. The audience understands Thomas instinctively. They know he is reaching out to them but cannot quite effect the meeting. The reaching ends in a tantalizing excitement, a frenzy. It is not a literary frenzy, the kind that ends in a riot with the police defending Edith Sitwell after a reading of *Façade*. On the contrary, it is the muttering of awakening, a slow realization about poetry, a totally unexpected apocalypse. This audience sees Thomas as a male Edna St. Vincent Millay, or perhaps a Charlie

Chaplin; they hear the extraordinary vibrato, a voice of elation and anguish singing over their heads. They know it is acting. They know this is poetry and they know it is for them.

He is like the old cliché of vaudeville in which a tragicomic figure engaged in some private act (such as keeping his pants from falling down) wanders onto a stage where a highly formal cultural something is in progress. Naturally the embarrassed clown steals the show. One must remember Thomas' own story about himself in which he gets his finger stuck in a beer bottle. He goes from place to place, beer bottle and all, meeting new people. The beer bottle becomes Thomas' symbol of his natural self: it is his passport from the common people to the literary life, and back again. It is both his symbol of self and his symbol of other-self. But to Thomas it is mainly a horror symbol. It is the key to No Man's Land. Because Thomas is an uncivilizable Puritan and a hard-shell fundamentalist of some undefinable kind, the puritanism sets up the tension in his poetry—a tension based upon love and fear of love: the basic sexual tension, the basic theological tension. The greatness of Thomas is that he recognizes the equation; and the weakness of Thomas is that he takes to his heels when he has to grapple with it.

Everything I have said can be said better in the little poem by Thomas that takes nine lines. The last line of the poem is so much like a line of Whitman's that I have searched through Whitman's poems to find it. I am sure it is there and yet I know it isn't. The line reads "I advance for as long as forever is."

> Twenty-four years remind the tears of my eyes.
> (Bury the dead for fear that they walk to the grave in labor)
> In the groin of the natural doorway I crouched like a tailor
> Sewing a shroud for a journey
> By the light of the meat-eating sun.
> Dressed to die, the sensual strut begun,
> With my red veins full of money,
> In the final direction of the elementary town
> I advance for as long as forever is.

D. H. LAWRENCE:
THE FIRST WHITE ABORIGINAL

D. H. LAWRENCE has more in common with Walt Whitman than any other man has, and it was Lawrence who called Whitman the first white aboriginal. Coming from Lawrence, the epithet was the highest praise. Lawrence's quest was for the aboriginal, the pure energy of the soul. Being an Englishman, he fled from the white man and his white religions and the terrible whiteness of consciousness (which he called mentality) and raced with all his strength to the dark races and beyond, to the blood religions, the spirit of the serpent, and all that. Lawrence made a magnificent leap across civilization into the aboriginal darkness. He is one of the supreme heretics of white, modern civilization. And so for him to bless Walt with the title of the first white aboriginal is a matter of tremendous import. Lawrence is one of the great spirits of our age, as Whitman is, although from Lawrence stems a good deal of the negativity of modern creative life. From Whitman stems much of what there is of the opposite. Lawrence sprang from a modern industrial hell which he never forgave and was never far enough away from to understand. Whitman did not have to spring; he sprouted, he vegetated, he loafed out of nowhere into the role of prophet and seer. At a single stroke, apparently without preparation, he became the one poet of America and Democracy. He is the one mystical writer of any consequence America has produced; the most original religious thinker we have; the poet of the greatest achievement; the first profound innovator; the most accomplished artist as well (but nobody says this nowadays). Yet in the twentieth century Walt Whitman is almost completely shunned by his fellows. He has no audience, neither a general audience nor a literary clique. Official criticism ignores him completely;

modern Classicism, as it calls itself, acknowledges him with embarrassment. (Ezra Pound "forgives" Whitman because he "broke the new wood," meaning he broke iambic pentameter). And modern scholars, happily confused by the scholarly complexities of contemporary poets, look upon Walt as a grand failure and an anachronism or a bit of Americana, the prow of a clipper ship, perhaps.

Lawrence, in his search around the world for a pure well of human energy, acknowledged Whitman with love. It is a rare thing for Lawrence. He says:

> Whitman, the great poet, has meant so much to me. Whitman the one man breaking the way ahead. Whitman, the one pioneer. And only Whitman. No English pioneers [says Lawrence], no French. No European pioneer-poets. In Europe the would-be pioneers are mere innovators. The same in America. Ahead of Whitman, nothing. Ahead of all poets, pioneering into the wilderness of unopened life, Whitman. Beyond him, none. His wide, strange camp at the end of the high-road. And lots of new little poets camping on Whitman's camping ground now. But none going really beyond. . . .

But at this point Lawrence changes his tune and explains how Whitman failed. He says that Whitman fell into the old fallacy of Christian love, confusing his great doctrine of Sympathy with Love and Merging. Nothing was more loathsome to the puritanical Lawrence than Merging, and when Whitman merged Lawrence disgorged. How Lawrence longed to merge! And how the mere shake of the hand horrified him! Lawrence in thousands of passages obsessively records his taboo against touching. *Noli me tangere!* It is the opposite of Whitman's obsession *for* touching:

> Is this then a touch? quivering me to a new identity,
> Flames and ether making a rush for my veins,
> Treacherous tip of me reaching and crowding to help them,
> My flesh and blood playing out lightning to strike what is hardly
>   different from myself,
> On all sides prurient provokers stiffening my limbs,
> Straining the udder of my heart for its withheld drip,

Behaving licentious toward me, taking no denial,
Depriving me of my best as for a purpose,
Unbuttoning my clothes, holding me by the bare waist. . . .

(This is the passage in "Song of Myself" which, after a parenthesis, "What is less or more than a touch? leads into "I think I could turn and live with animals, they are so placid and self-contained, I stand and look at them long and long . . ."—one of the greatest moments of poetry.)

Lawrence, with his deep love of animals and his irritable suspicion of mankind, was the inferior of Whitman. Whitman had the natural love of man which Lawrence, rightly, called American. Lawrence was fascinated, hypnotized, and slightly sick in the stomach. Lawrence says if Walt had known about Charlie Chaplin he would have assumed one identity with him too. What a pity, Lawrence sneers. He'd have done poems, paeans and what not, Chants, Songs of Cinematernity. "Oh, Charlie, my Charlie, another film is done—"

But in the end Lawrence gives in; he knows a kindred spirit when he sees one. He looks down his nose at Whitman's paeans upon Death—Lawrence, who is one of the true poets of Death—and then adds:

> But the exultance of the message remains. Purified of merging, purified of Myself, the exultant message of American Democracy, of souls in the Open Road, full of glad recognition, full of fierce readiness, full of joy of worship, when one soul sees a greater soul.—The only riches, the great souls.

That is the last line of Lawrence's book called *Studies in Classic American Literature*, and I submit that it is a fine concession to be wrung from Lawrence, the archetype of tortured modern man, the man without heroes. Lawrence and Whitman are two modern poets with the deepest concern for mankind, the furthest insight, the widest sympathy, the simplest and best expression. They are scriptural writers in the long run, despising professionalism and literary fashion. But Lawrence fails to do more than pose the problem of modern civilization versus the individual intelligence. He has no answer. He half invents fascism; he is torn between the image of the free natural male (the father who is always leaving home to become a Gypsy) and the image of the leader, the aristocrat. He had it both ways: he remains unresolved. But he also had the vision. He became, in effect, an American, an American among Red Indians and rattlesnakes, close to that darker America betrayed by the white religions, Mexico, which he also loved. But it was Whitman's America that he held out for, "the true democracy [as Lawrence said] where soul meets soul, in the open road. Democracy. American Democracy where all journey down the open road. And where a soul is known at once in its going." Strange words coming from the author of *Kangaroo* and *The Plumed Serpent*.

Lawrence suffers somewhat the fate of Whitman today. He is declassed. He enjoys a kind of underground popularity among writers, but he is outside the pale of the Tradition. He is too violent, too special, too original. And he is too outspoken. But Lawrence could never survive within a tradition, any more than Whitman. And he has, at his best, a style so lean, it matches the burnt-away clean language of prophets. Most of Lawrence's disciples, it seems to me, misunderstand him; but at least he has disciples. Whitman has no disciples and practically no living literary reputation. He is only a name.

What has happened to Whitman in the century since *Leaves of Grass* was published? There were the usual false praises and the usual false deprecations, and enough of the true acclaim to give us a little faith in criticism. There has never been anything we could call popularity for Whitman. Publishers are inclined to prepare elaborate editions of *Leaves of Grass*, in the same way that they release erotic editions of The Song of Songs: in a wrong-headed way it is a compliment to Whitman. But the best minds of the present century have not closed with Whitman, in my opinion. And the leading poets of the twentieth century have coolly and with relentless deliberation suppressed Whitman and kept him from exerting his force. Any Whitman advocate of great talent, for example Hart Crane, is forced to apologize for this allegiance before he is admitted to the company of Moderns. There is no question that an Act of Exclusion has been in perpetual operation against Whitman since 1855 and is carried on today by the leading "Classicists" of English and American poetry. Walt just won't do. He is vulgar; he is a humbug; he copies the names of rivers out of the sixth-grade geography book; he is an optimist; he is unlettered; he is a theosophist; he abhors institutions; he is auto-erotic; he loves everybody; he is a Rotarian; he goes to the opera; he can't distinguish between good and evil; he has no sense of humor; he cannot solve his own paradox about the greatness of the individual and the greatness of the En-Masse; he has no style—etc., etc.

All such accusations are true, and one could multiply them for pages and pages. Yet in the last analysis, they do not matter. Emerson saw a little humor in Whitman, though he called it wit. But Whitman thought he was writing a kind of bible! And it is the biblical quality of Whitman (as with Lawrence) that is so offensive to lovers of Literature. What insolence! they say, and they are right. For neither Whitman nor Lawrence were "writers"; they were prophets. Literature makes it its business to stone prophets.

Whitman is indeed full of humbug, as when he talks about his experiences as a wound dresser:

> One night in the gloomiest period of the War, in the Patent Office Hospital in Washington city, as I stood by the bedside of a Pennsylvania soldier, who lay, conscious of quick approaching death, yet perfectly calm, and with noble, spiritual manner, the veteran surgeon, turning aside, said to me, that though he had witnessed many, many deaths of soldiers, and had been a worker at Bull Run, Antietam, Fredericksburg, etc., he had not seen yet the first case of a man or boy that met the approach of dissolution with cowardly qualms or terror. . . . Grand common stock! to me the accomplished and convincing growth, prophetic of the future; proof . . . of perfect beauty, tenderness and pluck, that never feudal lord, nor Greek, nor Roman breed, yet rivalled. Let no tongue ever speak disparagement of the American races, north or south. . . .

This sounds like Winston Churchill at his worst.

Whitman is not a complicated case of poor manners, confusions and paradoxes; of philosophical muddle and literary naïveté; of good intentions, high passages and bad dreary bogs. He is the one and only poet of America who has ever attempted to adumbrate the meaning of America. The twentieth-century American poet avoids this commitment, by and large: he considers it fitting and proper to take refuge in History against the horrors of progress; or in pure dialectic; or in the catacombs of established faith; or, failing that, in what is called the Language. Whitman's vision has degenerated into a thing called the Language; that is, the American Language, the natural nonhieratic language out of which a mythos might germinate. But Whitman contended that the mythos was at hand. He defined it; he sang it; he argued it; he poured it out. To no avail.

Twentieth-century poetry is a poetry of perfections. It is the least spontaneous poetry since—whatever date for the birth of artificiality you call to mind. It is the pride of twentieth-century poetry that even Yeats was brought to heel by critics who called for a "hard brittle technique." It is the pride of twentieth-century poetry that one publishes a poem once a decade. It is the boast of our poetry that it is impersonal, and that it can mean more or less what you think it means, and be right in the bargain. All of which is "traditional." Whitman and Lawrence were death to Tradition. Yet Whitman did not repudiate the past; nor did he look with any unctuousness upon the present, the America of a hundred years ago.

> Never was there . . . more hollowness at heart than at present, and here in the United States. Genuine belief seems to have left us. The underlying principles of the States are not honestly believed in . . . The spectacle is appalling. We live in an atmosphere of hypocrisy throughout. The men believe not in the women nor the women in men. A scornful superciliousness rules in literature. The aim of all the literateurs is to find something to make fun of. A lot of churches, sects, etc., the most dismal phantasms I know, usurp the name of religion . . . The depravity of the business classes of our country is not less than has been supposed, but infinitely greater. The official services of America, national, state, and municipal, in all their branches and departments, except the judiciary are saturated in corruption, bribery, falsehood, maladministration; and the judiciary is tainted. . . . In business, (this all-devouring modern word, business), the one sole object is, by any means, pecuniary gain. . . . I say that our New World democ-

racy . . . is, so far, an almost complete failure in its social aspects, and in really grand religious, moral, literary, and esthetic results . . .

Whitman sees the corruption and persists in his faith that the principle of democracy will overrule the corrupt. Let us call it the romantic position. But Whitman (like Jefferson) does not feel that the written word of democratic principle is sacrosanct. He goes to the heart of the matter. Man must do good, he says, because that is his ultimate nature. The man who falls a prey to corruption, dandyism, superficiality, selfishness, is a fallen man. Whitman despises him. He believes it natural to be pure: nature purifies. He has a kind of worship of chemistry, shared by his countrymen, an animal faith in the god of the sun, and the god of water. It is precisely his contempt for ideas of sin and evil which places him among the great teachers of mankind.

> What chemistry!
> That the winds are really not infectious,
> That this is no cheat, this transparent green-wash of the sea which
>   is so amorous after me,
> That it is safe to allow it to lick my naked body all over with its
>   tongues,
> That it will not endanger me with the fevers that have deposited
>   themselves in it,
> That it is all clean forever and ever,
> That the cool drink from the well tastes so good,
> That blackberries are so flavorous and juicy. . . .
> That when I recline on the grass I do not catch any disease . . .

He did not have a simple faith in the frontiers of "science"; on the contrary, he held a limited belief in physical achievements.

> Not to you alone, proud truths of the world,
> Nor to you alone, ye facts of modern science,
> But myths and fables of eld, Asia's, Africa's fables,
> The far-darting beams of the spirit, the unloosed dreams,
> The deep diving bibles and legends
> . . . You too with joy I sing.

America to Whitman was not a laboratory, but a place in the journey of mankind where the best in man might flower. America was not the goal; it was a bridge to the goal. In "Passage to India" he says of Columbus:

Ah Genoese thy dream! thy dream!
Centuries after thou art laid in thy grave,
The shore thou foundest verifies thy dream.

But the dream is not satisfying enough. We must steer for the deepest waters and take passage to the skies themselves. We must go where mariner has not yet dared to go, risking the ship, ourselves and all. It is not a geographical poem or a historical poem, much less a "war poem," although when Whitman talks about the Atlantic cable and its eloquent gentle wires, he sounds silly enough. But the physical achievement is his symbol of, not progress but goodness! It is axiomatic to Whitman that we shall lay cables, build the Union Pacific Railroad, and fly airships to Jupiter. That is the childlike and wonderful faith of the ordinary modern man who is not thrown into reverse by the terror of it all. Whitman is not even talking about that. It is the twentieth-century "classical" poet who is material- istic and who writes scathing books of poems against the electric toaster. For Whitman says in the same poem that the seas are already crossed, weathered the capes, the voyage done. Everything is already known. The advancement of man physically seems to him good but only a trifle. What really concerns him is that man shall explore the soul.

Passage indeed O soul to primal thought, . . .
Back, back to wisdom's birth, to innocent intuitions,
Again with fair creation.

Whitman is a mystic and he admits it. This is one more reason for his unpopularity. The best modern poets are allowed to admire the mystic but aren't allowed to be one. Whitman is too close for com- fort. Furthermore, he has no theology worth sorting out, except a kind of Quakerism, and religion isn't his concern. Man is his concern. And not American man. Whitman is not only the first white aborigi- nal; he is the first American; or that may be the same thing. When I read Whitman, good or bad, I always feel that here is first and foremost an American. The fundamental religiosity of Whitman plus the contempt for religion is American.

Whitman dissociated himself from mere poets and other writers. Who touches his book touches a man and men of all faiths.

> I do not despise you priests, all time, the world over,
> My faith is the greatest of faiths and the least of faiths,
> Enclosing worship ancient and modern and all between ancient and modern,
> Believing I shall come again upon the earth after five thousand years,
> Waiting responses from oracles, honoring the gods, saluting the sun,
> ... Helping the lama or brahmin as he trims the lamps of the idols,
> Dancing yet through the streets in a phallic procession, rapt and austere ...

and so on, down to the Mississippi Baptists with the jerks and spasms.

Whitman is too faithful in his belief in man to lay down the rules for a creed. It is unnecessary. If man is of Nature, and Nature is good, good will triumph. Evil is the failure of man to be as good as he can. For man to become all that is utterly possible is divine. And as every man is divine, inside and out, even the lowest are divinities. What is commonly looked down on nowadays in Whitman's talk about the divine average, is the average. Whitman emphasized the divine, rather than the average. Each person to him possessed divinity, and to repudiate that divinity was criminal. It is the god in each man and woman (which Lawrence called the Holy Ghost) that we can communicate with. I have rapport with you (Whitman's hieratic terminology is always couched in some kind of American French)—I have rapport with you because my divinity has a mouth to speak with. My lower self cannot speak; it can only commit acts of instinct. Yet there is a hierarchy of acts. Each thing to its nature:

> The moth eggs are in their place.
> The bright suns I see and the dark suns I cannot see are in their place,
> The palpable is in its place and the impalpable is in its place.

And Whitman says he is not stuck up and is in his place. Being "in place," of course, is not humility; nor is it a sign of any known orthodoxy.

Whitman asserts his divinity and he cannot evade it, despite a passing show of humility. He has the vision of himself as well in the scale of things. But he acknowledges the god in oneself—and here he makes a break with conventional poetry and conventional thought which is the core of his philosophy.

> Divine am I inside and out, and I make holy whatever I touch or
> am touched from.

It is Whitman's creed of the equality of the body and the soul. The body is not cursed; it is the miraculous materialization of the soul. The origin of this body-soul Whitman does not explain; he merely states that it is holy and the holy of holies. If he can find an object of worship more worthy than another it shall be his body or a part of his body. And while he is doting on himself he slips without warning into sun worship, nature worship, love worship, and then back to himself.

> If I worship one thing more than another it shall be the spread of
> my own body, or any part of it,
> Translucent mould of me it shall be you!
> Shaded ledges and rests it shall be you!
> Firm masculine colter it shall be you!
> Whatever goes to the filth of me it shall be you!
> You my rich blood! your milky stream pale strippings of my life!
> Breast that presses against other breasts it shall be you!
> My brain it shall be your occult convolutions!
> Root of washed sweet-flag!
> Timorous pond-snipe! nest of guarded duplicate eggs! it shall be
> you!
> Mixed tusseled hay of head, beard, brawn, it shall be you! Trick-
> ling sap of maple, fibre of manly wheat, it shall be you!
> Sun so generous it shall be you
> Vapors lighting and shading my face, it shall be you!
> You sweaty brooks and dews it shall be you!

Winds whose soft-tickling genitals rub against me it shall be you!
Broad muscular fields branches of live oak, loving lounger in my
    winding paths, it shall be you,
Hands I have taken, face I have kissed, mortal I have ever touched,
    it shall be you.
I dote on myself, there is that lot of me and all so luscious. . . .

He begins with his own corpus, which he finds so luscious; he forgets himself and begins looking around the park, then he recalls the
amorous uses of parks; and after a breath, he comes back to himself
and "the lot of him." If you read on and on you see that Whitman is
not talking about himself at all and acting like a baby discovering its
toes—but that is the superficial trick of it; he is talking about the primal discovery of self. He is talking about consciousness in the only
way it can be talked about: physically. I do not think for a second that
Whitman was either narcissistic or ego-maniac; he was trying to
obliterate the fatal dualism of body and soul. All his monotony about
keeping as clean around the bowels ("delicate" was the word he used)
as around the heart and head is not a swipe at Victorian convention; it
was his way of acknowledging the physicality of the soul, or the spiri-
tuality of the body. Lawrence shied away; and most American writers
in more or less the same Puritan tub get the backwash of revulsion
from this physical "obsession" of Whitman's.

But this is only the beginning. Whitman wanted to create the full
individual *in order to put this free man into the world.* The dialectical
conflict in Whitman, as in everyone else I suppose, is the free individual versus the crowd of mankind. The twentieth-century poet slinks
into his study and says, No crowds for me. But Whitman took it on.
He is the only modern poet who has the courage to meet the crowd.
And falling back into his demotic French he delivers the abstraction
En-Masse. "Endless unfolding of words of ages! And mine a word of
the modern, the word En-Masse." This becomes one of the most
ridiculed passages in Whitman, in which he drunkenly chants: "Hurrah for positive science! long live exact demonstration!" and "Gentle-
men, to you the first honors always!" But these funny passages of
Whitman are there, not because he is a fool, but because he has the
courage of his convictions. For just after this idiotic hurrahing for

exact demonstration comes another of the great bursts of poetry, the
one beginning "Walt Whitman am I, a kosmos, of mighty Manhattan
the son, / Turbulent, fleshy, sensual, eating, drinking, and breed-
ing. . . ." (Whitman is always aware of the comic possibilities of his
position, like many prophets.) The balanced man, the free man, the
man who meets his potentiality is a fit man for the new world, the
democracy he envisions. "The purpose of democracy," says Whitman
in prose, "is, through many transmigrations, and amid endless
ridicules, arguments, and ostensible failures, to illustrate, at all haz-
ards, this doctrine or theory that man, properly trained in sanest
highest freedom, may and must become a law, and series of laws, unto
himself, surrounding and providing for, not only his own personal
control, but all his relations to other individuals, and to the State; and
this as matters now stand in the civilized world, is the only scheme
worth working from, as warranting results like those of Nature's laws,
reliable . . . to carry on themselves."

The concept of En-Masse is not absurd and not laughable, as
other expressions of his certainly are, such as Democracy, Ma
Femme. But even Whitman's tendency to view Democracy as femi-
nine is penetrating. Whitman was the first great American feminist.

A great poet is not merely a poet of his nation but a poet of all
peoples. Whitman, who had little enough reward for his book, and
has little enough today, looked beyond literature and beyond the
greatness of art. His true personality went out beyond America, beyond religions and even beyond mankind. His poems about the self
and the mass of America were written before the Civil War, but the
war between the North and South brought everything home to
Whitman. His vision might well have been destroyed, but with his
natural passion for unity he embarked on a new discovery, not of the
body and soul, or rapport, or the En-Masse, but of the exploration of
Death. Whitman had always believed in Death as the purposeful continuity of existence, but he had had no significant experience of it.
One can barely imagine what the Civil War was to Whitman, this fa-
natically intense American, this New World man, the first white aboriginal, with his lusty physical joy of life, his love of comrades, his
genius for poetry, and his natural mysticism. Whitman was stricken

by the war but he was recreated by it. Columbus had been a rather nebulous hero; Lincoln was the reincarnation of the American god to him. Half of Whitman's great poetry is war poetry and poetry on Lincoln and his death, and death poetry, though it cannot all be dated from the war. Whitman accepted death as he did sex and otherness, self and not-self. The war returned to him the particularity of death, and it produced in him not bitterness but love. He triumphed over it. He saw beyond history and beyond America. But what he saw was with the American vision. In Whitman's dialectic, you do not give up the past for the vision: the past is of the vision as much as the future. In the open air "a great personal deed has room" and it is such a deed that seizes upon the hearts of the whole race of man. And this deed is not discovery or triumph or a formula of belief: it is the giving one-self—the Whitman in oneself—to the other, the comrade. Whitman knew that giving in the past had always been a form of taxation and protection. This new kind of giving is reckless and mystical, differing from the old giving because Whitman gives body and soul without sacrificing one to the other. Whitman is no "humanist" and no ordinary libertarian but a seer who dreams of free individuality in a world of free souls. The open road may be a commonplace symbol, but it is a deliberate symbol, and it stands for an actuality. That actuality is America as Whitman sees America in himself. The anti-Whitman party of our time attempts, of course, to deny the vision of the New World with its physical materialism, experimentalism, and the whole concept of man for the world of the present. It turns out that Whitman is not for the "people" and not for the impressively learned poets of our time. He is for man who begins at the beginning—all over again. There is more to poetry than books, he says.

> I think heroic deeds were all conceived in the open air, and all free
>   poems also,
> I think I could stop here myself and do miracles . . .
> Here a great personal deed has room . . .
> Here is realization . . . here is adhesiveness . . .
> Do you know what it is as you pass to be loved by strangers? . . .
> These are the days that must happen to you:

You shall not heap up what is called riches . . .
What beckonings of love you receive you shall only answer with
    passionate kisses of parting,
You shall not allow the hold of those who spread their reach'd
    hands toward you . . .
Allons! after the great companions, and to belong to them!
They too are on the road—they are the swift and majestic men
They are the greatest women . . .
They go, they go! I know that they go, but I know not where they
    go,
But I know that they go toward the best—toward something
    great . . ."

It is all there: the greatness of the body and the greatness of the soul;
the touching of the world and the heroism of departure; the magnificent motion of death; the expanding cycle of consciousness; the essential holiness of all things. And always at the center, the self, the
moment of incarnation, the Walt Whitman of oneself. The aboriginal or, if you like, the American.

The power of Whitman in the world is incalculable. In literature
it has long been calculated as nothing. It is because of poets like
Whitman that literature exists but it is always Literature that determines to exterminate its Whitmans, its Blakes, its Lawrences, its
Henry Millers. The probability is that Whitman will never be "accepted" as one of the great writers of mankind; acceptance is always a
function of the writers who assume the power of literature, for whatever reasons, and who make literature one of the arms of the law. Because Whitman is beyond the law of literature he is condemned to
extinction from generation to generation. Like Lawrence, who res-
cued him in our century, Whitman is beyond the reach of Criticism,
beyond the library and the curriculum, beyond Congress and
Church, and yet there, right under your nose, as you step out of
doors.

HENRY MILLER:
THE GREATEST LIVING AUTHOR

I CALL Henry Miller the greatest living author because I think he is. I do not call him a poet because he has never written a poem; he even dislikes poetry, I think. But everything he has written is a poem in the best as well as in the broadest sense of the word. Secondly, I do not call him a writer, but an author. The writer is the fly in the ointment of modern letters; Miller has waged ceaseless war against writers. If one had to type him one might call him a Wisdom writer, Wisdom literature being a type of literature which lies between literature and scripture; it is poetry only because it rises above literature and because it sometimes ends up in bibles. I wrote to the British poet and novelist Lawrence Durrell last year and said: Let's put together a bible of Miller's work. (I thought I was being original in calling it a bible.) Let's assemble a bible from his work, I said, and put one in every hotel room in America, after removing the Gideon Bibles and placing them in the laundry chutes. Durrell, however, had been working on this "bible" for years; I was a Johnny-come-lately. In fact, a group of writers all over the world have been working on it, and one version has just come out.

There is a commonplace reason why this volume is very much needed. The author's books are almost impossible to obtain; the ones that are not banned are stolen from libraries everywhere. Even a copy of one of the nonbanned books was recently stolen from the mails en route to me. Whoever got it had better be a book lover, because it was a bibliography.

I will introduce Miller with a quotation from the *Tropic of Cancer*: "I sometimes ask myself how it happens that I attract nothing but crackbrained individuals, neuroesthenics, neurotics, psychopaths—

and Jews especially. There must be something in a healthy Gentile that excites the Jewish mind, like when he sees sour black bread." The "healthy Gentile" is a good sobriquet for Miller, who usually refers to himself as the Happy Rock, Caliban, "just a Brooklyn boy," "Someone who has gone off the gold standard of Literature" or—the name I like best—the Patagonian. What is a Patagonian? I don't know, but it is certainly something rare and *sui generis*. We can call Miller the greatest living Patagonian.

How is one to talk about Miller? There are authors one cannot write a book or even a good essay about. Arthur Rimbaud is one (and Miller's book on Rimbaud is one of the best books on Rimbaud ever written, although it is mostly about Henry Miller). D. H. Lawrence is another author one cannot encompass in a book "about" (Miller abandoned his book on Lawrence). And Miller himself is one of those Patagonian authors who just won't fit into a book. Every word he has ever written is autobiographical, but only in the way *Leaves of Grass* is autobiographical. There is not a word of "confession" in Miller. His amorous exploits are sometimes read as a kind of Brooklyn Casanova or male Fanny Hill, but there is probably not a word of exaggeration or boasting to speak of—or only as much as the occasion would call for. The reader can and cannot reconstruct the Life of Henry Miller from his books, for Miller never sticks to the subject any more than Lawrence does. The fact is that there isn't any subject and Miller is its poet. But a little information about him might help present him to those who need an introduction. For myself, I do not read him consecutively; I choose one of his books blindly and open it at random. I have just done this; for an example, I find: "Man is not at home in the universe, despite all the efforts of philosophers and metaphysicians to provide a soothing syrup. Thought is still a narcotic. The deepest question is *why*. And it is a forbidden one. The very asking is in the nature of cosmic sabotage. And the penalty is—the afflictions of Job." Not the greatest prose probably, but Miller is not a writer; Henry James is a writer. Miller is a talker, a street-corner gabbler, a prophet, and a Patagonian.

What are the facts about Miller? I'm not sure how important they are. He was born in Brooklyn about 1890, of German ancestry, and in certain ways he is quite German. I have often thought that the Germans make the best Americans, though they certainly make the worst Germans. Miller understands the German in himself and in America. He compares Whitman and Goethe: "In Whitman the whole American scene comes to life, her past and her future, her birth and her death. Whatever there is of value in America Whitman has expressed, and there is nothing more to be said. The future belongs to the machine, to the robots. He was the poet of the body and the soul, Whitman. The first and the last poet. He is almost undecipherable today, a monument covered with rude hieroglyphics, for which there is no key . . . There is no equivalent in the languages of Europe for the spirit which he immortalized. Europe is saturated with art and her soil is full of dead bones and her museums are bursting with plundered treasures, but what Europe has never had is a free, healthy spirit, what you might call a MAN. Goethe was the nearest approach, but Goethe was a stuffed shirt, by comparison. Goethe was a respectable citizen, a pedant, a bore, a universal spirit, but stamped with the German trademark, with the double eagle. The serenity of Goethe, the calm, Olympian attitude, is nothing more than the drowsy stupor of a German bourgeois deity. Goethe is an end of something, Whitman is a beginning."

If anybody can decipher the Whitman key it is Miller. Miller is the twentieth-century reincarnation of Whitman. But to return to the "facts." The Brooklyn Boy went to a Brooklyn high school in a day when most high schools kept higher standards than most American universities today. He started at CCNY but quit almost immediately and went to work for a cement company ("Everlasting Cement"), then for a telegraph company, where he became the personnel manager in the biggest city in the world. The telegraph company is called the Cosmodemonic Telegraph Company in Miller's books, or in moments of gaiety the Cosmococcic Telegraph Company. One day while the vice-president was bawling him out he mentioned to Miller that he would like to see someone write a sort of Horatio Alger book about the messengers.

I thought to myself [said Miller]—you poor old futzer, you, just wait until I get it off my chest . . . I'll give you an Horatio Alger book . . . My head was in a whirl to leave his office. I saw the army of men, women and children that had passed through my hands, saw them weeping, begging, beseeching, imploring, cursing, spitting, fuming, threatening. I saw the tracks they left on the highways, lying on the floor of freight trains, the parents in rags, the coal box empty, the sink running over, the walls sweating and between the cold beads of sweat the cockroaches running like mad; I saw them hobbling along like twisted gnomes or falling backwards in the epileptic frenzy . . . I saw the walls giving way and the pest pouring out like a winged fluid, and the men higher up with their ironclad logic, waiting for it to blow over, waiting for everything to be patched up, waiting, waiting contentedly . . . saying that things were temporarily out of order. I saw the Horatio Alger hero, the dream of a sick America, mounting higher and higher, first messenger, then operator, then manager, then chief, then superintendent, then vice-president, then president, then trust magnate, then beer baron, then Lord of all the Americas, the money god, the god of gods, the clay of clay, nullity on high, zero with ninety-seven thousand decimals fore and aft . . . I will give you Horatio Alger as he looks the day after the Apocalypse, when all the stink has cleared away.

And he did. Miller's first book, *Tropic of Cancer*, was published in Paris in 1934 and was immediately famous and immediately banned in all English-speaking countries, and still is. It is the Horatio Alger story with a vengeance. Miller had walked out of the Cosmodemonic Telegraph Company one day without a word; ever after he lived on his wits. He had managed to get to Paris on ten dollars, where he lived more than a decade, not during the gay prosperous twenties but during the Great Depression. He starved, made friends by the score, mastered the French language and his own. It was not until the Second World War broke out that he returned to America to live at Big Sur, California. Among his best books several are banned: the two *Tropics* (*Tropic of Cancer*, 1934, and *Tropic of Capricorn*, 1939); *Black Spring*, 1936; and part of the present trilogy *The Rosy Crucifixion* (including *Sexus*, *Plexus*, and *Nexus*).

Unfortunately for Miller he is a man without honor in his own country and in his own language. When *Tropic of Cancer* was published he was even denied entrance into England, held over in custody by the port authorities and returned to France by the next boat. He made friends with his jailer and wrote a charming essay about him. But Miller has no sense of despair. At the beginning of *Tropic of Cancer* he writes: "I have no money, no resources, no hopes. I am the happiest man alive."

George Orwell was one of the few English critics who saw his worth, though (*mirabile dictu*) T. S. Eliot and even Ezra Pound complimented him. Pound in his usual ungracious manner gave the *Tropic of Cancer* to a friend who later became Miller's publisher, and said: Here is a dirty book worth reading. Pound even went so far as to try to enlist Miller in his economic system to save the world. Miller retaliated by writing a satire called *Money and How It Gets That Way*, dedicated to Ezra Pound. The acquaintanceship halted there, Miller's view of money being something like this (from *Tropic of Capricorn*): "To walk in money through the night crowd, protected by money, lulled by money, dulled by money, the crowd itself a money, the breath money, no least single object anywhere that is not money, money, money everywhere and still not enough, and then no money, or a little money or less money or more money, but money, always money, and if you have money or you don't have money it is the money that counts and money makes money, *but what makes money make money?*" Pound didn't care for that brand of economics.

But all the writers jostled each other to welcome Miller among the elect, for the moment at least: Eliot, Herbert Read, Aldous Huxley, John Dos Passos and among them some who really knew how good Miller was: William Carlos Williams, who called him the Dean, Lawrence Durrell, Paul Rosenfeld, Wallace Fowlie, Osbert Sitwell, Kenneth Patchen, many painters (Miller is a fanatical water colorist). But mostly he is beset by his neuresthenics and psychopaths, as any cosmodemonic poet must be. People of all sexes frequently turn up at Big Sur and announce that they want to join the Sex Cult. Miller gives them bus fare and a good dinner and sends them on their way.

Orwell has written one of the best essays on Miller, although he takes a sociological approach and tries to place Miller as a Depression writer or something of the sort. What astonished Orwell about Miller was the difference between his view and the existential bitterness of a novelist like Céline. Céline's *Voyage au Bout de La Nuit* describes the meaninglessness of modern life and is thus a prototype of twentieth-century fiction. Orwell calls Céline's book a cry of unbearable disgust, a voice from the cesspool. And Orwell adds that the *Tropic of Cancer* is almost exactly the opposite! Such a thing as Miller's book "has become so unusual as to seem almost anomalous, [for] it is the book of a man who is happy." Miller also had reached the bottom of the pit, as many writers do; but how, Orwell asks, could he have emerged unembittered, whole, laughing with joy? "Exactly the aspects of life that fill Céline with horror are the ones that appeal to him. So far from protesting, he is *accepting*. And the very word 'acceptance' calls up his real affinity, another American, Walt Whitman."

This is, indeed, the crux of the matter and it is unfortunate that Orwell cannot see past the socio-economic situation with Whitman and Miller. Nevertheless, this English critic recognizes Miller's mastery of his material and places him among the great writers of our age; more than that, he predicts that Miller will set the pace and attitude for the novelist of the future. This has not happened yet, but I agree that it must. Miller's influence today is primarily among poets; those poets who follow Whitman must necessarily follow Miller, even to the extent of giving up poetry in its formal sense and writing that personal apocalyptic prose which Miller does. It is the prose of the Bible of Hell that Blake talked about and Arthur Rimbaud wrote a chapter of.

What is this "acceptance" Orwell mentions in regard to Whitman and Henry Miller? On one level it is the poetry of cosmic consciousness, and on the most obvious level it is the poetry of the Romantic nineteenth century. Miller is unknown in this country because he represents the Continental rather than the English influence. He breaks with the English literary tradition just as many of the twentieth-century Americans do, because his ancestry is not British, and not American colonial. He does not read the favored British writers, Milton, Marlowe, Pope, Donne. He reads what his grandparents knew was in the air when Victorianism was the genius of British poetry. He grew up with books by Dostoyevsky, Knut Hamsun, Strindberg, Nietzsche (especially Nietzsche), Elie Faure, Spengler. Like a true poet he found his way to Rimbaud, Ramakrishna, Blavatsky, Huysmans, Count Keyserling, Prince Kropotkin, Lao-tse, Nostradamus, Petronius, Rabelais, Suzuki, Zen philosophy, Van Gogh. And in English he let himself be influenced not by the solid classics but by *Alice in Wonderland*, Chesterton's *St. Francis*, Conrad, Cooper, Emerson, Rider Haggard, G. A. Henty (the boy's historian—I remember being told when I was a boy that Henty had the facts all wrong), Joyce, Arthur Machen, Mencken, John Cowper Powys, Herbert Spencer's *Autobiography*, Thoreau on "Civil Disobedience," Emma Goldman—the great anarchist (whom he met)—Whitman, of course, and perhaps above all that companion piece to *Leaves of Grass* called *Huckleberry Finn*. Hardly a Great Books list from the shores of Lake Michigan—almost a period list. Miller will introduce his readers to strange masterpieces like Doughty's *Arabia Deserta* or to the journal of Anaïs Nin which has never been published but which he (and other writers) swears is one of the masterpieces of the twentieth century. I imagine that Miller has read as much as any man living but he does not have that religious solemnity about books which we are brought up in. Books, after all, are only mnemonic devices; and poets are always celebrating the burning of libraries. And as with libraries, so with monuments, and as with monuments, so with civilizations. But in Miller's case (*chez* Miller) there is no vindictiveness, no bitterness. Orwell was bothered when he met Miller because Miller didn't want to go to the Spanish Civil War and do battle on one side or the other. Miller is an anarchist of sorts, and he doesn't especially care which dog eats which dog. As it happens, the righteous Loyalists were eaten by the Communists and the righteous Falangists were eaten by the Nazis over the most decadent hole in Europe; so Miller was right.

Lawrence Durrell has said that the *Tropic* books were healthy while Céline and D. H. Lawrence were sick. Lawrence never escaped his puritanism and it is his heroic try that makes us honor him. Céline is the typical European man of despair—why should he not despair, this Frenchman of the trenches of World War I? We are raising up a generation of young American Célines, I'm afraid, but Miller's generation still had Whitman before its eyes and was not running back to the potholes and ash heaps of Europe. Miller is as good an antiquarian as anybody; in the medieval towns of France he goes wild with happiness; and he has written one of the best "travel books" on Greece ever done (the critics are unanimous about the *Colossus of Maroussi*); but to worship the "tradition" is to him the sheerest absurdity. Like most Americans, he shares the view of the first Henry Ford that history is bunk. He cannot forgive his "Nordic" ancestors for the doctrines of righteousness and cleanliness. His people, he says, were painfully clean: "Never once had they opened the door which leads to the soul; never once did they dream of taking a blind leap into the dark. After dinner the dishes were promptly washed and put in the closet; after the paper was read it was neatly folded and laid away on a shelf; after the clothes were washed they were ironed and folded and then tucked away in the drawers. Everything was for tomorrow, but tomorrow never came. The present was only a bridge and on this bridge they are still groaning, as the world groans, and not one idiot ever thinks of blowing up the bridge." As everyone knows, Cleanliness is the chief American industry. Miller is the most formidable anticleanliness poet since Walt Whitman, and his hatred of righteousness is also American, with the Americanism of Thoreau, Whitman, and Emma Goldman. Miller writes a good deal about cooking and wine drinking. Americans are the worst cooks in the world, outside of the British; and Americans are also great drunkards who know nothing about wine. The Germanic-American Miller reintroduces good food and decent wine into our literature. One of his funniest essays is about the American loaf of bread, the poisonous loaf of cleanliness wrapped in cellophane, the manufacture of which is a heavy industry like steel.

Orwell and other critics tend to regard Miller as a kind of hedonist and professional do-nothing. And morally, they tend to regard him as one of that illustrious line of Americans who undermine the foundations of traditional morals. Miller quotes Thoreau's statement, which might almost be the motto of the cosmic writer: "Most of what my neighbors call good, I am profoundly convinced is evil, and if I repent anything, it is my good conduct that I repent." One could hardly call Thoreau a criminal, yet he had his run-ins with the law, just as Miller has, and for the same reasons. The strain of anarchism and amorality is growing stronger in American literature, or that branch of it that I am talking about, and Miller is one of its chief carriers. It is not only Emma Goldman, Thoreau, Mark Twain, Whitman, and perhaps Salinger, but that whole literature of Detachment from political hysteria and overorganization. I am influenced enough by these people and by Miller to tell my students, the poets at least, to cultivate an ignorance of contemporary political and military events because they do not matter. I tell them not to vote, to join nothing. I try to steer them toward their true leaders and visionaries, men almost unknown in the polite literary world, Reich for instance. Wilhelm Reich furthered a movement in Germany called "Work Democracy"; not machine politics, no politics at all, but democracy within one's immediate orbit; democracy at home. America is still the only country where social idealism and experimentation have elbow room; there are still communities that practice primitive Christianity, such as the Catholic anarchists; and just plain little homemade gardens of Eden such as Miller's cliff at Big Sur. The life he describes in *Big Sur and the Oranges of Hieronymus Bosch* is a far cry from the little fascist dreams of the New Classicists. And it is a far cry from the bitter isolationism of Robinson Jeffers or even of Lawrence. Morally I regard Miller as a holy man, as most of his adherents do—Gandhi with a penis.

Miller says in a little essay on Immorality and Morality: "What is moral and what is immoral? Nobody can ever answer this question satisfactorily. Not because morals ceaselessly evolve, but because the principle on which they depend is factitious. Morality is for slaves, for beings without spirit. And when I say spirit I mean the Holy Spirit." And he ends this little piece with a quotation from ancient Hindu scripture: Evil does not exist.

Whitman, Lawrence, Miller, and even Blake all have the reputation of being sex-obsessed, Miller especially. Whereas Whitman writes "copulation is no more rank to me than death is," Miller writes hundreds of pages describing in the minutest and clearest detail his exploits in bed. Every serious reader of erotica has remarked about Miller that he is probably the only author in history who writes about such things with complete ease and naturalness. Lawrence never quite rid himself of his puritanical salaciousness, nor Joyce; both had too much religion in their veins. It is funny to recollect that

Lawrence thought *Ulysses* a smutty book and Joyce thought *Lady Chatterley* a smutty book. Both were right. But at least they *tried* to free themselves from literary morality. Miller's achievement is miraculous: he is screamingly funny without making fun of sex, the way Rabelais does. (Rabelais is, of course, magnificent; so is Boccaccio; but both write against the background of religion, like Joyce and Lawrence.) Miller is accurate and poetic in the highest degree; there is not a smirk anywhere in his writings. Miller undoubtedly profited from the mistakes of his predecessors; his aim was not to write about the erotic but to write the whole truth about the life he knew. This goal demanded the full vocabulary and iconography of sex, and it is possible that he is the first writer outside the Orient who has succeeded in writing as naturally about sex on a large scale as novelists ordinarily write about the dinner table or the battlefield. I think only an American could have performed this feat.

We are dealing with the serious question of banned books, burned books, and fear of books in general. America has the most liberal censorship laws in the West today, but we have done no more than make a start. I have always been amused by the famous decision of Judge Woolsey who lifted the ban on *Ulysses*, although it was certainly a fine thing to do and it is a landmark we can be proud of. Woolsey said various comical things, such as that he could not detect the "leer of the sensualist" in Joyce's book, and that therefore (the logic of it escapes me) it is not pornographic. In excusing the use of old Saxon words he noted that Joyce's "locale was Celtic and his season Spring." And, in order to push his decision through, Judge Woolsey stated that *Ulysses* "did not tend to excite sexual impulses or lustful thoughts," and he closed his argument with the elegant statement that although the book is "somewhat emetic, nowhere does it tend to be an aphrodisiac." Emetic means tending to produce vomiting and I doubt that Joyce savored that description of his masterpiece. The implication, of course, is that vomiting is good for you, and lustful thoughts not. Now everyone who has read *Ulysses* knows that the book is based largely on the lustful thoughts and acts of its characters and that Joyce spared no pains to represent these thoughts and deeds richly and smackingly. *Ulysses* is, since the Judge used the word, a pretty *good* aphrodisiac, partly because of Joyce's own religious tensions. Miller, on the other hand, is no aphrodisiac at all, because religious or so-called moral tension does not exist for him. When one of Miller's characters lusts, he lusts out loud and then proceeds to the business at hand. Joyce actually prevents himself from experiencing the beauty of sex or lust, while Miller is freed at the outset to deal with the overpowering mysteries and glories of love and copulation. Like other Millerites I claim that Miller is one of the few healthy Americans alive today; further, that the circulation of his books would do more to wipe out the obscenities of Broadway, Hollywood, and Madison Avenue than a full-scale social revolution. But I very much doubt whether any Judge Woolsey will ever admit Miller's banned books to legal publication. They are too intelligible. Even an innocuous little book like Allen Ginsberg's *Howl* had to fight its way through the San Francisco courts. Miller was one of his adherents, as was Professor Mark Schorer of the University of California. Schorer is one of our best critics, the author of a fine study of Blake, and the man who helped to get *Lady Chatterley* taken off the banned list.

Miller has furthered literature for all writers by ignoring the art forms, the novel, the poem, the drama, and by sticking to the autobiographical novel. He says in *The Books in My Life* (one of the available works), "The autobiographical novel, which Emerson predicted would grow in importance with time, has replaced the great confessions. It is not a mixture of truth and fiction, this genre of literature, but an expansion and deepening of truth. It is more authentic, more veridical, than the diary. It is not the flimsy truth of facts which the authors of these autobiographical novels offer but the truth of emotion, reflection and understanding, truth digested and assimilated. The being revealing himself does so on all levels simultaneously." Everything Miller has written is part of this great amorphous autobiographical novel and it must be read not entirely but in large chunks to make sense. Many of the individual works are whole in themselves, one dealing with his life in Paris, one with his life as a New Yorker, and there is, in fact, a definite span of years encompassed in the works. But the volumes of essays are also part of the story and there is no way to make a whole out of the parts. Miller is easy to quote if one quotes carefully; the danger is that one can find massive contradictions, unless there is some awareness of the underlying world and the cosmic attitudes of the author. These views are by no means unique, as they are the same as those of all those poets and mystics I referred to in a previous essay. What makes Miller unique is his time and place; he is the only American of our time who has given us a full-scale interpretation of modern America, other than the kind of thing we find in the cultural journals. Incidentally, we do not find Miller in these journals, which, presuming an interest in letters and art, are really organs of social and political opinion.

Readers of Whitman recall that Whitman was blistering about the materialism of this country a century ago, and its departure from the ideals of the founding fathers. Miller is worse. Now it is a commonplace of modern poetry that the poet dissociates himself from life as it is lived by the average American today. Whitman and Miller heap abuse on the failure of the country to live up to its promise. Miller writes as a poet about the demonic hideousness of New York City, Chicago, the South, or he rhapsodizes when there is anything to be rapturous about. But it is not Art that he cares about; it is man, man's treatment of man in America and man's treatment of nature. What we get in Miller is not a sense of superiority but fury, even the fury of the prophet of doom.

Miller knows America from the bottom up and from coast to coast. In the same way he knows Paris as few Frenchmen do. But when Miller describes slums it is usually with the joyous eye of the artist, not with the self-righteous sneer of the social reformer. Here, too, one might describe his psychology as "Oriental" rather than modern. The cultural situation is a matter of complete indifference to him. Miller frequently immerses himself in such modern Indian mystics as Krishnamurti and Ramakrishna, but without any of the flapdoodle of the cultist. He is himself one of the foremost of the contemporary men of Detachment. His influence (like that of Lawrence) comes as much from his life as from his writings. Here it is better to quote. This is Myrtle Avenue in Brooklyn:

> But I saw a street called Myrtle Avenue, which runs from Borough Hall to Fresh Pond Road, and down this street no saint ever walked (else it would have crumbled), down this street no miracle

ever passed, nor any poet, nor any species of human genius, nor did any flower ever grow there, nor did the sun strike it squarely, nor did the rain ever wash it. For the genuine Inferno which I had to postpone for twenty years I give you Myrtle Avenue, one of the innumerable bridlepaths ridden by iron monsters which lead to the heart of America's emptiness. If you have only seen Essen or Manchester or Chicago or Levallois-Perret or Glasgow or Hoboken or Canarsie or Bayonne you have seen nothing of the magnificent emptiness of progress and enlightenment. Dear reader, you must see Myrtle Avenue before you die, if only to realize how far into the future Dante saw. You must believe me that on this street, neither in the houses which line it, nor the cobblestones which pave it, nor the elevated structure which cuts it atwain, neither in any creature that bears a name and lives thereon, neither in any animal, bird or insect passing through it to slaughter or already slaughtered, is there hope of "lubet," "sublimate" or "abominate." It is a street not of sorrow, for sorrow would be human and recognizable, but of sheer emptiness: it is emptier than the most extinct volcano, emptier than a vacuum, emptier than the word God in the mouth of an unbeliever.

This is a man describing his own neighborhood, but the street is a type that runs from the Atlantic to the Pacific, with variations:

The whole country is lawless, violent, explosive, demoniacal. It's in the air, in the climate, in the ultra-grandiose landscape, in the stone forests that are lying horizontal, in the torrential rivers that bite through the rocky canyons, in the supranormal distances, the supernal arid wastes, the over-lush crops, the monstrous fruits, the mixture of quixotic bloods, the fatras of cults, sects, beliefs, the opposition of laws and languages, the contradictoriness of temperaments, principles, needs, requirements. The continent is full of buried violence, of the bones of antediluvian monsters and of lost races of man, of mysteries which are wrapped in doom. The atmosphere is at times so electrical that the soul is summoned out of its body and runs amok. Like the rain everything comes in bucketsful—or not at all. The whole continent is a huge volcano whose crater is temporarily concealed by a moving panorama which is partly dream, partly fear, partly despair. From Alaska to Yucatan it's the same story. Nature dominates, Nature wins out. Everywhere the same fundamental urge to slay, to ravage, to plunder. Outwardly they seem like a fine, upstanding people—healthy, optimistic, courageous. Inwardly they are filled with worms. A tiny spark and they blow up.

The passages on Times Square repeat and catalogue, like Whitman; they are a little too painful to read out of context. Here is a bit of Chicago; Miller is wandering in the Negro slums with a fellow visitor:

We got into the car, rode a few blocks and got out to visit another shell crater. The street was deserted except for some chickens grubbing for food between the slats of a crumbling piazza. More vacant lots, more gutted houses; fire escapes clinging to the walls with their iron teeth, like drunken acrobats. A Sunday atmosphere here. Everything serene and peaceful. Like Louvain or Rheims between bombardments. Like Phoebus, Virginia, dreaming of bringing her steeds to water, or like modern Eleusis smothered by a wet sock. Then suddenly I saw it chalked upon the side of a house in letters ten feet high:

GOOD NEWS! GOD IS LOVE!

When I saw these words I got down on my knees in the open sewer which had been conveniently placed there for the purpose and I offered up a short prayer, a silent one, which must have registered as far as Mound City, Illinois, where the colored muskrats have built their igloos. It was time for a good stiff drink of codliver oil but as the varnish factories were all closed we had to repair to the abattoir and quaff a bucket of blood. Never has blood tasted so wonderful! It was like taking Vitamins A, B, C, D, E in quick succession and then chewing a stick of cold dynamite. Good news! Aye, wonderful news—for Chicago. I ordered the chauffeur to take us immediately to Mundelein so that I could bless the cardinal and all the real estate operations, but we only got as far as the Bahai Temple . . .

Or, again—in explanation:

Oh, Henry, what beautiful golden teeth you have! exclaimed my four-year-old daughter the other morning on climbing into bed with me. (That's how I approach the works of my confreres.) I see how beautiful are their golden teeth, not how ugly or artificial they are.

Combating the "system" is nonsense. There is only one aim in life and that is to live it. In America it has become impossible, except for a few lucky or wise people, to live one's own life; consequently the poets and artists tend to move to the fringes of society. Wherever there are individuals, says Miller (like Thoreau) there are new frontiers. The American way of life has become illusory; we lead the lives of prisoners while we boast about free speech, free press, and free religion, none of which we actually do enjoy in full. The price for security has become too great; abundance has become a travesty. The only thing for nonenslaved man to do is to move out to the edge, lose contact with the machines of organization which are as ubiquitous in this country as in Russia. "Instead of bucking your head against a stone wall, sit quietly with hands folded and wait for the walls to crumble . . . Don't sit and *pray* that it will happen! Just sit and *watch* it happen!" These sayings the culture literateur condemns as irresponsible. Miller follows through with the complete program of nonparticipation in our machine society, which is organized from the cradle to the grave. "Just as Gandhi successfully exploited the doctrine of nonresistance, so these 'saints of the just' practiced nonrecognition—non-recognition of sin, guilt, fear and disease . . . even death." Whitman also believed in nonrecognition of death. His view of death as part of life is one of the many reasons for his unpopularity in America, where death is considered a crime against society. "Why try to solve a problem? *Dissolve* it! [says Miller]. Fear not to be a coward, a traitor, a renegade. In this universe of ours there is room for all, perhaps even need for all. The sun does not inquire about rank and status before shedding its warmth; the cyclone levels the godly and the ungodly; the government takes your tax money even though it be tainted. Nor is the atom bomb a respecter of persons. Perhaps that is why the righteous are squirming so!"

All of this is about modern America and the high cost of security. Do we really have a high standard of living? Miller says not, as most poets do. If living means appreciation of life we have the lowest standard of living in the world, in spite of the fact that it costs more to live in America than in any country in the world. Miller says "the cost is not only in dollars and cents but in sweat and blood, in frustration, ennui, broken homes, smashed ideals, illness and insanity. We have the most wonderful hospitals, the most fabulous prisons, the best equipped and highest paid army and navy, the speediest bombers, the largest stockpile of atom bombs, yet never enough of any of these items to satisfy the demand. Our manual workers are the highest paid in the world; our poets the worst . . ."

And Miller gives this answer, letting Krishnamurti say it:

The world problem is the individual problem; if the individual is at peace, has happiness, has great tolerance, and an intense desire to help, then the world problem as such ceases to exist. You consider the world problem before you have considered your own problem. Before you have established peace and understanding in your own hearts and in your own minds you desire to establish peace and tranquillity in the minds of others, in your nations and in your states; whereas peace and understanding will only come when there is understanding, certainty and strength in yourselves.

To place the individual before the state, whether the Russian state or the American state, is the first need of modern man. To interpret Miller, man is like the common soldier on the battlefield; he can know nothing of the battle at large or of its causes; he can know only the fifty feet or so in his immediate vicinity; within that radius he is a man responsible for himself and his fellows; beyond that he is powerless. Modern life, having made everyone state conscious, has destroyed the individual. America has as few individuals today as Russia, and as many taboos to keep the individual from coming to life as the USSR. First, we have contaminated the idea of society; second, we have contaminated the idea of community. Miller writing about his little community at Big Sur frowns on the idea of community itself. "To create community—and what is a nation, or a people, without a sense of community—there must be a common purpose. Even here in Big Sur, where the oranges are ready to blossom forth, there is no common purpose, no common effort. There is a remarkable neighborliness, but no community spirit. We have a Grange, as do other rural communities, but what is a 'Grange' in the life of man? The real workers are outside the Grange. Just as the 'real men of God' are outside the Church. And the real leaders outside the world of politics."

"We create our fate," says Miller. And better still: "Forget, forgive, renounce, abdicate." And "scrap the past instantly." Live the good life instantly; it's now or never, and always has been.

Miller is "irresponsible" as far as official and popular politics go, or as far as common church morality goes, and as far as literary manners go. But he is not a poseur, he has no program, yet he has a deep and pure sense of morality. I would call him a total revolutionary, the man who will settle for nothing less than "Christmas on earth." In his remarkable study of Rimbaud, a prose-poem of one hundred and fifty pages called *The Time of the Assassins*, Miller discourses on the spiritual suicide of modern youth.

> I like to think of him as the one who extended the boundaries of that only partially explored domain. Youth ends where manhood begins, it is said. A phase without meaning, since from the beginning of history man has never enjoyed the full measure of youth nor known the limitless possibilities of adulthood. How can one know the splendor and fullness of youth if one's energies are consumed in combating the errors and falsities of parents and ancestors? Is youth to waste its strength unlocking the grip of death? Is youth's only mission on earth to rebel, to destroy, to assassinate? Is youth only to be offered up to sarifice? What of the *dreams* of youth? Are they always to be regarded as follies? Are they to be populated only with chimeras? ... Stifle or deform youth's dreams and you destroy the creator. Where there has been no real youth there can be no real manhood. If society has come to resemble a collection of deformities, is it not the work of our educators and preceptors? Today, as yesterday, the youth who would live his own life has no place to turn, no place to live his youth unless, retiring into his chrysalis, he closes all apertures and buries himself alive. The conception of our mother the earth

being "an egg which doth contain all good things in it" has un-
dergone a profound change. The cosmic egg contains an addled
yolk. This is the present view of mother earth. The psychoana-
lysts have traced the poison back to the womb, but to what avail?
In the light of this profound discovery we are given per-
mission . . . to step from one rotten egg into another. . . . Why
breed new monsters of negation and futility? Let society scotch
its own rotten corpse! Let us have a new heaven and a new
earth!—that was the sense of Rimbaud's obstinate revolt.

Miller calls for an end to revolt once and for all. His message is
precisely that of Whitman, of Rimbaud, of Rilke: "Everything we are
taught is false"; and "Change your life." As a writer Miller may be
second- or third-rate or of no rating at all; as a spiritual example he
stands among the great men of our age. Will this ever be recognized?
Not in our time probably. The Rimbaud book ends with a Coda, a
little recital of the literature of despair which has surrounded us for a
hundred years. Listen to it. It is a fitting close to the present book.

Rimbaud was born in the middle of the nineteenth century,
October 20th, 1854, at 6:00 A.M., it is said. A century of unrest, of
materialism, and of 'progress,' as we say. Purgatorial in every
sense of the word, and the writers who flourished in this period
reflect this ominously. Wars and revolutions were abundant. Russia alone, we are told, waged thirty-three wars (mostly of conquest) during the 18th and 19th centuries. Shortly after Rimbaud
is born his father is off to the Crimean War. So is Tolstoy. The
revolution of 1848, of brief duration but full of consequences, is
followed by the bloody Commune of 1871, which Rimbaud as a
boy is thought to have participated in. In 1848 we in America are
fighting the Mexicans with whom we are now great friends,
though the Mexicans are not too sure of it. During this war
Thoreau makes his famous speech on Civil Disobedience, a document which will one day be added to the Emancipation Proclamation. . . . Twelve years later the Civil War breaks out, perhaps
the bloodiest of all civil wars. . . . From 1847 until his death in
1881 Amiel is writing his *Journal Intime* . . . which . . . gives a
thoroughgoing analysis of the moral dilemma in which the

creative spirits of the time found themselves. The very titles of the books written by influential writers of the 19th century are revelatory. I give just a few . . . *The Sickness unto Death* (Kierkegaard), *Dreams and Life* (Gérard de Nerval), *Las Fleurs du Mal* (Baudelaire), *Les Chants de Maldoror* (Lautréamont), *The Birth of Tragedy* (Nietzsche), *La Bête Humaine* (Zola), *Hunger* (Knut Hamsun), *Les Lauriers Sont Coupés* (Dujardin), *The Conquest of Bread* (Kropotkin), *Looking Backward* (Edward Bellamy), *Alice in Wonderland, The Serpent in Paradise* (Sacher-Masoch), *Les Paradis Artificiels* (Baudelaire), *Dead Souls* (Gogol), *The House of the Dead* (Dostoiefsky), *The Wild Duck* (Ibsen), *The Inferno* (Strindberg), *The Nether World* (Gissing), *A Rebours* (Huysmans). . . .

Goethe's *Faust* was not so very old when Rimbaud asked a friend for a copy of it. Remember the date of his birth is October 20th, 1854 (6:00 A.M. Western Standard Diabolical Time). The very next year, 1855, *Leaves of Grass* makes its appearance, followed by condemnation and suppression. Meanwhile *Moby Dick* had come out (1851) and Thoreau's *Walden* (1854). In 1855 Gérard de Nerval commits suicide, having lasted till the remarkable age of 47. In 1854 Kierkegaard is already penning his last words to history in which he gives the parable of "The Sacrificed Ones." Just four or five years before Rimbaud completes *A Season in Hell* (1873), Lautréamont publishes privately his celebrated piece of blasphemy, another "work of youth," as we say, in order not to take these heartbreaking testaments seriously. . . . By 1888 Nietzsche is explaining to Brandes that he can now boast three readers: Brandes, Taine, and Strindberg. The next year he goes mad and remains that way until his death in 1900. Lucky man! From 1893 to 1897 Strindberg is experiencing a crise . . . which he describes with magisterial effects in the *Inferno*. Reminiscent of Rimbaud is the title of another of his works: *The Keys to Paradise*. In 1888 comes Dujardin's curious little book, forgotten until recently. . . . By this time Mark Twain is at his height, *Huckleberry Finn* having appeared in 1884, the same year as *Against the Grain* of Huysmans. . . . By the fall of 1891 Gissing's *New Grub Street* is launched. It is an interesting year in 19th century literature, the year of Rimbaud's death. . . .

What a century of names! . . . Shelley, Blake, Stendhal, Hegel, Fechner, Emerson, Poe, Schopenhauer, Max Stirner, Mallarmé, Tchekov, Andreyev, Verlaine, Couperus, Maeterlinck, Madame Blavatsky, Samuel Butler, Claudel, Unamuno, Conrad, Bakunin, Shaw, Rilke, Stefan George, Verhaeren, Gautier, Léon Bloy, Balzac, Yeats. . . .

What revolt, what disillusionment, what longing! Nothing but crises, breakdown, hallucinations and visions. The foundations of politics, morals, economics, and art tremble. The air is full of warnings and prophecies of the debacle to come—and in the 20th century it comes! Already two world wars and a promise of more before the century is out. Have we touched bottom? Not yet. The moral crisis of the 19th century has merely given way to the spiritual bankruptcy of the 20th. It is "the time of the assassins" and no mistaking it. . . .

Rimbaud is indeed the symbol of the death of modern poetry. This seer, this visionary deserts poetry at the age of eighteen to make money, by gunrunning, even by slave-trading, ending with a death-bed conversion. His is a life of slander, beginning with the motto "Death to God" chalked on the church door and ending with extreme unction and the money belt under the bed. I think the message of Rimbaud to Miller is the death of poetry, the death of history. The whole romantic agony of the nineteenth century is summed up in this adolescent genius, a curse laid on us. Miller obliterates the curse; he pronounces the benediction over Rimbaud, over the death of poetry, over the death of civilization itself but with a side-splitting laugh without an iota of animosity in it. Miller leads us away from the charnel house of nineteenth-century poetry; he does not even recognize the existence of twentieth-century poetry. For poetry has lost its significance, its relevance, and even its meaning in our time. To begin again it must repair to the wilderness, outside society, outside the city gates, a million miles from books and their keepers. Almost alone of the writers of our time Henry Miller has done this; I would guess that his following is enormous and that it is just beginning to grow. Like Nietzsche, like Lawrence, his word somehow spreads abroad and somehow cleanses the atmosphere of the mind of its age-old detritus of tradition, its habits of despair, its hates.

One word more: at the close of his beautiful clown story, "The Smile at the Foot of the Ladder," Miller talks about the clown, the hero of so much of the best contemporary literature.

> Joy is like a river [says Miller], it flows ceaselessly. It seems to me that this is the message which the clown is trying to convey to us, that we should participate through ceaseless flow and movement, that we should not stop to reflect, compare, analyze, possess, but flow on and through, endlessly, like music. This is the gift of surrender, and the clown makes it symbolically. It is for us to make it real.

> At no time in the history of man has the world been so full of pain and anguish. Here and there, however, we meet with individuals who are untouched, unsullied, by the common grief. They are not heartless individuals, far from it! They are emancipated beings. For them the world is not what it seems to us. They see with other eyes. We say of them that they have died to the world. They live in the moment, fully, and the radiance which emanates from them is a perpetual song of joy.

And Miller is certainly one of these who have died to the world, like the clown. The ponderous absurdities of modern literature and the world it perpetuates dissolve in the hilarities of this almost unknown American author; this poet who dissociates himself from the so-called modern age and whose one aim is to give literature back to life. There are not many of these emancipated beings left in our world, these clowns and clairvoyants, celebrants of the soul and of the flesh and of the still-remaining promise of America. And of these few great souls the greatest is—the Patagonian.

THE DEATH OF
RANDALL JARRELL

𝕀̃ THIS IS NOT a eulogy, not a memorial, not one of those exercises in the objective perception of value for which the age of criticism is justly infamous. Randall Jarrell was not my friend, nor was he my enemy. But he was the poet whose poetry I admired and looked up to most after William Carlos Williams. This I said many times in many ways in my criticism. I praised his poetry more and more wholeheartedly than any other of his contemporaries. My praise, it may be, did not sit comfortably with him, for he spotted me as an outsider, or one who was constantly battling to get on the outside. Jarrell was very much an insider. There was a terrible conflict in his soul between his instinct for freedom and his desire for cultural asylum. This conflict gave him his style, his literary style, his lifestyle. It is a style deceptively free. His bookplate might be the question mark. The most common and significant expression he uses at crucial points in his poetry and in his prose is *and yet*. . . . I thought of naming this essay "Randall Jarrell—And Yet," but I decided to be more ambitious. I shall try to situate Randall Jarrell among his fellows rather than doing his portrait. I think there is a message in his death, for me and for this generation.

Let me dispose of a little personal data first, a few observations which will perhaps illumine my not too extensive relationship with him. When I was editing *Poetry* magazine, and after I had published hundreds—could it have been thousands?—of poets, I noted that the manuscripts of Randall Jarrell, whether poems or prose, were the only perfect manuscripts I ever saw. I mean that they were letter-perfect. There was no question of a typo or any other kind of graphical error. He was my only scrupulous poet, for most poets write the way they dress and their manuscripts look like somebody else's laundry, thank God. And this minor perfection of Jarrell's was reflected in the precision of thought, especially in his prose, which all the same sometimes took on a slightly euphuistic contour. I think euphuistic is the word; *baroque* describes certain of his stylistic processes, a style of inlay in which quotation is so exquisitely handled that everything Jarrell quotes sounds as if he wrote it. He was a great, you might say a dangerous, listener. And yet his style of reportage is comic, for he fears loftiness and bombast like the plague. One looks forward to the publication of his letters. We can be sure that the voice of the poet and of the cultural gossip is there. Charm is overwhelming in all his writing; *wit* is too platitudinous a word for his work, and the sharply outlined involutions of his thought deserve a better word than *wisdom*.

He gave a marvelous summation of contemporary poetry in a lecture four years ago. I asked him if I could publish it in the *Prairie Schooner*, which I then edited. His reply was: "I'd be delighted for you to print the lecture in the *Prairie Schooner*. You've always been my favorite editor because you're not like an editor at all." I put the best construction on this remark that I could, especially as I knew it to be true, more than true, a complimentary reprimand of *my* style of life and letters. Except for an early merciless review of one of my books, he was always understanding about me—and acidulous. We were of the same group, so to speak, and had fought all the same wars, and he had a right to cry *Whoa!* when I came galloping by.

All the poets sat on the edge of their seats while Jarrell, whom everybody had to admit had earned the right to do so, put together the jigsaw puzzle of modern poetry in front of our eyes. When I was finally fitted into place, with a splash of color, I felt a relief that I *fitted* and a regret that that puzzle had been solved. I will repeat what he said of me because it is germane to my evaluation of Jarrell: "Karl Shapiro's poems are fresh and young and rash and live; their hard clear outlines, their flat bold colors create a world like that of a knowing and skillful neo-primitive painting, without any of the confusion or profundity of atmosphere, of aerial perspective, but with notable visual and satiric force." He then goes on to mention my influences, Auden, Rilke, Whitman, and he does not need to say that these are also his influences, more his than mine, because Jarrell assimilated his Auden and Rilke and Whitman, along with his Corbière and Grimm and even Robert Frost. I assimilated nothing but was only influenced by. I rejected Influence out of hand and waged a one-man children's crusade against the Past, the Graeco-Judaeo-Christian thingamajig, so that Jarrell could say of me with amused amazement: "Both in verse and in prose Shapiro loves, partly out of indignation and partly out of sheer mischievousness, to tell the naked truths or half-truths or quarter-truths that will make anybody's hair stand on end; he is always crying: 'But he hasn't any clothes on!' about an emperor who is half the time surprisingly well dressed." There is a slight concession here: Jarrell admits that the emperor is dressed like an emperor only *half* the time, while I contend that he is badly dressed even when he is naked.

I will be done with this "interrelationship" in a moment, but I am leading up to something important, a whole or half- or quarter-truth which I am bound to utter. I will read a poem I wrote about Jarrell; it is a prose-poem, as prosodists say when they run out of verbiage, and is in my last book. I don't remember Jarrell's reaction to the poem, but I aimed to please him when I wrote it.

> Randall, I like your poetry terribly, yet I'm afraid to say so. Not that my praise keeps you awake—though I'm afraid it does. I can't help liking them. I even like the whine, the make-believe whiplash with the actual wire in it. Once when you reviewed me badly (you must) I wrote you: "I felt as if I had been run over but not hurt." That made you laugh. I was happy. It wasn't much of a triumph but it worked. When people ask about you I am inclined to say: He's an assassin (a word I never use). I'm inclined to say: Why are you always yourself? Your love of Rilke—if it's love— your intimacy with German and God knows what all, your tenderness and terrorization, your prose sentences—like Bernini graves, staggeringly expensive, Italianate, warm, sentences once-and-for-all. All the verses you leave half-finished in mid-air—I once knew a woman who never finished a sentence. Your mind is

always at its best, your craft the finest craft "money can buy," you would say with a barb. I'm afraid of you. Who wouldn't be? But I rush to read you, whatever you print. That's news.

And this is also news. I am quoting from the News Notes section of *Poetry* magazine of last spring. "There was a public ceremony at Yale on February 28th to honor the memory of Randall Jarrell, who was killed last autumn in an automobile accident. John Berryman, Richard Eberhart, John Hollander, Stanley Kunitz, Robert Lowell, William Meredith, Adrienne Rich, Robert Penn Warren, Richard Wilbur, and Peter Taylor came together at Yale to participate in the tribute, for which the chairman was Norman Holmes Pearson. Mary Jarrell, widow of the poet, read 'the last recently written poem that truly pleased him,' 'The Player Piano,' as yet unpublished. The Yale *Daily News* reports that she 'received an impassioned standing ovation as she walked to the lectern.' Elizabeth Bishop, Cleanth Brooks, Robert Fitzgerald, Marianne Moore, John Crowe Ransom, and Allen Tate, who could not attend, sent testimonials which Professor Pearson read. . . ."

When I read this little notice in *Poetry* I was dismayed at my conspicuous absence from the list. Had Jarrell left it in his will to keep me off the Yale campus? Impossible. I had a blood-boiling moment of suspicion or paranoia that the Bollingen Committee or Professor Pearson or Robert Lowell had blackballed me from the club. My anti-cultural-committee activities span many years, and I have tried to sabotage organized culture whenever possible—not always successfully, of course. When the National Institute of Arts and Letters elected me as a member, I declined. But when their officers called me and said nobody had had that much cheek since Sinclair Lewis declined, and who the hell did I think I was, I chickened out and let them enroll me. When I went to watch the President sign the Arts and Humanities bill, some writer said: What are you doing here? Spying, was all I could say. And now Randall had been organized in death by some cultural subcommittee and all I could think was: Now he knows what it feels like to turn over in his grave.

Between the instinct for freedom and the desire for cultural asylum others can make a choice, and always do. Culture Committees love funerals. There is, even in one's fellow poets, a touch of the vulture; when the poet lies on the roof of the Tower of Silence you can bear the shuddering of ragged wings.

I remember once that Robert Lowell and Randall Jarrell were playing a game. The game was Who's First and it was Lowell's game. The idea is to grade the poets until the downgrading wipes most of the competition off the board. Two or three remaining contenders then engage in a death struggle. Jarrell played this game with a will, but his winning instinct was no match for Lowell.

In Jarrell's bibliography published in 1958 there is a good introduction which contains this sentence: "Most critics predicted the emerging greatness of a Robert Lowell or a Karl Shapiro, but few guessed that Jarrell would outstrip them, especially in so short a time." This judgment is sound as far as I am concerned and certainly as far as Lowell is concerned. I'm not playing Who's First, I hope, because I don't think the game is worth my time or anyone else's. Comparisons of Lowell and Jarrell are irrelevant anyhow. Lowell is primarily a figurehead which he himself personally carved out of solid rock. The effort was immense, Churchillian in blood, sweat, and tears. But one feels that Lowell writes poetry to *get even*, while Jarrell became a poet because he couldn't help it.

Some years ago I volunteered to write an article for the *Evergreen Review* about Lowell. I said I would call it "Robert Lowell *as* T. S. Eliot." A while later I said I would change the title to "Robert Lowell as Cassius Clay." I finished up by not writing the article at all. It was not Lowell I was after but the *maître d'hôtel* psychology of literature which Lowell espouses.

In the Jarrell lecture which I published in the *Prairie Schooner*, Jarrell says this of Lowell (I am paraphrasing): Robert Lowell is the poet of shock. His style manages to make even quotations and historical facts a personal possession. "Make it grotesque" could be Lowell's motto. (In the context Jarrell is contrasting Lowell with Richard Wilbur, a poet who makes poems out of the things of life rather than out of life itself.) Jarrell thought that Lowell possessed and wrote out of a life, yet he knew that this life was at least as unreal as Wilbur's life-by-virtue-of-the-things-of-life. Here is a direct quote: "Lowell has always had an astonishing ambition, a willingness to learn what past poetry was and to compete with it on its own terms." My comment is what Jarrell politely implies, that competition is the sole inspiration of such a poet. Jarrell says in a parenthesis that Lowell bullied his early work, but his own vulnerable humanity has been forced in on him (a statement of tremendous humanity and pardon) with a shadow of fear above. Of Lowell's poems he mentions their stubborn toughness, their senseless originality (an expression to conjure with), and their contingency. Some of the poems justify the harshness and violence and what Jarrell calls their barbarous immediacy; he ends by complimenting Lowell, without having convinced us why, for his largeness and grandeur, and throws him a fish in this sentence: "You feel before reading any new poem of his the uneasy expectation of perhaps encountering a masterpiece." In an earlier treatment of Lowell in *Poetry and the Age*, Jarrell wrote: "Cocteau said to poets: *Learn what you can do and then don't do it*; and this is so. . . . As a poet Mr. Lowell sometimes doesn't have enough trust in God and tries to do everything himself; . . . But probably the reader will want to say to me . . . what Lincoln said about the drunkard Grant: 'If I knew his brand I would order my other generals a barrel.' "

Our generation—the generation of Jarrell, Wilbur, myself, Roethke, Lowell, Schwartz, Bishop, Ciardi, Berryman, Kunitz, Nemerov, Whittemore—one is almost inclined to add Merrill, Lynch, Pearce, Fenner, and Smith—our generation lived through more history than most or maybe any. We lived through more history even than Stendhal, who fell, as he says, with Napoleon. We were reared as intellectuals and fought the Second World War before it happened and then again when it did happen. We witnessed the god that failed and helped trip him up. We predicted the Alexandrianism of the age and like everybody else we throve on it. We drove our foreign cars to class to teach. And we bit the hand that fed us, but not very hard, not hard enough. The hand went on signing papers. Once upon a time we were all revolutionaries of one stripe or another, but when we got married and settled down, with tenure, we talked technique instead of overthrow. Half of us stopped rebelling and not because of middle age. The age made it so easy to be a poet, or to survive on lobster, the age gave in so sweetly to our imprecations, the age so needed us to help it hate itself, this spineless age ended by softening the backbone of poetry.

Dylan Thomas was the anti-symbol of our group, that Dylan who died after he saw the faces of mice in the Bristol crystal. It was Thomas who taught poetry to stop thinking, and we resented that! Though we were not all drunks and suicides, we had our goodly share. But all of us felt the rot of institutionalism in our bones. Jarrell got it down in a novel, the kind of novel the age demanded, the exposé of sensibility. Jarrell's novel *Pictures from an Institution* is so brilliant that it defeats itself as a fiction; it becomes a hornbook of avant-gardism, sophisticated to the point of philistinism. Jarrell is misleadingly philistine, say, about Modern Art of all varieties. It is because he is impatient with failure or imperfection or goofing around with the Muse. But this impatience of Jarrell's is also a veritable lust for perfection; and both the impatience and the philistinism are what you might call Texan. Jarrell was a good Texan in the sense that President Johnson is a bad Texan. *And yet*, what Jarrell does to Gertrude, his anti-heroine in the novel, is almost beyond belief. Can any one be that worthy of hatred? One wonders what Gertrude thought when she read her portrait. Gertrude is one of those savage Southern female novelists who leaves the world in terror of the art of fiction.

The setting of the novel is Benton, a very expensive higher education academy only six versts from Sara Lawrence or Bennington. Benton's President Robbin doesn't fare any better than the loathed Gertrude, and the only lovable character in the book is a German-Jewish composer-in-residence named Rosenbaum. Jarrell attacks avant-garde institutionalism and everything it implies immolating President Robbins and all his kinfolk in the way Gertrude might. He attacks dehumanized letters in his lip-smacking crucifixion of Gertrude. True humanity, true culture, true wisdom are preserved in the broken-English Rosenbaums. Jarrell's love of the Good German led him deep into the Black Forest, deep into German childhood. I shared with him his love for *Der Ros kavalier*, for Elisabeth Schwarzkopf (who was not very kosher German), and even for Mahler. Germany is the preconscious of Europe, almost all, no, all geniuses are maniacs, Germany itself is a maniac, bright dangerous offspring of the Western soul. "Must you learn from your makers how to die?" Jarrell asks of war spirits in one of so many of his Germany-inspired poems. In a note to the poem "A Game at Salzburg" he says that there is a game that Austrians and Germans play with very young children. The child says to the grownup, *Here I am*, and the grownup answers, *There you are. Hier bin i': Da bist du.* Then Jarrell says: It seemed to me that if there could be a conversation between the world and God, this would be it." There is an almost unbearable sorrow in this colloquy, a German-Jewish sorrow, so to speak. Jarrell lets Dr. Rosenbaum say: "The people in Hell . . . say nothing but *What?*" To which Jarrell adds: "Americans in Hell tell each other how to make martinis."

I am not reviewing the novel, but I give it a central place in Jarrell's work as a kind of negative plate of the poetry. The empty intellectualism of America is pinpointed at Benton: the author says, "Nowadays Benton picked and chose: girls who had read Wittgenstein as high school baby-sitters were rejected because the school's quota of abnormally intelligent students had already been filled that year." Jarrell, not quite a Des Esseintes, suffers from a disillusionment of America which all our best artists share, suffers from the disappointment at the failure of the healing-powers of poetry in this nation. Benton—American higher education—is only a rarer kind of custom-built Cadillac. One can almost begin to see the coat of arms emerging on the enameled door. One is already afraid of who is inside. He says, lapsing into what he thinks: "Is an institution always a man's shadow shortened in the sun, the lowest common denominator of everybody in it?" It is bitter to answer yes, but so it is in the modern Institution. In his anthology of short Russian novels, Jarrell quotes Turgenev on Tolstoy. Tolstoy "never believed in people's sincerity. Every spiritual movement seemed to him false, and with his extraordinarily penetrating eyes he used to pierce those on whom his suspicion fell." The early Jarrell published the beginning of a massive attack on Auden, the most conspicuous idealist of the age. Later he forgave Auden, ideals and all.

Jarrell's generation, my generation, inherited the question of Culture, Mass Culture versus True Culture. It is our *pons asinorum* and we all had to cross it. Jarrell worried the problem more than most of

us because he could not take for granted the purely elite aesthetic of
Eliot, the motto of which is High Culture Only: No Foreigners Allowed. Those of us who grew up with the *Partisan Review* on our
kitchen tables and who wrote for it with great pride had a slightly al-
tered version of High Culture. With us it was High Culture plus social revolution. We won the Second World War but lost the social
revolution. We lost it to what Jarrell called the Medium, the Medium
being a kind of symbol for Mass Culture. In the backwash of power
and prosperity that engulfed America after our victory, the writers
fled to those island citadels called Institutions. Whether it was Benton or Harvard or Berkeley, each of these Mont St. Michels harbored
its refugees from the world, from Mass Culture, from the Medium.
Jarrell said the acceptably righteous things about Mass Culture, that
it either corrupts or isolates the writer, that "true works of art are
more and more produced away from or in opposition to society." And
yet he knew the writer's need for contact with the mass and qualified
his rejections of the Medium. Part of the artist, he said (I am quoting
from *A Sad Heart at the Super-Market*): part of the artist "wants to be
like his kind, is like his kind, longs to be loved and admired and successful." Part of Jarrell longed to be accepted by the Medium, but the
thought of that depressed him. He asked, "Is the influence of what I
have called the Medium likely to lead us to any good life? to make us
love and try to attain any real excellence, beauty, magnanimity? . . ."
The answer has to be no. The middle-aged woman in the supermarket who buys All and Cheer and Joy for her gleaming washing machines sees only the image of death staring at her in her rear-view
mirror. Let me read this poem, which in my mind is already a famous
poem.

NEXT DAY

Moving from Cheer to Joy, from Joy to All,
I take a box
And add it to my wild rice, my Cornish game hens.
The slack or shorted, basketed, identical
Food-gathering flocks
Are selves I overlook. Wisdom, said William James,

Is learning what to overlook. And I am wise
If that is wisdom;
Yet somehow, as I buy All from these shelves
And the boy takes it to my station wagon,
What I've become
Troubles me even if I shut my eyes.

When I was young and miserable and pretty
And poor, I'd wish
What all girls wish: to have a husband,
A house and children. Now that I'm old, my wish
Is womanish:
That the boy putting groceries in my car

See me. It bewilders me he doesn't see me.
For so many years
I was good enough to eat: the world looked at me
And its mouth watered. How often they have undressed me,
The eyes of strangers!
And, holding their flesh within my flesh, their vile

Imaginings within my imagining,
I too have taken
The chance of life. Now the boy pats my dog
And we start home. Now I am good.
The last mistaken,
Ecstatic, accidental bliss, the blind

Happiness that, bursting, leaves upon the palm
Some soap and water—
It was so long ago, back in some Gay
Twenties, Nineties, I don't know . . . Today I miss
My lovely daughter
Away at school, my sons away at school,

My husband away at work—I wish for them.
The dog, the maid,
And I go through the sure unvarying days
At home in them. As I look at my life,

I am afraid
Only that it will change, as I am changing:

I am afraid, this morning, of my face.
It looks at me
From the rear-view mirror, with the eyes I hate,
The smile I hate. Its plain, lined look
Of gray discovery
Repeats to me: "You're old." That's all, I'm old.

And yet I'm afraid, as I was at the funeral
I went to yesterday.
My friend's cold made-up face, granite among its flowers,
Her undressed, operated-on, dressed body
Were my face and body.
As I think of her I hear her telling me

How young I seem, I *am* exceptional,
I think of all I have.
But really no one is exceptional,
No one has anything, I'm anybody,
I stand beside my grave
Confused with my life, that is commonplace and solitary.

So in that life which is our Way, there is no excellence. But one wonders, to use Jarrell's pun on the great word *All*, if that is really all. When
the prophets of High Culture (I called it Hi-Cult in one of my own essays) all died out, leaving only Dwight Macdonald to rave against the
Medium and Kitsch and Camp and all those once-fashionable diseases of
the age; when Eliot fell in love and died, and Pound discovered silence—
in short, when the Twenties and Thirties ended, it was already the Six-
ties, and had become hard to say where the Medium ended and the
isolate poet began. How could a specialized study of the intellectual, say,
Herzog, be a best-seller? What mass audience was it that picked that up?
Even the woman in the supermarket quotes William James. The question with us, with Jarrell, was the probability of accepting the supermarket and its brightly packaged values. Or must one be an Allen Ginsberg
and situate Walt Whitman in the supermarket, only to say: "See, I told
you so! America has to start over from scratch."

In *Poetry and the Age*, one of the best handbooks of anti-criticism criticism we have, there is an essay on the obscurity of the poet. My edition of the book is dated 1955, a fatal year for pronunciamentos about the Audience, the year when some giant beast slouching toward the City Lights Bookshop gave birth to "Howl." "Tomorrow morning," Jarrell was saying, "some poet may, like Byron, wake up to find himself famous—for having written a novel, for having killed his wife; it will not be for having written a poem." Jarrell was wrong; the whole generation was wrong about the Audience and the Poet; "Howl" gave us the lie. For myself, I was delighted and immediately sent in my resignation to my generation. They accepted it gingerly but with inquisitorial silence. In the same essay Jarrell had said, "The general public . . . has set up a criterion of its own, one by which every form of contemporary art is condemned." This statement too, which had for so long been so widely accepted, was already obsolete. A decade after "Howl"—and I see that poem as a symptom rather than as a cause—the general public itself has become the contemporary art audience. There are very few places in our geography any more which resemble a Nebraska of the spirit; and in any case, philistinism today is no longer spontaneous but organized, political. Condemnation of the artist today is no longer mere provincialism; it is, to use a not very old-fashioned term, a form of fascism. And the general public, whatever that is, is choosing up sides. The Medium still dominates the sensory experience of the masses of people, but the Medium itself has become an initiate of Hi-Cult. The Medium has also had courses in modern poetry and electronic music.

The Berkeley or California Rebellion, like the Whiskey Rebellion, was a protest against a central culture. The California Rebellion struck out at every form of institutionalism it could clap eyes on. This too was a generational revolt and continues to be world-wide; it is, as most writers about it have noticed, more a sociological upheaval than a new motion in the arts. There is no innovation in Beat arts; the poetry stems from traditional rebel poets, Rimbaud, Pound, Whitman, Artaud. And the counterrevolt against Beatism stems from what was left over from the old-guard elite and also from members of Jarrell's generation. Jarrell would not, I believe, commit himself to the new barbarians, as some writers call them. He could not; he was too urbane, too civilized, too much a lover of the perfect. I cannot imagine him favoring for any reason the later phase of Beat art, the jazz-poetry of Bob Dylan and all those electric guitarists who carry their echo chambers with them wherever they go, portable Aeolian winds, and whose motto seems to be Death By Motorcycle. Perhaps finally Jarrell recognized how much of an institution *our* generation had become, how much an institution he had become. I was in more of a position to face the music, the music of the electric guitar, because of my resignation. It was no surprise to me when I published a collection of essays called *In Defense of Ignorance* to receive a letter from a prominent member of our generation that complimented me highly on the book and said how much it was needed, a letter which ended, "but I would appreciate it if you didn't tell anybody." It was of course not Jarrell who penned this. Lowell questioned my adherence to William Carlos Williams. Williams is the godfather of "Howl."

Jarrell's beautiful fable called *The Bat Poet* is, like all true fables, open to various readings. A child can read as well as a philosopher as well as a poet, each with the same comprehension. A little light-brown bat leaves the pack to go out into the world of daylight to "hang there and think." The real bats don't understand the poet bat, who uses such things as colors in his poems, for the bat poet is a poet. Busy work-a-night bats don't care for color and have no truck with poems. After trying out his poem on such creatures as the mockingbird, who criticizes the bat poet's prosody and complains how hard it is to be a mockingbird; after failing to write a poem about the cardinal, who is perhaps too beautiful even for a poem; after bargaining with the chipmunk, who is the bat poet's most sympathetic critic (although naturally a poem about the owl gives the chipmunk the primordial Angst), the bat poet writes his best poem about, of all things, a mother bat zigzagging through the night with her baby clinging to her body. The chipmunk decides that everything the bat does is upside down. At last the bat poet decides to go and read his bat poem to the bats themselves, but when he gets to the barn where the bats collect, he has curiously forgotten his most important poem and just hangs upside down and goes to sleep like all the other bats.

Whether to be a bat or a poet: that is the question. Maybe the poets of Jarrell's and my generation were all hybrid bat-poets, going back to the institutional barn and then lighting off in broad sunlight to write poems about the righteous and dyspeptic mockingbird, the rich-bitch cardinal, the kindly and existential chipmunk, the Owl who gets us all indiscriminately in his claws. When I got my first copy of *The Bat Poet* I couldn't read it. The title and the drawing bothered me. It was the only thing of Jarrell's I didn't leap to read, and I gave my copy to a student. When I went to find a copy I found that my library at the University of Nebraska had never heard of it, that no bookstore in my part of the world had ever heard of it, that nobody I knew within hailing distance had ever heard of it, except that there was a mint copy in the state capitol building, which I obtained.

The basic assumption, the basic critical theorem of our generation was that poetry didn't really *go* in this age, that the age demanded everything of the artist except his art, and that the poet was still declassed. Insofar as there was any truth in the assumption it was a minor truth. When Jarrell defended Robert Frost in calling attention to "the other Frost" he was reminding his intellectual contemporaries that even a popular poet could make the grade. But Jarrell was really saying about Frost that he was a poet whose popularity was perhaps accidental. Conversely, Dylan Thomas, whom Jarrell thought correctly one of the most obscure poets of the age, was popular by default. It might be truer to say that Frost and Thomas were not only creative but also performing artists, not only performing artists but artists in action. Frost and Thomas lived their poetry, on stage and off; they were one with it, while our generation tended to hide or to collect in small conspiratorial groups. We barely learned to *read* poetry, because, as we said a little wearily, we *wrote* it. And because we wrote poetry that we were not necessarily committed to read, because we held to the cold North American delivery, we could seldom muster more than a token audience. Even Robert Frost, finally one of our great readers, insisted on the verb *say* for his recitations. Jarrell's bat poet picks up the idiom: he says he is going to *say* a poem to the mockingbird, and so forth. The opposite of *to say* is to *sing*, and even tone-deaf Yeats chanted his works. Pound revived a chant for the *Cantos*: it was one of the qualities that attracted him to the Beats. But the classroom voice and the High Church voice were dominant in the generation of Jarrell. And yet, what else were we to do in America, we argued, in a language which is inflected only in moments of violence? We shift between the nasal monotone and the double spondee. Jarrell is the one poet of my generation who made an art of American speech as it is, who advanced beyond Frost in using not only a contemporary idiom (although in Frost it is necessarily fictitious) but the actual rhythms of our speech. Here Jarrell is unique and technically radical. No other poet of our time has embalmed the common dialogue of Americans with such mastery. And because he caught our bourgeois speech he caught our meaning. Here is part of the marvelous essay-poem about, of all uncapturable things, Woman.

WOMAN

"All things become thee, being thine," I think sometimes
As I think of you. I think: "How many faults
In thee have seemed a virtue!" While your taste is on my tongue

The years return, blessings innumerable
As the breaths that you have quickened, gild my flesh.
Lie there in majesty!

                    When, like Disraeli, I murmur
That you are more like a mistress than a wife,
More like an angel than a mistress; when, like Satan,
I hiss in your ear some vile suggestion,
Some delectable abomination,
You smile at me indulgently: "Men, men!"

You smile at mankind, recognizing in it
The absurd occasion of your fall.
For men—as your soap operas, as your *Home Journals*,
As your heart's whisper—men are only children.
And you believe them. Truly, you are children.

Should I love you so dearly if you weren't?
If I weren't?
                    O morning star,
Each morning my dull heart goes out to you
And rises with the sun, but with the sun
Sets not, but all the long night nests within your eyes.

Men's share of grace, of all that can make bearable,
Lovable almost, the apparition, Man,
Has fallen to you. Erect, extraordinary
As a polar bear on roller skates, he passes
On into the Eternal . . .
                    From your pedestal, you watch
Admiringly, when you remember to.

Let us form, as Freud has said, "a group of two."
You are the best thing that this world can offer—
He said so. Or I remember that he said so;
If I am mistaken it's a Freudian error,
An error nothing but a man would make.
Women can't bear women. Cunningly engraved
On many an old wife's dead heart is "Women,
Beware women!" And yet it was a man
Sick of too much sweetness—of a life
Rich with a mother, wife, three daughters, a wife's sister,
An abyss of analysands—who wrote: "I cannot
Escape the notion (though I hesitate
To give it expression) that for women
The level of what is ethically normal
Is different from what it is in men.
Their superego"—he goes on without hesitation—
"Is never so inexorable, so impersonal,
So independent of its emotional
Origins as we require it in a man."

(It is a long deep poem of a couple of hundred lines such as)

You call to me, "Come"; and when I come say, "Go,"
Smiling your soft contrary smile . . .

two lines packed with as much meaning as "The Death of the Ball-Turret Gunner."

An age's poetry does not purify the dialect, or any of that non-sense which aesthetic moralists believe, but an age's poetry fixes the age for those who care to gaze upon it in another age. Most of the poets of Jarrell's generation, when they were not simply describing, setting up the landscape of the city dump or suburbia or attacking the gleaming machinery of our brilliant kitchens, most of our poets dealt in minor points of ideology, lives of the saints or of boxers, or the symbolism of automobiles. Our technique was irony and nothing but irony, more kinds of irony than the Arabs have words for *camel*. But Jarrell, for all his indirection, spoke directly to the theme and in the direct idiom of our semiliterate educated classes. He listened like a novelist—I have already alluded to his ear—he heard the worst of us as well as the best. Things like iambic pentameter hypnotized him not. He used it as one sits in a Victorian chair in a friend's house, but how well he knew a Victorian chair when he saw one.

No one has ever caught a French writer or a German writer or an English or Irish or Scotch writer asking what a French, German, English, Irish, or Scotch writer is. But American writers ask practically nothing but What is an American writer? Meaning. What is an American? It is the great theme of American literature and in a sense the "If some day a tourist notices, among the ruins of New York City, a copy of *Leaves of Grass*, and stops and picks it up and reads some lines in it, she will be able to say to herself: How very American! If he and his country had not existed, it would have been impossible to imagine them."

Jarrell is almost as pro-American as Whitman himself. He applauds Marianne Moore's saying about America only one. Jarrell says, for instance, about Walt Whitman that it is not Niagara Falls, the calico horses, and the war-canoe that matter, nor the resources nor the know-how; "it is not the plunder, but 'accessibility to experience.'" He praises her Americanness and makes more famous the famed line about our language: "grassless / linksless, languageless country in which letters are written / not in Spanish, not in Greek, not in Latin, not in shorthand, / but in plain American which cats and dogs can read!"

For *Paterson Book I* Jarrell reserved greater praise, predicting, because it was the most American poem ever, that it might become the "best very long poem that any American has written," *Paterson* didn't pan out that way, for Jarrell or for anyone else, but Williams did. Williams revealed America, New York on its horizon, "a pillar of smoke by day," says Jarrell, "a pillar of fire by night." Williams and

Jarrell play with the remark of Henry James that America has no ruins; America is full of ruins, says Jarrell, the ruins of hopes.

M. B. Tolson, the great and practically unsung Negro poet—he too is dead—says somewhere in *Harlem Gallery* that the dilemma of the Negro between the white and the black bourgeoisie is: To be or not to be—a Negro. The Negro has a choice, is what Tolson argues, and he (and I) would rather the Negro become a Negro. But this dilemma does not exist for the paleface American: there is no choice of to be or not to be an American. Once an American, once an American poet, one can only ask: I am an American (or an American writer); is there anything I can do about it? American poets, even as late as Jarrell's generation, tried to do something about it by remaining only as American as their passports demanded. A few of us, following Williams, wore the stars and stripes in secret, like The Man Without a Country. Jarrell and I are two of these. The generation of our fathers wore the flag with the cross of St. George or the flag of the stars and bars, and some of them sported the ribbon of the Legion of Honor and one or two the Red, White, and Black. None of my generation sported the Iron Cross, which one sees nowadays in dime stores in America for little boys to play Nazi. But almost all of the generation of Jarrell at one time or another played Red or Pink.

The value and the quality of poetry, unfortunately or fortunately, have nothing to do with moral or political contents. *The Divine Comedy* is banned in Pakistan or used to be, for religious reasons; modern art and poetry are or used to be banned in Red Russia, also for religious reasons. Sad to say, many poets are political or moral idiots, even among the great. In our own time we have to fight the tendencies which threaten what is dear to our own lives and ideologies. But in Jarrell's generation we were almost to a man humane humanists, and, unlike our predecessors, were democratic in politic, agnostic in religion, and baroque in literature. Among us only Robert Lowell and myself could be described as extremists, and our extremism had different derivations and opposite goals.

Jarrell suffered deeply through the Stalinist-Francoist-Mussolini-Hitler years, hoping against hope for a betterment in the human condition. His first book was called *Blood for a Stranger* and was printed in 1942, a war book. He retained only a few of these poems when thirteen years later he published his selected poems, but the themes of war and fascism—war as fascism—were always in his mind. Jarrell has written more good poems about the wars and about Jews and Germany, the good Germany perhaps, than anyone else. He has written also the most famous and the best war poem of anyone in the twentieth century, in five lines.

The volume called *Little Friend, Little Friend*, though it has some of his best-made single poems, is a thematic book, a war book in which the poet is personally absent. The title page carries the penetrating explanation of the poem, the pathos of modern war in the code language of flyers: ". . . Then I heard the bomber call me in: 'Little Friend, Little Friend, I got two engines on fire. Can you see me, Little Friend?' I said 'I'm crossing right over you. Let's go home.'"

The anguish of the soldier is shown less in his anonymity, his exile from the human race, than in his emotional, sentimental desperation. The chief symbols—though Jarrell did not write to manipulate symbols qua symbols—are the mother and the cat. It is no Baudelairean cat (woman the destroyer), no T. S. Eliot cat (a kindly figure from the bestiary); Jarrell's cat is the object of love, if not a love-object, a cat who listens. The mother is pure mother who "thinks heavily: My son is grown." That's all; he's grown, therefore he is a soldier. The pilot falling from his plane sees the smoking carrier and its guns as children's toys. For it is true that in the elemental iconography of war everything is stripped down to a child's arithmetic: mother, soldier, cat, gun. There is a salient difference between our war poetry such as Jarrell's and that first great war poetry written in our fathers' war by Wilfred Owen and Sassoon and Rosenberg and Blunden and so on. The British war poets who showed everyone how to write anti-war poetry were themselves all outstanding warriors and heroes. They cried out against war but were as conversant with blood as Lawrence of Arabia. None of my generation were war heroes, that I remember, nor even outstanding soldiers. It says in a note in one of Jarrell's books that he "washed out" as a combat pilot and became a celestial navigator, a much more suitable classification for a poet. In a sense we waited out the war in uniform. Jarrell's ball-turret gunner is also washed out—of the turret with a hose. Unlike the war poets of the

First World War, who never recovered from the experience, our generation did. We inherited an historical perspective which was denied our fathers. We foresaw and witnessed the whole world turning into the State. The war was of secondary importance to us even while we were part of it. When we came home there was grass growing on all the highways of the forty-eight states, but not for long. Our army went from demobilization to college or to television school; our poets became the university poets. But the tragedy of our generation—and I believe it is the tragedy—was that our army never melted away. It remained, it grew bigger, it was more and more all over the world. It became the way of life, the state; if not the garrison state itself, then something resembling it mightily. The war never came to a stop; only the protocols of armistice were suspended. Our poetry from the Forties on records the helplessness we felt in the face of the impersonal organism of the age—the Impersonal itself which is always death to poetry.

There is a literary commonplace that American literature is essentially a child literature. That *Moby Dick* is a boy's book—I was given a copy when I was seven—that every American hero is Huckleberry Finn in disguise, that poets are really little girls in mufti, that the artist has to prove his masculinity, and so on. A culture without mythos is forced into ideology. Whitman is an ideologue; his negation of mythology is 100 per cent American. Our poets when they deal in the myths do as Jarrell did, following Rilke and other modern artists, analyze and psychologized Orestes or Orpheus. We understand without belief. This is the opposite of using comparative mythology in order to revive and enforce belief, as Eliot did. Our poetry studies behavior and leads us back to the child. With Jarrell too the child becomes the critic and the center of value. Our mythology is the First Impression, the earliest consciousness; all the big people are giants out of Grimm and most of them are bad. When a little girl is moving to a new house she thinks:

> The broody hen
> Squawks upside down—her eggs are boiled;
> The cat is dragged from the limb.

She thinks:

We are going to live in a new pumpkin
Under a gold star.

Theodore Roethke was a modern kind of nature poet, a biology poet
with the eyes of a microscope. Jarrell was the poet of the *kinder* and
the earliest games of the mind and heart. All those wounded soldiers
and shot-down men turn back into children, for a wounded man is
again a child. In the poem called "The State" the child says:

When they killed my mother it made me nervous;
I thought to myself, It was *right*:
Of course she was crazy, and how she ate!
And she died, after all, in her way, for the State.
But I minded: how queer it was to stare
At one of them not sitting there.

In his earliest collected work, one of those five-sided anthologies
which New Directions invented to launch young poets, Jarrell worried the bone of Romanticism, trying to find a rationale for his departure from what he called Modernism. The crux of the problem of our
generation was the Modernism which Eliot and Pound and Joyce
represented and which Jarrell said did not apply to him or to us. He
pretended that Modernism was dead but knew how well it would
flourish in the academies. He catalogues the faults of Modernist poetry as well as has been done: the emphasis on connotation, texture,
extreme intensity, forced emotion, violence, obscurity, emphasis on
sensation, perceptual nuances, emphasis on the part rather than on
the whole, and much more. He even enumerates the Modernist
poet's attitudes: anti-scientific (Jarrell was one of the few poets of our
age who was not anti-scientific and who understood that Science was
not necessarily the intruder in the house); anti-commonsense, and
anti-public. He ends this essay, which is very early and very fine, with
a touch of the style to come. He has his hypothetical reader ask him a
question: ". . . the reader may have thought curiously, 'Does he really
suppose he writes the sort of poetry that replaces modernism?' " And
he replies with an ambiguous, a diplomatic yes.
    It was, say, Eliot, who is yet the most convenient target of attack
for new poets, because Eliot erected targets wherever his mind led

him; it was Eliot who invented Modernism and had it patented. And it was Auden who first shot at the target and missed. Jarrell took care of Modernism in practice better than in theory, as later he took care of Auden. It became necessary for everyone my age to attack Auden, as sculptors must attack Mount Rushmore. Nevertheless, Auden and Mount Rushmore still stand and probably always will. Jarrell, I think, failed to help establish our generation as a separate force and simply, not so simply, went his way to write some of the most quietly agonizing poetry of our time. His overestimation of Lowell represented a kind of fear that, generationally speaking, we did not exist. He half-feared being ingested by the Lowells. But I am a child, said Jarrell, I am the bat-poet; let me go and I will send you many much juicier poets. I will send you my mother and father and a fat girl in the library and even my cat. When John Ciardi put together an anthology of our generation with self-introductions, Lowell was too busy to write his (as I was too) and Jarrell reprinted his encomium about Lowell for Lowell's introduction. The roster of the generation in that version of it reads: Richard Wilbur, Peter Viereck, Muriel Rukeyser, Theodore Roethke, Karl Shapiro, Winfield Townley Scott, John Frederick Nims, E. L. Mayo, Robert Lowell, Randall Jarrell, John Holmes, Richard Eberhart, John Ciardi, Elizabeth Bishop, and Delmore Schwartz. It is an impressive list, in my view, a loose confederation of states which had no president.

I must say something about Schwartz. Dwight Macdonald wrote a memorial about him in the September 8th issue of the *New York Review of Books*. In it he said all the things an editor of the *Partisan Review* should say, all the hi-cult clichés which the *Partisan Review* takes as gospel. It is strange, to say the least, that this great publication, one of the great intellectual quarterlies of our century, should always have been so obtuse about poetry, as if (which I believe was the trouble) they didn't understand it. They took a Stalinist view of poetry, which is that poetry should go back where it came from, and then modified that view with Trotsky's rather nineteenth-century bohemian view of poetry, which reminds one touchingly of perhaps Verlaine. They could swallow the *Four Quartets* hook, line, and sinker and turn on the Beat poets like the OGPU. Macdonald, politically brilliant, a jaded libertarian with the old Marxist leadership principle in his heart, Macdonald says that Schwartz was killed by America, a statement that wouldn't stand up five minutes in a provincial psychiatrist's office, any more than that same college cheer that went: America killed Dylan. Macdonald says: "Poetry is a dangerous occupation in this country, as the biographers of too many of our best twentieth-century poets show, from Ezra Pound on, including the recent deaths of Randall Jarrell and Theodore Roethke. This is not a new thing . . ." And then Macdonald launches into Baudelaire on Poe. ("For Poe the United States was nothing more than a vast prison . . ." and so forth.) This dismal, sociologically oriented view of poetry (now being taught in junior high but no further) was shared neither by Schwartz nor Jarrell nor myself nor by any of the poets I know of. Whether poetry is a more dangerous occupation in America than tree surgery or insurance salesmanship is hard to say. Macdonald points to Delmore Schwartz's tremendous urge toward self-destruction but contents himself with the easy out that America got Delmore. It is one of those facile aesthetic lies which lead to the formation of poetry committees.

There is this about Schwartz as about Jarrell: both refused that lie, and both were tormented by the strategy of escaping from the elite committees which survive by virtue of the lie. Macdonald, discussing his friendship for Schwartz, cites the Jewish-Gentile difference between them, as if this were an area of misunderstanding for an editor of the *Partisan Review* or even *McCall's*. Jarrell, unlike Schwartz, did not become a part of *PR*, although he edited poetry and did the poetry reviews for the *Nation*, a magazine which is intellectually unidentifiable. The *Nation* in our time was more congenial to poetry than the great quarterlies, which always subordinated the poem to the ideology of the magazine. Jarrell wrote some of his best critiques for the *Nation*, in that kindly intellectual morass where one was allowed to Become rather than Be. In the quarterlies one must have already arrived.

So, after all, Jarrell was hung up, as we all were, by the sense of common sense, Thomas Paine's or Henry Ford's or the Scientist's. And after all, Macdonald has a truth in his craw, that poetry (he meant, I think, *being* a poet) is dangerous. *In danger* would be a better phrase, as children are in danger. It comes to the sadness about us that poets are not loved or are loved in the wrong way for the right reasons or—whatever that saying is. It comes to the fact that America the Mother wants to love her children but is much more successful at killing them off, or just making them successful. Jarrell had a brilliant, sure, and subtle mind, and would have been the greatest poet since whoever the last great poet was, had he not lacked the sense of power. He lacked it, to his disaster. It is what you might call a psychological factor, *the* psychological factor. He came of a generation that could not hate Mother America but which was afraid of her and for her. There is no one of our generation who betrayed her or who tried to topple the Victorian Statue of Liberty into the drink. Jarrell was the least anti-American of all of us, and the most. He recoiled from the boredom and the horror and the glory of the day-to-day life. But what he did in his poetry, which had never really been done before, was to face the modern scene and to—what more is there to say—to face it. He faced the music of the American Way of Life. But the subject wasn't anything that Dwight Macdonald would know about, because the elites never stoop to the observation of the actual. It wasn't anything that the power-mad poets would ever see, because they are so busy climbing Mount Everest that they don't know what millennium they are in. Jarrell tried to do the impossible: to observe and make poetry of a chaos, without being either inside or outside of it. He did it better than anyone else, better than it can he done. He did it passionately and with superb control. He did it with lies and subterfuge and great prose. He did it by hiding and spying, reporting and keening. I would imagine that he wept himself to death, out of frustration for the Kafka-like manias of our time, including those of the intelligentsia; out of the ambition which he denied himself because he was more intelligent than any of us; out of the love of the natural which denies the political. He died, you might say, because his heart was in the right place and his heart was even stronger than his intellect. Jarrell was split between his heart and mind. He was modern, which means hating being modern. He was born after Humpty-Dumpty fell off the wall, and he knew that T. S. Eliot Scotch tape couldn't put anything back together again.

II

Poetry and Protests

IS POETRY AN
AMERICAN ART?

AS POET, EDITOR, essayist, anthologist and professor, I have been involved in American poetry all my life. And as poet, editor, essayist, anthologist, and professor, I have finally had to confront the question, Is poetry an American art? The question implies a negative. If we assume the question has any authenticity—that is, is more than the braying of an amateur critic—what are its implications for the American poet, editor, essayist, anthologist, and professor?

American poetry nowadays has the reputation for having accumulated a large and impressive body of works. In the English language we are said to be the present leader in the art. Numerically as well as qualitatively, we make the best showing. Nevertheless, I believe that American poetry is a European transplantation which has never really taken root with us and never will. Ours is a hothouse poetry, kept alive by artificial respiration and fluorescent light. Otherwise, it is a poetry of brickbats.

We've all heard this *ad nauseam*. Our poetry is either academic or vandalistic. And yet I think it is so.

I remember a remark by the British poet George Barker which used to offend us. Barker said: American poetry is a very easy subject to discuss for the simple reason that it does not exist. Today, the remark makes better sense to me. I recall T. S. Eliot's aside which used to rub me the wrong way. Speaking of Walt Whitman, Eliot said that he was a great *prose* writer. I did not really understand Eliot's condemnation until I found something like it in Whitman's own notes. Whitman wrote that the barriers between prose and poetry must be broken down once and for all. He said:

In my opinion the time has arrived to essentially break down the
barriers of form between prose and poetry. I say the latter is
henceforth to win and maintain its character regardless of rhyme,
and the measurement rules of iambic, spondee, dactyl, etc., and
that even if rhyme and those measurements continue to furnish
the medium for inferior writing and themes (especially for persi-
flage and the comic, as there seems henceforward, to the perfect
taste, something inevitably comic in rhyme, merely in itself, and
anyhow), the truest and greatest poetry (while subtly and necessarily always rhythmic, and distinguishable easily enough), can
never again, in the English language be expressed in arbitrary and
rhyming meter, any more than the greatest eloquence, or the
truest power and passion. While admitting that the venerable and
heavenly forms of chiming versification have in their time play'd
great and fitting parts—that the pensive complaint, the ballads,
wars, amours, legends of Europe, etc., have, many of them, been
inevitably render'd in rhyming verse—that there may have been
very illustrious poets whose shapes the mantle of such verse has
beautifully and appropriately envelopt—and though the mantle
has fallen, with perhaps added beauty, on some of our own age—
it is, notwithstanding, certain to me, that the day of such conventional rhyme is ended. In America, at any rate, and as a medium
of highest aesthetic practical or spiritual expression, present or
future, it palpably fails, and must fail, to serve. The Muse of the
Prairies, of California, Canada, Texas, and of the peaks of Col-
orado, dismissing the literary, as well as social etiquette of over-
sea feudalism and caste, joyfully enlarging, adapting itself to
comprehend the size of the whole people, with the free play, emotions, pride, passions, experiences, that belong to them, body and
soul—to the general globe, and all its relations in astronomy, as
the savants portray them to us—to the modern, the busy Nineteenth century (as grandly poetic as any, only different) with
steamships, railroads, factories, electric telegraphs, cylinder
presses—to the thought of the solidarity of nations, the brotherhood and sisterhood of the entire earth—to the dignity and heroism of the practical labor of farms, factories, foundries,
workshops, mines, or on shipboard, or on lakes and rivers—re-

sumes that other medium of expression, more flexible, more eligible—soars to the freer, vast, diviner heaven of prose. . . .

That last sentence—Faulknerian or something—reduced to a beginning and end and avoiding the middle reads in effect: The Muse (of America) soars to the freer, vast, diviner heaven of prose. . . . In my limited knowledge Whitman is the first poet ever to speak of the *heaven of prose*, and I would like to nail that expression on the desk of every American poet.

Whitman is the one great poet we have produced, and by that loose term I mean simply a great world poet. He is also our one innovator. Yet, it was Whitman who demanded the obliteration of the art as it had been known.

We can, I believe, understand the character and importance of American poetry, so-called, when we perceive that the art is not native to us and that it can be produced only under laboratory conditions. And many corollary facts can be adduced from the same premise, for example, the fact that most of our poets are products and functionaries of the university. The fact that this poetry is almost completely, literary, that is, that it depends on predigested cultural contents for its health. The fact that self-destruction is more of an occupational hazard among our poets than among any other writers. (This is not true of our novelists, for example.) The fact that there is not and never has been an audience for poetry in the United States. The fact that we have substituted scientific and critical analysis, of poetry for the use of it, whatever that might be. The fact that poetry has failed to reach the drama qua poetry. And the fact that our most influential poets, such as Pound, Eliot, and Williams, all moved poetry as far in the direction of prose as they were able but without succeeding in bringing about a permanent *rapprochement* or fusion of the two.

I notice with some wonder that a similar process may be taking place in England. I have in mind the strange poem *The Anathemata* which David Jones published in this country roughly a decade ago.

This poem by Jones could hardly have been written without the example of the *Cantos*, to which it is greatly indebted in form. The poem itself, however, is a Christian poem, rich in the mythologies and liturgies of Britain. It is not inconsequential that Eliot and Auden have both given *The Anathemata* their highest praise. Jones has very possibly made the kind of breakthrough for English poetry which the other twentieth-century British poets failed to do. The true influence of Pound and Eliot may be felt in England in this way: the mythic form is broken, prosaic prosody may well be the salvation of English poetry, which has fallen on hard times, though this form I think insufficient for the needs of American poets. Mythography with us is artificial and all but meaningless; in England it retains its validity. The peculiar situation of American culture imposes upon us our cultural amnesia, our most salient and formidable characteristic. Even what we have left of the classical and religious forms, symbols, and ikons is blurred and vestigial, in conflict with the forms and ikons of our actual life. I can now understand and be more tolerant of W. H. Auden's return to the English Church. The American Void must have terrified him, as in fact it terrified Eliot. And Pound's wild-eyed quest for order led him to a more secular mythos of the Virtuous Banker and the Precise Definition. Much of Auden's best poetry, incidentally, is prose, but I doubt if European poetry can ever be as freewheeling as the American in this respect. It cannot be, in fact. American poetry must be *sui generis* if it is to progress. I would like to reintroduce the term *progress* into the literary consciousness, for our poetry has been standing still for generations.

Whitman had the greatest insight after all. This might account for his monumental unpopularity in America. For Whitman is unpopular not only with Americans at large—*nonexistent* would be a better word—but with poets. Whitman is dangerous to American poets, like a pesticide. Even a poet with the great gifts of Hart Crane could only view Whitman as the good gray poet or great pink mother. For despite his admiration of Whitman, Crane could never free himself from the most formal European poetics, a pseudo-Elizabethan rhetoric and the "iambic" line. Crane is one of our finest twentieth-century poets—and of the most self-destructive variety. And what are we to make of the paradox, for example, of Pound's dependence on Whitman's prosody while rejecting the sense of Whitman's poetry? And Hart Crane's identification with the sense of Whitman while rejecting the revolutionary forms?

In a footnote kind of way, I think also of Eliot's rejection of Milton during his free-verse years and his ultimate acceptance of Milton as Eliot drifted back into the traditional European forms. I beg the theological and psychological questions, not knowing how to deal with them. I'm inclined to judge a poet by his prosody, not his "philosophy." Unless I'm deluding myself, in prosody all the cards are laid on the table. Milton was as revolutionary as Eliot; rather, we might say, Milton is to English poetry what Whitman is to American prose. Both were "translating." Milton was "translating" the idea of the epic. Whitman was "translating" the mystique of American politics. Milton was improvising on pagan rhythms. Whitman was improvising on the Constitution and on the *Brooklyn Eagle*. Both in fact were drifting out of versification at different and appropriate rates of speed. To use a happy vulgarism, we can say both were in orbit. I admire *Paradise Lost* in the same way that I admire *Leaves of Grass*, and I recognize that both books are failures, that is, they are monuments, not living forces. They are the Stone Guests of Anglo-American poetry. They freeze us in our tracks.

American poetry, however, is polarized between Poe and Whitman, not Milton (until Eliot raised that ghost). The Poe-Whitman syndrome is the clue to the failure of our poetry. Or perhaps we should say that because of Poe and Whitman we have great prose.

Poe is the death of our poetry; Whitman, the midwife of our prose. Let me fall back on D. H. Lawrence, who can do this better than I can.

Lawrence is excellent on this theme, and his own vacillations are very much to the point. Lawrence was quite American in his disdain for poetry. Poe horrified him because Poe was pathologically incestuous, tearing down the delicate barrier between brother and sister, male and female, past and present. But Whitman disgusted Lawrence also when Whitman spoke of *merging*. Whitman wanted all mankind to form a kind of daisy chain of love. Lawrence stamped his foot at that kind of cowardice. He ended by nominating Poe a ghoul and Whitman a Great Soul (whatever that is). But Lawrence had the scent: the purely destructive Poe, with his scientific detachment—the last thin disguise of ego; and Whitman, whirling us into the spiral nebulae—daddy pushing the cosmic swing, endless rocking. And

Lawrence had the common sense to elicit Whitman, who would go beyond oneself instead of insisting on oneself.

But Poe had no self. Poe preferred to become potting soil, night soil, to borrow a beautiful Irish expression.

It is precisely this circumambience or space program of Whitman's which accounts for his unpopularity among our contemporaries. If we leave out the poem about the learned Astronomer, Whitman is all learned astronomy, geography, and television. I'm not the first critic to suspect that the collected poetry of T. S. Eliot and Ezra Pound is a redaction of *Leaves of Grass*, an attempt to hush up the joyous sense of vision in order to keep mankind's nose to the grindstone.

When Poe had successfully and scientifically disintegrated the psyche, he died and went to Paris. And there, as we know, he was made the patron saint of Symbolism. This bizarre form of literature is the foundation of modern poetry, with its belief in nuances, effects, spooks, and cultural memory. We find this Gallicized Poe working a great influence on the moderns, even though the *American* Poe is repudiated by Eliot and the other moderns. The *American* Poe in the United States is, of course, the man of postmortem effects which Lawrence had in mind. And curiously, it is this popular Poe—despised by the Literati—which bears the greatest resemblance to the literature of the absurd. "The Bells" or "Ulalume" or the whodunits are literature of such low caliber that they approximate the anti-literary. Intentionally or not, Poe is still one of the great destructive forces of literature. This explains T. S. Eliot's fear and contempt of Poe, for Eliot would like to salvage and revive literature. Eliot would like to retain the ratiocinative Poe without the romantic slag. And the disembodied, Gallicized Poe is pure in this respect. Poe is the author of the doctrine of the uncontaminated poem, which I refer to as the laboratory poem.

Whitman could not possibly affect Europe. Whitman is more or less on the wavelength of India, the cosmic wavelength, but in Europe it just sounds like a lot of United States static. Swinburne found Whitman attractive for a time but dropped him. Only a dissident European like Lawrence could stomach Walt. And similarly, very few Americans can stomach him either. Our own wavelength as far as poetry is concerned is still European: reason, form, continuity, fear of spontaneity and originality. This is why we can produce only a variant of English poetry and why we have no American poetry except for a few followers of Whitman who are mainly pseudo-Orientals. The pseudo-Orientalism of Whitman and our New England Transcendentalists is repeated by our contemporary Beat poets as Zen or Yoga.

The rational line of modern poetry, when it flirts with the East—the line of Eliot and Pound—is quietistic and orderly and is directed toward a controlled politics and a state church. We get Confucius in Pound, a variant of the eighteenth-century Jefferson, or we get a mysticism of surrender and passivity, as in Eliot.

The irrational line of modern poetry, when it flirts with the East, is anarchic in politics; it is apolitical and religiously egocentric. Such is the American variant of Zen, which sees this psychology rightly or wrongly as a technique of self-expression. Not as a way of making peace with nature or history, but as a way of thumbing one's nose at life and time. American Zen is about on the level of the American fascination with judo and the haiku; both are techniques of combat. With my minuscule knowledge of the Japanese, I yet think we have not understood them very well.

Nevertheless, the ambition to separate our art from Europe is a healthy ambition, and the drive to the East was inevitable. It was equally inevitable in the time of Whitman and in our time. We must appreciate this intellectual flight in Eliot's Vedism, Pound's Confucianism, and the Beat writer's Zen. What such writers share is an intolerance for American hedonism and violence, what is called The American Way of Life.

Modern American poets, for the rest, have held to an uneasy compromise with French poetics, in Cummings or Wallace Stevens, or to a mindless adherence to the standards of English literature. And this Anglo-American poetry, as I have suggested, is quite naturally the province of our "English Departments."

American poetry—what there is of it—has a powerful centrifugal force. It throws itself out of its country. I know of no other poetry which has done this. Think of the pride of the British poet for Britain, of the almost religious adoration of the French poet for

France, even a Rimbaud or the poets of the Resistance. Then look at American poetry with its bitterness, disillusionment, its striking-back, its treason; it is even in Whitman. What does it mean? Why is there so little good American poetry which is not self-consciously anti-American?

Years ago I put together an anthology of American poetry for college students. The chronology ran from Anne Bradstreet to Allen Ginsberg. A secretary at the publishing house objected so violently to the latter item that she had a nervous breakdown and had to be led away. The Ginsberg poem was "Howl," and the publishers themselves were concerned about sales, especially in parochial schools. They included the poem nevertheless. In compiling this anthology I did my one and only piece of original research. I went back and read all the books of American poetry that had been called that. Little if any of it was. My scoreboard ended up something like this: seventeenth century, Anne Bradstreet and Edward Taylor (no Wigglesworth). Eighteenth century, nothing. Or rather, Philip Freneau, mostly because he had the good sense to ignore the Hartford Wits. He is probably our first American poet, but unfortunately he isn't much of a poet. Nineteenth century, Bryant, Emerson, Longfellow, Whittier, Poe, Holmes, Jones Very, Thoreau, Whitman, Melville (a perfectly awful poet), Bayard Taylor, Henry Timrod, Emily Dickinson, Lanier, and Father Tabb. The rest of the gallery, the bulk of it really, is given over to twentieth-century poets.

It is an extremely unimpressive record for a nation born and conceived to remake the world in its image. Taking a dismal view of the anthology, we might say with accuracy that we have given birth to only one poet before the present century, Walt Whitman. There are a few false starts, such as Poe and Emily Dickinson. The rest is padding.

As far as I can tell, Whitman was the first American writer to be conscious of the fact that the language of England no longer applied to us, though we speak it. It was a language dissolving. A curious linguistic process obtains with us: it is a destructive process and it is fascinating. It works this way. We admit, in greater or lesser numbers, immigrants from all over. We immediately destroy their language, simultaneously destroying our own. What we get rid of are the cultural vestiges and overtones. We cultivate what used to be called broken English. Now, no one seriously suggests that we have a new and separate language or even a derivative language, but everyone agrees tacitly that we have scarcely a language at all but only a medium of communication.

After the Civil War everyone was indoctrinated into the Northern mentality. This meant (aside from the love of the factory and the office, the industrialization of the farm, and the hatred of nature) the accelerated demolition of cultural vestiges. An Old Country language became a matter of shame; the very trace of an accent was distasteful. It has taken a mighty effort on the part of the present government to institute foreign-language programs, for unconsciously we resist them. We do not wish to come that close to the recent and ugly past. Next to the French, with whom we have so much in common, we are linguistically the most intolerant people in the world—and proud of it.

It cannot be said that Americans have a mother tongue. We have removed the singing organ of the nightingale. On the other hand, all the arts in this country *except poetry* are flourishing, as everyone is aware. Painting, sculpture, theater, music, the novel and short story, and much other prose—we are creating very lustily in every direction except that of the poem. Our poetry is still English, still written in the hieratic language which is to us about as meaningful as Etruscan. We speak a variant of English certainly. Yet we associate the language inevitably with its greatest form of expression, English poetry. Now what can English poetry mean to a third-generation Czechoslovakian used-car dealer in Nebraska whose children are my students? For my part, I am on the side of the student.

What is the rationale of visiting this poetry upon millions of central and southern Europeans, Scandinavians, Jews, Negroes, Japanese, or Navajo Indians? Classical Greek would make more sense—or Latin certainly. Yet most English professors in America can't read two words of Greek and only six of Latin. This has never ceased to amaze me. The great bulk of English literature was created by men saturated in the classical languages, men whose sensibilities were shaped by the endless discipline in those languages. How many English professors know Italian, and how can one be knowledgeable in English literature without knowing it? I am speaking as an outsider, an impostor really, for I have too much respect for the scholar's profession to think that I am any more than a guest in any university. But as a writer I know that English poetry was not conceived in a vacuum, that it is a part and only a part of European literature, and that American literature is perhaps the first original point of departure from that great culture.

There is little evidence that Americans have ever clutched poetry to their hearts. Jefferson was more interested in Italian and German music than in Shakespeare. Benjamin Franklin packed a copy of *Fanny Hill* in his luggage when he went abroad as an ambassador. Lincoln, a great writer, was no litterateur. Our great prose writers of the nineteenth century wrote execrable poetry, for example, Melville and Thoreau; Mark Twain was the opposite of poet (or, from my viewpoint, a great poet who wouldn't stoop to verses). All of our great writers ("poets" in quotes, if you like) are prose writers. William Carlos Williams made English poetry his chief target of abuse. Cummings tried to veer toward a divorce from English forms by cultivating the graphic atomic forms of Apollinaire. Stevens beat prosody to a new flatness. The only good poet in the *English* tradition we have produced in our time is Robert Frost. I myself have never been able to see anything in the slightest American about Frost. Oxford and Cambridge knew this. He was our last Colonial, the shining light of that group of British poets who called themselves the Georgians. It can scarcely be said that he lived in America. His habitat was that mythological New England which, since it does not exist, might as well be Old England. We know very well that Frost is not read in the United States; he is studied. I won't go into the question of Frost as our Establishmentarian poet or Virgil. Or why William Carlos Williams, our most American poet since Whitman, who was once supposed to serve as poetry consultant to the Library of Congress, was unseated before he could exercise that function. The government feels safer with a poet of the Tradition, European tradition, that is.

Frost, it goes without saying, is a master. But it is no accident that he had to go to England for recognition and that to the end, except for the great honor given him by President Kennedy, his audience was English.

I think also of the almost catatonic depression of E. A. Robinson, a poet displaced in America, or the bitter self-hatred of Robinson Jeffers, a Whitman without joy. Jeffers had hoped to spend his life in Ireland and escape this country forever. The fact that Jeffers wrote in Whitman's forms—traducing them, really—only reinforces the irony or paradox of the expression "American poet."

It would be tedious to rehearse the present situation in our poetry, this poetry so endlessly and cruelly satirized by our novelists, and rightly so. The poet in the academy, the Writers Conference or Writers Colony, the Fulbright poet, the poet-critic—these are what posterity shall know us by. I will not discuss this phase of the business but simply touch upon the types of poetry we get from this environment.

First of all, we have many, many poets, all highly trained and expert in the skill of writing poetry. I am not trying to be witty when I say that the average graduate student who works a little at it can write a poem as well as Yeats. My opinion of Yeats has suffered considerably from this discovery. Was Yeats a graduate student?

The huge majority of these poets of ours are nestled in or around a college or university. The American university has taken on the responsibility for the care and feeding of poets. For a long time I admired this hospitality but after engaging in it for a number of years decided that it was a snare and delusion. A poet on an American campus, if he is not a bona fide professor, is no more than an exotic insect, a zoology specimen, a Live One. He exists entirely in the third person. He fled from the town where he had no identity. In the university he has so much identity that he might as well be under a microscope. Freshmen pull his wings off and deans wear him like a scarab. But I am off the subject.

Where are the poems themselves published? In university quarterlies, naturally; in secular monthlies, governed or influenced by university culture; and in magazines such as the *New Yorker*, which entertains a slightly gamy approach to literature. Or else in certain select little magazines far from any public view.

For me it is impossible to distinguish between one of these marvelous mechanical poems and another. They always seem to me to be written by the same person or Thing. I can't name five poets writing in the English or American language today who have enough individuality or style to be distinguished from one another. That some get ahead of others in reputation is purely a matter of chance. Or so I believe.

But there is also a poetry of revolt in the United States. This poetry of revolt is better, more engaging than the university poetry, but in the end, it too is Academic.

In a larger sense, of course, all our poetry has been a poetry of revolt or at least of complaint. This is the most significant fact of all. Such a poetry rejects the very basis of its existence. It rejects what I call the poetic situation, that which is characteristic or what Williams called the *local*. Our poetry is criticism, very nearly in a technical sense, as our criticism is very nearly philosophy. We have a poetry of violence and a poetry of wit. The violence may be inner or outer in direction. And I notice about my two favorite United States poets, Whitman and Williams, that they report upon the violent but do not themselves become violent. Perhaps it was because Whitman and Williams knew the street and not simply the writer's colony, the European salon, or the academy that they developed a sense of proportion about American life. Whereas the *poète maudit* is committed to cursing a society he does not know, the academic poet is committed to cursing the street. Or rather, he does not curse; he witticizes and versifies. Yet the poetry is good, well made, and made to last. It's for the "quality." And the violence is real and records true horror and frequently ends in blood. But I cannot be content with either poetry. Our poetry reflects only corners of the city; the poet flees from university to university like a pilgrim in the Dark Ages hurrying from one distant cathedral to the next. Our poor modern poet, full of self-pity, booze and pot, his pockets stuffed with stanzas and passports. Or else he flows from the Left Bank of the Seine to the Left Bank of the Ganges miraculously, being a mendicant. I have no quarrel with any of that except to ask him once in a while: Where are you from? Why don't you sit down and take a load off your feet?

American poetry in our time has been a brilliant form of introspective photography. But the famous photograph album of the modern anthology is only to leaf through in some unborn dentist's office, a momentary and mindless distraction before the consolation of the novocaine. In different ways our opposite poets, the Academes and the Bohemes, are both anesthetized. Isn't this because they are trying to write poetry, on the one hand, and *be poets*, on the other? To *be* a poet in America—what is this like? To write poems in America—isn't that turning back the clock?

Some young poet recently wrote an article in which he was saying about me and others: Leave us alone. Shut up about Whitman and Williams and prose and let us write our poems in peace. Maybe he is right. An overnight collapse of the stanza might be as dangerous as the abolition of the army. Poets still need close-order drill and the barracks mentality. It's too bad that they do. Novelists don't, nor does any other kind of artist I know of. But poets are still the hostages of convention.

What would an American poetry be like should we have one? Certainly it would not be recognizable as such. It would be nonsensical, hilarious, and obscene like us. Absurd like us. It would be marked, as we are, by cultural forgetfulness and lack of principle. It would be void of values and ideals, sensual, joyous, bitter, curious, gossipy, knowledgeable to the last minute detail, ungrammatical, endlessly celebrating the facts, objects, neuroses, murders, love affairs, and vulgarities of America. Certainly it would develop favorite forms, but these would be soluble in prose. It would be comical and slack and full of junk; impure, generous, bookish, and cheap. It would be mystical, savage, drab, and as hateful as Joyce Kilmer's "Trees." As sloppy as Whitman and—well, it would be like the great American novel which every American poet ends up writing as a tribute to "the diviner heaven" of prose.

For poetry is—let us admit it—a minor art of America, like pottery. Our poetry becomes more and more ceramic as the decades roll by. And outside the pot shop the boys with their hammers and rocks peer in at the window. The novelists of this country pay their respects to poetry out of courtesy and professional esprit, but they know, as we know, that the jig is up. Poetry has long since become a pastime, a way of puttering around. Henry Miller wrote me once that he had been puzzled all his life by his suspicions about so much famous poetry and that usually in his reading he sought great poetry in prose. He admired certain German, French, and Oriental poets and Whitman in this country. But on the whole, he drew back from the sacred object called the poem. I had helped him understand this, he said, for which I felt pleased. And for myself, I also seek poetry in prose and in foreign poets. Notice the tremendous pull toward translation in our time. Our poets, the best of them, have turned translation not into an art but into a new poetic medium. What does this point to except a failure of our own medium? Doesn't it mean that our poetry can no longer digest the contents of our life? For this kind of translation is not scholarly or even culture-tradition translation; it is a lifeline or a feeding tube from afar, a temporary supply of life to revive our sickly poetry. We will translate Cavafy one day, Catullus the next, Evtushenko, Lorca, or Gottfried Benn. We do this as if to reassure ourselves that poetry is possible in the old manner. But at bottom we don't believe it. We don't believe the spatter of questions at the close of "The Waste Land" or the beautiful gleaming lines of Homer and Ovid and Cavalcanti in *The Cantos*. *Dove sta memoria.* But we have no memory. Memory is a luxury Americans cannot afford.

Everything in our literature tends toward the dissolution of what people usually call poetry. We happen to have great literature—the political works, the strange and wonderful novels and tales, the polemics, sermons, speeches, asides, criticism, even journalism and reports—and a few unexpected flashes of poetry. But poetry itself we do not have, except that poetry which flowers under the light of prose. How typical it is of our poetry, even a century back, that it is tortured into existence. Emily Dickinson's heartbreaking style or Emerson's the same, repeated in our time in the exquisite timidities of Marianne Moore and the stylized elegance of our university wits. I suffered through Cummings' struggle against the great monuments of the Tradition and his momentary honeymoon in France, Jeffers' gigantic bitterness, Sandburg's hiding in the shawl of Lincoln, and Roethke's roving back and forth between Yeats, the *New Yorker*, and *Leaves of Grass*. Trying to write poetry in the old manner is murder for us. All of which sounds like the lengthy obituary which Rexroth did when Dylan Thomas died.

We have tried so hard—and failed—to produce a poetry of sensibility. Let us give it up. We have experimented with every extreme to no avail. The art of poetry is foreign to us. To some this is a bitter pill

to swallow, but we'd better take our medicine. I think I understand finally the flight of our great exiles, the lonely achievement of Whitman, and the triumph of other arts of language in this country except
ours. "The heaven of prose"—that is a corny expression to conjure
with and to nail on the walls of Yaddo or the MacDowell Colony. But
it makes sense. For if some Tibetan or Amazonian were to ask me to
name the great poems of this country I would name a couple of poets
and add something as preposterous as the works of Thomas Jefferson
and Thoreau, *The Rosy Crucifixion, Huckleberry Finn, Henderson the
Rain King*, etc., etc. The poetry might well be placed in the archives
of Washington, not even in a library. Nobody reads it except students, who have no choice, and the teachers who think it necessary to
talk about. Nobody loves it. Nobody wants it. It's mostly a great stack
of Confederate money which you can hold sorrowfully in your hand
and wonder: Did people ever really think you could spend it?

As a summing up, I would like to share the responsibility for what
I have said. I am in earnest when I argue that American poetry is yet
to be born and that what we have optimistically called our poetry is
only a garden of chemical flowers. I share the responsibility with
Whitman, who laid it on the line when he denied the possibility of a
formal poetics in America. I elicit the support of Eliot, who shrewdly
named Whitman a great prose writer. Pound, who demonstrated how
the Old World forms might be broken. Williams, who struggled so
long to locate in language the rhythm of American life at its worst.

I have been trying in my small way for years to help devalue the
false currency of our poetry. We need a poetic stock market crash.
Yet, we have had it; we had it really at the Boston Tea Party; we have
it in every generation which rebels against the Old World cultures.
The saying goes: Every nation gets the poetry it deserves. Is this what
we deserve? Why don't we turn the question around to ask: Do we
deserve a poetry at all? Our history shows very little inclination toward the art. The one brief upsurge of poetry we have had was during
the 1920's: Sandburg, Fletcher, Lindsay, easy poets who wanted
American listeners. The Americans listened more or less politely and
then went about their business. Fletcher killed himself. Lindsay killed
himself. Sandburg became a famous historian. It was almost as if
the muse of America had muttered: Give them enough rope. . . .

Exile or monasticism became the only method of survival for the poet: abroad or behind the campus wall, anywhere, elsewhere, even Skid Row. The Southern poets exiled themselves to the North.

For years I've battled publishers to print more poets, sometimes succeeding in getting some new man's work in print. Now I don't know but that the publishers weren't right. For generally the publisher is only shamed into printing poetry. The Old World is drilled in the superstition that poetry is the highest form of art. If so, it is certainly not the highest in this country.

Perhaps we should teach our children that once upon a time there was a thing called poetry, that it was very beautiful, and that people tried to bring it to our shores in boats but it died. And a few people couldn't live without it, so they went back to the Old World to see it. And others built elaborate greenhouses, called English Departments, where they kept it breathing. And they watered it with the most expensive electricity, but it didn't like it here and died anyhow. And some fractious students lost their tempers and began to smash the greenhouse windows. And then everybody started reading and writing prose.

THE TRUE ARTIFICER

ↂ THE MYSTERY OF art is the presence of form. The poet arrives
at a knowledge of its own kind, a knowledge which we can share, we
are led to believe, without form. Herein lie all the disagreements
philosophers and critics have ever had about the nature of poetry. For
this knowledge cannot be shared, cannot come into being, until it is
formed. The world is always on the verge of thinking art trivial because the reasoning mind cannot take form seriously. Form, says the
reasoning mind, is bound to be play, and some philosophers at their
wits ends throw up their hands and declare that art is only a higher
kind of amusement. Why it should be "higher" than bullfighting or
quoits then becomes the second hard question. The reasoning mind
cannot imagine how serious utterances can really be serious unless
they are put directly, that is, in prose.

This attitude about the triviality of form is puzzling because it
does not seem to apply to anything except works of art; for all knowledge of any kind is formal, and not simply poetic knowledge. The
formality of philosophy resides in logic and dialectic. The formality
of natural science resides in the selection and organization of data;
mathematicians even go so far as to talk about the formal *beauty* of an
equation, thus leading some people to think that mathematicians are
as unbalanced as poets. The formality of supernatural knowledge resides in rite, sacrament, and the repetition of formulas. Why, then, is
it preposterous for the artist to express himself in form?

Perhaps the answer resides in the paradox that artistic material is
made of human experience. Human experience itself is formless,
chaotic; at any rate we cannot comprehend the "form" of human experience satisfactorily. Human experience is chaotic, but human experience in art is orderly. The poet discovers an order for his own
experience; the expression of this discovery is by definition formal.

How can it be otherwise? For he has entered into ties with the world where apparently no ties existed. He has not "sought" form nor "achieved" form nor "invented" form: he has experienced it. He has entered its presence and it exists by virtue of his presence. And when it comes into existence it shows certain characteristics, which are these.

Beauty: a work of art is beautiful. Symmetry and harmony: beauty is symmetrical or partakes of symmetry, and is harmonious or partakes of harmony. Wholeness: beauty must be whole, not fragmentary. Symmetry plus harmony plus wholeness equal formal beauty: that is our equation. And poetic artifice consists of finding the symmetrical, harmonious whole for a given poetic (personal) situation. The natural difficulties of finding such a solution for experience in all its actuality and economy and authenticity make the poet an artisan and the labor of his days painstaking, niggling, and seemingly unworthy of one who is known as a voyant, prophet, singer, idealist, and heaven knows what.

Once we accept the equation of symmetry and harmony and wholeness for art we can proceed rapidly to those uses of symmetry and harmony which are peculiar to each kind of art: in poetry, repetition and melody and rhythmic plot. The rhythm of poetry has to do not only with meters but with melodies (alliteration and rhyme and sound-development) and with the rhythm of ideas and the rhythm of images; more than that, with the rhythm of feeling.

Rhythm is the most obvious and the most profound quality of art. To understand the role of rhythm in art is to understand the very nature of art. To regard rhythm as a secondary characteristic of art is to fall into the hands of the rationalists of art and the people who talk about form and content.

Poetic rhythm can be reduced to meter, and meter can be analyzed minutely (though it seldom is) for its bearing on other elements of symmetry and harmony in the poem. Meter also bears a direct relationship to the language it represents. Eventually any particular language decides on a rhythmic norm—a certain number of syllables to the typical line and a certain distribution of rhythmic values within the line. Seemingly, this is the height of convention and inelasticity, and yet the poet is never at a loss for new ways to vary the formula.

The reason is that meter in the abstract has no applicability, while applied meter is as various as the words which make up the line.

Meter in the abstract bears a relation to the language it uses, but meter in the particular bears a relation to and an identity with the sense of the words. Where this is not the case we feel a dislocation of form, and suspicion sets in that something has gone wrong with the poem. The meter in any particular case gives the exact linguistic emphasis the poet is after: thus we do not feel meter separately from meaning; we feel the double weight of the right thing said with the right pressure and the right speed. And this form must also correspond with the poet's own peculiarities of speech, his own vocabulary and grammatical needs. It seems impossible to accomplish all these acrobatics at once, but there is plenty of evidence to prove that it can be done.

The meter of poetry gives it its obvious and visible symmetry, but to think of meter as anything except the symmetry of the sense is to fall at once into the form-content delusion. Meter exists because of the laws of symmetry, harmony and wholeness. The poet is bound to these laws and has no respite from them.

This is the barest possible statement about poetic symmetry. I wish now to touch on the simplest point of harmony, which in poetry is alliteration.

If someone in conversation uses an alliteration, he is likely to be laughed at. This laughter expresses uneasiness, the suspicion of affectation and even of insincerity. The presence of as simple a form as an alliteration indicates art-making, artifice. Perfection in common discourse would make anybody think the speaker had rehearsed his lines: we would wonder what he had up his sleeve. There is also the fact that an alliteration creates a point of tension when it occurs, or a reflection that throws the hearer back to a prior place.

On the other hand, a poet comes upon the idea that everything everywhere is falling through space. No matter where he got the idea, from a Greek philosopher or a Princeton mathematician; he is brought to this idea in his own life by seeing leaves falling from the trees in autumn. The dying season reminds him of human death, the slow death of the world, the universe, etc. Of course, the poet is saddened by so much impending disaster and he is going to try to act

this out in the poem. This he does all the way through his work, and I
shall take the little line of climax which says—this being a German
poem—*Wir alle fallen*. There are two points of harmony here, both
alliterative. One comes with the repeat of the *all* sound (which, by the
way, runs through the whole poem). Repetition of the same sound is
itself an expression of tension and denotes a pitch of emotion. Again
it should be said that if one used two such sounds together in prose
he would run the risk of ridicule, while in poetry he is obliged to create such harmonies.

The other point of repetition is the lettering, the repeat of the *f*
sound. Anyone who thinks alliteration is trivial thinks poetry itself is
trivial. Alliteration works in several ways at once: it adds a rhythm to
the other rhythms of meter and sense; it heightens feeling in the
reader's mind; and more important, it gives finality to the idea by setting it off as a separate figure. In a sense it traps the idea so that it can
never again escape. Perhaps this is what people mean when they say
that good poetry is memorable. I prefer to say that, in a case like this,
the poet has proved what he thought and felt.

All poetry is rhythmic but not all poetry is metered. When it is
not metered the poet usually has to supply some other regulating artifice to create symmetry and harmony. Often a non-metrical poetry
is highly imagistic, the images bearing the weight of the whole form.
In some cases image-making is almost the primary business of the
poet and there are poets who can get by almost completely with images. As I mentioned earlier, image-making and imagination are two
different things and sometimes opposites. The child who makes a
bush of a bear is not making an image; he is making a mistake of
imagination. The poet making images does not seek hallucinations
but realities, as when Lawrence speaks of the Bavarian gentians "giving off darkness, blue darkness." This "reality," I should add, is not a
matter of objective observation but of poetic involvement. It is
produced by emotional contact, like the expression we create in
someone's eyes by looking into them.

Poetic imagery is not simply picture-making and picture language. Imagery works through all the senses, sometimes separately,
sometimes together. But the eye and the ear are the senses most affected, although the sense of touch is probably more at work in poetic

imagery than we usually suppose. The poet produces image sensations in very devious ways, and with the aim of breaking through dull
usage and exposing the naked sensory quality of his statement. This
act in itself comes as close to a description of the poet's artifice as we
can get, for the ability to make images out of words presupposes
everything else about the poet: his personal involvement with language and with his desire to turn experience into language. It can be
said of the poet that he feels in language, and that sometimes feeling
does not come alive in him until it has been verbalized. It is difficult
for other people to believe in the poet's sense of the physical reality of
words; critics try to understand poetry with a more limited sense of
language, and this relative insensitivity makes the critic bestow magical powers on the poet. The image-making sense in the poet is really
not as futuristic, as "creative," as critics think: it is more the desire to
get it right, to say the thing accurately, to find the true value of the
locution for each case. Imagery affects everything in a poem except
perhaps meter. Indeed, if there is any dichotomy in the whole work of
art, it is not form and content, or image and idea, or feeling and statement, but image and meter. Image includes every verbal function in
poetry, and meter, of course, is not verbal but temporal. It may be
that it is the time element of poetry which, in fact, takes the poem out
of flowing chronological time and puts it into a time-world all its
own.

The most important class of image is metaphor. This is the bold-
est of language figures and is even a synonym for image. Metaphor
takes to itself the properties of all words and is concerned with those
properties. Metaphor can assign new properties to words but not
with license. In fact, it is the business of metaphor to find out the sensory and ideational possibilities of words which are inherent in them
and which they acquire through use and abuse. Only in this way can
metaphor bring about the metamorphosis in poetry which the poet
needs.

A good image is a good picture, a proper likeness, a physical truth,
and a symbolic truth. When the poet calls England a precious stone
we get a vision of something small and precious; we get a feeling of
indissoluble hardness which resists ages of change; and we get a sense
of eminence also, that which is the center of something. The poet

then speaks of the sea in contrast. The sea is soft, less precious, fluid, the element in which we find the precious stone. The line reads, "This precious stone set in the silver sea." In metaphorical terms the meaning "beautiful, safe, beloved England" becomes "this land, the king's which he wears forever in his crown."

The difference between a poetic and a rational statement about England is that the latter is more abstract. The historian would say "the power of England." The poet images this power by talking about England as a jewel of the sea. And the artifice of metaphor here consists in finding the symbolic particular for the abstraction.

There is one other element of poetic artifice I wish to mention, this one the most difficult to say anything sensible about. That is the music of poetry. The chief sensory quality of language is music, but the music of language cannot be coded and reduced to scales and harmonic tables. Still there is no question that the sound of words in poetry does most of the work of producing images and sensory meaning. Every language has a melodic system of its own and every poet within his language has a melodic system of his own. And this sound system is based on inherent sensory meanings and inherent verbal meanings.

There are some people who say that no word has inherent meaning, only given meaning. I have even heard of one of these men telling his children that on Monday they would call meat *bread* and bread *meat*. On Tuesday they would call meat *wood*, and on Wednesday *ice*. By Saturday, I imagine, the children would be ready to burn all the family poetry books in the fireplace. On the other hand, a poet like Paul Claudel believes so deeply in the inherent meaning of words that he even argues for the graphic extension of meaning; a word to him even looks like what it means. But let that go. George Saintsbury, a nineteenth-century critic, used to say that inherent meanings in sound do not exist: he was a semanticist of sorts. Saintsbury said that there was nothing somber or lugubrious about the sound of *gloom* or *doom*, as poets contended, for if that were so, how could you account for the word *bloom*?

The rationalist of language believes in the story of the Tower of Babel, namely that more than one language is a curse. Semanticists are always trying to take the curse off words by reducing all languages to one, and one so useful that with it the Hottentot could converse with the biphysicist about the House of Lords. The poet believes in the endless multiplicity of language and dialects and personal styles: he glories in every change the language makes, and he knows that each change comes from a deep necessity in the language and that the language will reject every change which is not a true change. There is a natural French Academy in language which holds court over every nuance and innovation: it may be that this is the assembly in which the poet is the unacknowledged legislator.

Every word in every language is intrinsically and extrinsically meaningful. Every word that comes into existence has the esthetic and moral approval of the people who made it and used it. When we have two words which are supposed to mean the same thing, we may be sure that they mean different things. Is there no difference between *flower, fibs, fleur, blossom, blume, bloom?* Is it an accident that the word *bloom* may refer to a lump of wrought-iron? Or that the word *love* has residual meanings of pleasure and belief?

The highest compliment we can pay the poet is to say he has "ear." Ear is the ability, the genius, for feeling simultaneously the harmony of the whole poem and the sense of the sound for each particular word. The function of ear is not musical purely and simply: it is the ability to know the musical sense of the line. We can understand this on the elementary plane of onomatopoeia, where sound imitates meaning.

With ear the poet can do almost anything, yet he can never depart from the sound possibilities inherent in a word-form. If a word with a loud sound has a "soft" meaning (for instance, *bough*) the uses of the word in poetry will be quite restricted. The fact that there is always wind where there is a bough increases the loudness of meaning slightly. The quality of the word is limited by this internal sensory conflict. The word *bloom*, because of its heavy sensuous sound, will always cast something of a shadow over the line in which it appears. If the word *bloom* were more important than the word *flower* in English, we would be a different kind of people with perhaps a more tragic, more melodramatic view of nature.

There is a simple proof of the ruling power of sound in poetry, namely, translation. Everyone is familiar with the terrible loss that occurs when a poem is taken out of one language and put into another. Indeed, the loss is practically total. But what is lost is not merely a pleasing and harmonious series of sounds of the original: what is lost is the very meaning of the original poem. A Chinese proverb says that translation is the reverse side of the brocade. Needless to say, the reverse side of the brocade is useless. Translation is practically as useless; we see only a rough design and a maze of horrid knots and loose ends on a dull field. The sound may be no more than color in one sense: in a deeper sense it is everything that creates the meaning of the poem. This does not mean that the sound *corresponds* to the meaning. It means that the sound produces the imagery, that the inherent sensory meanings of the words are revealed by the choice of the word for its context. The poet knows that there can be only one choice for every particular case. After he has turned over hundreds of candidates in his mind, he comes upon the one and only choice. And what can the translator do but recreate the whole poem from the bottom up?

II

To speak of poetic artifice is always risky because the very mention of artifice assumes that it involves a separate and distinct creative act. But no reference can be made to artifice without pointing to particular cases. Artifice does not come into action until poetic knowledge is born. To speak of one without the other is meaningless. For this reason I wish to retrace what I have just said about rhythm, meter, image, metaphor, and ear, this time in terms of what we can call sincerity.

The poet has a dual obligation to sincerity, one to himself and one to the poem. This is a far different matter from the form-content equation. Sincerity to self in art means the power of accepting the reality of one's milieu in terms of oneself. This sounds the simplest and most commonplace of requirements, but it is the most difficult, and in fact the all-but-impossible human requirement. It is this attribute which we associate with saintliness and the utmost wisdom. It is the essence of humility before actuality. But acceptance of the milieu does not mean resignation, surrender, or blind praise. It means belief in existence. It means a break with every other situation, the recognition of the inescapability from the unique situation. It means a divorce from the historical function and a marriage with the poetic-creative function. This attitude is neither revolutionary nor traditionalist; it is impossible for the poet to generalize his condition so far in either direction. Yet in sincerity he breaks through to new land, a symbolically disruptive act which is recognized by conventional minds as dangerous. The true poet makes this breakthrough without ill intention and without malice: the "experimental" poet does it with evil intent. Since the time of Baudelaire the notion that poetry is malicious has become so widespread that poetry boasts of its destructive powers. Modern poetry represents official sincerity, or the myth of sincerity (called integrity), but little modern poetry is sincere except in relation to its myth. That is, modern poetry says that this is a bad world and we will not say anything about it except that it is bad. Anyone who says it is good desecrates the myth. Thus, the approach to the myth of language must be that in this world the language is debased—etcetera, etcetera.

Acceptance of the situation for the poet is the sign of sincerity to self. This acceptance implies less rather than more involvement in the outside situation. The scene is where he is. He does not seek out the scene. Of the poet who goes out into the scene we always ask the question: Is he sincere? The great nationalist poets, the great rhetoricians, the makers and users of systems convince us, if at all, in spite of their giantism. These poets substitute will for sincerity and they carry with them our suspicion that their real aim is to dominate the scene, and not necessarily to know it.

Sincerity to the poem follows naturally from acceptance of the scene. Sincerity to the poem is the expression of the other deeper sincerity. The old aphorism "style is the man" strikes close to what I am saying. It is not that the poet achieves style as a highjumper achieves height, as much as it is that he achieves selfhood and personality. When we say *style* we are apt to think of surfaces, but it is our duty as readers to distinguish between style which is only a mask and style which is the outer form of inner reality. The poet of masks does not fool anyone for long. The true poet is incapable of imitation. We do not think Shakespeare was unoriginal because he used Plutarch and Holinshed. The story is always there, always in existence: it is what the poet experiences from it that is his theme. The leaves are always falling, the ladies are always fickle, the soldiers always dying, the poor always suffering. Some of this sinks into the poet's soul and cheers him or hurts him, and changes his life. And being changed he changes how to say it.

The poet's artifice consists in making his lines conform to the degree of change he has experienced. The alterations he makes time and time again in a single phrase or a single word are not for "effects"; they are a search for the exact degree of change which he has lived and which is part of him. This is sincerity to the situation. But the search for the right word is carried out also in the other direction, in terms of the possibilities of the language. This is sincerity to the poem. Thus it is that all authentic or sincere poetry is new and surprising and all insincere poetry trite. The trite is bound to be untrue because the degree of the situation has not been taken. The trite can only be "universal"; it can have only general statistical truth, not human poetic truth. The term *trite* is also coupled with the term *sentimentality*: both imply half-truth.

Sincerity in terms of rhythm means finding the rhythm of the language itself and finding the personal expression of this collective rhythm. The rhythm of poetry differs radically from language to language, but in one language it never goes very far from a norm. Even in extreme cases in English rhythm—for instance Hopkins, Whitman, and Eliot, who all tried to escape the norm—the basic meter is present. What is astonishing is the infinite variety that exists within the norm of our simple English line. American poets today are making the mightiest effort to turn the wheel of rhythm, and may succeed—but so far we have no proof that a new era has been reached for English rhythm. The most widely used new rhythm is modelled on a tri-syllabic rather than a di-syllabic meter; in Pound it takes an abbreviated form of the classic hexameter:

Surrounded by herds and by cohorts looked on Mt. Taishan

The rhythm is sincere in terms of modern English and it is sincere in terms of the classical aims of the poet. But the form is limiting be-

cause it can be sustained in English only by an elaborate use of con-
junctions and other connectives:

And the flute lay there by her thigh

. . . .

And then went down to the ship

The whole form spreads because of the meters, requiring the largest
possible canvas for work. Modern metrics in general show more tendency to compromise than this.

The poet cannot know what to say until his ear has heard it. Up to
that point, experience is still in the realm of sensation, locked in. But
by being doubly aware of his situation and the condition of the language, the poet does something for the poem and for the language.
Language itself seeks form. There is a kind of poetic soul in language
which everyone contributes to and takes from. The poet immerses
himself in this language-consciousness; he is at home in this element
above all. But his task only begins at this juncture.

Meter is the frame of poetry. It frames not only the whole with
symmetry but it frames each part within the larger frame. Without
meter, as we know from free verse poets, there is no principle of selection, unless the poet supplies one. Meter drives rhythm into pattern: it does the same with imagery and sound. The lines of force in a
poem can be traced through meter: without it everything else is in
danger of dislocation. Sincere meter permits natural word order, natural to the language, natural to the poet's language, and natural to the
particular poem. Sincere meter permits the flow of feeling through
imagery and the sounds of the lines.

A poem must do what it says. This dictum can well sum up the responsibilities of the poet to his craft. If the poem says *I love you* the
words must act out this conviction and feeling in such a way as to
convince a reader that the act of love is beyond question real. Most
poems that fail merely say; they do not do. But the good poet goes to
infinite pains to re-create the scene and mood and quality of what he
says. Each word is exploited for its image content, and here the poet
must concern himself with the sensory possibilities of the words in
terms of their truth to the situation and to himself. The situation can
be made real only if he finds it in himself to be capable of the experi-

ence he is writing about. He searches for meanings in terms of the senses. The intelligence of art is sensory intelligence, the meaning of art is sensory meaning: unless the poet can argue through language colors, language shapes, language sounds, and through the natural image-making genius of language, he fails as a poet.

Through ear we can trace the poet's total sense of harmony, as through meter we can trace the invisible field of force which holds the poem's body in shape. Ear, specifically, is the ability to find the sensuous correspondences of meaning: ear makes physical what is only implicit in meaning. Ear is harmony itself, from one point of view: it is also the guide to sincerity to the poem and sincerity to self. Ear is the critical faculty of the creative mind, but ear cannot function unless the poet is wholly involved in the situation and the situation wholly involved in him. It is an active, not a passive faculty, and it is this which distinguishes it from the faculty of judgment or the faculty of observation. As soon as one speaks of ear he becomes involved in the presentation of the total poem, the wholeness of which is its meaning. Ear, from the poet's point of view, is equivalent to his own total experience of the finished poem: a vision of it. Ear, to the reader, is his acceptance of the poem because it is good.

The artifice of poetry is without science, without philosophy, without religion. You cannot write or understand a poem philosophically, you cannot write or understand a poem religiously, you cannot write or understand a poem scientifically. The uniqueness of a work of art is its primary characteristic. Outside the work of art there is no rationale which can shed light on it. The poet therefore has no obligation to "explain" his poem in other terms, for there is nothing to explain unless something has gone wrong.

Criticism which usually tries to view poetry in the light of other knowledge thus has the double meaning of explanation and negation. But the attempt to make poetry "mean" more than it does is a sign of desperation about other things. Esthetics, I daresay, flourishes in a time of pessimism. Art flourishes at any time when the individual spirit is left free. True poetry does not require explanation, in any case, because of the law of beauty which demands immediate response to the whole work. Good poets never play with meaning: on the contrary they make meaning foolproof. There is no such thing as a good unintelligible work of art. And there is no such thing as a good work of art which is not immediately apprehensible in the senses. This dictum can be tested against Homer and Dante and Shakespeare and a handful of contemporaries: there is always the handle by which the cup is held, be it plot or logic of circumstance, or something else.

The artifice of poetry is essentially dramatic, and no drama is effective without immediate response. The poet is a playwright who dramatizes his experience; he is the actor who acts it out. Most poets, even when their poems fail in immediacy, defend their work by claiming that their poems leap the gap from poet to reader, even when they don't. But there are some poets who believe that the difficulties of understanding are natural to poetry. Such poets are usually amateur philosophers or theologians. Poetic knowledge is at its best profound and manifold, but poetic artifice demands that this knowledge be made to transform the poem into an immediate perceptible whole.

Modern metaphor is sometimes spoken of as a form in which the literal term is buried: the reader has the job of picking the lock. Supposedly, the poetry gains from this extrusion of meaning and the senses are set free to deal with the secondary results of the meanings. But it is quite obvious that the poem loses more than it gains by this method. In any case, such a method throws into jeopardy the entire basis of art. Nearly all contemporary art that goes bad does so as much because of the "suppression of the missing term" as because of lack of talent. To take away from the artist the primary obligation of immediacy is to leave him a prey to intuition and every license of the imagination. Also it permits the theory, used not only by poets but by critics of poetry, that a poem can mean more than it says, and that it can mean several things. A poet who talks about the four, six, eight or ten "levels" of meaning either has his tongue in his cheek or is trying to impress the police. Any such theory is an invitation to bedlam. Every artist by instinct should fight against the principle of multiplicity of meaning: when for some reason he finds it impossible to form his work any other way, he should admit this as failure in himself, and not try to blame the state of civilization, the collapse of culture, the rise of "mass language," and other circumstances which are not properly his business. It is the poet's job to discover the way to integrity of meaning, not his job to destroy integrity of meaning. Poetry that defends fragmentation borders on apocalyptic knowledge and insane knowledge. Poetry that defends the derangement of the senses, synesthesia, associationalism and the like, drifts rapidly towards a religious state of mind in which poetry itself becomes a religion and an art of prophecy. The good poet is known for the limitations he puts upon his material as well as for the wholeness he creates out of it. It is for this reason that the best artists frequently seem to be doing the same thing over and over again. The inferior artist, who abhors limits, becomes napoleonic and thinks all he has to do is turn his face like a bright light on any scene, and the scene will become illuminated.

Poetry creates a total scene only by implication. The scene within the work is whole but it does not signify a system. This kind of knowledge is the opposite of philosophical knowledge, which seeks a whole order. It is the opposite of scientific knowledge, which seeks a whole order of a different kind. It is the opposite of religious knowledge, which seeks a total order in its own way. Poetry lies eternally outside any order of things which seeks or finds a self-contained system of ideas or beliefs. The current of poetry continually crosses these other currents in a counter-direction. Yet the limited personal truth of poetry and art gives the only permanent evidence of human reality we have. This is why philosophers and politicians and even scientists quote poetry: there is nothing else in human knowledge to prove what they are saying. The accurate quotation of poetry is equivalent to a point of evidence.

Artifice itself is proof. It proves to the poet that what happened could happen. The poem brings into physical existence the always dying reality of experience and the bright or blurred sensations of memory. And artifice brings into existence for the reader the reality of the poet's vision. Let us not abuse the word vision: it is an ocular term, not a fortune teller's. It is not the vulgar conception of poetry as ideal knowledge or future knowledge or transcendental knowledge or pure knowledge or any of the things we read about in books of poetics.

The twentieth century has made the discovery, among so many others, that poetry must be written. This discovery has not yet led to a revision of poetics: so far it has led only to a mechanistic view of art.

We have given up the notion of oracular poetry, poetry of the depths, trance poetry, and so on, but we have swung over to the extreme on the other side. Nowadays critics talk about structure, tenor, function, texture, using the language of mechanics. They approach poetry through the language of psychology, whereas the vocabulary of emotion among them is considered primitive and even obscene. If a critic pronounces a poem beautiful, everyone hangs his head in shame. Nevertheless, we are better off than the critics who used to talk about inspiration and imagination, and it is even possible that we are coming close to a civilized poetics. The obstacle at present is the existence and even growth of a mythopoeia which would raise poetry to an even higher status than government, ethics or religion. The public has instinctively fought off this religion of poetry, but most of the literary public has been weakened or disaffected by the pretenses of mythos. Myth is easily changed into culture propaganda, as was the case in Russia and also in countries where the artist changed to the seer. It makes no difference whether the poetry is supposed to be for the peasants or for the aristocracy: as soon as poetry becomes *for* something or somebody, it is doomed. A poetry that distills values or sets standards or projects myths is at once official poetry. It is tragic for poets and for everyone else that poetry in our time cannot be taken seriously unless it poses as *something like* philosophy or *something like* religion or *something like* science.

And yet the discovery that poetry has to be written is a good sign. This could only have happened in America, where there was no poetry until a century ago and people set about (as Americans will) to find out how it is done. We even started schools for this purpose, to the vast amusement of Europeans. The discovery that poetry must be written has unfortunately helped those zealous people who believe in something called Communication. Both historic poets and mythic poets believe that poetry is a kind of higher Morse Code which can be translated into ordinary language if one knows the signals. But poetry does not communicate in this way at all. The poet does not communicate to the poem; nor does the poem communicate to the reader. The very term "communicate" is a propaganda word which expresses a false reality. A poem is a perfectly intelligible thing in itself: it is coherent; it is whole; it is beautiful; but it is not winking at anybody. This is why the poet has a choice about publication itself: it would not necessarily change his poetry if he locked it all in a strong-box. Most poets probably release their work because of a variety of psychological reasons and not because the poem is *for* someone else. Even the common experience of viewing a particular work is, in a sense, fortuitous, for the creator has no obligation to anything but his creation: he knows, of course, that a given work should have a pre-dictable effect on an audience, but he cannot be sure. I do not think the good poet intentionally hides his work, nor does he shout it from the rooftops. He gives it because he is proud to have made it, but it is given to no one. The giving in art consists in the making—when the poet has finished the poem and it lies on the table before him, he has done his supreme act of charity. It would be wicked, if knowing it to be good, he then destroyed it, but the poem says only: This is what I am. When the poet writes a poem "to" his mistress, the dedication can only be an afterthought. The poet has experienced the lady's beauty and his love for her (which is colored by her love for him) but the work of the poem takes place quite apart from this maze of feel-ings. The poet at the point of creation sits down with the question: What happened to me? Where was I when it happened? His spirit then gives witness of injury or exultation, his memory remakes the scene, he begins the search for words to tell the story. And the *time when* he does these things determines whether they will be done at all. Shelley's glorious image of inspiration as a fading coal tells what happens to the poet who waits. Waiting is death to art. Almost any-one can recover from experience: only the artist can arrest the quality of experience.

At the bottom of every poem lies the personal history of poetic ar-tifice, the ceaseless engagement of the poet with the quality of experi-ence itself, the efforts to reach the poem without violating his own truth or without violating its verbal possibilities. This can only be done by finding the wholeness of the situation itself. Wholeness is achieved through the virtues of symmetry and harmony. And symme-try and harmony in a related and complete work result in a thing of beauty. *Beauty is a quality of poetry and not its aim.* Its aim is to give fi-nality to the particular personal human truth.

There is a legend about the end of the world which pictures a poet standing in the doorway of his lonely cottage, watching the approach of a pestilent cloud. He knows he is the last living man and he knows that death will come to him in a few hours. What does he do? How does he prepare for his own death and the death of the world? He does not sink down in thought or prayer; he does not attempt to record his final hours; he does not seek an escape from the inevitable destiny. He turns back into the house and goes to his writing table; he takes up the poem he is writing and studies it again. He begins the new corrections.

This is the legend of the true artificer.

THE CAREER OF THE POEM

A DELICIOUS obliquity one sometimes hears at literary conferences and such places is the question: Are you a writer or a poet? The question, of course, is a high compliment, if one happens to be a poet. It bestows on the poet the keys to the kingdom; it takes him out of the realm of mere literature and installs him in the empyrean; it frees him from any of the normal ties to the world with which other men are bound; it makes him a kind of god.

There is a part of the world which wants to sanctify the poet and make him an object of worship. For is not the poet incorruptible? Is not his integrity beyond reproach? Is he not a man of wizardly insight and towering intelligence? Is not his learning instinctively deep even when it is not broad? Is he not the sole symbol of freedom in a regimented universe? Is he not impervious to the lust for money, power and position? Is he not also that Tiresias who sees into the future, who descends to hell and flies up to heaven?

These are hard questions to say no to, but let us say no, for the sake of truth, and then see what there is, if anything, that makes the poet a superior being. For certainly the poet is as corruptible as anybody else, and more times than not displays the manners of a corporal and the morals of a bellboy. His integrity, although he wears it on his sleeve, is very much to be doubted. His insights into anything but poetry—and very often poetry itself—are apt to be as wrong as anyone else's: we have only to think of the political writings of poets. His intelligence varies as much as that of other men and bears only an indirect relationship to his talent. His learning is always suspect. His love of physical freedom is another superstition: many poets would be perfectly happy in jail if they didn't have to work. As for freedom from money-lust, power or position, one has only to read the lives of

214

the poets to be disabused of this fantasy. A history of literary politics would read like a combined version of the more lurid pages of Gibbon and the Marquis de Sade.

Poetic fame, poetic honor, or what you will, is part of the iconography of history. The fame of Byron on the Continent had nothing to do with his poetic stature and everything to do with his role of hero. Being a poet helped his heroics; the heroics did not always improve his poetry. History seizes on the heroic element in the artist and hugs it for dear life. And sometimes the artist himself adopts this quixotic pose, and he then becomes a party to a literary conspiracy and begins to confuse poetry with history, logic, science, system-making and God.

Nevertheless, the world wants the poet for what he is not, and the foolish poet goes to the world. This liaison results in the two false uses of art which we have been discussing: the one that makes the poet a man of the people, or a man who leads people, or a man who makes the whole world kin, or a man who states universal truths. This is the idea of the historic poet. And the other that makes the poet a purveyor of myths, an oracle, a seer, an almost-philosopher, an aristocrat of the spirit, a being who perceives transcendental relationships. This is the idea of the mythic poet.

Literature of this kind always produces doctrines and fiats and manifestoes. After a time it becomes anathema for the historic poet to write anything which is not a folksong, a patriotic ballad, a rhetorical screed, an epic, or a Methodist hymn. In the other camp it becomes anathema to write anything which does not add to a symbolic system of ideas, or which does not code or decode the mythos of culture. Perceiving this strife, the readers of poems, if there are any left, decide that it is a fight between pessimists and optimists, intellectuals and emotionalists, romantics and classicists, or some other misleading dualism.

Now and then we get a really consistent poet who will align his politics, his religion, his science, and his philosophy so that they all work together. We then have what is called a Great poet. Even if in the nature of his system this poet must decide to eliminate people themselves, he is still called Great. The term refers to a kind of military genius. On the other side, we have the poet who perpetuates

myths of the ideal world or the dream world, and this one is called a
Major poet. Yeats is Major but not Great. Pound is Great but not
Major. A minor poet, incidentally, is one who has no master plan of
strategy either for the world or for the cosmos. Rilke, who is probably the best modern poet, is neither major nor minor nor great and is
something of an embarrassment to critics. He is both emotional and
"intellectual," both obscure and simple, both metaphysical and symbolist, both formalist and anti-traditional: in short, he is himself, like
any poet who abdicates from theory and literary politics.

Both historic and mythic poets regard themselves as official poets.
They acquire aides-de-camp among the estheticians and the press,
and conduct their affairs along the lines of any other business or political enterprise.

The desire of these official poets to provide answers to all questions is indicative of the intellectual temper of the times we live in,
and is not confined to artists, by any means. A man who makes a discovery about the mind develops a psychology to explain all human
behavior. A historian will explain all history by means of a theory of
cycles. An economist will retell the story of man from the point of
view of physical want. One man will explain everything about the
human race from the dogma of the Fall of Man. A later prophet will
see all history as a noble struggle to improve—the dogma of the Rise
of Man.

Literature is contaminated by systems. The libertarian poet, the
religious poet who plies the dogma of his church, even the "scientific" metaphysical poet: these look for an absolute doctrine of life on
which to build. In a healthy world this slavery to ideas does not exist
and the members of my quadrivium do not contaminate each other.
Philosophy pursues the absolute and calls itself the love of knowledge. Science pursues demonstrable knowledge and calls itself the
love of natural law. Religion pursues goodness and calls itself the
love of God. And poetry pursues human personal knowledge and
calls itself the love of beauty. With poetry, as with other forms of
knowledge, there is no crossing the line, no violation of the nature of
the thing, without contamination. All art that does so is marked by
insincerity, whether intellectual insincerity (the poet who takes a system of ideas to his bosom and writes verses to hang upon his Tree of

Life) or emotional insincerity (the artist who tries to experience history).

What claim, then, has the poet to any knowledge except the personal knowledge of truth or beauty? Absolutely none. What claim has he to be a specialist in culture, morals, politics, religion, philosophy, science or even esthetics? Absolutely none. But if that is the case, what claim has the poet to any fame at all? Is there then no basis for poetic reputation, no reason for exalting poetry among the works of man?

Certainly there is. The seeker after truth and the seeker of truth through beauty are necessary to the world. But they are not rulers of the world or leaders of the world. The idea of the sacred poet is one of the most unsavory and dangerous ideas in our civilization. How and when the sacred poet was born I do not know, but in our own age this superstition has grown steadily for a century and a half. In Mozart's time the composer and performer were seated at table with the valet and the cook. This strikes us as cruel and degrading, but our exaltation of the artist is just as shameful. Perhaps it was when kings began to topple that the artist began the march up the table. This is one of the points of contamination I have been talking about. Those poets who staked out claims on the frontiers of time are the ones I call mythic and historic poets. Their descendants set themselves up as arbiters of history, or of morals, or of standards of taste—practices which have nothing fundamentally to do with poetry. Mythic poetry and historic poetry are both corrupt forms of art, and both are corrupted by power.

A civilization in equilibrium does not make the poet a sacred cow, which when it barges into a citizen's house is hung with garlands of flowers. A civilization in equilibrium needs the poet as much as it needs the priest, the scientist, the scholar and the abstract thinker; he is never made a superior symbol of authority in any way. A civilization without poets is a moribund civilization: it has no love of its way of life. But a civilization in which the artist is worshipped is on the point of suicide. The artist should be treated as the equal of all other people who contribute to the sum total of knowledge, but no more, except within his own guild, when he deserves their honor.

There is no such thing as a subject for poetry; that subject is a matter between the poet and his poem. But if this is so, why rule out myths and the diatribes of historic poets? One reason is that such poetry is false knowledge: the poet cannot possibly have the experience of the whole of the race or nation, any more than anyone else. But another reason is that such poetry is supposed to be sacred, hieratic poetry, and this I consider evil. We should strip the poet of his false honors, false titles and false powers. Of course, if someone were to draw up an *index expurgatorius* of all the mythic and historic poems in history, the world's anthology would weigh a good deal less. But matters are not as bad as all that. Most poets write true poems in spite of their divine mission to purify something or other. Most of Whitman's poems stand among the masterpieces of literature: his pseudo-philosophical-political ramblings we can forgive. Yeats was one of the finest poetic talents of our time, but being caught up in an all-explaining magic, he turned to Madam Biavatsky's metaphysical cookbooks. Even so, he wrote magnificently to his dying day. But why should we allow this license of intelligence to Yeats any more than we would allow it to Millikan or Whitehead? There is no answer.

Poetry springs from the love of personal truth and it results in a thing of beauty. Beauty is a condition of art, an absolute condition, and an instrument of the kind of truth which we are here concerned with. But the worship of beauty is a form of idolatry which is little better than worship of the golden calf. People went to churches during the Renaissance, not to worship the pictures, as we do now, but to worship God; yet we do not question their love of art. Mozart was made a papal knight but he was not canonized. Yet in our time a French scholar has proved the existence of a religion built around the adolescent poet Rimbaud.

There is always the tendency to find some more noble use of art than the mere search for the personal truth of life—as if that were not sufficient. Art must lead others, art must improve others, art must even cure others. Yes, art leads us to perceive truth in beauty. But art is not medicine; art is not pedagogy; art is not jurisprudence; art is not the decalogue. The true poet does not fall into these attitudes of doctor and teacher and priest. He is detached from such quarrels. Other poets in their pride accept the world's challenge and purvey all sorts of real and quack remedies for readers who ask for them.

The apologist for knowledge, and not only poetic knowledge, always takes it on himself to explain how he is really king of the cats. Poetic apologists are plentiful and I will cite only two typical credos. The first was written over a century ago.

> Poetry is indeed something divine. It is at once the centre and circumference of knowledge; it is that which comprehends all science, and that to which all science must be referred. It is at the same time the root and blossom of all other systems of thought . . . what were our aspirations . . . if poetry did not ascend to bring light and fire from those eternal regions where the owl-winged faculty of calculation dare not ever soar? . . .

These wild sayings need no comment except this: Shelley redeems them, and all but refutes them, in the same essay. And yet it is precisely the hysteria of apologists which we must guard against. I quote next from an essay written in our time by a man whose object is to justify to the world the ways of modern poets. This is typically the contemporary position about the value of poetry.

> It seems likely that one reason there has been so little great literature is that at most times so little has been required of it: how often has a Virgil felt obligated to create the myth of imperial culture? . . . how often has a Dante turned up to put into actual order all that had been running into the disorder of the rigid intellect and the arbitary will? Ordinarily, past times have required little of literature in the way either of creating or ordering a culture. The artist's task was principally to express the continuity of his culture and the turbulence that underlay it. . . . Those who seem to be the chief writers of our time have found their subjects in attempting to dramatize at once both the culture and the turbulence it was meant to control, and in doing so they have had practically to create . . . the terms, the very symbolic substance, of the culture as they went along. . . .

It is not easy to understand this excerpt from Mr. Blackmur, chiefly because it is so loaded with pseudo-scientific jargon, but in essence it does not differ from Shelley. Or rather, it is Shelley with the interposition of modern science midway and Matthew Arnold three quarters of the way. And it is a retreat from Shelley in that it concedes the abdication of the poet-king: the king of knowledge is now in a university library brooding over the usurpation.

The true poet is a constant prey to the world and its leaders because of his inability to accept knowledge he has not tested for himself. This almost scientific intransigence makes him both untouchable and desirable. He is fair game for the world's rulers and is as subject to kidnaping as those physicists who end up in a closed city built for the dreams of science. Hence the poet sometimes becomes the tool of the objective thinkers of the world and betrays his nature and purpose by trying to make his truth available to others. That, in fact, is the antinomy in poetic knowledge; that the artist is restricted to his own world and cannot universalize what he knows. He can do no more than find the form of what he knows and relive himself through creativity. Thus poetry is neither historic nor prophetic but occupies a separate world of time and value. The implication that the poet is a spiritual brother of God, both being members of the same profession, is intolerable. The poet cannot even enjoy as much spiritual intimacy with God as the mystic or the saint, nor can his knowledge of God be as intelligible as that of the metaphysician. The poet's spiritual rapport with God is relatively crude and is like that of the magician and the psychologist rather than that of the mystic. For the poet, the unitive experience is forever blocked by the nature of creative work, art being an embodiment of personality and not a surrender of personality to the larger Being.

But poetry is not solipsistic knowledge, nor is it knowledge of the infinite, nor even of the distant. Poetry is knowledge of the self only, but there is no self without a world, and no embodiment of self without art. To extend the poet's meaning beyond this point is to render him and his work meaningless. This is what usually happens when we touch art with the wand of doctrine.

History is a precious and noble fiction. Without it we would be living in a temporal chaos. Only saints can live without history. History indeed is the vital core of civilization: it gives us the symbology of our lives. History might even be called the world's poem, the poem by all hands, because history does for the world what the poet does for himself; it creates its image. But the poet himself, the true poet, must live outside history like the saint. This is self-evident: if he accepts history he will be silent to the truth in himself.

The fate of works of art is always a matter of chance. The history of art is a history of chance. The historian of art, to be convincing, must be as much artist as historian, for history, like all other knowledge, must be formal and exclusive. The hierarchy of values is also a fiction, and is always being upset by new turns of history and by the advent of new works of art. For this reason, no good historian attempts to write history while it is happening, any more than a poet tries to write a poem while he is making love.

The French symbolists attempted to evaluate poetry by evolving a sempiternal time-formula for the work of art. The poet was conceived as body, the poem as soul. It was indeed a perversion of the old Manichaeist theory in which the world was considered evil. The symbolist was a potential suicide who spent his holidays in the cemetery; he was the author of the clever and infamous doctrine that the poem begins to live when the poet is lain in the tomb. And it was this flattering unction that gave the blessing to all future "purists" in art.

Poetic reputation, like the career of a work of art, cannot be understood in terms of value. Poetic reputation has to do with the fact that value is attributed to a particular piece of work. There are so many examples of this in the history of art that it is difficult to find the exceptions. It pleases our historical sense to say that Hopkins was "in advance of" the Victorians and had to wait for the understanding of a later generation. But the *Rubaiyat* had the same career as *The Wreck of the Deutschland*; someone had to pin the label of greatness on it. In one sense, the history of poetry is no more than the history of opinion.

The non-historicity of art is one of its most significant characteristics. For the poet there is no progress, no evolution: for poetry there is no progress, no evolution. There is only the eternal problem of rebirth. Literary historians know this well. A man at the height of his powers may produce his worst work. In art there is a refinement of skill, as in any other trade, but no assurance of success. This fact is true because the poet enters a new and different world with each poem. The other worlds are lost to him and he can re-enter them only like any other reader. This constant re-entry into the world of new relationships makes of the poet neither messiah nor explorer but only a man fully alive in spirit and in body to existence itself.

Poetry intersects with the fiction of history, as it does with philosophy and science and religion. But all this is accidental and unpredictable. True poetry memorializes the scene, the time and place, and the world takes this as tribute. But the poet did not set out to memorialize anything. It is only as a by-product of art that art brings the past to life. There are "periods" of art, no doubt, but they tell us nothing about the individual work or the individual artist. Period does little more than point to the poet's vocabulary. Poetry helps create history: it helps rewrite it. This also is a by-product of the creative act. The history of literature is filled with men who attracted no attention in their lifetime and who did attract it later. It is filled with men who attracted attention in their lifetime and did not attract it after they died. And it is filled with men who attracted attention both during and after their lives, but never steadily, never eternally.

Even the great mythological characters come and go like the lost Pleiad. There is really only one way to perpetuate myth: that is by turning it into belief. But this form of contamination (which exists actively in our period) needs no further comment. The "universality" of a particular myth does no service to art; on the contrary it deadens art. The lively medieval myth of Tristan and Yseult was originally a tale of the triumph of love. In our period it became weakened to a tale of the triumph of death. Which is the right version? Both are "right." But there is a dangerous didacticism in the 19th-century version, with its awful wallowing in the sty and its dark message that love and death are one. The original tale is rich with authenticity and credibility: the latter-day version is obviously more concerned with a formula—and a deadly one—directed to history. It is interesting to note that the symbolists worshipped the art of Richard Wagner and saw him as a priest and the opera house as a church. It is equally interesting to note that Wagner himself was a political writer who was one of the advance founders of the Super-Germanic racial myth. The conjunction of myth and history occurs in actuality in Wagner and by implication in the theorists of the symbol.

There is no rationale to success in works of art: anyone who has read the life of one poet knows this. On the other hand, there are certain works which are taken as touchstones of the age in which they appear. Such poems or works of art color the very atmosphere of life for a time. I suppose there are many examples: *Hernani*, *The Raven*, the painting *The Night Watch*, even Whistler's *"Mother."* But these works are not necessarily the best works of the period nor the best works of the author. I am inclined to think that these symbolic works, so-called, are really the brain-children of History. In any case, they are carried about as standards for a time and are then entered into the chronicles of the age.

There is nevertheless a true fame for the work of art, one which the poet himself values, one which the world values as well. This fame has nothing to do with the esotericism of myth or the power of public appeal. It has to do with authenticity. In art we refer to truth in terms of authenticity: that is the only way we have to get at it. How this authenticity is established by the poet and how it is recognized by the reader is another question. But suffice it to say that if this quality did not exist we would be living in a chaos in which every work of art would be the equal of every other work of art. This truth is personal truth. It is not universal truth nor is it merely what is called a point of view. It is a truth which the writer does not doubt and which the reader is convinced of in spite of himself; and the means of persuasion is beauty. Probably it is this relationship which makes some writers think of beauty and truth as interchangeable. In any case, in a work of art we as readers can vouch for the beauty. The truth we take on faith. If we doubt its beauty we doubt its truth. One of the worst criticisms we can make about a work of art is to say that it is unconvincing.

The personal truth of works of beauty cannot be equated with mythic truth or universal truth. We do not pretend to believe or not to believe what the poet says in order to follow, appreciate, or love the poem. All we have to believe is that the poet is sincere. Let one shadow of a doubt fall across our minds and the poem disintegrates. But the term belief is somewhat misleading; for poetry is more an act of passion than act of thought. Poetry occurs because a "belief" has been kindled by passion and made incandescent. There cannot be a cold poem. And the belief is more often than not a matter of emotion; that is, a belief which pulls the emotions into it. The creator of beauty is engaged in a constant struggle with the reality of his own emotions. Emotions do not exist in a vacuum; they are produced by contact with the world. The poet never moves out of this world of struggle in which his emotions ("beliefs") lock with experience. His recollections of these struggles are the subjects of his poems.

But how does this affect someone else? What is my poem to you? It is an embodiment of myself or part of myself, which would otherwise be lost, as most men's lives are lost to others, except in memory. It is the rescue of my passion from disintegration. The poet wrests from the world the revelation of his personal reality. I need not point out that this is one of the most common themes of poets of all ages. When the sonneteer cries that his poem will make the lady's beauty live forever, he means that her beauty has become part of him; that part which creates his poem. Thus the poet triumphs over formlessness, the formlessness of his own life and of all life, the design of which is hidden from us. For many people, reality does not come into existence except through art. Through art we see with another's eyes, but we see no more than one truth. This truth may be the affirmation of our own reality. Indeed, that would be a lofty enough reason in itself for the high position of art.

The love of beauty, like the love of knowledge and the love of God, may be the metaphysical affirmation of man's divinity. At least, it is deeply satisfying to think so. Personal experience plus obedience to the laws of beauty—those strange laws which every artist discovers for himself—this is the equation for the creative act. And obedience to the laws of beauty implies a belief in the harmony of all things.

The poet's fame and honor are based on his love and knowledge of beauty: he does not love religion, science, or philosophy more, or as much. And it is love of beauty which other men sometimes interpret as love itself. The poet is a man of love. But he differs from others in that he is so fired with the love of beauty that he must create beauty itself. Beauty feeds him with the desire to create beauty. No good poet departs from the obsession with beauty for a second. The moment he does he is lost—off on the journey to historic life or mythhood. If the poet must play priest, philosopher, or politician, he takes care to watch that his poem is not crushed by the burden of preaching, philosophy, or politics.

Looking back on the 20th century, readers will have a difficult time explaining the prevalent attitude of hatred among our artists. But once they separate the conventional myths and attitudes from the poetry, they will find that modern poets behaved in much the way that other poets have. And they will discard the poetry of stereotyped emotions and official intellectual strategies. Culture poetry will find its way to the encyclopedias. The other poetry will remain, more or less, barring the accidents of time.

The poet leaves an actual record of his passion in the presence of world reality. He creates the image of himself, sometimes only a part of himself, sometimes his full self. With Shakespeare we have the whole image; with Baudelaire we have a stylized and fragmentary image. But whole or fragmentary, the image is not always pretty. Yet when it is a good likeness, we recognize it and appreciate its handiwork. And the creation of this image takes place, like any other creation, through love. What the poet loves helps create his poetry and himself.

Let us give up the old pedagogical idea that the effect of poetry on the world is salutary. To believe that men are bettered by poetry is as narrow as to believe that they are worsened by it. Let us think of it another way. Let us think of creation in art as the vocation, and only the vocation of a certain kind of man. Let us then give it the honor of any vocation for knowledge. But let us admit also that the sum total of the creation of an artist can equal only himself.

Such knowledge would seem useless to most men and, in fact, the usual view of poetry is precisely that. What poetry does is to ennoble the man who writes it by developing in him an almost habitual love of beauty. This may be the basis for supposing that poets are better than other people. Perhaps the vocation for art and the occupation with beauty do purify the writer; but this purification can take strange and exotic forms.

The fame due to poetry should not be exaggerated. A poet creates out of the necessity for seeking truth through the medium of beauty. The thing of beauty sets out on a career in the world. Sometimes it becomes legendary: sometimes it fades quickly from the face of the earth. But where it remains it leaves an image of its maker. Seeing it, other men have the sense of one man's affirmation of life, whoever he was, wherever, whenever he lived. Then we recognize, if we can read these works, the intelligence, the talent, the acts of a man who placed love of truth above all things and who could not find truth except in beauty. Thus tragedy and death itself turn beautiful in art.

It may be that everything reaches toward its absolute, the condition in which form can live harmoniously with freedom. The absolute of the poet is not abstract knowledge, not phenomenal knowledge, not knowledge of God, but knowledge of life. Life is the absolute he reaches for. And insofar as he creates himself he has fulfilled his purpose.

The fame of art rises from the world's dream of freedom of spirit. The poet is not the buoyant and volatile singer of visions; on the contrary, he is more the Doubting Thomas who finds it hard to believe in the accepted abstractions, and who must prove them all over again for himself. One might say that the poet's freedom really consists of scepticism. The world admires the poet the more when the world begins to distrust its own laws of conduct. It is in times of disbelief that art is taken most seriously, because then the artist appears to others to be a veritable rock of personality. In such times also the poet is inclined to accept the position of superiority to his fellows.

There is reason enough to exalt poetry. The artist is the only person whose work immortalizes life itself—his life and the lives of those who happen into the picture. It is this work which gives us a true knowledge of the maker, the poet, and of his world. It is knowledge of doubtful value, perhaps, but it is nonetheless true knowledge. One can learn nothing from art, really, except a kind of curious wisdom—the wisdom of love.

I have tried to avoid using specific illustrations and even quotations in these remarks, but I want to point up what I have been saying by citing one poet whose career embodies many of the pitfalls and perplexities I have mentioned. The poet I have in mind has already become legendary in modern literature, and he is generally regarded as a martyr of modern society. I refer to Hart Crane. Crane in the generations since his suicide has become a leading poetic symbol for

American poets. He has all the qualifications for the hero of modern culture. Crane came from the Middle West, he was poorly educated, he became "urbanized" and an exile from his own world; subsequently he was a drunkard and a masochist. But what is of greater significance, he combined the aspirations of the mythic and the historic poet in one flesh. Crane had neither the background nor the personal stability nor the humility to resist history and myth. As soon as he discovered mythic poetry he made the leap to the world of symbols and its attendant dreams of transcendental knowledge. But he was also a young American who wished to celebrate his nation, and he was pulled as strongly in the other direction, toward history. These were the two forces that tore him apart. What his actual talent was we shall never know, because it is obscured by theory-ridden symbolism, on the one hand, and by quixotic yearnings for the future, on the other. In Crane, myth meets history, and we witness the inevitable collapse of personality which is so characteristic of modern poetry.

What causes this dissolution and violent destruction of personality in modern art, this nihilism which the poet sometimes directs against himself and sometimes against the world? What turns the man of love into a thing of bitterness? Why does almost every title of a modern book of poems contain a negative? What is the significance of our official acceptance of the artist's drunkenness, perversion, crime, insanity and suicide?

I do not know the answers to these terrible questions, but I have tried to suggest one: slavery to doctrines of culture under the guise of history and myth; a slavery to which the young poet is offered no alternative.

The just honor of poetry comes from the admiration of mankind for the creation of one personality or one facet of personality. It is not unlike the honor we pay to the athlete or to the man who achieves wealth or success in his affairs. Our pride in him is the pride of created identity. But there is this difference: the poet who creates out of his life has done so because he was part of a particular place and time, part of a particular milieu and nation, and part of a particular age. The truer, the more authentic his work, the longer will last the soil from which he sprang and the clearer the character of his nation will appear to others. The treason comes with those artists who set out to become a touchstone of their time and place; the treason comes with those minions of culture who try to produce the poet who will represent them before the world. Culture says: We must have Art; let us set about having it. And the mythic poets and the historic poets flock to the banners. Meanwhile there is the true poet who has perhaps never published a line, who lives in a town from which no poet has ever come before, and whose greatest peril lies in his indoctrination with the false mythos of culture heroism.

This mythos inculcates in him the vices of exile as against participation in life; specialization as against wholeness of personality; anxiety and despair as against acceptance of the scene; analysis as against creation. Powerful fanaticisms converge on the newborn poet: one is the fanaticism of symbolism which betrays the poet into thinking that he reaches the absolute and returns to the world to sing about it. A second is the fanaticism of world-creation which deludes the poet into thinking that he, the poet, is the maker of all things. These are the two major causes of false poetry which I have discussed. But there is a third fanaticism which tends to come into existence when the other two have been banished: this is the fanaticism of ego which has as its slogan, "All things are nothing to me." Indeed, it is this attitude of the absurdity of things which is today most likely to subvert the new poet and turn him toward some form of philosophical indifference and egotism.

Is it not because of the poet's commitment to total knowledge or his egotistical rejection of all knowledge that there is so little authentic poetry in our world? The artist cannot live by art alone, nor can he live by any of the absolutes of knowledge. He must live among *all* absolutes, however; he must recognize the laws of contradiction; and he must believe in the human imperative of sympathy and the poetic law of *Einfühlung*. Only then will true creation be permitted him. Our poets today are sent out into the world by their writing masters into what they believe to be an enemy civilization and a hostile universe. Little wonder that they behave ever after like soldiers on their first patrol. Little wonder that they all mouth the same stereotypes about our dying world and our dying way of life. Little wonder that the poetry of cultural anthropology and cultural history make up the bulk of the twentieth-century anthology.

It is hard to imagine how the next true poet will escape all the masters lying in wait to receive him, but that is uniquely and eternally the problem of the young true poet. Nor do I imagine for a moment that he will spring into being filled with love of country and sweetness of mind. We have not yet drunk all the hemlock of the age. And yet I believe the way can be prepared for the next poet by encouraging in him neutrality of mind and charity of feeling; by leading him to those works of art which are the beneficent products of personality, as well as those which are not. And not only to works of art but to works of science and philosophy and mysticism. This job of preparation, almost impossible in an atmosphere of cultural fanaticism, can nevertheless be accomplished if we draw volunteers from the belligerents themselves, and from the long-since dispersed audience. The first step must be to destroy the religion of specialization which relieves scholars and intellectuals of their obligation to evaluate contemporary works of art. Every teacher of literature, every professor of science, should take it on himself to pass judgment on new works of poetry; every serious user of words should do the same. We should respect also the man who is not interested in poetry; he is a man for all that. This reading of new works should be done with good subjective gusto, not with a manual of criticism in hand. It should be done in the first flush of feeling, when the mind is still warm with the pleasure or displeasure of the work. The mortuary gloom which fills most poetry lecture halls resembles nothing so much as a students' operating theatre: the clinical, almost morbid curiosity of the listeners, the attitude of strain, even the applause for the cautery of the bleeding poem, all emphasize the life-and-death grimness of the affair. This is the opposite of a joyous occasion.

The ruling vice in literature today is an absolutism based on one of many doctrines of cultural acceptability, all of which are intent on the unconditional surrender of all others. We should not let the historic poet or critic tell us that he is the defender of social values; we should not let the mythic poet or critic tell us that he is the defender of the Tradition and the true works of the spirit. Instead, we should judge their works, bringing to them all the sympathy and intelligence and training at our command. But as long as we fail to observe our final and supreme obligation as readers, which is to pronounce upon the particular work with our own personal opinions, we give our sanction to the rule of Culture over art. The new poet is always the one who outwits the guardians of the prevalent systems— and mostly because he is not even aware of their existence.

Whatever the value of the poem *sub specie aeternitatis*, it should be given as a fresh, complete, instantaneous thing; for these are the qualities which make for long life in works of art, and even for what we fondly call the immortality of poems. The career of the poem exists only in those moments when the poem is being given and being received.

AMERICAN POET?

℔ FOR ABOUT A quarter of a century I have been putting together lectures and talks about poetry, criticism, modern literature, politics, religion, and culture. Most of these have ended up in journals or books. I have always written these with gusto and sassiness, with the delight of an amateur filling in. I do not think of myself as a critic or a litterateur or a "spokesman" but merely as someone who responds to an invitation. I rise to the bait.

Now, for the first time, I have been stumped. Roy Basler asked me to speak here, following Ralph Ellison, on what would appear to be the easiest subject of all—myself. All at once I was tonguetied. I hardly ever write about anything else and seldom conceal the fact, yet a head-on confrontation with myself threw me out of gear. Perhaps I had never written about myself after all. I began to have the anxieties of a man who hears himself on a tape recorder or watches himself on television for the first time and thinks—My God, am I that phony!

The suggestion, of course, was not to regale you with my autobiography but to discuss my writing in relation to my milieu. But my writing *is* my milieu, and insofar as I am I, this is the only I, I know. A student said to me the other day, "I enjoy the way you deliberately mispronounce French." I was flabbergasted. And once a woman came up to me before a lecture I was about to give on anarchism and said, "I don't believe a word you are going to say, and I don't think you do either." I am a prey to rudenesses like this, but having an easy disposition, I blame myself for these intimacies. I wrote a glowing panegyric about Henry Miller a few years ago and have been asked a million times how much of it I meant to be taken seriously. People who disagree with me tend to consider me a liar. High-powered critics consider me a clown. A religious magazine once called me the Mort Sahl of criticism. I took this as flattery though it surely wasn't meant that way. I am a member of a sect sometimes called anticritics and I cannot in good faith expect to be treated with the dignity accorded to an Aristotle or a T. S. Eliot. It is part of the program of my sect to laugh criticism out of business, to play practical jokes, and in general to harass and demoralize the enemy. It is serious play.

I began this lecture about six months ago and have worked on it steadily and with an increasing feeling of failure. I filled three medium-sized notebooks with small script and typed about a hundred pages trying to develop my ideas. Only a minute quantity of this matter remains. It is more or less what I go through in writing a poem. I will write a poem many times and one day throw it all away and write a completely different one. But the "different" one could not have been written without the wrong ones. This is the process of getting at oneself. Only, in this case, I am not sure I succeeded.

Now, it is absolutely of no interest to you how much time and waste of time go into a man's poem or essay and I think it is ill-mannered for a writer to brag about his herculean efforts, but on this particular occasion I think the subject calls for it. For the subject here is that I do not know what the subject is. I have never asked myself what I am in relation to my poems. I am afraid to. The answer might turn out to be—nothing. What if I am no more than the sum of poems? What if the poems are not worthy?

Eventually I made a pattern of my notes and found I was trying to get at myself from several directions. One was "racial" (I debated about whether to put that word in quotes, and finally did). Another was autobiographical. A third had to do with my withdrawal from the Serious World into poetry. A fourth was an account of how I returned to the Serious World after having gained a reputation. To me this return signified the surrender of the prodigal wandering of my mind. And finally my present direction, which I am not sure about.

These are the things I am going to talk about, personally and in the abstract. I will apologize for "that frightful quantity of I's and me's" later.

Let me get the race business out of the way first. Anthropologically I would describe myself as an American Russian-Jewish Southerner. I think I have the items in the correct order. The word *Jew* in the Western World is certain to make anyone's skin twitch, including a Jew's. Some years ago I collected all the poems I had written having to do with this word and called the volume *Poems of a Jew*. The title aroused indignation from Jews and Gentiles alike. My chief reason for the book was to make people and myself say the word without any feedback. It would be a word like any other.

Now, when Ralph Ellison and I received the invitation to speak in the Whittall series we both had a slight attack of anxiety. I think we both experienced a fleeting fear that we were about to revive the minstrel show, with a Negro novelist and a Jewish poet as the end men. A perfectly innocent and gracious come-on can produce a severe attack of shyness.

I read *Invisible Man* again. It is not only the best novel about the American Negro, it is probably the Great American Novel itself. Ellison has got it all down. The Negro is invisible and that is his grief. He is not a single separate person but only a member of a category. The applicable expression, the significant folk prejudice about other races, goes: They all look alike to me. One refuses to recognize the other race except as a phylum. The individual is not to materialize, under any circumstances. I have an aunt who as a child walked from the white side of a Virginia town to the black side to hear Booker T. Washington speak from the back of a train. She was the only white person in the crowd. Her father, my grandfather, was a Russian Jew. Somewhere in this incident was a recognition of a visible Negro. For this I am proud.

But as visibility goes, the Jew is the opposite of the Negro. The Jew is always and only the individual and is so recognized. Jewish culture in modern history, as well as in the mythology, is the triumph of the visibility of the one self. In the West, only the Germans evidently have persisted in seeing the Jew as a collectivity. This might account for the fact that Germany could produce super-Jews such as Marx, Freud, and Einstein, while the Jewish mass was fated for obliteration. The German technique of non-recognition by obliteration is only the logical development of the technique which white people in Europe and America have carried out for centuries against people whom they do not wish to see.

It is practically impossible for a white person to understand the training a Negro must undergo to conceal his individuality. The Negro who made himself distinct, much less distinguished, was asking for the rope. For years I puzzled over the absence of Negro poetry in this country. The Negro had created jazz and jazz poetry, which had revolutionized music the world over. But he had no poetry with a capital P. What Negro would so assert himself or debase himself to write the Poem, that white and sacred object which sanctifies the white book? All we had was the Negro spiritual, the weakest example of Negro art—Uncle Tom on Sunday.

But with me visibility was a curse. I was raised as a middle-class Jew and underwent the formal training of a bar mitzvah, after which I lost all interest in what I had learned. My family was observant but only sporadically and without fanaticism. Fundamentally, religion was for old people and Europeans. As we know from American-Jewish novels, a generation ago the children of immigrants were pulled away from the old culture by the breathless and somewhat mindless opportunism of the New World. The new acculturation had to wait for a third generation, my generation. The formula has been stated often and applies to me. All of my uncles and my father are business people. Almost all my cousins are professional people. And my children and their contemporaries have a strong leaning toward the arts, perhaps even by encouragement. What will happen to the fifth generation I don't know. According to writers like Philip Roth, there is a strong possibility of character degeneration as a result of too much material or professional success.

Anyone writing about himself who says, "I became a writer because," and then enumerates causes, is guessing. But I guess about myself that I became a writer for some of the following reasons: a lack of interest in study (I went to three high schools and two universities and am without a degree); a hypersensitivity to my Jewishness, aggravated by complex social distinctions in the South and in Baltimore; a sense of inadequacy to face the street; boredom; self-pity; eroticism; lack of seriousness; bad memory; fear of lightning and dogs; love of impressions and hallucinations; a tendency to speak in analogies (which perhaps led to a love of rhyme); a love of the obscure and esoteric; and a desire to impress by being witty or profane or irreverent. I have said nothing about a love of poetry, for such a thing could hardly be more than a sum of a great many causes. All I know is that by the age of seventeen I spent most of my time and all of my money in secondhand bookstores. The poetry shelves were the ones I searched most closely. I stole a rhyming dictionary from my high school in Baltimore and also a beautiful edition of the *Odes* of Anacreon in Greek (which I could not read).

In my family's circle of friends there was no literary atmosphere, yet my father encouraged my older brother to write and perhaps even to become a writer. My brother won a literary reputation while still in high school. A poem of his won a state contest in Virginia, and he read it at the University in Charlottesville, where he later distinguished himself in every field of study he undertook. I tried to impress him once by showing him a book I was reading. It was a psychopathic study of Poe—that was perhaps the subtitle—and was my first introduction to the pathology of poets.

Yiddish, a rich Chaucerian language, was not taught to us, although my parents spoke it sometimes as a private language or with elders. I was not aware of a Yiddish literature until long after I had become a poet. The cultural attitude among our class of people was generally that of middle-class people everywhere—that culture belongs to the leisure class. As far as culture for Jews went, that belonged to the German Jews, who were somehow culture aristocrats. Culture in my mind was vaguely associated with Germany and in its negative connotations still is.

These few facts and observations scarcely add up to a vita. I am at present attempting to write a kind of novel in which I will be able to deal with realities regardless of the facts. Unimportant details are often the most significant for our understanding of a man's life and work, and I think that a novel itself is some such construction; whereas the autobiography of a writer is liable to be lusterless and wooden, when not full of misinformation. What poets have written well about themselves? Yeats' friends complained about his *Autobiographies*. Yeats himself in one of them catches himself in a lie and then asks, "Why did I tell that lie?" Yeats is not the best example, however, with his psychology of the mask, his ritualistic posing, and his sad love life. I suggest that poets cannot write well about themselves because what they consider important in themselves, the Seri-

ous World considers trivial. Furthermore, poets have difficulty distinguishing between reality and fantasy. This sometimes, rather frequently in fact, makes the poet a clinical case. I have never quite
believed that rigamarole of Coleridge's about Kubla Khan, but it is as
good a "truth" as any about the poem.

Saul Bellow, speaking here last year, quoted the well-known line
from Stendhal's autobiography: "that frightful quantity of I's and
me's!" In a new book of poems I have coming out I use three quotes
from this book, the one mentioned and also: "How many precautions
are necessary to keep oneself from lying!" And a third: "What! is it
nothing but that?" Stendhal was always being surprised by his disappointment in experience. He says about his love affairs and about the
Battle of Waterloo—"What! is it nothing but that?"

Stendhal's real name was Henri Beyle, but in writing his autobiography he didn't call himself either Beyle or Stendhal but Henri Bru-
lard. It is the typical act of the artist, who knows less than his
neighbors who he is. The world is about to celebrate the birthday of
Shakespeare, yet after four hundred years the world still does not
know who he was.

It is a social convention of immemorial standing that only certain
people are permitted to speak of themselves in public. Artists fall in
this class, as do comedians, criminals, and alcoholics. But on the
whole, society and the guild of artists are content to leave this area of
expression to a very few Augustines, Rousseaus, Gandhis, Cellinis,
and now and then a Stendhal. Moreover, there is a strong tendency in
literature today toward the "veridical"—the novel that tells all and
the poem that expresses sentiment. But no one is any wiser about
Henry Miller or Allen Ginsberg for having read their books. I think
it was Keats who said that the poet is without character. It is even
something of a platitude that the artist is a man in search of himself.
For that reason, I am always suspicious of the poet who has found
himself and who has delineated himself clearly and unmistakably to
the world. Yeats, Eliot, and Baudelaire are such poets. Sartre felt the
need to write a "pathography" of Baudelaire, which he calls an existential biography. He completes Baudelaire's personality, a necessary
service in the case of a poet who invented the man called Baudelaire.
Sartre coldly ferrets out the mother love of Baudelaire, his fetishism,

and his inability to surrender to any experience except the peripheral. It is a study of the poet as onanist. We do not need a biography of Shakespeare, even if all the facts were laid before us. We definitely need one or many about the self-invented poet.

The writer's apprenticeship is a long and lonely affair from which he emerges cured of his loneliness, if he is fortunate. But in that case he may be cured of his writing as well. The density and unintelligibility of much youthful poetry is caused not so much by lack of skill as by the fear of communicating. The theory of poetic hurt has always been with us since ancient times—the lame foot and the cherished wound. "Mad Ireland hurt you into poetry," says Auden in his elegy for Yeats. And something or other does hurt the poet always "into" his poem. The youthful poet may withdraw first from the vision of ugliness which he sees everywhere around him; he would and does remake this world that wrongs the image of beauty. This is the typical withdrawal of the poet and is the world's explanation of what he is. This same hurt poet may later become a passionate public poet, a man of ringing ideals or a revolutionary. A good example is Swinburne, who graduated from Our Lady of Pain to the Statue of Liberty. Byron is the most celebrated poet of this kind.

I am talking about the poet, not about poetry. Modern criticism has made it a taboo to talk about the poet and has taken the poem out of context so completely that little or nothing remains of it but its sensibility. It is perhaps the triumph of the wound theory of art. And modern society being what it supposedly is, the enemy of the individual, the poet and all other artists inherit the wound. Sometimes I think we should call them the poets of the Purple Heart.

But an ancient distinction was made also between the poet with a happy gift of nature and the poet hurt into madness. Of the poets with a happy gift of nature we have few. We are not ready for that. Poetry as celebration we have little of. Our joys are carefully disguised, so as not to offend the canon.

I went through all the ritual stages of anger and denial and enjoyed a long and lonely apprenticeship during the Depression. The Depression was a fine time for me; it substantiated my anger and prevented me from getting a job. My family was not poor. It was the time for young Communists but I was saved from them in several

ways. I detested meetings, I hated majority opinion (and so pretended
to be a Trotskyite), and I carried on a private flirtation with Catholicism. In those days of political involvement I studied piano and had
myself tutored in Latin.

But the only activity I pursued in good faith was writing poetry, or
trying to. When I was twenty-one, I published a book of my poems.
Like most such volumes the less said about it the better, yet it served
the purpose of getting me a scholarship to a university. That was not
the intention of the book but was the only form of recognition it
received. The poems were imitations of William Carlos Williams
and William Shakespeare. The Shakespeare ones were terrible, the
Williams pieces much better. Over the years, Williams has superseded Shakespeare in my taste. I don't mean that he is the greater
poet but that he speaks to me still. I was attracted by Williams' simplicity and his obscurity, the way he would let a piece of a poem stand
for a poem, and the way he loved typography. But it was many years
before I understood his theory of the object. The New Critics were
beginning to take hold in the journals and I was infuriated by the theorizing without understanding it. I hated to think that Williams had a
theory. No one was more opinionated or more given to generalizations than I, yet I could not bear the opinions of others who were
more entitled to have them. I still think I am right in this denial of
the equal rights of criticism. It has always seemed to me that good
poetry is obviously good and the discussion of it qua poetry is a waste
of time. The career of a poem, on the other hand, has always in-
trigued me—how far it goes in the world.

In the midthirties, Auden and Spender began to be printed in this
country, and it was through them that I learned what I needed to
know about writing my own poems. I could imitate Williams but not
proceed beyond his style. The big Pound-Williams influence later
helped form the generation of Beat poets, but I have always failed to
be Beat, no matter how hard I tried. I went on a trip to Tahiti and
took with me Spender's 1934 *Poems*. They were the hardest, clearest,
loftiest, and most hurt lines I had ever seen in modern English. For
me they were a textbook I had been looking for. While I was in
Tahiti, the Spanish Civil War broke out. I returned home, not to join

the Abraham Lincoln Brigade but to sun myself on the beaches of Atlantic City and write.

Auden, as every poetry professor knows, remade the whole fabric
of diction for poets. He did the necessary and the seemingly impossible job of bringing poetic language up to date. Because of him poets
today can use the language of technology and the theoretical sciences
at will and without the self-conscious overtones of a word like *gramo-
phone* or *motorcar* in Eliot. A line like "Here is the cosmopolitan cooking,/The light alloys and the glass" had the same impact on me as
"For God's sake hold your tongue and let me love" had once had.
Auden presented modern English to poetry.

When he came to this country in 1939, I wrote him a long letter
explaining carefully that New England is not a part of the United
States. I forget what this was about. He replied with a beautifully
written postcard that said succinctly, "Thank you."

I continued my retreat, which ended with two years of undergraduate study in Baltimore. Ostensibly I was to enter graduate study in
English, though in the back of my head was a plan to study classics. I
never got to that stage of the game but was drafted into the Army
about a year before Pearl Harbor. There was a one-year conscription
law, my name was drawn from a hat, and there was no deferment. But
by that time, A.D. 1940, I was beginning to publish poetry in national
magazines and could carry this vice with me to the barracks.

The Army was a kind of echo of my Depression years. In the
Army one is totally isolated as a person. Soldiers can only lead fantasy
lives, with a few brutal hours or days of freedom in between the
shouting and the ritual of training. The din is so great and so inces-
sant that it acts as a silence. One can write because everyone writes
in the Army. People who have never put pen to paper spend hours
composing letters. I found I was in a Writers' Colony. And because
I was in Virginia, in a strange way I felt I was home. By the time I
went overseas, I had had published my first large group of poems in a
volume of new poets. It was well reviewed by well-known reviewers
and I felt my first gratification for my years of effort. Just then my or-
ders came through to be shipped to Australia; I was almost insane
with fury.

During the space of three years in the Pacific, I published four books, which must be some kind of record for a foot soldier. That term doesn't sound quite right. I was a company clerk in the Medical Corps and something of an adept at goofing off to write poems. It had long since become expected of me in my outfit, and I do not recall ever having suffered any abuse because of my "hobby," as it was thought to be. Until the time I reached home I received very heady praise from the critics. The tide began to turn when F. O. Matthiessen praised one of my books written in New Guinea as perhaps the most important literary achievement to come out of the war. The review was on the front page of the *New York Times Book Review*, and a large Signal Corps photograph showed me sitting on the wooden steps of a tropical tent reading one of my own works. I would like to say a word about this book, which was widely resented by poets and critics alike, perhaps because Matthiessen attached such great importance to it.

My outfit was one day informed that we would be deactivated for ninety days preparatory to going to the Dutch Indies. I sat down and sketched out a critique of poetry which I wanted to write in verse. I would write about thirty lines a day (which I did) and at the end of three months have what I wanted, a kind of 20th-century neoclassical treatise on the art of poetry. The book was divided into three parts called The Confusion in Prosody, The Confusion in Language, and The Confusion in Belief. Everything was going to be straightened out. As the subject was contemporary poetry, I had to use contemporary poets for my examples. The foreword opened with a salvo against criticism in general. It then announced that 20th-century poetry is a kind of zoo. The whole work was two thousand and seventy lines long; I numbered the lines to make them look incontrovertible. It was my initial anti-intellectual essay, one of a long series to come, and I neither remember why I wrote it nor why Matthiessen, who had written one of the definitive books on T. S. Eliot, praised it. William Carlos Williams has an essay about it in which he is generously ambiguous. But to most of the poets my age, I had announced myself as a Philistine.

The fact is that I had never had any ideas about poetry but only overpowering predilections and prejudices. My antipathy for criticism was almost constitutional, though I did not begin to read it seriously until I became a professor several years after the war. My last retreat occurred in this library. The books I read here when I was poetry consultant were esoteric and mystical books, the Kabala, theosophy, Jung, Ouspensky, Plotinus, and so forth. Orthodox philosophy did not attract me.

I taught modern poetry for three years at Hopkins, awkwardly, for I had never taught. I wrote out vast dull lectures on Francis Thompson and AE and the Georgians, thinking I would work my way up to the interesting stuff but somehow never quite got there. I fiddled around with prosody a lot. At the first opportunity, I left the University and went to Chicago to edit *Poetry*. I have taught in universities off and on for twelve years but have never felt at home in what cultural symposiums call the academic atmosphere. Like most writers of today, I have written my share of criticism about the Academy and its literary produce, but I doubt if I have contributed any solution to the argument about the effect of teaching on writing and writing on teaching.

In any case, I breathed a sigh of relief when I gave up my professorial role and sat down in Harriet Monroe's old chair. *Poetry* magazine was going on forty years old when I got there and was about as formidable a literary institution as any in the country. More than that, one had the feeling that if it collapsed, the entire city of Chicago would crumble into dust. That was the impression I got from the mighty personages of the town who guarded over it spiritually, while keeping it on a starvation diet. I have never understood the marriage of wealth and culture, but I soon discovered that my real job was not editor but money-raiser. I am about as good a money-raiser as I was a soldier. Once I passed Tony Accardo on the street, and the thought flashed through my mind that perhaps the Syndicate would help support *Poetry*. I didn't follow that up, but in the end we founded a drinking club on the premises and that promised a solution until the whole thing unaccountably blew up, the *Poetry* offices were banished to the attics of the Newberry Library, and I went West. I once again became a professor and am likely to remain so.

So much for literary adventure.

Randall Jarrell gave a very courageous talk here a little over a year ago in front of the largest collection of live poets I have ever seen. In this talk he played the schoolmaster and gave all the American poets of the modern anthology a name or a grade. When he got to me he said I was neoprimitivist. Or rather he said my poems were like neoprimitive paintings. I must say I was pleased. I paint, not on Sunday, but whenever I find paint lying around. And in my paintings, which I find always make people laugh, I am ashamed to use shadow or perspective. I feel there is something dishonest about shadows and distances, but then I have never learned to draw. Nor do I wish to learn.

In poetry, I dislike shadows—"without any confusion or profundity of atmosphere," as Jarrell put it. Over a long period of time I have been charging quixotically at a huge shape called Culture without ever knowing whether I have scored against the leviathan. These tilts have taken various forms: against mythic form, symbolism, the Tradition, and so on. It is a kind of guerrilla warfare in which I am not the only assailant. Still, the battle against the Tradition and the continuity of culture and the presentness of the past, and so on, has become tedious. In the long run, criticism can't change anything. Only new works of art can do that.

American poetry is in a unique situation. At least I know of no other poetry which has its particular problems. I am referring to the English language. We have the language of England more or less by accident, for we might, giving and taking a battle here and there, be French- or Spanish-speaking people. Be that as it may, we have the language of England without the culture of England. The culture of this country is so multiplex that it is indescribable. In my state, for instance, there are dialects of German spoken which no longer exist in Germany. But the question is deeper than dialects. It is one of contents. There is also the fact that most Americans are descendants of uneducated populations and that whatever cultural aristocracy existed here in the 18th century has long since been swamped by wave after wave of subcultures. As poetry goes, we are precultured.

A century ago one man tried to create an American poetry with his bare hands. He did not succeed in that, but he did succeed in writing our greatest poems or some of them. The great literary works of America are predominantly prose, political works, fiction, even criticism. And in a sense the same thing holds in the 20th century. The attempt to impose the European mythos on our poetry has in part determined the character of what we call modern poetry, but this had to be done by missionaries, such as Pound and Eliot. And it had to be done through the agency of the American university. Pound's criticism consists of innumerable epistles directed to what he calls the Beaneries, our institutions of higher learning. Eliot's essays, the most formidable body of criticism in modern literature, helped set in motion a practical school of criticism which revolutionized the literary sensibility in our universities. (Eliot disclaims too great an influence here, though he is commonly thought of as the originator of the New Criticism.) And in turn this criticism affected not only the pedagogy of poetry but poetry itself. Many people, myself included, nowadays speak of university poetry. The battles, or rather skirmishes, between university poets and street poets have occupied our attention in the past few years.

All of this is related to something like a class conception of the art. The missionaries or exiles were addressing a newly arrived educated class, not a small elite but a vast army of Ph.D.'s or graduate students in literature. And these people by and large are themselves critics, instead of scholars, and frequently poets or people who want to write poems. And they have developed an expertise in the techniques which makes it sometimes impossible to tell who is a real poet and who is a technician.

I won't annoy you by trying to define Real Poet. Everybody has his own criteria. And I see no reason why there can't be poets, actual live ones, in the university or in the nightclub or on the assembly line. But I think that the poet is always nostalgic for the street, since he has become so urbanized that that is his only alternative to the university.

The most recent lecture I've given was called "Is Poetry an American Art?" The answer was: probably not. Some people asked why *American* poet; why can't one just be a poet? The answer is that you can't. A poetry is part of the character of the place. The place is inherent in the language. All of which is stated in the philosophy of Dr. Williams, who fought against the European influence on our poetry all his life and who said that *The Waste Land* was to modern poetry what the atom bomb was to mankind. (It was a necessary exaggeration.)

There is a legend that Apollinaire once stole the *Mona Lisa* from the Louvre. And there is the artist who decorated her with a moustache. They were trying to pry this criterion off the wall. It had become an idol, practically in the religious sense, though it is the opposite of a Madonna. Masterpiece or not, this picture had acquired the power to judge all other pictures.

I sympathize with the thief of the *Mona Lisa* and with the artist who added to her charms. The motto of such poets is: let the past take care of itself. Everything is new.

It appears to me that American poets have begun to admit that the English influence is dead and that it never really obtained in this country as poetry. As an English professor, I foresee as a side effect to this discovery the withering away of the English department. The fact that English departments are at present the largest in most universities indicates some kind of sickness. More and more poets, even of the educated variety, have begun to drop the mannerisms of the conventional poem and to play with the more intricate rhythms and tonalities of prose and speech. In a way, we are back to where we were when the new poetry began in the second decade of our century, back to the image, the cadence, and the statement without embellishment. And we have discovered the new poetry of the Old World and not simply the classics and the metaphysical poets. We are closing the gap between prose and poetry.

To allow standards to take root in this country, we have had to devalue the standards of the past. Someone or other is everlastingly trying to impose a literature a thousand or two thousand years old on a nation that is less than two hundred. Thus most of our poetry has been as rigid and unoriginal as the architecture of banks. But we find poets now arguing in favor of "bad" poetry. I am one. Bad is in quotation marks. Bad means good. It means not great or major or monumental or mythic or epic. Poets in my situation, poets who have withdrawn from the high culture, are more interested in the art of children, the untrained, the hallucinated, even the psychopathic and the criminal. I think this is true of most artists today except the poets of—if I may use the well-worn word—the Establishment. And if one works himself clean through the poem and comes out on the other side, into empty space, and finds himself poem-less, what then? I sometimes think I have done this.

It has been about five years since I wrote what I used to think was the best kind of poem I could write. That was the poem with a beginning, a middle, and an end. It was a poem that used literary allusion and rhythmic structuring and intellectual argument and the works. I had written for years for a famous New York magazine which one sees on cocktail tables the world over (I don't know why I am being coy about it, but at one point I was practically the poet laureate of that publication). One day I shook myself and said, "No more." I think it was because I started to collect those poems for a book and found too many I didn't want to see in a book.

So I began to backpedal. I worked for several years trying to break the style I had become habituated to. Eventually I came up with something more free which I could use. I had always been a fan of those D. H. Lawrence epigrams called *Nettles* and *Pansies* and especially those glowing bunches of poetry called *Birds, Beasts and Flowers*. My new rhythm, however, sounded too much like Lawrence and I knew I had not gone far enough back. Then I started reading French prose poems, Baudelaire, Rimbaud, and the *Éloges* of St. John Perse. While I was at this library Perse had once seen a prose poem or two of mine and hinted that that was the technique that mattered. But I had only written one or two such poems and waited a long time before I was ready to tackle the thing in earnest. This sounds as if I am about to present the great American prose poem, but all I mean to say is that I finally felt at ease in the form. What I was searching for was a medium in which I could say anything I wanted—which for poets is something like finding the philosophers' stone or the elixir vitae. For one thing, I wanted to be able to use the ridiculous, for another the nonsensical, for another the "obscene." I wanted to be as personal as I liked, as autobiographical when I felt like it, editorializing or pompous, in short, to be able to drop into any intensity of language I liked at any time. None of this was particularly original, but it was new to me. I wrote a huge stack of these poems, the form of which was governed by the size of a sheet of paper in the typewriter. When the publisher saw the manuscript he commented dryly that the only limits to the book seemed to be physiological. And not wanting to violate the fashion of slenderness for volumes of poems, we cut it down to about twice the size of the usual seed catalog.

It is as important to learn how to use one's skills as to acquire them in art, and just as difficult. The kind of poem I am talking about may be indistinguishable from that of the high school composition or the worst polyphonic prose of Amy Lowell, but that is inevitable. The writer must learn from his underlings as the painter learns from the billboard or the composer from the trombonist blowing the blues. This is what I think has been deficient in so much modern poetry—a fear of coming to grips with the raw material. That and too much attention to stock intellectual attitudes. The modern artist and sculptor are fascinated and delighted with the industrial world, but the poet has not yet heard of it.

On the last day of a Creative Writing class of mine last week—I have taught myself to say Creative Writing without wincing; nobody would ever think of saying Creative Painting or Creative Music—after we had gone through the last purple stack of mimeographed student poems and had once again demolished the split-level house, bombed the second car, the streamlined church, and the powder room; Freud having been buried with the air conditioner and the last corybantic prose poem in praise of sex or LSD analyzed, I gave a valedictory. It was a little talk about the *Oxford Book of English Verse, 1250–1900*, and I contrasted it with the modern anthology. I hadn't thought of the *Oxford Book* or looked at it for many years, but it all at once crossed my mind that this book had been my bible when I was the age of my students and that in all probability they had never heard of it or anything like it.

It is true that this famous anthology is the product of Victorian taste, yet it would be difficult to imagine a much different version of the seven hundred years of English poetry. The Quiller-Couch *Oxford Book* (He did many of the Oxford anthologies) begins with the fresh and beautiful "Sumer is icumen in," dated around 1250, and ends with a muggy religious poem or hymn called "Dominus Illuminatio Mea." This final poem is anonymous, and one senses the editorial hand in this concluding work or benediction.

But in between the "Sumer is icumen in" and the "Dominus"

poem there are seven centuries of the greatest poetry of the European culture, even with the omission of the great plays, narratives, and epics. And in all that poetry there is scarcely ever more than a suggestion of philosophical despair. It would be a tour de force to compile a minority report of the centuries, gleaning a darker side of the English creative spirit, opposing Rochester's ode "Upon Nothing" to Milton's faith in order and Providence, or paying more attention to the satanic Swinburne than to Tennyson or Alice Meynell. But such an anthology would tell nothing, for until the magic year 1900, English poetry as we know it is essentially joyous. It is true that the Oxford editor would not even include "Dover Beach" and could see no thing better in Whitman than "O Captain, My Captain"; nevertheless the book is triumphantly representative and great.

By now there are several generations of students, at least, who began the study of poetry with the 20th century, that is, with the proclamations of failure, the failure of love, the failure of history, the prophecies of imminent darkness. *The Waste Land* is probably the first classic that impinges on their minds; however it was intended or has since been reinterpreted, it embodies the modern poet's code of the banality of modern existence and the evil of 20th-century man. And if not this poem, then one of a dozen others. The 20th-century reader of poetry must regard any poetry before our time as something as far away as the poetry of classical Greece.

I am not expressing a preference for the Oxford collection or suggesting a compromise. I am merely making the observation that the 20th-century anthology has closed the *Oxford Book*, perhaps forever. In this country, at least, we have broken the circuit between the poetic past and the poetic present. And I do not see how it can be otherwise with us.

What does this do to us as poets and to our poetry? American literature in a quite real sense is a boy's literature. From Fenimore Cooper to Salinger, it is a literature of youth. I was given a complete copy of *Moby Dick* as a child because it was a boy's book, and I read it as a boy's book, though it had some tough passages. And poetry was always something far away and long ago; Americans couldn't write poetry. There was one American poet, Edgar Allen Poe; one didn't press the point too far. I do not recall the name of Whitman from public school, though my memory may trick me. I think I discovered Whitman on my own.

The American poet has from the beginning been faced with a choice, whether to accept or to reject the *Oxford Book*, using that term as an oversimplified symbol. And in modern poetry the choices have been made. Of our four greatest 20th-century poets, Pound, Eliot, Frost, and Williams, two went abroad to repair the fences of the Tradition and to create, intentionally or not, a criticism which became a pedagogy which became a poetics. Frost refused to believe that the fences needed mending and quietly amassed a wealth of poems which all but proved that English poetry was still solvent. Williams nearly lost his mind watching these antics.

American binary psychology lends itself to poetry as to politics. We have in our century created two poetry parties called whatever anyone wants to call them, Paleface and Redskin, Academic and Beat, Classic and Romantic, or Republican and Democrat. And it is unfortunately true that the Redskins are pink with rage and the Palefaces blue with indignation. And it is also true that these two literary parties end up in the same anthologies—in one big unhappy family of poetry.

So many times have the characteristics of these parties been described, at least to those who read the literary journals, that there is nothing more to say about them descriptively. But there is much to say otherwise. I will stick to the usual nomenclature of Academic and Beat to avoid confusion.

The Beat professes Innocence, with or without a capital I. The Academic professes Guilt with a capital G. The Innocence of the Beat of course identifies him with American literature, even though the Beat chants hymns to Castro. The Beat extracts the quality of rebellion and revolution from American literature and then sits back and waits for the police to prove his point.

The Academic gaily assumes a metaphysical guilt, possibly a Christian guilt; in any case a kind of mandarin Hollywood guilt which presumes the nature of literary violence and destruction on the part of the Beat. The Academic forgives and protects the Beat. The Beat is overwhelmed by the failure of success.

This kind of nonsense seesaws back and forth. But modern poetry never seems to escape this biparty system, this wrangle over precedent and originality. In reality, both parties are literature-centered (to invent a typical vulgarism of our speech); and because literature is the center of value of both schools, neither can know much about anything except literature. Beat poetry is as academic as the Academic. Academic poetry, which has become noticeably gamy, is as gossipy (you might say "subversive") as the Beat. And both end up as a variety of social criticism, but of such a hieratic style that only the highly trained in poetry would even care to notice it. Both Beat and Academic, however, subscribe to the 19th-century hope, the hope of the *Oxford Book*, that in the end poetry will reinstate human virtue or national virtue or the virtue of oneself.

Modern poetry is a kind of lobby. It has something to sell, it is not sure what, yet it knows it has a corporation of power behind it, either a thousand years of reputation or the idea of genius or sainthood. And it knows that this power is real, for Culture, with whole armies and navies behind it, has said so.

It is only with the greatest effort and charm that the Beat can convince us of his assertion of innocence; and only with the greatest diplomacy and wit that the Academic can convince us of his culpability.

Possibly poetry in America is obsolete or not yet born because it is literature-centered. This is precisely the thing that has always separated poetry from the other arts of writing. Even in this country one distinguishes between the poet and the writer—I am always pleased to be confronted with the question at those Nabokov-like places called Writers Conferences: Are you a writer or a poet? Poetry has always been the ultimate enemy of literature, and if poetry is good for anything, that is what it is good for.

And yet, how, in a nation where books are as plentiful as food, or more so, can the poet escape literature? How, where literature is also an industry, can poetry breathe? Here, where the latest literary movement is put on sale after the first manifesto is written, where every writer (and poet) hopes to be "controversial" in order to rise above the din of the linotype, how can the poet ever dream of such a thing as an audience when the audience is rejected both by the Beat (as bourgeois) and by the Academic (as bourgeois). For the Beat pretends to be the proletarian and the Academic pretends to be the aristocrat. And both—whatever bourgeois is supposed to mean at this late date—share in this bourgeois sensibility and morality. Both kinds of poetry are in a secret alliance to uphold Literature.

All I am saying is that, for me, American poetry has long since ceased to hold my attention, because it seems to me to aspire to a place in society. That is, the poet-in-residence in a university is no different from the poet-in-Skid Row. Both are on Culture Relief. Both are trying to prove to themselves that the fate of nations is bound up with their personal fates. Both, in the back of their minds, think in the way that Pound and Eliot and Yeats thought: *that poetry will tell people what to do.*

One can forgive poets for these hallucinations. It is harder to forgive governments for egging them on. I said earlier that I could never understand the marriage of wealth and culture. Even less can I understand the marriage of government and culture. I know I am standing at the moment somewhere on Capitol Hill, but I have always tried in a little way to keep State and Poetry separate. This is not in the Constitution. I hope the Constitution will never have occasion to think about such things as institutionalizing Poetry.

There was a fine young British poet killed on the battlefield in the First World War who wrote the famous line: "The Poetry is in the pity." He was referring to the pity of War. He was too late for the *Oxford Book* and a little premature for the 20th-century anthology. Wilfred Owen came into that no man's land between the end of the old poetry and the beginning of the new. He said that he was trying not to console but to warn; he went so far as to apologize for telling the truth about war. But the true poet must be truthful, he said.

The 20th-century poet is not so embattled except ideologically. He has somehow earned or inherited an intellectual leisure which has made him a parvenu of sensibility. The 20th-century poet cannot locate the poetry, either in the pity or anywhere else. He locates it, or tries to, in vague and anxious dissatisfactions within himself or within what he thinks are the crimes and sins of society. He can't decide whether to be a peacock or a phoenix or an ostrich and takes turns trying to be each.

I mentioned Wilfred Owen to paraphrase him. With us the poetry is not in the pity, but the poetry is in the situation. As the *Oxford Book* failed the situation of war, for example—it would have ended with Rupert Brooke's "The Soldier" if it had had to face the trench war of 1914–18, and could not have ended with an antiwar poet without spoiling the whole illusion of the great tradition. Everyone at the turn of the century had the premonition that time had run out on the Tradition; it is extraordinary how many writers knew in their bones that what lay just ahead would be unlike anything that had ever been known before.

When Yeats later put together his *Oxford Book*—the *Oxford Book of Modern Verse, 1892–1935*, he enshrined the *Mona Lisa* on page one, taking a famous prose sentence from Pater, a bit of high mystification about her, and turning it into a piece of free verse. And there she remains, the patron saint of Academic poetry. And the Beat has failed to pry her off the wall.

American poetry is irrelevant. It does not pertain to our situation. It pertains only to language and literature and sensibility. It pertains only to form and to "philosophy" or to the personalized anguish of the socially angry. America is more than a campus, I am convinced, and more than a picturesque and disaffiliated slum. What it is is for the artist to reveal in every way he can. And, as I have said, all our artists have been busy revealing our world, with the exception of the poets. The modern poet has closed his eyes to life, as it has long since closed its eyes to nature. To the modern poet, nature may sometimes provide a bestiary, and, in fact, we have written the finest allegories about moths and ants, praying mantises and flies. But all the apples are dead, except the Genesis apple. People in the modern anthology are dead or somnambulatory. The modern anthology might just as well be copyrighted on the moon. I forget the date of the death of the moon.

Perhaps I haven't progressed at all from the time I wrote my verse critique in the tropics. I still wait for the poetry of the situation. Our poetry has everything to do. It has to escape from itself first of all. It has to liberate itself from literature before it can do anything else. Most poets, I think, have agreed that poetry is not an art of language and not even an art. It is one of the techniques of revelation, one of the powers through which we control relationships and conciliate nature. The sculptor who drives to the junkyard, who makes beauty out of trash is performing this function. Poetry has been making trash out of beauty for the most part. This is tempting fate. Or if I am exaggerating, let us at least concede that it is the function of poetry to propitiate, to quiet the anger of things. I am not talking about affirmation and negation; that is a question of circumstance. I am talking about the poet in situ. If he is in place, he is where he belongs. Whitman had a long recital of things in their places, small things and cosmic things. Williams took the least likely objects for poems—least likely for the *Oxford Book*—a piece of brown wrapping paper rolling in the street or a rotten apple. These poets revealed things in their situation. There is something like this in the Marquis de Sade, who says that in Tartary there is a people which creates a new god for itself every day. This god has to be the first object encountered on waking in the morning. If by chance it happens to be an object of great revulsion, that thing is still the idol of the day.

Our poetry has been so industrious manufacturing values that it has practically forgotten how to do anything else. That is why it must empty its mind of its moral and ethical contents and of its esthetic contents as well. When it does so, it will be in a position to experience the world as our painters, our musicians, and our novelists have experienced it.

For myself, I have solved the problem of the racial wound, which drove me into the various retreats where I could assert myself and create myself. But it is too late for me ever to be assimilated into the Serious World. I can only play at responsibility. I am yet to be convinced that those who make the decisions by which we live are not play-acting. I hope that this sense—or perhaps gift—of amazement will never leave me.

THE POETRY WRECK

☞ THE TITLE of this chapter is not autobiographical, but I will say something about my background as a librarian. I studied to be a public librarian at the Enoch Pratt Library in Baltimore. It was an excellent course of study and I was within a few weeks of final examinations when I was drafted by the Army and not allowed to finish. I would probably be a professional librarian today had my name not been fished out of the goldfish bowl. Five years later, on being discharged from the Army, my first job was Consultant in Poetry at the Library of Congress. Subsequently I became editor of the Newberry Library journal of acquisitions and worked at that library for three years. I consider myself more or less of a professional in library affairs, more so at least than most professors and writers.

At the center of all human culture stands the library. At the center of civilization stands the library. But now and then the apocalyptic question crosses our minds: Is the library still standing? If the university is moving toward a new Dark Age, if all public institutions are facing a new Dark Age, what of the library? If standards of value in every department of modern life are being threatened by barbarism and savagery, what of the books themselves and their keepers?

I am no Jeremiah and will leave the ranting to others. But as a teacher of reading and writing, as a reader and writer myself, as a literary critic and professor of literature for some twenty years, as a functionary of the teaching world, a proud member of the Establishment and what one poet calls a shameless patriot, I wish to report to you my version of the degeneration of the literary intelligence and its attendant confusions everywhere in our lives.

I call it the degeneration of the literary intelligence; others have other names. To book people this degeneration may seem to be local and, hopefully, of short duration; and to the "outside" world the degeneration may seem to be a signal for the arrival of the barbarians. When a professor at a venerable university has his life's work destroyed by student vandals, society may well begin to tremble. Who would have thought, at least since the defeat of Hitler, that American professors would begin to remove their notes and files from their offices and take them home; that they would begin to remove their best or their irreplaceable volumes; that libraries would begin the reduplication of indexes as a safety measure; that specially trained police and guards and firemen would replace the old innocuous campus cop. I apologize for evoking these commonplaces, and yet who, except Lewis Carroll perhaps, would have dreamed of students acquiring the power to fire faculties, presidents and chancellors, to determine curricula, and worst of all, to force personal political opinion and dogma upon the teaching community at large, and upon society itself. All under the name of Idealism, of course.

I would like to place an image in your minds. A professor at a famous west coast university told me that at the first meeting of the class, the students flicked through the assigned textbook, a newly published poetry anthology, flung it on the floor, and stalked out. They said that the textbook was not "relevant." Relevant to what is not known. The modern illiterate thinks that you will finish the sentence that he has forgotten how to formulate. I see this act of boorishness as a hair's breadth from book-burning.

And everything that follows book-burning. My experience as librarian-writer-professor is relatively unusual, and I believe I have a perspective upon the degenerative process in literature which should be shared. For example, I have been engaged in creative writing programs for twenty-odd years, virtually from the beginning of this kind of teaching. These programs have corroded steadily and today have reached the point of futility. Early writing programs, such as the one at the Johns Hopkins University, turned out novelists such as John Barth (at least Barth studied in their program). Students in similar programs today, according to my experience all over the United States, can no longer spell, can no longer construct a simple English sentence, much less a paragraph, and cannot speak. We have the most inarticulate generation of college students in our history, and this may well account for their mass outbreaks of violence. They have no more intelligent way to express themselves. But what is really distressing is that this generation cannot and does not read. I am speaking of university students in what are supposed to be our best universities. Their illiteracy is staggering. But of course they claim to read. They may slam the professor's anthology on the floor but they will go to the bookshop and buy the innumerable paperback bestsellers of Their Generation, which are almost always trashy rewrites of current sociological or philosophical fads. The kitsch-camp-op-pop-absurdist-revolutionary sweepings and swill with which they fill their wordless minds are what they bring to class. They do not want to read; they want to "experience." They do not want to learn; they want to "feel." They have become almost impossible to teach. By accident, I have discovered in recent years that the only students in poetry-writing classes who know how to write as simple and universal a thing as iambic pentameter have gone to Catholic schools. Iambic pentameter is not Catholic; it happens to be the metrical form in which almost all English poetry since Chaucer has been written and is still. Not only do the students not know what it is; *they do not want to know*, and say so.

I use *illiteracy* in the proper sense: the inability to read and write. As this condition becomes endemic in the American educational system the value and meaning of literature becomes obscured, literature falls into desuetude.

As far as I can tell, the high school has now reached the level of the grade school; the college is at high school level; the graduate school at college level; and whatever reading and writing is being done is being done by professors—the people who are taking their libraries home. Creative writing has hit the level of playschool, a kind of adult kindergarten.

One other note about the new university illiteracy. For at least a full generation the American educational system has been trying to abolish languages, not only Latin and Greek (which have practically disappeared) but all modern European languages, and it seems to me English itself. We are losing the battle to maintain even the most elementary language requirements, and every humanities professor will tell you in dismay in one manner or another that his graduate students are by and large linguistic cripples. The written dissertation has long been an academic joke, I maintain because of the bad writing. One can foresee the abolition of even this ultimate test of superior ability and knowledge.

It appears that the modern student enters the university with a contempt for the university, a contempt for society, a contempt for literature, and a contempt for himself. Where did he learn this? Not from his own school; not from the library. I don't think so. He learned it from what the new illiterates call the Media: TV, radio, newspaper, phonograph, rock festival, magazine and paperback bookstore. He learned it from what the new illiterates call their counterculture; he learned it from his contemporaries and the exploiters of cults. For the first time in history the illiterates have a literature of their own: op-pop-camp-kitsch-existential-occult-nihilist sweepings and swill. Armed to the teeth with this quasi-literature it is little wonder that they slam the textbook on the floor and stomp out to their cars, barefooted.

I will now introduce the hero, or anti-hero, if you like. He is a real person and all the information I am going to give you is true and accurate, except for his name. I have changed his name not for any legalistic reason but because I feel humiliated to have to bring up his name at all. Here then is Dylan MacGoon.

The good Welsh name Dylan has been appropriated and desecrated by pop singers since Thomas's death. It is unlikely that these show-biz and rebel Dylans have read or could understand Thomas's poetry, which is some of the finest and most obscure poetry of our time. The pseudo-Dylans, however, regard Thomas as a casualty of modern life (which he wasn't) and therefore a symbol of their own shabby and talentless selves. Thomas drank himself to death, as all the world knows and regrets, but he was the farthest thing from the pudgy Lenin or cherubic Castro his namesakes make him out to be. Anyhow, I call our latter-day hero Dylan because he is one of the many pseudo-Dylans who are passed off by the Media as today's poets.

I first heard of Dylan MacGoon as I was checking out of a hotel in Milwaukee. The girl behind the desk, who must have seen in the local paper that I was lecturing on poetry, asked me what I thought of the poetry of Dylan MacGoon. Who? I said. In the ensuing months the name began to come at me from all directions. In one university where I gave a poetry reading I was challenged by a student from the audience who wanted to know what I thought of MacGoon. I had seen some of his verses by then and answered that I didn't think anything of them; they were not even trash. The student then wanted to know what right I had to pass judgment on him. I mumbled something to the effect that I had earned the right, a divine right, so to speak.

MacGoon however would not go away. He followed me to every lecture I gave; he entered my classroom, via the mouths of my students; even when I turned on television he was there. Especially there. True, he was there as a balladeer-and-guitar-slinger, yet he was also designated as famous poet. One day I saw him interviewed by one of the top news commentators, the kind of reporter who is assigned only to prime ministers and field marshals. Mr. MacGoon, said the commentator in tones of authentic awe, you are the foremost best selling poet in the United States (I think he said world), and then proceeded to ask about his creative regimen—the sort of questions one would ask Michelangelo or Picasso perhaps. MacGoon tried to answer as best he could (language is not his strong point) and succeeded, between the awe of the commentator and his own honest dissimulations, in presenting the image of poet. His millions of readers and listeners—all under nineteen, I hope—must have been gladdened.

Millions of readers cannot be an exaggeration. An advertisement in a San Francisco paper a couple of weeks ago, an ad, by the way, for some *new* books of poems by MacGoon, said that he has already sold more than fifty million of his recordings.

I went to the little public library in the little town I live in, hoping against hope that there would be no MacGoon. There was. Still, I said to myself, the library is next door to a high school, and MacGoon is better for the kids than marijuana. Then again, maybe he isn't. In a desperate attempt to exorcise MacGoon I finally succumbed to the public prints and reviewed one of his three current

best-sellers in a weekly New York book review. I called my remarks
"The Rise of American Cockney" and they went more or less as follows:

Whoever visits an American bookstore in search of poetry can be
sure of finding only one staple. Whether in San Francisco or
Dubuque, Dallas, Boston or New York, and no matter what the size
of the shop, he will find himself facing a row of cream-colored volumes by—Kahlil Gibran. If there is only one volume it will be
Gibran's *The Prophet*, a quasi-mystical, quasi-poetic placebo which
has trickled through the bloodstream of American adolescence for at
least a generation. The book, in print for over forty years, must be
rated as a minor sales miracle. It also throws a baleful sociological
glare upon the poetics of the young.

Esthetic has become Statistic. Wallace Stevens, whose *Harmonium* remains one of the finest achievements of modern literature,
sold two hundred copies of the book over a period of a decade, very
nearly driving an exquisite poet to suicide. But MacGoon is written
up in mass magazines and newspapers as a poet and as a publishing
phenomenon, which indeed he is. Yet it is irrelevant to speak of Mac-
Goon as a poet; his writings are not even trash.

The cockneyizing of American poetry began with *Howl*, a highfalutin put-on which started up the seismographs of Berkeley and elsewhere. The name of the game was the inversion of values and it
worked for everybody "under thirty" and everybody over who was
bored, hysterical or narcissistic. Freak-out culture coincides with this
poetical document. Poetic decomposition and *faisandage*, in America
at least, date from this bored, hysterical and narcissistic drivel.

The downhill speed of American poetry in the last decade has
been breathtaking, for those who watch the sport. Poetry plunged
out of the classics, out of the modern masters, out of all standards,
and plopped into the playpen. There we are entertained with the
fecal-buccal carnival of the Naughties and the Uglies, who have their
own magazines and publishing houses, and the love-lorn alienates,
nihilists, disaffiliates who croon or "rock" their way into the
legitimate publishing establishment. MacGoon falls into the latter
category.

What hidden message have we here? Is the Beatleization of American poetry becoming a reality? Are the negative values on the rise in poetry also? Will the bilge work its way up to the library and the graduate school and to the art of writing itself? The answers to all these questions is a dismal groan.

Entertainment is a healthful and lifegiving diversion of the masses, and even the high-decibel howls of the pseudo-poets deserve a niche in the wall of time. But the deliberate obtrusion of the howler or the rocker-crooner upon the literate minority can serve no other purpose than to destroy the sensibilities of everyone concerned. Discrimination is a dirty word in the vocabulary of politics, but in literature it is one of the holiest of concepts. Without it all is offal.

Publishers, even those who formerly prided themselves on the quality of their publications, are now miring themselves in the dismal swamp of the adolescent revolution. They seem to drool at the sight of a rock festival, which attracts a quarter to a half million of the new humanoids. They cannot resist the temptation. They seek out—Mac-Goon—and pay their overhead.

The aftermath of my little critique was typical. There were letters and phone calls and a dressing-down from a reporter in Los Angeles who called to ask me to explain myself. He had been assigned to interview MacGoon. The crooner, it seems, had also read my diatribe. When asked what he thought of it he answered: who cares what *he* thinks?

And the weekly book review dropped me.

In one of the more literate sub-culture magazines I notice a serious *explication de texte* of a poem? song?, a very weak something-or-other written by a poet? named Buffy Sainte-Marie. Buffy's lines "Little wheel spin and spin/Big wheel turn around and around," which resemble the speech of the mental defective and are the norm of the new poetry, are explicated thus: "In Buffy's song the medieval and Elizabethan image of the microcosm mirroring the macrocosm becomes saturated with historical and political content." The article is on Herbert Marcuse.

We are experiencing a literary breakdown which is unlike anything I know of in the history of letters. It is something new and something to be reckoned with. We have reached the level of mindlessness at which students and the literate public can no longer distinguish between poetry and gibberish. Ten years ago nobody would have dreamed of comparing Robert W. Service or Edgar Guest (poor Edgar) or even Joyce Kilmer with Andrew Marvell or Robert Browning. But today I read in a California paper that a "serious critic . . . has likened the Beatles' lyrics to Shakespeare's work." I read that Bob Dylan is "the major poet of his generation." Arrogance and ignorance always go hand in hand, and now we are having both shoved at us from all sides: from publishers, from professional intellectual saboteurs, and from many dog-in-the-manger professors as well.

Some of you know, and I am proud to say, that I have been in the forefront of the fight against censorship all my life. Any schoolboy who buys his first copy of *Tropic of Cancer* will find my introduction in the front of it. It was my introduction which helped win the battle for that book in the Massachusetts courts and subsequently everywhere. I have defended and will continue to defend the principle of absolute unqualified freedom to print and present anything and everything the human mind and sub-mind are capable of advancing. I shudder to think of some of the stuff I have given my sanction to.

But I believe equally in the principle of self-regulation and the wielding of professional judgment and authority. We have to assert endlessly and in every generation, and in every way we can devise, standards of worth in literature. Teaching has become cowardly and lax at every level, giving way to the pressures of special pleaders and mischief-makers. The greed and cynicism of even the best publishers appalls me; the wild exploitation of primitivism by the Media has rendered us insensible and made us a prey to every disease of esthetic decadence which the lower reaches of the imagination can concoct. Every healthy mature culture needs folk art and popular art, entertainment, show-biz, and amateur creativity. But where the elemental forms of art become dominant and aggressive forms, the culture dies of shock. We need only remind ourselves what the arts were like under Hitler and Mussolini and what they still are in Russia. When critics and university students can no longer tell the difference between rock lyrics and songs of Shakespeare, teaching is no longer possible; standards of good and inferior disappear; discrimination dies; and the true artist goes into hiding. We are in the time that Yeats predicted and when everyone is quoting his famous lines: "The best lack all conviction, while the worst/Are full of passionate intensity."

One wonders whether it is too late to reverse the course of the fashionable bourgeois revolutions, or college-kid revolutions, if you prefer. Personally, I am pessimistic and believe that cultural barbarism has already arrived. The Media love it; the university is too demoralized and debilitated to exercise any real discipline against it; the public is buffeted back and forth by demonstrations of violence and Dadaist hijinks and finds itself shoved farther and farther to the right of reasonable center; the honest artist finds himself once again moving to the periphery of society; real poets are supplanted by guitar-slingers and high-decibel mocking-birds; the long and successful battles for freedom of speech and publication are filthied by entrepreneurs and commercial smuthounds; the textbook is thrown on the floor by the barefoot radical rich; and—to sum it up—chaos is come again. Yet, in its quiet majesty and unfathomable humility, sits the library, not yet overwhelmed by the tides that push the rotten stuff along the shore.

It is always possible, of course, that cultural illiteracy will reach the point at which nobody will sack the library because they won't know what it is.

At highbrow, "high-level" symposia of educators and social scientists, one of the main issues of debate is the definition of a university. One would think that professors would not need a *definition* or a justification of the university—this twentieth-century talk-show would not amuse Plato, for example. Yet it is symptomatic of our times that the leaders of culture question their own right to exist. These symposia, by the way, are conducted almost exclusively by humanists and social scientists. Real hard-core scientists already know that a university is a place where one trains the young in what one knows to be proven knowledge. The symposiasts, however, are not sure, and the main question that exercises them is whether the university is a place where the student seeks his identity or studies his lessons, the lessons of experts and professionals. There is no question in my mind that the identity crusaders are the villains of the cultural upheaval and can be held accountable for the dissolution of educational standards and values in this country. All of us are the victims of their guilts. In the

Walpurgisnacht of campus upheavals, which are always led by faculty identity-seekers and could not exist without their leadership, all society becomes the victim, not merely the institutions which bind a civilization together.

The use of the university as an intellectual testing-ground of the personality is criminal. The university has one function only: to train the qualified student to the height of his capacity for learning, productivity in his skills, and imaginative research. Sensitivity training for twenty-year-olds is obscene. We have seen the results of the prolongation of adolescence into manhood and womanhood and the sanction of childish behavior in maturity. Far from being attractive or interesting, many students of twenty are already driveling old men and women who even have the physical characteristics of the aged. Their only equipment seems to be a smoldering and murky indignation against what they think is Society. Their sole emotion seems to be self-pity. They may be studying John Donne and Longinus but they are reading and quoting Dylan MacGoon.

WHAT THE POET KNOWS

℟ FOR THE SAKE OF ARGUMENT, let us divide knowledge into four kinds and assume that each kind is free and independent. Let us assume also that all four kinds are equal in value, none being superior to another. This device will keep us from trying to compare poetry with things outside it, as nearly all writers about art have done. Aristotle, for instance, says that poetry is "more philosophical and a higher thing than history," which is only his way of saying that poetry is not quite as good as philosophy. And a contemporary esthetician says that "Art is prayer." One could compile an anthology of sayings about art based upon attempts to compare poetry with other things. Today, we live in a world in which art is considered by some to be a form of mental hygiene, by others to be a form of unorganized religion, and by others to be a form of unofficial philosophy. I prefer to think of art as a kind of knowledge which is neither better nor worse than other kinds, and which cannot be compared with them at all.

The four kinds of knowledge are natural, supernatural, abstract, and poetic. Or we can call them scientific, religious, philosophical, and artistic. Or we can call them rational, mystical, ideal, and creative. The ground between them we can mark off without much dissent.

Rational knowledge is what we think of as science, and it is, of course, the dominant kind of knowledge in our age. I mean to say that we live more according to the rules of science than to the rules of religion or art or philosophy. But science does not dominate poetry in our time. Science has little effect on art for us because of the nature of rational knowledge. This kind of knowledge excludes man from its universe; it will admit an arm or a leg, a circulatory system or a job, an act of violence or a deed of sale, but not the whole man. If rational knowledge did so, it would of course be "useless" and irrational knowledge. Science is wise enough not to invite man into the universe: that would violate the integrity and the meaning of science. There was a time when men would write a philosophic or scientific treatise in verse—but such works contributed neither to science nor philosophy nor poetry. It was when science shook off the forms unnatural to it that it leapt forward out of the Dark Ages into the brilliant light of a true knowledge of its possibilities. In achieving its purity, science put all other forms of knowledge in the shadows and even began to dominate them. The practical arts of economic life, government, and education have become the colonies of science. At a certain point, science has even tried to colonize the "fine" arts and philosophy and religion, but this is beyond its power to do.

The official cultural doctrine of antagonism to science is one of the most shameful aspects of our literature and accounts as much as anything for the cultural doctrine of "exile." The young poet thinks there is nothing in the universe more satanic than neon light; D. H. Lawrence hated wheels; the Henry Miller type of poet has contempt for anything marked "Made in U.S.A." Ninety-nine out of a hundred contemporary poems are aimed at factory windows. But poetry should be neither pro-science nor anti-science: it should neither reject nor "assimilate" the machine (as one poet thought). To take an abstract position about science or about anything else is to deflect art from its purpose.

Nevertheless, there are certain mixed forms of science which are irritants to the artist. These are the social sciences, as they are termed. The scientific historian, for one, is almost a natural foil for the poet. All social scientists, as they are called, seem to be trespassers against art. Social science is reason's apology to man, and these apologies take peculiar forms. One of these is to make a science of man himself. Another is to make a science of man's habits. There is a science of society and a science of culture and, for all I know, even a science of art. A biologist who has collected a million gall wasps is considered competent to collect human beings who have been stung with sexual desire. Economics, psychology, semantics, sociology, all the "sciences" that deal with the whole man are necessarily imperfect. Pure science makes a discovery which can be superseded only by a more inclusive discovery; but social science is always being disrupted by the unpredictability of—people. Most artists and many scholars now look upon the "sciences of people" with suspicion.

Supernatural knowledge, revelation, or whatever you want to call it, does the opposite of natural knowledge for man. It tends to make man all spirit, or spirit trapped in mortal coils until some happier hour. I mean to say that there is no religion of life, so to speak, nor can there be. Poetic knowledge, on the other hand, loves the world more frankly than it loves God, and this creates a natural barrier between poets and holier men. Some poets, to be sure, are men of God and some men of God are poets, but, in general, churches are weak in esthetics and the glory of this life, while most religious poets, so-called, are weak in talent. The reason is not far to seek: the closer one approaches the mystical experience the more the world falls away, the closer the substance of the world comes to annihilation. The mystical is the opposite of the creative process: to the mystic a poem is just as much a "false reality" as any other phenomenon.

Supernatural knowledge, when it is written about, sometimes moves close to philosophy and sometimes close to poetry. This is because of the strange demands religion makes on man: it must deal with the individual life and soul, like poetry; but it must also deal with the absolute, like philosophy. In a time like ours it must even accommodate itself to some extent to scientific knowledge. Religion has the supremely difficult task of relating the individual to the universe and to all time. And its attention to the individual gives religion a great similarity to art.

Abstract knowledge, knowledge of the ideal, is the all-embracing category of knowledge; at any rate, philosophy must take everything into account, and relate all things to principles. The completeness of philosophy is its most famous characteristic: science can ignore religion and art; religion can ignore science and art; poetry can ignore science, religion, and philosophy, if it likes. But philosophy must deal with God and number and beauty, sooner or later, and what is harder for it, must try to put them together. Philosophy touches poetry specifically at esthetics: I have already mentioned two esthetic convictions which have nothing in common. There are thousands of esthetic dogmas which have nothing in common, and we can understand this only if we recognize that any esthetic is only a part of some larger philosophical system. This is not to say that all poetics are wrong or are merely dogmatic abstractions. Nevertheless, there is no one poetics, no one view of art which has satisfied many people for long. Poetics sometimes determines the external character of poetry, as in the convention that a play must take place within a period of twenty-four hours; but these rules do not trouble poetry deeply. Aside from poetics, there is a deeper way in which philosophy affects poetry, and that is, directly. Now and then we find a poet or a group of poets to whom philosophy is a vital form of knowledge. But this happens rarely and we should not think that because there are "philosophical" poets that poetry is philosophical. Nor should we think that because there are "religious" poets that poetry is religious.

The idea that all knowledge must be unified seems to be characteristic of the human mind, and it is a mischievous and even malignant idea. In an age of cultural fanaticism there is a tendency to tear down the barriers between disparate functions of thought: we have the phenomenon of social knowledge as proof. Even in picking up a review of a new work of poetry, one cannot know in advance whether he is going to be treated to a psychological, an historical, a philosophical, or a religious treatise. The same thing occurs in other branches of learning. For instance, there are educators who draw up lists of books and call them Great; they then extract the ideas from these books and make a list of Great Ideas. Students are then taught these ideas in such a way as to suggest that they are Truth itself. Or, to take a specific example of how one kind of knowledge can contaminate another: I once read the extraordinary statement that the philosopher Descartes had "cut the throat of poetry." This was perhaps a reference to the effect he had on separating thought and feeling, or something of the sort. Now Descartes, whatever else he was responsible for, did not cut the throat of poetry, even in this fine metaphor. A statement of this kind leads us to believe that, at the very least, all poets had read Descartes or somebody else who had read Descartes, and that everybody everywhere believed him. In reality, nothing of this sort ever happens in art, the reason being that poetry has a knowledge of its own kind which does not depend on other kinds of knowledge. There are so many incompatible notions about the nature of poetry that it would take an encyclopedia to recount them. I do not say this in a spirit of pride, or because I know the true formula, but because, quite obviously, the theories of poetry which disagree with each other cannot all be right. The worst offenders in this realm are the philosophers and the poets themselves.

Of the many false paths which poetry can take, because of its attraction to other forms of knowledge, there are three which are the most conspicuous. One is toward classicism, formalism, and myth. In this category we find most poetry which is symbolic and metaphysical; and such poetry eventually turns into philosophy or religion. The second false path is toward public speech, rhetoric and history. In this category, we find most of the poetry and art which advocates human progress and discourses on man's fate. The third category is toward self-regard, ego, and sentimentality, but as this kind of art usually represents no more than failure of talent, we shall not discuss it at all.

Mythic poetry and historic poetry are the two banners under which most modern literati today range themselves, and most of my remarks will be concerned with their habits, their desires, and their manner of waging war. Specifically, I want to deal with these general faults of poetic theory and practice: the idea of poetry as something that has happened to prose; the idea of poetry as a figment of the imagination; poetry as transcendental knowledge and religion; poetry as history. In the last two categories (which I shall devote the most space to) there is the common factor of language-worship. Language-worshippers sometimes cross the line from myth to history and back again. The fight between them is a fight for power.

Literary theorists have nearly always thought of poetry as some kind of transformation of prose. If they have not found it to be prose transformed, they have found it to be an inspired code, the voice of hidden oracles, the gods, the buried consciousness of man or some such mystery. Between the artisan poet and the oracular poet there are many fixed theories, but these two represent the extreme positions. And yet poetry does not come out of "embellishment" (a term without meaning in art) nor does it come out of trance, as mystic knowledge is supposed to do. In order to give poetry meaning, philosophers and critics have had to say that poetry is at bottom the voice of the gods, or the voice of all men or that it pertains to the conscience of all men or to the nature of all men; they have had to say that it is either imitation or expression. The desire to make poetry "universal" is apparently irrepressible: equally irrepressible is the idea that the poet is a trumpet through which sound all the rumblings of Hell and the suspirations of Paradise. And the most rationalistic theory of poetry says that it is only somebody else's best thoughts put into memorable snippets of song.

We are always taught that poets get their ideas and plots from other people, and that they then put these ideas and plots into poetry. Poetry is something that holds ideas and the container is called Form. It seems perfectly sensible to look at it that way, and many critics are content to let it go at that. But this view is just about as meaningful as the description of man as a spirit encased in flesh.

A slightly more sophisticated school of pedagogy teaches that poetry is not a casing that holds ideas but a kind of stomach in which the ideas are digested and transformed. This is a much more diplomatic approach to poetry and is one that even contains some truth. In any case, it could hardly offend anyone, except poets. Critics are constantly studying poets to find out how they have digested their reading, and this probing drives some poets to look for books that practically nobody has heard of. One poet once wrote a young poetess that by the time she was forty she would thank God to find a book she hadn't yet read. This is odd advice, considering that poetry existed before books and even before writing. Poetry is bound to be something more than warmed-over philosophies, uncopyrighted plays, and misinterpreted history. It is indeed.

The most orthodox idea about poetic knowledge, the one we are usually taught (by inference) in school, is that it doesn't exist. When we begin to *study* poetry—for it is assumed that poetry is a dialect—we are soon led to the books which our poet read in his college. We track down the source of "trailing clouds of glory," and that is that.

Most poetry does not seem to offer much poetic knowledge of a primary kind: it does not deal with an obvious metamorphosis in the poet's life; and this fact gives aid and comfort to the people who think poetry is unoriginal. For every poem that presents an original character, like Caliban, or an original philosophic idea, there are a thousand, just as good, which seem to repeat a character or idea. These poems, however, are concerned with the personal conflict between the poet and "common" knowledge. The knowledge may be out of mythology or out of the almanac; it can come from any source. The contribution to poetic knowledge here consists of the conflict itself and the degree to which the poet has been changed by this type of intellectual experience. The plot or the character may or may not be changed: that is incidental. The poet and consequently the poem must show metamorphosis: that is what is crucial.

Shakespeare gives Polonius, whom he calls a fool, much rational poetry to say: "neither a borrower nor a lender be," "be thou familiar but by no means vulgar," and even the noble γνῶθι σεαυτόν, "to thine ownself be true." Then he has him killed. We cannot expect anything of polonian knowledge except the universal. And of course rational people seize on the poetry of maxims to show that poetry is "natural" and that it has a basis in common experience. *But there is no basis of common experience in art except the work of art itself.* Far from diminishing the value and the wonder of art, this dictum seems to me to raise art to a place of eminence among the works of man.

Another misleading theory about poetic knowledge is that it is imaginative knowledge, and this idea has been greatly abused by poets as well as critics. A century ago certain poets tried to limit the meaning of the term *imagination* but only succeeded in making it a synonym for what we call the creative process. I am no philologist, but I think the mix-up over the term *imagination* comes from its connection with the word *image*. The poet makes images, poetry is image-knowledge, but it is not imaginative knowledge. The imagination is the fool in the house, says a mystic, and it is so with poetry. Poetic knowledge is not a leaping to the unknown; on the contrary, it is a painful engagement with the known. In poetry the imagination can produce pleasure domes, but more often the imagination works like a toy-factory which turns out toy and sometimes real monsters. Imagination can only yield intuitions, some of which are true and some not. Intuitive poetry is just as unreliable as intuitive science. Theories of the imagination usually come from very quixotic poets who are really in love with progress and destiny. It seems to me that imagination is more the property of inventors like Thomas Edison than of poets like Shakespeare. Shakespeare himself poked fun at the imagination which makes weasels of clouds and bushes of bears; he used the term otherwise to mean the image-making and name-giving genius of poets.

There is one development of recent art—it happened sporadically in the past—which is a true form of imaginative art; it is called surrealism. Surrealism tries to break down all barriers between the subject and the object and to produce a delirium of reality. But this delirium is as artificial as an invented dream, lacking both spontaneity and selectivity. Surrealism is one of the more advanced forms of public speech and it is popular with the poet who is most interested in translating dogma into sensation.

Next, there is the idea of poetry as transcendental knowledge. At present, the two chief schools of poetry are the ones called metaphysical and symbolist. In point of fact, they are not very important in terms of production, but they are the most talked about. Indirectly they have had a small (local) effect on poetry and a large effect on poetics. But in general all the discussion we hear about them only obscures the fact that there is more discussion than poetry. Metaphysical poetry is said to be concerned with myth, and myth in modern terminology does not mean a belief that no one any longer believes in: it means a belief that people would like to believe in, if they knew what to believe. Hence, to say that you don't care about myth is, to a lover of the metaphysical school, as bad as saying that the universe doesn't exist. Not to believe in myth is even more serious than not believing in Original Sin, because without myth there could be no Original Sin in the first place. Any discussion of metaphysical poetry is bound to be academic, however, because there is almost no such poetry today. A few poets have tried to imitate John Donne and George Herbert, but without much luck. On the other hand, there are poets whose experience of life is largely philosophical, in a real and literal sense, and some of these even talk about metaphysics in their poetry. But that is quite another kettle of fish from writing a poem, say, like *The Ecstasy*. Metaphysical poetry is also concerned with scientific method of a peculiar homemade variety. It looks for formulas to explain extra-physical sensation (as in Donne's poem); it uses the vocabulary of mechanics; and it imitates the inorganic rather than the organic in life. "Metascientific" would be a more accurate term for this kind of poetry, for "metaphysical" poetry seldom progresses beyond popular science.

Symbolist poetry, however, does exist, although it is "officially" dead. The French have been trying to pin symbolism on Poe for a hundred years, and they may succeed yet, but symbolism is something that will always be associated with the country of its origin.

The poet Mallarmé describing a bicyclist once said that he is "one who unwinds between his legs the image of an endless rail." He did not say this in a poem but in a poetry notebook; nevertheless it is the kind of poetic knowledge that interested the symbolists. The curious thing about this sort of knowledge is that it is neither poetic nor rational nor religious nor even mythic knowledge. It is knowledge arrived at by that amazing faculty of the mind which we call the sense of humor. I would describe symbolist knowledge as poetic humor which is not funny. Nothing, in fact, could be more serious, for the symbolist searches for the higher reality beyond words and beyond ideas. The quality of Mallarmé's statement is complex: it is brilliant, precise, and senseless. I do not know what true poetic knowledge about a cyclist would be—that would depend on the poet—but this example of Mallarmé's comes pretty close to abstract knowledge. Many symbolists, of course, end up as amateur philosophers, causing such poets as Wallace Stevens (the most French of American poets) to mutter abjectly that poetry is only a kind of unofficial philosophy. Symbolist poets tried to get as far away from literal meaning as possible, in theory at least, and at other times tried to collect every possible meaning of a word into one usage. When James Joyce says *shaving-mug*, you have to think of the Great Chalice of Antioch, female fertility, and lilies-of-the-valley. The symbolists ran so far from what they called Rhetoric that the very mention of ideas sent them scuttling. This attitude has been taken as a justification for poetry in which the arts of persuasion are taboo. But even a symbolist work is "rhetorical" to the extent that it persuades the reader of its credibility; and any poem goes bad that leaves credibility for argumentation, generalization, and abstraction.—I am not attempting to define symbolism and metaphysical art, as you see, but only to make a comment about the kind of knowledge these schools are concerned with.

One of the results of symbolist and metaphysical poetry has been to encourage a religion of language. Every poet loves language almost more than anything else, but this is not the same thing as adoration of language. Modern poets and critics have the two things so mixed up with each other and with the mystical Logos that one despairs of ever seeing a clear statement on the subject. The adoration of language is of course a "myth" in the sense that modern critics use the word—they say that language is sacrosanct. Now it may be true that language is sacrosanct, but we can respect this belief only in the way in which we respect the savage's belief in amulets. The mischief, however, comes with those poets who pin the destiny of the world on the state of the language. It was Mallarmé who raised the battlecry about purifying the dialect of the tribe—an odd thing for an anti-rhetoric man to do, unless he was being funny. And this was done in an elegiac poem about Poe, of all people. Whatever else Poe did, he certainly did not purify the dialect of the American, or any other tribe. Be that as it may, this purification ceremony takes a lot of time and energy of living poets: they talk about the debased state of language, mass language, official language, and so on, as if they were members of an Inquisition or of a Health Department. Certainly there are forms of language which are debased, but I do not see why this should worry the poet any more or less than it does the corner policeman. But the point is that the myth of language is one of those false messiahs which many people take seriously and even mistake for the meaning of poetry. Such a high-sounding doctrine approaches being a religion: I bring it up for that reason. A religion of language is degrading to art, when it is not simply absurd. Poetic knowledge can sometimes be located completely in love of language, but such a poetry will be a special and self-limiting variety. To make language the be-all and the end-all of poetry, and not only poetry, but life itself, even symbolically, is a form of literary madness. Language worship is widespread today; the one acceptable "mythic" plot for the modern poet seems to be the Death of Language and the Rebirth of the Word. Mighty libraries are being written about this piece of solemn nonsense.

Language-worship in one form takes the road to transcendental knowledge, religion, or philosophy. In the terminology of modern criticism, the kind of poet who takes this path is called Major, because of his influence on other people's ideas through what are termed myths. But there is an even more prevalent form of Language-worship, which takes the road to History, and its standard-bearers are called Great. "Great" in this meaning of the word refers to general-ship in art and the politics of art. The Great poet may cross the line to the field of myth and come back again—in fact, there is consider-able traffic in arms behind the scene of battle.

The poet of public pretensions, the poet of history, is the one who is also known as the experimenter, the innovator, the revolutionary. It is my intention here to avoid naming names unless I can mention them favorably or at least with neutrality; but I feel obliged, for the sake of clarity, to give at least one example of the artist of history. I choose as my example the painter Picasso, in the belief that things said about one art are true of the other arts.

The artist like Picasso declares war on the world and especially on the world of his medium; that is, he is nihilistic even about language. Having no real center in love, no rooted attachment to his situation, the revolutionary artist tries conquest after conquest, each more dar-ing and destructive than the last. Many of the works of such an artist are themselves without center, violent, empty, destructive, sentimen-tal. He converts everything into his version of it—a war, the organs of the body, the periods of art, statistics, the gods. In most cases this kind of artist develops intransigent political or religious views which would impose a new order of life on mankind. For the worshipper of language, it is only one step from the slogan "Remake the Language" to "Remake the World." Other innovators are finalists, so to speak, who dream of creating the novel to end all novels, or the last poem. The spirit of competition is heavy among them.

We must not oversimplify the behavior of the historic poet and expect him to be a noted Fascist or Communist like Pound or Pi-casso. Often the historic poet is a democrat and a libertarian: the basis of similarity between them is in adoration of art and the use of language as an instrument of power. Most poets in the modern an-thology are language-worshippers of the historic rather than the mythic persuasion. Many of them give the impression of tremendous objectivity and even saintliness in their lives and work. But nearly all of them believe in the redemption of the world through art.

I have mentioned four misleading theories of poetry: poetry as a form of prose, poetry as imagination, poetry as myth, and poetry as history. It remains now to describe what I believe true poetry to be.

II

Someone has said that poetry is everywhere at its goal. That is so. Many of the disagreements of critics throughout history over what poetry is results from their approach to poetry. Most critics come to poetry with a split consciousness: they are as interested in the cause of the poem (which they call its meaning) as they are in the poem itself, or they are interested in the poem's effect on history, or they are interested in the mechanics of the poem and will not approach it until they have put on the white overalls of analytical criticism.

To say that poetry is everywhere at its goal is to say that poetry gives us knowledge of its own kind, a unique, unrepeatable, intelligible form. Poetic knowledge is neither intuitive, nor provable, nor ordered, nor consistent, but self-contradictory, beyond demonstration, beyond proof. We accept it by conviction or not at all. We accept it as we accept the belief in another's pain or pleasure, or we reject it as unconvincing, not sincere, or a symptom of disorder. How much bad poetry is only pitiful bravado, a falsetto cry of self-assertion! Poetic truth is in fact personal truth itself, that which comes out of the experience of life, and *only* out of the experience itself. Poetry is not universal, nor is its knowledge; it is not the truth for all, nor the whole truth, nor the real truth, nor the truth in a flash. Above all, it is not the truth of the Outside, of the State, or of Nature, or of God, or of the Cosmos. It is the personal particular human truth which cannot be ordered or reasoned or preconceived. It can only be lived in life and it can only be *made* in art. Poetic knowledge shows no development and cannot be pieced together like rational knowledge, nor even made consistent, like knowledge of the gods. Nor are there any absolutes in poetry, except the absolutes of the particular poet. It is as though there were an infinite number of atomic systems, all mutually contradictory, all provable, all believable. With poetry it is never a question of true and false but only of the credibility of the work. Nat-

ural knowledge tells us that the world turns; religion tells us to forgive; poetry tells us that my love is like a red, red rose. Poetry tells us
that ripeness is all, and it tells us that nothing is so beautiful as spring
(two truths which "contradict" each other). We call a poem a true
poem when we do not hesitate to believe it—when it is impossible in
its artfulness not to believe it.

Poetic knowledge differs from other knowledge in this also: it
does not seek, it does not ask; it affirms. But poetic affirmation is neither for better nor for worse, and we must not be deceived into thinking, as poets sometimes are, that poetry is praise. It is sometimes
praise, sometimes damnation, sometimes neither. Almost all youthful
poetry does ask the philosophical questions, Who am I? and What
am I? But the poet who writes this is still outside poetic knowledge
and trying to approach it.

Poetry is innocent, not wise. It does not learn from experience,
because each poetic experience is unique. The Madonna is painted a
million times by a million hands and is never achieved—or always
achieved, depending on whether you take the rational or the poetic
view. The assertion is ever new and not a reassertion, not an act of
faith but an act of innocence. The poet lives in the eternity of himself
and is beyond the reach of worldly historical time or other-worldly
eternal time. His knowledge is not of the world, nor of himself, but of
himself-as-world. Yet he is far from thinking himself omnipotent.
"Oh, I am wonderful!" says the poet. "I cannot tell how my ankles
bend, nor whence the cause of my faintest wish." This is sometimes
mistaken for egotism, when it is only innocent wonder, innocent happiness. Nor does the true poet feel omniscience; he sees only as much
of the world as the soldier sees of the battlefield. If he attempts to see
as much as the general he will see nothing and probably be destroyed
for his curiosity. Poetic knowledge puts us in the midst of experience;
in the midst of particular experience, which is the only kind of experience valid for art. Conceivably, one can experience, say, the brotherhood of man, or so we are led to believe by the historic artist who has
the soul and the ambitions of Genghis Khan, but this can only be
done by putting personality to the sword and by sowing salt on the
land from which personality springs. The question of how to particu-
larize universal experience, such as a social revolution, besets the his-

toric poet and changes him into a mockery of personality. It is imperative for this kind of artist to think in terms of change; it is unbearable to him that there are limits to experience and limits to form. Such a poet becomes a prey to history. In the public poet the historical sense is overpowering; it is his main message. And such poets, when they return to themselves, suffer from the most acute sentimentality: they record the agonized flight from history to self. This becomes typically the music "yearning like a god in pain," the music of repentance, and a hopeless search for something nobler than ego. The true artist, on the other hand, is unconscious of history and never lives in the future or the past; he is pre-eminently the man of the present, the one in whom the convergence of times is possible, but only if he is free in spirit and personality. It does not matter for the artist whether the civilization he lives in is compulsory or voluntary; it matters only that personality and spirit are free to grow. Thus it is that we sometimes have great art under terrible despotisms and sometimes no art under the happiest democracies. One can have liberty, equality, and fraternity and still be a spiritual slave.

I give as two examples of the greatest of true artists in our civilization, Shakespeare and Mozart. In both men ego and time-consciousness are practically non-existent: the personality is practically everything. We do not experience these men in terms of pride or humility or will. We experience them as man, the complete image. In Mozart, who historically is a mass of contradictions—Freemason, Catholic, Romantic, Classicist—we find the eternity of the particular, serenity without voluptuousness, tragedy without self-pity, joy without hysteria, glory without bombast. In him the particular is so vivid, so completely lived, that we enter world after world of pleasure and pain and re-live long stretches of his spiritual life. Through his music we learn his landscape, the preciseness of his vocabulary, the shades of his feeling, the turn of his thought, the people in his view. It is the same with Shakespeare. But with those poets who are trumpets of prophecy, we get everything that belongs outside poetic knowledge—philosophy, rhetoric, politics, and eventually violence in action and social nihilism.

The way in which the poet puts himself in the midst of experience is by poetic sympathy, or what a German poet has called *Einfühlung*.

This One-Feeling, or In-Feeling, is very necessary to poetic knowledge but it can easily become an aberration. *Einfühlung* is the utmost
sympathy for the Other, and it is rooted in love. But this feeling must
be held in check by a sense of probability. The imagination cannot
run away with it. When the poet feels that he is experiencing history
or the universe, you may be sure he is about to make a fool of himself.
The good poet sticks to his real loves, those within the realm of probability. He never tries to hold hands with God or the human race. Religious knowledge can sometimes do this, but extreme religious
knowledge is characterized by trance, annihilation, and nirvana. Rational knowledge excludes the subject from the scene and experiences
without the experiencer. But the poet includes the scene: it takes
place in him: above all, he is involved in it. I have heard that Chinese
poetics also excludes the subject, and this may be the reason why certain Chinese poems can be written on a postage stamp: Too little *Einfühlung* leads to the poetry of ego and sentiment. Too much leads to
insincerity and the trumpet calls of history and mysticism. But poetic
knowledge need not go as far as mystical knowledge and cannot,
without violating its nature. Poetic knowledge is not all-inclusive but
definitely limited. This does not mean there are certain "subjects" for
the poet and certain subjects for the saint and certain subjects for the
mathematician. Poetry is not a matter of subject but of presence, the
presence of the poet in a given scene. Anything is subject matter for
poetry, even philosophy, even history, even the daily news. The question is always whether the poet is poetically involved in that part of
the action of the world into which he has wandered.

The true poet lives in a whole world rather than a part world from
which he excludes certain varieties of experience. He lives not only
with his wide-awake mind but with his deeper memory and with his
foreconscious mind of probability. Thus his thinking and his living
run counter to the orderly chronological fictions of history and the
static eternities of religion. It is this cast of mind too which gives the
poet the appearance of madness, and which sometimes drives him
mad, and which, in any case, admits to him the company of bed-
lamites. This is quite a different thing from poetic "divine madness,"
so-called, and we should not be taken in by the unhappy doctrine that
the artist is a lunatic. We cannot imagine madness in Shakespeare or

Mozart; we do associate it with the artist who gives himself to myth and history. It is a sad commentary on our world that there is an official doctrine of poetic madness, the reasoned derangement of the senses, and such romantic nonsense. The modern artist who cannot accept the poetic imperative of wholeness of personality moves over into a dream world of nihilism and pseudo-insanity. Pseudo-insanity describes the rationales of most bad modern works of art.

Our modern world is a rational world par excellence and, to be sure, man as personality feels more and more excluded from it. Hence all our talk about loneliness, the artist's talk of exile, the individualist's talk of standardization. This shutting out of man from the world has helped divide poetry into the two hostile camps which I have called historic poetry and mythic poetry. The historic poets try to celebrate the historic state of affairs, or failing that, try to celebrate human nature or the universality of feeling. Mythic poetry does not celebrate the world at all: it prefers to forget this world for an external world, a world beyond the senses.

The true poet does not live in a world of his own, nor an imaginary world, a symbolic world, a transcendental world, a world of ideas, an historical world, or a world in which everything is made of words. The true poet is neither a revolutionary, nor an innovator, nor an experimenter, nor a visionary; he is neither an architect of the greatest thoughts nor the discoverer of unknown realms and new horizons. How many hundreds of things the poet is said to be, none of which he is! And yet he is something quite as wonderful. He is the man to whom everything is a wholeness, the man whose mind and whose senses glow with the wonder of the immediate. And, uniquely—for the poet is not the only man endowed with endless wonder and delight—the poet is the man who must *create* the wholeness of the world he knows. Hence his childlikeness; hence the prevalence of poetry in youth. The poet is in a perpetual state of learning the world; and the poet's learning is by love and wonder, learning by fascination of the beautiful and the ugly, but learning, above all, by making a thing of wonder and wholeness with his own hands. Make it he must: that is the law of his nature, for in creation he creates himself.

This work of self-creation I shall next try to describe.

THE DECOLONIZATION OF AMERICAN LITERATURE

AMERICAN LITERATURE has been in the throes of decolonization since America first put pen to paper.

This literature began as a country-cousin literature of England. We were beholden to England for "culture" and broke with that culture through politics. For the great literature of this country until lately is political. In fact, it is the great political documents of America which have broken the back of cultural slavery all over the world. The writings of Jefferson, the Constitution, the Emancipation Proclamation are the basic artifacts of American literature. Decolonization is born in these documents. We are just beginning to feel the consequences. We are still at the dawn of those fabulous political words.

Three hundred years passed before the first words of cultural independence were set down, three centuries of holding on to the Old World, the European mother. We might have been a French country or a Spanish country or English like Canada, but we turned out to be none of those. One of the main reasons was that we had slaves, we had Negroes. The presence of slaves forced the ideal of liberty to its conclusion.

When America decolonized itself from Europe, from England, it opened the door to decolonization everywhere. We pressed a button and opened Pandora's box. It is this country that gave France the example of revolution. And even today we are the admiration and the horror of the Old World. We have not broken with those documents.

We were England's, Robert Frost said; we were colonials. When we stopped being colonials, all hell broke loose.

To be colonial means to live in a faraway place and to long for home. American literature was this way until little more than a century ago—until a few writers began to say, like Emerson, Europe is not home; until Thoreau pulled back even from the village of Concord; until Whitman rewrote the Constitution in poetry and sang the one great poem about the death of Abraham Lincoln.

To be colonial means not to cut the umbilical cord with Home and also to create the Native. America created two Natives, the Indian and the Negro. The Indian was banished to the unconscious mind of America (what is left of the Indian is a record of cultural shock which is phenomenal in modern history). But the Negro could not be banished. He was an industrial army, fuel to be burned and to be replenished of itself. He was the American "native." Richard Wright called his first novel *Native Son*; he understood "native."

But we were still colonial when we began to write. We would even send a Negro slave girl to England as a poet in the eighteenth century! I want to quote verbatim the biographical note from an old anthology of Negro poetry, edited by Langston Hughes and Ama Bontemps in 1949. This is colonialism in a nutshell.

Phillis Wheatley (Senegal, West Africa, 1753–84) was captured and sold into slavery in early childhood and brought to Boston in 1761. She became the property of John Wheatley of Boston whose wife and daughter soon noted the alert sensitivity of the young African girl and encouraged Phillis's efforts to acquire learning. Within a few years she was completely at home in the language and literature of her captors. She began writing poetry, and in 1770, at the age of seventeen, published, "A Poem, by Phillis, A Negro Girl in Boston, on the Death of the Reverend George Whitefield." When her health began to fail, Phillis was advised by doctors to take a sea voyage. This was arranged by the kindly mistress, who also gave the girl her freedom before she sailed for England. In London, Phillis was a success. It was there that her only collected volume of verse was first issued under the title *Poems on Various Subjects, Religious and Moral*, 1773. Then one by one the patrons of this talented ex-slave girl died and she returned to Boston. Her marriage was unhappy, and she died as a servant in a cheap lodging house at the age of thirty-one.

The ironies of this footnote are staggering and would require a Dostoevsky to handle them. Phillis Wheatley's poetry is as bad as all eighteenth-century colonial poetry, though better than that, say, of the Hartford Wits, which isn't saying much. Yet this experiment in colonial "culture" contains a message. The message is negative all down the line: slave girl, Boston at the dawn of revolution, guilt about rebellion from the Old World, neo-classical poetry, "the kindly mistress," and so on.

In every case except ours, a new culture is based on Home Country, Settler, and Native. But in America nobody knows where the Home Country is, for the Settlers come from Home Countries all over the world; and the Natives are no more. We have no Natives and no common Home Country. We have no peasantry. We have only expatriates and ex-slaves. This is a country of Runaways and Captives.

When the literature of America got under way it fascinated the world: runaways and captives, cops and robbers, cowboys and Indians, palefaces and blackskins, Jews and Goyim, Syndicate and Chamber of Commerce. Nobody wanted to be a native—the natives were dead and done for; everybody wanted to be a "settler." Those who would not "settle" went back to some Old Country of the mind: Eliot, Santayana, Pound, Hemingway, Henry James. Others mourned their "rootlessness"; we have a whole literature of that.

The cultural history of our country is one of decolonization, every element trying to sever itself from its origins. We are something like the white Australians, who are not eager to trace their ancestry back more than three or four generations because their original ancestors will have been sent over in the "hulks," the convict ships that were sent from England to the farthest place England could think of. Every FFV in Australia was a convict. We are in the same boat; we have only a paper aristocracy, and our aristocrats were revolutionaries who fought for their lives. In this sense the Daughters of the American Revolution are subversive. Only they have forgotten what their ancestors were subversive about.

Our literature took a long time to decolonize from English literature, and the process hasn't ended yet. In the beginning we were "Anglo-Saxon," about 90 per cent, for the blacks were not counted in the population and the immigrants hadn't arrived. Excuse a few sentences of facts, which I think mean so much. A generation after independence the Germans and Irish began to arrive in force. Before the Civil War, hordes of Irish, Dutch, Danes, Swedes, Norwegians, Swiss, and Jews swarmed in. Toward the end of the century came larger waves of Italians, Russians, Poles, Bohemians, and Hungarians. A smaller number of Asiatics seeped in, for this country is still anti-Asiatic (we invented our first concentration camps for American citizens of Japanese ancestry during the Second World War). In all this the English element was inundated and, so to speak, contaminated. The language of the King was lost in the shuffle.

A language in itself is nothing. A literature in itself is nothing. A literature is the expression of a nation's soul, and a great literature leaves nothing out—that is its greatness. But to leave nothing out means to go against the grain; it means to dissent. Our modern literature is a literature of dissent, monotonous and endless dissidence. This dissidence gives modern literature its authenticity. Yet this literature of dissent is only in its infancy. Dissent is contagious, and every day we find new areas of eruption everywhere in the world. But dissent is also a drop in the bucket of literature, a drop of pigment in the skin or in the blood.

American literature is unique; it is the only literature I have ever heard of in which all elements have tried, more or less simultaneously, to decolonize themselves. It is the only literature which practices cultural amnesia as a doctrine. The few famous American writers who refused to surrender the past, who insisted on memory (Henry James or Eliot), surrendered their nationality to the idea of European cultural supremacy. They could maintain a continuity with Europe only by becoming Europeans again.

English literature is a dead literature in America, a memory. The English language is practically a memory. Only a few English professors in America pretend that English and its great literature are continuous with ours.

A decolonized literature in an African country or in a free Arab country or in Israel is different from ours. Those nations have a culture to go back to. They go back to where they began when history interrupted their life. In Israel the Hebrew language was reinvented

overnight after a sleep of two thousand years. It seemed the most natural thing in the world, for it was that language and its great book
which held those people together who became the new Israelites. In
India people fight in the streets to retain their ancient tongues, the
source of their culture. In Africa, French and English will not long
remain the medium of literature, not in the European forms at least.
But in America we have only vestiges of culture *to which we do not wish
to return*. The first thing the American immigrant tried to do was to
prevent his children from inheriting the old language, the old culture. (In my case, for instance, Yiddish was used as a private language
of jokes and confidences which we, third generation Americans, were
not supposed to know. I have found the same to be true with students
of mine who are of Czech descent or German or Swedish or Dutch
or Greek.)

In a sense, all cultural languages are banished from America. A
country settled by runaways and slaves did not carry much high culture with it. And the tides of immigration engulfed what high culture
there was. The half-educated American has long been a byword
abroad; in fact, it is impossible for the American to be educated in the
European sense. We cannot be nor do we have to. As I ask my fellow
teachers: In what way am I to present, say, English poetry to the
grandson of a Latvian farmer from a ranch in western Nebraska? As
the poetry of his culture? In what way am I to present Chaucer or
T. S. Eliot to my Negro students? Is that their heritage? Is the great
complex of European culture their heritage? And do they have any
such heritage at all? Even to me, an English professor and a writer of
the English tongue, all things English are somewhat foreign.

I gather from Sartre's writings about Africa that European culture
is no longer capable of influencing world culture. Europe is now the
colony. It is European culture which is thirsty for replenishment from
outside. American culture shows a similar thirst for replenishment
but can slake this thirst from within.

The great theme of American literature is rootlessness. And this
fact also makes us unique. Many writers have even said that there is
no relationship between the American and the land. It is as if the
spirit of place were hostile to us. We become the greatest technicians
and mechanics because we fight the spirit of place; we are bent upon

conquering place by force. We have never made peace with the land but have taken it by storm. D. H. Lawrence felt this about us; Henry Miller and Faulkner have it in their books; the urban poets, who have forgotten what a tree looks like, substantiate it in their dusty poems.

The price our writers have had to pay for rootlessness, for cutting ties with all the different pasts behind us, is the neuroticism we know so well in our literature. And yet we have no choice; insofar as the American writer is true to his situation, he is a neurotic, ridden with the anxieties of separateness from the past. Freedom is one of the beneficent symptoms of this anxiety. We are suddenly confronted with an alphabet of freedoms ranging from civil rights to freedom of the banned book and the spoken obscenity. Our literature is engaging in a Socratic dialogue with all previous values; we do this with increasing recklessness and frequently with cynicism, for what is there to lose? The fact is, there is no place to go back to; we have nowhere to go but forward. We cannot help ourselves; that is our condition.

So long as America held on to the mother literature it was colonial. This was the case until the twentieth century and even into it. The criterion of the poem was the English poem; of the novel, the English novel. The exceptions are few and can be counted on one hand. It was only with the recognition of rootlessness that a strong and massive American literature came into being. This theme coincided with all the forms of radicalism that swept through the intelligentsia in the early years of the century. Anarchism, various forms of Marxism, and more recently existentialism are all expressions of the rootless, those peoples set adrift by history who have nevertheless become articulate. The Jewish writer was among the first to speak from this void.

The Jew is the mythic wanderer, but the American Jew is the one who has forgotten where he wandered from. The American Jew has no longing for Israel and possibly only an intellectual sympathy with it. He has little or no cultural memory of the religion or of the tradition. All he has is the invisible yellow badge, which still shows up in certain lights. This badge, this psychology of self-consciousness, makes the Jew want to be absolutely visible. He insists on his identification. He is the opposite of Ellison's "invisible man." If the Jew does not stick out like a sore thumb he is very restless. Hence all these books by and about Jews. Why does the Irishman James Joyce choose a poor, uninteresting Jew to be his main character in *Ulysses*? Because Leopold Bloom not only has a faulty memory of his fabulous past as a Hebrew but is lost. Bloom is a symbol of the modern bourgeois drifter. He doesn't belong in Ireland or anywhere else. He is cultural ectoplasm.

In America we are all cultural ectoplasm; and the Jew can stick out his sore thumb, look in a mirror, and say like Job: Whence cometh thou?

What is the fascination for the Jewish-American writer today? It is the fascination of the American for one of his own type, the man who at last debates with himself the question, What does it mean to be a Jew, an American, a Negro, an American Jew, an American Negro, an Afro-American, an American of Jewish descent, and so on?

What it means, of course, is that the question has been raised. The question was not raised in the nineteenth century, except perhaps by Walt Whitman. And the question refers art back to the political artifacts: Are those things real? Do they mean what I think and hope they mean? The Constitution of the United States has been backed into a corner by writers. No constitution can answer all the questions we are asking it. Every time the Constitution answers a question it asks a new one.

But American-Jewish writing is already obsolete. The Jew qua Jew is no longer a major premise in the creative equation. The Jewish writer can in effect sit back and chew his cud and watch the Negro. The Jew has achieved decolonization in America; though not by himself, it was going to happen somehow. I lived through it and even had a hand in it. Maybe I should explain that.

Very early in life I decided upon being a poet. (I won't go into the motivations of "being a poet," which are very complex and also irrelevant here.) I knew only one language, English, and so fell in love with English poetry. Falling in love with English poetry, which is still my old flame, meant living an imaginary English life. Living an imaginary English life meant living a phony life of the mind, for I was not English in any sense of the word. And living a phony life of the mind meant eventually becoming an English professor. One day, when I had learned how to write poetry, I had to make a decision about my name. Nobody in the *Oxford Book of English Verse* was named Shapiro. In fact, nobody was named Shapiro except tailors and junk dealers. What was I to do? Change my name? This was my first crisis as a poet.

In those days, believe it or not, it was impossible to get a poem published if you did not have an "Anglo-Saxon" name, but I decided to stick to my name; that decision made me "Jewish." And since I had made the decision I wrote poems about Jewishness.

My name itself had no content whatever. Most Jews' names are more recent than the last names of Negroes. That is, most Jews got names when Napoleon broke the ghetto system in Europe and the Jews either were given the names of a German or Polish town or made up one. *Shapiro* comes from a German town named Spira, I am told. I couldn't care less. So it was not the name that held me, as you might hold on to *Vanderbilt* or *R. I. Reynolds*; it was the foreignness of the word. I hung onto that; I wanted to know why my name was a kind of curse.

Years later I published a book called *Poems of a Jew.* That was when I was finally decolonized. When I printed that book I was already American. I was as rootless as a Texas millionaire with Negro and Indian blood in his veins.

When our literature got under way, it began like a census to list our cultural deaths. There was the grand gesture of Whitman like a captain on the bridge waving goodbye to the Past. There was Captain Ahab hunting down the great white "blood consciousness" and sinking the ship of white civilization along with it. There was Huck Finn, who lit out for the wilderness, running for his life, like his author, from respectability. There followed that long recital of the failure of the American hero—the epitaphs of Spoon River and Winesburg, Ohio; the brutal caricatures of the American bourgeois: the salesman, the evangelist, the politician; the corruption of pioneer and settler by the rootless materialism of the New World. Hemingway assaults the virility of the American male; Faulkner's vast gallery of Southerners portrays the decline and fall of a world under a curse—he calls it rightly the curse of slavery. Of the heroes of the American novel, only the artist is left unscathed. He is Ishmael in the cultural desert.

It is the motif of rootlessness that gives our literature its greatness to the outside world. Whatever the value of literary prizes, consider the names of Americans who have been awarded the Nobel Prize for literature: Eugene O'Neill, Pearl Buck, Hemingway, Faulkner, Steinbeck, and Eliot. These writers deal mainly with modern man in the void. If they are part of what is called the Western Tradition, they lie at the very edge of it. Each phase of American literature marks a further step away from that Tradition. As each "colonial" group in America finds its literary voice, we are moved deeper into the void. Huckleberry Finn, Ahab, Joe Christmas, Herzog—it hardly matters who the hero is; he leads us on the search for his authenticity. It is the unauthentic American artist who reaches back to the Tradition.

The Martinique writer and psychiatrist Frantz Fanon says in his book *The Wretched of the Earth* that when the African native "begins to pull on his moorings, and to cause anxiety to the settler, he is handed over to well-meaning souls who in cultural congresses point out to him the specificity and wealth of Western values." And he adds: "But every time Western values are mentioned they produce in the native a sort of stiffening or muscular lockjaw."

The Culture Conference or Congress is a twentieth-century institution which has never been looked at squarely. I myself make it a point to avoid those conferences, but I have attended enough of them here and abroad to know that they represent a more or less official machine dedicated to the status quo. They seek to hold the line for traditional values. For this reason the Culture Conference is supported by government, by foundations, and by writers and artists who have a stake in the tradition. The Culture Conference is opposed to decolonization, at least the decolonization of culture. The hidden premise on which it operates is the superiority of European culture. It must therefore work hard to reconvert the "native" and bring him back to a sense of cultural inferiority. I once attended one of these conferences in Tokyo, where it was agreed beforehand that politics could not be discussed. Here were a multitude of writers from all over the world, among them some of the most famous and some of the most political, who voluntarily emasculated all discussion at the outset. Instead they talked about the art of translation.

A few years ago you could ask in all seriousness: Is a Negro literature possible in America? The question implied a negative. I am among those who felt that the Negro had nothing to gain by becoming literary, that he had nothing to say according to the tradition of letters as we know this tradition. He could only create a pseudo-literature, the novel and poem according to Uncle Tom. We had seen this happen with Paul Laurence Dunbar and the early slave poets. Between a transliterated Negro dialect (itself a phony dialect) and *Oxford Book* English there seemed no choice. If there were to be an authentic Negro medium, where would it come from? Obviously it could not come from the standard classics of American literature, poetry, or prose. Perhaps something could rise from the church spiritual, a form of poetry which worked upon secret levels of meaning, or more likely from the blues. But almost nothing of the sort appeared to be happening. A literature is not created in a vacuum; it is created out of love for its medium. Could and should the Negro love the Anglo-American language? Or was it possible that he had his own version of it, as the Jewish writer had his?

But a literature is more than a version of language; a novel or poem is more than a work of art. Literature is an accurate transcription of the quality of thought and feeling of the writer and his people. What audience would such a literature have, if any? Was there a Negro audience to read *Native Son* or *Invisible Man* or Tolson's *Libretto*? You suspected that there wasn't, that such works would be for a small white or "mixed" audience. The publication of *Native Son* was a great shock to the white reader, not only because of what it said but because a Negro had written it. Negroes didn't produce works of that caliber, nor did they read them. Literature, so the mythos went, was white man's business.

Even the books by Richard Wright were in the white tradition; his audience was the traditional audience, as were the values implicit in the work. Ellison's *Invisible Man*, which I wrote about elsewhere as the Great American Novel, is a masterpiece, but again in the white tradition. Ellison might even be called a white Negro. Neither what he says nor how he says it is without precedent in the general literary consciousness. Like Wright he corroborates the white liberal's worst fears; like Wright he illuminates the guilt of the settler vis-à-vis the native. In fact, it seems to me there is more *negritude*, if I may use the word, in Faulkner than in either Wright or Ellison. Faulkner is better able to present the sensibility of the Negro, albeit the Mississippi Negro, because Faulkner's characters are not always at the point of dramatic crisis.

What Wright and Ellison proved was that the Negro can write a novel as good as a white novel, as good as anything in the Tradition. But this obviously was not enough. Especially as the Tradition was beginning to come apart at the seams. For a Negro literature to come into being, it had to start from the bottom, not from the top.

At some time in its career a people makes a decision to embrace the art of writing. It has no obligation to at any time. The Jews produced virtually no literature after the Old Testament except commentaries. The Jews were in a state of cultural withdrawal all during the diaspora. Scholars will disagree but cannot convince me that the Jews produced any literature or art or music worth mentioning until the great revolutions of the eighteenth and nineteenth centuries freed the Jew from cultured bondage. It is in our century that the Jew has suddenly begun to sing and paint and write, for this is the century of cultural liberation all over the world. Ours is one of the greatest periods of art in history, and it is great insofar as we have broken with the Tradition. To break with the Tradition does not mean to annihilate it; it means to place new values upon it. It means to pick up the pieces and maybe throw them down again. Malraux means this when he says about the greatness of modern art: The fragment is king.

The greatness as well as the horror of the twentieth century is that it is a last judgment. It is a time when every value is called into question everywhere and on every level of the human experience. It is the genius of our age to question.

The racial revolutions of our age are more effects than causes. They are the result of universal indignation over the failures of our culture. One country famed for its music and its philosophers tried to destroy a whole nation in its midst by murder. Another country famed for poetry discovered that it held a large part of the world in virtual slavery. Another country famed for its sense of liberty and its adoration of the arts suddenly collapsed from internal weakness and corruption. These were all European countries of great antiquity. In the East rose a superpolice state with a paranoid belief in its historical destiny. In America we assembled and exploded the ultimate weapon.

For many years I have been trying to loosen the hold of the academic or "colonial" mind over poetry. It encourages a poetry as well as an entire literature of reference, the kind that refers back in every case to prior commitments, historical, religious, or philosophical. In a sense it is a useless battle; attacking the Establishment only tends to strengthen it. It would be better to ignore the existence of the literature of reference and to create whatever we think valid than to go on tilting at windmills. This is what the Beat writers did; they were successful because they refused to take part in the academic dialogue. If someone asked one of the usual deathly questions, such as "What is the role of the artist in the modern world?" they would be likely to answer something like "Fried shoes." Refusal to "play the game" kept them safe. Refusal to play the game won freedom for India and is winning freedom for the American South. Refusal to play the game will turn the dehumanized "multiversity" back into a place of learning.

The importance of the Negro writer in the world today is far out of proportion to the number of books we have to go by. But the significance of Negro writing today is paramount because everywhere, not simply in America, the Negro is in the position to ask the questions. The "hyphenated" Jewish writer is no more. Time has solved that problem. The Jewish writer either is assimilated into the modern bourgeois world with all its neuroses or is a settler in the biblical land, carrying on skirmishes against the Philistines or the Egyptians as in the days of old. A few American Jews try to keep alive the mystique of the diaspora, but with little success. Most modern Jews themselves reject the myth of the dispersion for our time. They go to Israel and have a look and then hurry back to Detroit or Omaha. Today the American Negro faces the same dilemma; Wright, Ellison, Baldwin, Tolson know that Mother Africa is not for them. And the Africans know it too.

Everywhere decolonization is taking place we find the disappointment of the visitor who feels rejected from his dream. But this is part of the awakening, part of the process of freedom itself. If the African looks down on the American Negro, he has earned that right. If the Afro-American feels out of place in Nigeria or even Liberia, he knows at last the limits of his dream.

We can witness at the moment three phases of decolonization in our culture: *nostalgia, assimilation,* and *negritude. Nostalgia* is homesickness not for the good old days but for the bad old days. *Assimilation* means a cultural entente at the expense of any mystique. *Negritude* means assertion of the realities, historical and "mystical" as well.

The early literature of America, all of it, is nostalgic for the worst. It is as true of Anne Bradstreet as of Phillis Wheatley. And in fact the masses of people at any time fear the heavy responsibilities of freedom and pine for the bad old days when all choices were made for them. Not to have to choose is a freedom, the freedom of the slave. The Negro poets who cultivated a "slave" dialect were in fact in accord with their condition; they consented to the cultural authority of the white "prosody," as the white colonials acceded to the cultural authority of the Old World.

But assimilation too is nostalgic. It was often said of German Jews before Hitler that they were more German than the Germans. Which didn't stop Hitler from rooting them out. The nostalgia of the American-Jewish writer who is assimilated into American literature is curious. I was talking with a famous American writer who had made Jewishness the theme in his books. Speaking of the new Jews, the Israelis, he said: "But they aren't Jews any more!" I agreed. Those new Jews had lost their consciousness of the diaspora; they had fought their way back into the mythical homeland and were lost to the old Jewry. But cultural assimilation of Jews into American life was relatively easy and has all but been accomplished. A Jew does not have the problem of the Hindu, the Oriental, or the Negro; the Jew looks more or less "American" anywhere he goes; even his name is not held against him as it once was. But cultural assimilation also means national oblivion for the nation assimilated. You can only pretend to act like a Jew; the writer or artist can do this easily because that is his business. The American Jew of average sensibility, on the other hand, experiences the common cultural amnesia of Americans of any extraction. While the American-Jewish figure in fiction has a cultural nervous breakdown over American twentieth-century values, he longs for the bad old days when his father was a bootlegger or a peddler because he was suffering the crucifixion of the culturally underprivileged; the father would do anything to keep his family Jews, to turn them into doctors and lawyers or rich merchants. With economic freedom they could then be Jews. Only it didn't work that way, for Jewishness meant suffering, and an unsuffering Jew was an anomaly. An unsuffering Jew is a goy. Hence the nostalgia of the assimilated.

The Negro is luckier; he can never disappear from his condition in the Caucasian world any more than a Hindu or a Japanese. There he is, unassimilable and un-nostalgic, the biggest fact of life in the modern world.

Our century is very great because with us all the chickens have come home to roost, because great men of goodwill—statesmen, presidents, leaders of men, artists, and young people—have demanded the exaction of promises made to nations by visionaries and the spokesmen of freedom. This is happening under our eyes; we are all a party to it. Nostalgia is obsolete. Assimilation may well be. Neither is of vital importance. I prefer the idea of negritude. At least it is the first great idea or concept that can deal with the biggest fact of modern life without trying to water it down.

I will give three examples: Aimé Césaire, Léopold Senghor, and M. B. Tolson. Césaire is a Caribbean, Senghor is a Senegalese, and Tolson was born in Missouri. The first two use French for poetry; Tolson uses English or American. (My designation of Tolson's language is that he writes in Negro.)

Or rather, all three of these great poets write in Negro. That is what negritude means in literature. It does not mean accommodation to the standards of the settler or to his nostalgia for the mother or father country. It does not mean making peace through disappearance into the scene; nor, as Senghor has shown in his political writings, does it mean war. It means insistence on the pride of selfhood without hatred. No oppressed people in history has had less sense of revenge than the Negro. Retribution is not Negro.

Negritude is simply decolonization under the positive aspect. Senghor has no grudge against the Tradition (as I do) or against modern technology. On the contrary, he welcomes everything that will make possible greater harmony among men. This is the wisdom of the French in the decolonized man, the daring of the French to push an idea into action as far as it will go. There are, I believe, no African poets of the English language of his stature. The English are still the heirs of apartheid.

Césaire's discovery of negritude—he is pinned as the inventor of the name—is that of the disaffected assimilationist, the Parisian from the colonies who became a Marxist and by nomination a surrealist, even though surrealism is a luxury of the white civilization, a toy of people who can afford unconsciousness. It is also a desperate attempt to rejoin civilized brilliance with a *raison d'être*. Surrealism is an adrenaline shot in the heart under superb cultural conditions. It revives a culture which does not really want to live. Césaire, as I understand it, did not rise to the bait when André Breton elected him to the surrealist school. I am not criticizing surrealism, which is of fundamental value in all modern arts; I am pointing out the naiveté of the French in enlisting colonials in aesthetic causes which were far from the realities of the African or the American Negro.

Negritude in the famous poem *"Cahier d'un Retour au Pays Natale"* ("Memorandum on My Martinique" is one translation)—negritude is the realization of pity for the modern world with its great inventions and its great alibis. It shouts hurrah not for the "steel blue speed" of the modern but for those who have never invented anything:

> Hurrah for those who never invented anything
> Hurrah for those who never explored anything
> Hurrah for those who never conquered anything

I know of only one American poet who in genius and experience even approaches the concept—M. B. Tolson. And Tolson knows that the concept is different with us. In American culture, according to the ground rules, there can be no separatism even by race and color. What then? Is there a long road of assimilation and miscegenation ahead? Can there be an American negritude?

Tolson is an American who was also the Poet Laureate of Liberia. He lived in Oklahoma in an all-Negro town where he was twice mayor. In various capacities as editor, I have published more poetry by him than anyone in America. He has a superb reputation among a few poets and critics but is unknown to students and to the general reading public. This is not because he is difficult to read (which he is), for difficulty of text is the stock-in-trade of the poetry-teaching profession. *Tolson is not read because he was a Negro.* A blind spot in the white literary eye will not recognize a great Negro poet.

To complicate matters, Tolson's *Libretto for the Republic of Liberia*, commissioned by the first African republic, has in its American publication an introduction by Allen Tate. He sees Tolson as an exception because "for the first time . . . a Negro poet has assimilated completely the poetic language of his time and, by implication, the language of the Anglo-American tradition." Tate is one of the canniest critics in the business, the American T. S. Eliot, as it were. But the crux of the matter is that Tate says: ". . . the distinguishing Negro quality is not in the language but in the subject matter . . . ," for subject matter can only deal with your suffering and contaminate the beauty of poetry.

I have tried to counter this statement in my own introduction to Tolson's recently published *Harlem Gallery*. Tate considers that the use of Negro subject matter in poetry, which he calls "the tragic aggressiveness of the modern poet," limits the Negro poet to a "provincial mediocrity." But in trying to assert that Tolson has been assimilated by the Anglo-American tradition, he puts Tolson in quarantine and destroys the value of the poem—possibly this critic's conscious intention. Thus it took a Southern intellectual and poet to introduce Tolson's *Libretto*. That was the only possible literary context for a great Negro poet ten or fifteen years ago: he must in that context be captured and returned to colonization, to that Tradition which had enslaved his ancestors and would continue to do so if it could manage it.

The refusal to see that Tolson's significance lies in his language, Negro, and that only that language can express the poetic sensibility of the Negro at the door of freedom, is a final desperate maneuver to contain the Negro within the traditional culture. And for that it is too late. The Tradition is already antebellum.

The falsification I speak of is that of trying to assimilate Tolson into the Tradition when he was doing the opposite. The fact that Tolson's *Libretto* is unknown by white traditionalists gives the lie to the critic's assertion that Tolson has risen above Negro experience to become an "artist." The facts are that Tolson is a dedicated revolutionist who revolutionizes modern poetry in a language of American negritude. The forms of the *Libretto* and of *Harlem Gallery*, far from being "traditional," are the Negro satire upon the poetic tradition of the Eliots of our age. The tradition cannot stand being satirized and lampooned and so tries to kick an authentic poet upstairs into the oblivion of acceptance. But the Negro artist won't stay in the attic any more than he stayed in the cellar.

Tolson says it better in his big poem:

> The Great White World
> and the Black Bourgeoisie
> have shoved the Negro artist into
> the white and not-white dichotomy,
> the Afroamerican dilemma in the Arts—
> the dialectic of
> to be or not to be
> a Negro.

This essay stops at the threshold of the Black Revolution or the Black Recoil or whatever it is called. I prefer to think of it as a Black Apartheid, a deliberate withdrawal into racism for whatever gains it can produce. I doubt whether any non-black critic can deal with this phenomenon, not this early, at any rate.

THE JEWISH WRITER
IN AMERICA

IN THE COURSE of writing these chapters and delivering them as public lectures I made the awful discovery that I must define my Jewishness to the reader. What has being a Jew got to do with literary criticism? Quite a bit, evidently. The mere act of defending oneself against the shallow Jew-baiting of Pound or the profound racism of Eliot constitutes a "position." And insofar as I have a position, it is bound to be something of a "Jewish position." Even while I was delivering these notes as lectures I was accused of criticizing modern poetry on "Jewish" grounds. A philosophy professor conspicuously stalked out of the crowded hall where I was speaking unfavorably of Eliot; he gave it out later that my remarks about Eliot's Anglo-Catholicism offended him personally. The unphilosophical departure of this gentleman paved the way for the criticism which I heard frequently later on—my quarrel with the Pound-Eliot school was a *Jewish* quarrel. Against this accusation I must defend my book. And for the sake of my "religious" readers I must spell out my Jewishness, such as it is.

One of the chief strategic triumphs of the new Classicism has been its ability to quash the opposition, whether literary, sociological, or religious. Eliot carefully flattered the conservative mind in government, in philosophy, and in religion. Pound flattered the sense of culture aristocracy and the political authoritarianism which goes hand in hand with the religion of culture. The anti-Americanism of both writers is of that variety which connects commercialism with "mass taste" and "freethinking." What Eliot calls the freethinking Jew, Pound calls the international Jewish banker. Indeed, it is the medieval image of the Jew as Shylock and Christ-killer which the Classicists perpetuate in the twentieth century. And, miraculous to report, the intellectual Jewish writers do not resist this image but tend to accept it guiltily! I refer particularly to the Jewish editors of cultural journals who purvey Marxist-Freudian anti-Semitism (in the belief that a Jewish identity is an historical anachronism) and I refer to the many Jewish professors of literature who are "new critics" and who thereby deprive themselves of any humanitarian standard of judgment. A book of verse I published last year called *Poems of a Jew* was most bitterly assailed by Jewish New Critics, while the nonintellectual Jewish press tended to accept the poems as an awkward but serious expression of modern Jewishness.

The intellectual faction among Jewish professors, critics, and editors has been led quietly by the nose into the Pound-Eliot preserve. They were content to accept the Culture religion which in Eliot's criticism apparently subsumed any actual religion. They were content to accept Eliot's second-hand ideas of "pluralistic culture" which apparently subsumed mere nationalisms. Thus it was precisely the "freethinkers" whom Eliot despised who became his staunchest defenders. And those intellectuals who were not captivated by Eliot's version of the Tradition were taken in by his esthetic of the "objectivity" of the work of art. Even a critic as political in his thinking as F. O. Matthiessen convinced himself that it was somehow indecent to expose Eliot's beliefs to view. So holy was Eliot's reputation as poet, thinker, and man that criticism of his work became the chief taboo in twentieth-century literature. William Carlos Williams alone dared attack the master. And for a Jew to raise his voice against Pound, Eliot, or Hulme was considered an act of savagery by the New Criticism and the New Pedagogy. It is extraordinary how much the defense of Pound has been placed on a hypocritical "Christian" footing. With what relief the intellectuals seized on the trashy and meretricious canto about humility to prove old Ezra's purity of heart. Pound on the throne of humility evidently cancels out Pound as the Great Dictator.

As a twentieth-century American writer I grew up to respect the British literary tradition above all others and to share in the famous American "guilt" about our own heritage. As a Jew I was misled by Jewish intellectuals, ex-Marxists and Freudians, to minimize and even accept the fashionable anti-Americanism and anti-Semitism of the Moderns. In all probability I would never have been led to examine the ideas of these Moderns had I not been driven to do so—by participating in the Pound affair over the Bollingen Prize, and by having to teach modern poetry. Whatever Jewish consciousness I possess today I can trace to the writings of the American Classicists who made it their business to equate "American" and "Jew" as twin evils. This consciousness of myself as American Jew restricted and narrowed my writing for many years, erecting a private ghetto in my mind. To break out of this ghetto is one of the reasons for writing this book.

There is no Jewish writer *per se* in America. But the American writer, generally speaking, does not mention his ancestry, even if he happens to know what it is. The American writer tends to cut himself off from his past and even to deride it. There are exceptions, of course—the Henry Jameses and the Eliots—but most American writers favor the approach of Mark Twain: that dukes, kings, and ancestors are flotsam and jetsam one would do better to steer clear of. A poet from an old New England family wrote me when he saw my book *Poems of a Jew* and said, "You go back so much farther than I do!" He said this almost with a kind of envy, I thought. Then he added cryptically: "You write like an Arab," one of the strangest compliments I have ever had. At least, I think it was a compliment.

It is only in the last generation or two that an American Jew could write Jewishly and still be thought of as an American. Twenty years ago, when I was beginning to write for publication, I wrote an American poet whom I knew to be Jewish and asked him what obstacles one had to overcome to publish poems under a Jewish name. His reply was so ambiguous that I decided his own name wasn't very Jewish after all. I was not imagining things: many years later a non-Jewish poet said to me: "When I first saw your poems I thought you had an impossible name for a poet." This remark did not indicate anti-Semitism or anything of the sort, but it suggests the persistence of the British tradition in American letters until a very late date. In this respect I feel I have done a little pioneer work for American writers: changing of names has always shocked me deeply, even though it has always been a common practice among writers. But in poetry or

any other art, the question of race or religion is of the highest significance. Nowadays the Jewish writer in America meets with no obstacles *qua* Jew in publication or in other forms of recognition, but this
happy circumstance only brings us closer to the question: What is an
American Jewish writer?

To me the answer is—an American Jewish writer is a Jew who is
an American who is a writer. Everybody knows what an American is;
everyone knows what a writer is; but very few people seem to know
what a Jew is, including Jews, and including American Jewish writers.

A few years ago I participated in a symposium called "The Jewish
Writer and the English Literary Tradition." It was published in *Commentary*—itself a kind of literary phenomenon: an upper-middle-class
magazine sponsored by an American Jewish organization and the
highbrow editorship of the *Partisan Review*. The question for the
symposium was this: "As a Jew and a writer in the Anglo-American
literary tradition, how do you confront the presence in that tradition
of the mythical . . . figure of the Jew as found in the (anti-Semitic)
writings of Chaucer, Marlowe, Shakespeare, Scott, T. S. Eliot, Evelyn
Waugh, Thomas Wolfe, Henry Adams, etc. In what way do you find
this a problem to you? etc."

Reading between the lines, I took the question to mean: Do you
think the Jew will be able to break into high literary society? That is,
we were given a sociological question, one in which any element of a
Jewish *mystique* was distinctly absent. And the replies also struck me
as sociological, or, as we say more often, rationalistic. The replies ran
along these lines:

(*a*) The Jew defends a pluralistic culture; therefore he is attacked
as "international." (The term "pluralistic" has been popularized by
T. S. Eliot, whom most of the symposium felt it necessary to bow to
in passing.) (*b*) Anti-Semitism is pathological, a disease like the black
plague, and just as medieval. Get a well-doctored society and it will
disappear. (*c*) Jews are also secretly anti-Semitic, parochial, and self-
pitying. Let the Jewish writer be *more* cosmopolitan. (*d*) Writers like
Eliot really love the Jews, but you must learn how to take insults. (*e*)
Is anti-Semitism really real? (Stephen Spender answered this way.) If
a Jew didn't know he was a Jew he wouldn't think he was a Jew.

The summation of the other approaches was by Philip Rahv, an honest and ruthless logician. What we must do, said Rahv, is to "conduct a struggle against the new religiosity, along with those non-Jewish intellectuals who refuse to abandon the progressive and secular outlook. This . . . religiosity tends to divide rather than unite humanity; it is historically vacuous and metaphysically permeated with nostalgia . . ."

The best statement made in this list of responses was by Harold Rosenberg, who put his finger on the weakness of the question itself. Rosenberg noted that to move from a personification like Shylock to the sociological cliché is a serious mistake. For instance, some German critic sees *The Merchant of Venice* with the repulsive Shylock and writes a review that says in effect: Down with the Jews. Thus Shylock becomes the Jew-with-the-knife and an instrument for political propaganda. As a result the Jew tends to blame Shakespeare for anti-Semitism.

To me the symposium was meaningless because it took for granted that religion is obsolescent, and racism the product of religion. The writers who took part in it seemed to be saying that religion is evil but Culture is good (whatever Culture is). Let's save Culture and get rid of religion.

My own answer was this: We are Jews by popular consent of the Jewish-Christian community and not by choice or ambition. We accept our Jewishness because to reject it would be a betrayal not of our electors but of ourselves. In the same way I felt when I was conscripted that to avoid military duty would have been a betrayal of my identity as an American. If this is negative Americanism then I can also call myself a negative Jew. But my election to America and to Israel gives me my total identity, the kind of identity which has never been permitted to survive in all of Europe's history.

The most curious aspect of this affair is that the Jews who are recognized writers of one kind or another shrink back from Judaism but defend, however half-heartedly, their right to be Jews. In a sense they would welcome the extinction of the Jewish religion as long as they could maintain their identity as Jews. How this can be done in actuality is beyond me. And what sense it would make is also beyond me. I read somewhere that a Christian writer asked a Jew what it was to be a Jew. The Jew answered: We are a religion. This is a beautiful answer and a true one, but perhaps not true enough. We are even more than a religion.

Our symposium people seemed to interpret the expression "American Jewish writer" to mean one who infused into the American idiom something of the Jewish idiom or of Jewish psychology. To me this is trivial; and in any case the American idiom is a vast complex of such idioms, all of which are tending toward the making of a great national (American) literature. A brilliant novel like Saul Bellow's *The Adventures of Augie March* is saturated with Jewish witticisms and sentiments; the very language seems almost a transliteration of—what? I can't read Yiddish but I recognize the idiom. And the American reader need not know of the presence of this element in Bellow's writing, for by now it is as much American as it is Jewish. What is really Jewish in Bellow lies much deeper: it is the poetry of the Jew that makes his hero what he is, in Chicago, in Mexico, wherever Augie happens to be. Bellow has translated Singer's story "Gimpel the Fool" from Yiddish. It is one of the most side-splitting and yet painful tales I have ever read, but it might have been written in New York instead of Poland, or wherever it came from. This is Jewishness far beyond culture, social problems, history, and the rest. It is even beyond religion, as far as I can see.

Sociological Judaism seems to me completely pointless; and the preservation of national memory for its own sake, mere narcissism. The business of the Jewish writer is not to complain about society but to rise above such complaints. Nearly all social protest literature is superficial anyhow; the greater realities of difference lie below the bickerings of ideologists. I would say there are two kinds of Jewish American literature, the kind recommended by our symposium—a psychologically Judaistic literature—and the real kind, which I would recommend: a God-centered literature. That is a poor way of putting it but I will try to explain what I mean.

A merely Judaistic literature is only a kind of "regional" literature, even though this "region" takes in most of the world and all of history. In such literature the Jew may be good or bad, Shylock or the Wandering Jew or Leopold Bloom, but he is simply a man of memory, an anachronism. He is not the Jew who "lives life," as Martin Buber puts it. He is the Jew of the past, the Jew of the Wailing Wall.

Recently I read a new *Oxford Book of Irish Verse* and was struck by the centuries-old struggle of the Irish poets to regain their Irishness, to throw off the cosmopolitanism of the world-writer and to renew that particular consciousness which is not a "cultural heritage" but an identity. In the case of the Irish I can sense only dimly what that identity is. But in the case of the Jew I know what it is. The Jewish writer everywhere in the modern world has the problem of regaining the Jewish consciousness, which in our case is God-consciousness. I am not talking about religion; religion is only a by-product of this consciousness. For the Jewish writer who wants to turn his back on this consciousness we can only give him our blessing and let him go. But for the consciously Jewish writer in America or anywhere else we must recognize his obligation to establish this consciousness centrally in his work, the right, so to speak, of the existence of God. If this encourages religious progress that may be to the good; but I am not talking about religion. I am opposed to all organized religion, including Judaism.

Jewish creative intelligence has been driven into by-paths for centuries. We are just beginning to return to the era of Jewish philosophy, but our abstract thinking generally still belongs to the Middle Ages. We produce an Einstein, who from the religious or even political viewpoint is a baby. We produce a Freud who foists upon the world a surrogate religion while striving mightily to destroy both Christianity and Judaism in one breath. The fantastic intellectual powers of the Jews of our time go into everything under the sun except Jewish consciousness, or to use a really lofty word, holiness.

The Jews have written one of the greatest holy books. And that book is the beginning and the end of our literature. Jewish literature is not great. Jewish philosophy is not great. Jewish scholarship—perhaps. Our contributions to science, government, law and the humane knowledges, even the arts of music, and in our lifetime, painting, have been advanced by Jews. But the great arts of the written word have not been advanced by the people of the book. Not to any significant degree.

Our friends of the symposium on the Jewish writer in the United States were more interested in setting up fresh literary symbols than they were in understanding a religion or in seeking the *mystique* back of it. Consequently I think of them as literary social climbers and not poets.

As far as one can tell these things, there are only two countries in the world where the Jewish writer is free to create his own consciousness: Israel and the United States. Everywhere else the Jew seems to live on the past. Even Proust's re-creation of consciousness is a kind of Jewish nostalgia. In Europe it is either nostalgia or nightmare: Proust or Kafka. The European Jew was always a visitor and knew it. But in America everybody is a visitor. In this land of permanent visitors the Jew is in a rare position to "live the life" of a full Jewish consciousness. The Jews live a fantastic historical paradox: we are the spiritual aborigines of the modern world, and we are the ethical and sometimes intellectual conscience of the modern world. History has hated us so deeply because every Jew is regarded as a living witness of the Christian and Muslim revelations—which he is. The Jewish assumption of holiness and his rather *laissez faire* attitude toward religion make him a natural target in almost any historical situation. Only in America (as the expression goes) can the Jew be a natural Jew. There are fewer religious tensions in America than any place else in history—the national tendency to vulgarize religion and to experiment with new sects has allowed the American Jew to relax—to emerge from the historical consciousness to a contemporary Jewish consciousness.

I was speaking of the creative man and by that I mean not only the poet or novelist, painter or composer but the mystic and saint. Our rational modern upbringing prevents us from even thinking of God. In our time we say or think that God is for women and children. We go to houses of worship possibly, but only because it is too troublesome not to. Now, the true writer and mystic does not ransack the storehouse of religion for literary plunder; rather he adds to the spiritual storehouse. He does not take; he gives. He may never even go near a synagogue or church, and in many cases in the past he has been forbidden to enter the official house of prayer. Poets and mystics are always having the door slammed in their faces; especially the church door.

This full Jewish consciousness which is today possible in America as in Israel is a way of life, so to speak. And it does not necessarily involve ritual or anything of the sort, though it may in some cases. It does not involve piety and may in fact involve the exact opposite. I am paraphrasing the modern Jewish philosopher, Martin Buber—I hope I am not corrupting what he means. He says: "The true hallowing of man is the hallowing of the human in him . . . In life, as Hasidism [Jewish mysticism] understands and proclaims it, there is no essential distinction between sacred and profane spaces, between sacred and profane times, between sacred and profane actions, between sacred and profane conversations." I am not sure how many Jews accept this kind of belief, but I suppose very few. All the same, in my ignorance of my own religion, it seems to me the very core of Jewish consciousness. It is antiascetic and joyous—the Hasidim dance wildly with the Torah. "Man," says Buber, "cannot approach the divine by reaching beyond the human; but he can approach Him through becoming human." In the last century, when rationalism touched everything, a doctrine like this was thought of as the wildest superstition. To me it is like a breath of fresh air. It is the highest form of Humanism.

What does this have to do with the problem of the American Jewish writer? Nothing, probably. And yet I see a striking similarity between this mystical humanism and American secular humanism. It matters very little whether the American Jewish poet or novelist writes *about* the American Jew (the good artist is seldom that self-conscious anyway); it even matters little whether he lives as a Jew in the conventional sense of "living as"; what does matter is that he accept the consequences of Jewishness. He cannot escape them in any event, and I do not think he should *suffer* these consequences but revel in them.

The Jewish writer is presented with a kind of freedom which is almost inconceivable. The Jewish plus American combination only doubles this freedom.

Modern literature attempts to perpetuate the Jew as imaged in Christian theology and story. But this Jew is as dead as the Negro of the minstrel show. Both images come from the age of slavery. The Jew today is free in his mythological homeland Israel and free in America, the mythological homeland of freedom. Creatively he has begun to flourish as never before, nor can the medievalism of the

New Classicists prevent this flowering, as much as they fear it. Freedom in any form is anathema to modern Classicism. Even "free verse" is not really free, says the poor fettered Eliot. And the "free-thinking Jew" is, of course, a grave danger to whatever is the opposite of freedom.

THE CRITIC IN SPITE
OF HIMSELF

". . . a great deal of the best and most
sensible criticism of any age is necessarily
absurd."—RANDALL JARRELL

RANDALL JARRELL has had the last word on criticism. No one can improve on his blissful condemnation of the modern critic and the special languages and vested interests of criticism. No one has tried harder to curb some of the critic's wasteful activity. But whether he has done any good is hard to say; Jarrell is himself such a fine critic (at least when I can agree with him) that he may father a whole new family of critical minds. If he does, and if they are truly writers and not just "machines of sensibility," we may be able to see an end to the age of criticism, as he calls it. This is not very likely. We are indeed in the age of criticism and one can hardly put an end to the criticism without putting an end to the age.

I am one of that innumerable tribe of poets who was drawn into criticism at that tender age when one has published his first poems in a respectable place. I now look back on my initiation into criticism as something of a tribal investiture, for it was this ceremony that turned my hand to prose. As a writer of prose I eventually became an editor, which is to say a big brother to poets and critics. How many scores of young poets have *I* led by the hand into the kingdom of criticism. But I am not altogether sorry for it, any more than I am for my own initiation. Besides, there was nothing I could do about it. We live in a time when every swan really dreams of becoming a goose, and does.

But my own hope has always been to make poets speak openly and judge freely, without regard for established critical canons.

Please do not think I am trying to fill you in on my autobiography if I resort to personal anecdote in these remarks. I am not averse to autobiography, even in criticism, and in fact favor it over the obscurantist and dehumanized styles which we associate with the Best Criticism. No one has ever referred to me as one of the Best Critics, but as it is an honor that I do not covet, it contents me to write the kind of criticism I do. This kind of criticism has its own very high goals, although it may not be recognizable as the thing we are accustomed to call literary criticism. It strikes me that my career as a critic is little short of fantastic, and I want to mention why, if only to point out the high place criticism has attained as a public or cultural function. I say my *career* as a critic—comical phrase—and not my criticism itself.

My criticism, and not my poetry, has carried me around the world several times, though I detest long journeys. I have lectured on *Leaves of Grass* in Dublin and in Calcutta, on William Carlos Williams in Hyderabad, on Edgar Lee Masters in Salzburg and on free verse in Tokyo. Last winter an admiral called me from the Pentagon to ask me to fly to the Antarctic, on three days' notice, to talk to our troops about modern poetry. As a critic I live in a Salvador Dali universe. As a poet I live in Lincoln, Nebraska. In addition to these voyages through time and space in behalf of criticism, all my jobs may be traced to my prose, though my poems may have had something to do with it. My first teaching job was given me, I am convinced, because of a lecture in which I took issue with George Saintsbury on seven or eight points of foot prosody. Looking back on this lecture, I see it as a kind of exercise in literary hypnotism in which I mesmerized myself as well as my audience.

I could go on listing the literary juries and such bodies on which I have served as critic, not as poet; the Foundations which have employed my critical acumen to help them get rid of their money; and even the publishers who have consulted me about new works of criticism in manuscript (I have usually advised no publication, only to receive the printed book a couple of months later).

You must be thinking what a gay life the critic leads—why, it's like a mixture of Lord Byron, Admiral Byrd, and V. I. Lenin crossing the

Eastern Front in a sealed train! And it is. The life of the critic has
long since taken the place of the life of the poet. There are no Byrons
in the twentieth century; only poor bedeviled Dylan Thomases, who
would rather crouch behind the decanter or dive from the Golden
Gate Bridge than answer highbrow questions about their poems.
Only those and the poet-critics, as some unfeeling lexicographer calls
us. I wonder if it has ever occurred to the poet of our time that his audience prefers his criticism to his poetry because his poetry may be
lacking in something? Is this possible? People, after all, are going to
have literature in some form, and if criticism is all they can get, they
will have criticism. We hear of no critics in Shakespeare's day: maybe
one or two, but nobody who would be invited to address, say, a meeting of the National Council of the Teachers of English.

We must admit the sociological position which criticism has
achieved in our time, while we are trying to wean our writers away
from it. It is no accident that criticism occupies the place of honor
among the modern literary arts. And it is no exaggeration to say that
poetry is the weakest of the arts in the twentieth century because it is
a criticism-ridden art—hardly an art at all. Criticism is an attitude of
mind, not simply a method of elucidation. It is what remains when
literature itself has begun to expire. Criticism flourishes when literature has failed; is not this tragically true even in the case of the individual writer? But this axiom would signify that twentieth-century
literature is not the richly manifold art we tell ourselves it is. Is it time
we re-examined modern poetry? Is it possible that modern criticism is
only a handsome façade concealing a terrible poverty? Are criticism
and poetry really one and the same in our time?

You will recognize that the position I take is that of the anti-
intellectual, as sorry as the name may sound. My criticism has tried to
be anti-intellectual from the beginning, although a couple of times I
have been jockeyed into attacks on my own beliefs. What is an anti-
intellectual? The best way to define it is through its opposite. An intellectual is a person who reduces all experience to abstract ideas. He
need not be a writer, of course, or an artist of any kind. If an intellectual should come home and find his house in flames, he might rush
into the burning building to save his manuscripts or his record player
or even his children (for intellectuals are frequently men of action),

but he will be thinking all the time of the complexities of megalopolitan life or of Euripides' *Medea*, or something of that kind. The intellectual cannot experience anything without *thinking* about it. It was the intellectual whom Lawrence loathed above all modern creatures, and Lawrence was right. The Spanish intellectual Ortega once made the penetrating remark that the intellectual is not necessarily intelligent.

Very likely I am not a true anti-intellectual, only a lowbrow highbrow. The true anti-intellectual would not be writing an essay against criticism (and I have written many), nor would he be quoting Ortega; he would be sure to avoid him. But it is virtually impossible for a twentieth-century writer not to turn into an intellectual. Every inducement will be held out to him to "philosophize" upon his experience, to abstract it and turn it into cold, calculating prose. "You have only to tell us how you wrote that poem," says the intellectual to the unsuspecting poet, "and we will pay your electric bill for life." The poet today is, as everyone is uncomfortably aware, the hostage of the intellectual. Intellectual, of course, is a synonym for critic. So the battle against intellectualism must be waged by people like me, in the hope that others may be spared.

The word *intellectual* has never taken root in America and to this day remains a foreign concept. This is curious when you consider that modern intellectual criticism, like modern poetry itself, is largely the invention of a few expatriated Americans. In Europe or in Asia the term *intellectual* is highly respectable; in America it still remains a term of derision. Modern criticism, however, has gone a long way to make the term and the thing respectable in this country, and it is the business of the anticritic to deride intellectualism wherever it raises its head. In Europe the term also refers to a social class and not simply to the individual. The Russians use the term as a class distinction. Marx used it so, as did his followers. The intellectual class is as much a part of Marxist society as the proletariat. And similarly, outside Russia, the European intellectuals form a class and hold hands across vast ideological chasms. For what they have in common is the reduction of social and historical experience to Criticism with a capital C (using that word in all its iridescent aspects at once). It amused me a couple of years ago to see two well-known literary critics, one a

Catholic and the other a Marxist, dedicating their books to one another. No two writers could have less in common ideologically, but
what they did have in common was Ideology itself. The modern critic
has pulled criticism up by the boot straps to a position of cultural
power which in the twentieth century is staggering. No wonder all
those bright young men want to be critics, junior executives in the international culture conference of ideology. These intellectuals tell
themselves and the world that they are responsible for the social, esthetic, and even spiritual "values" of the age. They are value experts
all down the line. They have abolished the idea that esthetic values
are established by works of art alone and that social and religious values—what colorless terminologies they have put in our mouths—are
established by humanity, not by critics. Literary criticism hardly exists in our time; what we really have is culture criticism or theology ill
concealed. The critic today uses literature only as a vehicle for ideas;
he has bigger fish to fry than poets. The most insignificant book reviewer is really a social psychologist *in parvo*. Give him half a chance
and he will turn into an Arnold Toynbee or an Oswald Spengler or an
Ezra Pound overnight and regale you with theories of history that
will make your head spin.

If what I have said is true, we are dealing with a question of honesty. It is my contention that modern criticism is not honest, though
it may be sincere. Its dishonesty results from its undying loyalty to
generalities. I will give you an example. Ezra Pound in several places
decries the poetry of Shakespeare because it does not fit his system of
great books. This is typically the case with intellectual criticism.
Pound knows as well as you do that Shakespeare is the finest of all
English poets, but he must remain sincere to the system he has
blocked out. He thus engages in a fantastic act of dishonesty. Eliot
did the same with Milton and with dozens of other poets. Because of
some theory Eliot had about the "musicality" of verse he forbade
poets to read Milton. Eventually Eliot changed his mind, perhaps because his loyalty to Milton's puritanism finally got the better of him.
Sincerity to the idea always takes precedence in the mental life of the
intellectual, whether the idea comprises a total system or is some off-
shoot of one of the *isms*.

The honest critic has no system and stands in no dread of contradicting himself. And because he abhors systems he is in a better position to view a work of art in its wholeness and in its relations to other things. An essay like George Orwell's on Kipling is an example of honest criticism. Orwell rather dislikes Kipling and tells us why in clear English. Eliot, working from theory to fact, gives us a defense of Kipling. From what we think we know of the loftiness of Eliot's tastes this is something of a shock. Eliot admires Kipling by way of a typical act of intellectual dishonesty. He first tries to give the appeal of Kipling's kind of poetry a high-sounding name, in this case "ballad attention." Then he mentions in passing the more sophisticated forms in Anglo-Saxon, Welsh, Latin, Greek, Sanskrit, Persian, and Chinese, as if these languages have something to do with Kipling. To flatter his audience he talks about the "simple-minded," that is, people who didn't come to the lecture, and hides behind the mysteries of prosody to say something nice about "Danny Deever"! Eliot defending "Danny Deever" is a sight to behold; when he comes to the climax of the poem he says "the atmosphere has been prepared for a complete suspension of disbelief." The point is—I am not going to bog down in Eliot-on-Kipling or even Eliot—that Eliot is only *using* Kipling experimentally, in the best intellectual manner, as a guinea pig. Eliot is no more interested in Kipling than I am, but in his own ideas, such as "the willing suspension of disbelief," which Eliot adopted as one of his crucial ideas. The willing suspension of disbelief is almost as crucial to Eliot's criticism as Original Sin itself, but only one who believes in Original Sin (to paraphrase Eliot) will know what I am talking about. I don't happen to believe in it myself.

Milton is not good enough for the intellectualism of Eliot but Kipling is! The Uriah Heepishness of Eliot can almost make Kipling plausible, though not quite. Orwell, who is an honest fellow, though he got himself caught in Marxist intellectualism for a while, makes the simple observation that Kipling is a bad poet but that there are degrees of badness in poetry, just as there are degrees of goodness. Kipling, says Orwell, is a *good* bad poet. Eliot tried to arrive at something of the sort but ends up completely hamstrung in his own terminology. It is terminology that has made Eliot famous in an age of catchwords. That and Eliot's sincerity to his terminology. For Eliot does not talk about Kipling at all; he talks about Eliot talking about Kipling.

I bring up the matter of Eliot's criticism only incidentally here. What I am getting at is the difference between criticism and judgment. We have today the biggest and busiest criticism in the history of literature, but no judgment. The judgments we have are really precepts and are handed down from on high by Criticism. Most writers find out to their dismay sooner or later that the modern critic does not care about literature except as a bone of contention. To the critic, analytical or theoretical (one is bad as the other), a work of art is something that fits into a system or doesn't, and every new creation is a threat to already existing systems. It is not uncommon for the critic to complain of too much poetry in the world—if only there were!—and it is the critic who sees to it that there is only one poet recognized per decade, or whatever the quota happens to be. Modern criticism is highly orthodox, that is, based on exclusion. Nearly all such criticism deals with what it calls the elites. Now and then a Kipling is elected to the club, a writer who is admittedly rather common but who is orthodox at heart. This keeps the orthodoxy going and beefs up the blood stream.

The absence of judgment in modern criticism is beyond belief. Critics in fact no longer exercise judgment about literary works; they discourage it. They talk about poetry or fiction in terms of Myth or Symbol or Structure, anything at hand which can be intellectualized. The poem is only a conversation piece leading up to a discussion of the higher abstractions concerning society or religion. Originally, to be sure, the depersonalization of criticism was intended as a maneuver to attract attention to poetry, not to criticism. But very shortly the mightiest of tails began to wag one of the oddest-looking literary dogs ever beheld by man. Those of you who are exempt from reading modern criticism cannot begin to imagine the abdominous magnitude of this critical literature, even leaving out the textbooks and anthologies. The modem literary textbook is a thing to conjure with. Textbooks designed for the "understanding" or "exploration" of poetry have probably done more to warp the literary judgment of college students than the Collected Comic Books of the Twentieth

Century. Because they are based on the "depersonalized" view of literature and life, they all tend toward the extinction of the faculty of judgment, one of man's most vital characteristics. My experience with students who have been subjected to these dry and terrible tomes, the very paper of which seems impregnated with lead, is that they are utterly and permanently stunned into literary insensibility.

Authoritarian criticism precludes judgment; this fact is too obvious to pursue. In place of judgment this criticism sets up two barriers to judgment. The first is the morass of concepts, the second is a list of approved works (in effect an *Index Expurgatorius*). By taking over the terms of ancient rhetoric, esthetics, logic, modern anthropology and psychology and even chemistry, the critic situates himself behind impregnable walls. So situated, he can completely ignore his real job, that of discriminating between works of literature, even in the simple way Orwell does with *good* and *bad* and *good-bad*. Naturally this is a great relief to the critic. The prolonged postponement of literary judgment also leads to the creation of a hothouse poetry, the poetry especially written for the critic. A frightening quantity of modern poetry is written to the criticism; it is hothouse grown, factory made. Such poetry may even become famous, if criticism takes a shine to it.

Inferior poetry of the past can also be made a touchstone: I am thinking particularly of the Metaphysical poetry and other kinds of poetry bordering on the freakish. John Donne gives the critic much more to talk about than, say, Robert Herrick; that is the criterion. Whether Donne is as good a poet as Herrick is never discussed. If you can impress students with how complex the mind of John Donne is, you need not mention any such crucial questions as how good a poet he is. Donne, of course, is better brain food than Herrick, and the modern critic and textbook author will put a hard thinker at the top of the list any time. It looks better to people like scientists, who do practically nothing but think. I judge Donne to be a good poet about on a par with Marianne Moore, a poet who writes well only when she violates the precepts laid down for her by T. S. Eliot. One of Hart Crane's worst poems, "Voyages," appears in every comprehension and exploratory textbook. Especially "Voyages II," which has an almost religious appeal to the modern critical mentality. Nothing is ever said about the bad writing in this poem, which ranges from the bombastic to the maudlin. On the other hand, Crane's *The Bridge*, one of the few modern poems worth reading more than once, was condemned by criticism almost before it was published. The critics said such things as American culture cannot afford such a subject, and other nonsense having nothing to do with poetry.

The matter of "understanding" poetry is too important to pass by here; and I would like to use an incident involving myself to make my point clear. Just at the time when I had published my first poems in a good literary magazine, and was highly elated at this recognition, I had to take an examination in "poetry comprehension." The examination was given in a school for librarians and was part of a very serious training program which would certify me to become a librarian. On the examination as a whole I received one of the best marks; in poetry comprehension I received the lowest. (Imagine what a book reviewer could do with that statement!) I was the only member of the class interested in writing poetry and the only one who read it almost to the exclusion of everything else. But I failed to comprehend poetry. I confess that I mention this incident with a certain glee. What was it I did not comprehend about poetry which was so simple to people who accepted poetry much as they did bibliography or cataloguing—a subject to be mastered cold? Obviously I was not reading poetry the way my classmates were. All of them did fine and comprehended in a split second, while I, the poet in their midst, went blank before the poems on the examination sheet.

That was many years ago and I still have not learned to comprehend a poem in the accepted manner. My students know—they are reared on understanding poetry, and hate it—and even some of the poets of my acquaintance are adept in this art. I look upon them with a fishy eye but I certainly do not begrudge them this skill or hobby, or whatever you want to call it. In my own case, I never think of reading a poem for what it "means" unless there is so little merit in the thing that there is nothing else to do with it. The examination-meaning of a poem is usually so obvious that it is hard to think about it at all. The opening period of *Paradise Lost* is one of the most extraordinary sentences ever written and worthy of the name of sublimity which Longinus gives to the creation in Genesis—what does it *mean*? It means that Milton has found the "poetry" of his immense theme, that he is caught up in the terror and splendor of his vision, which exists only in his expression of it. There is no way to say what these lines mean except by reciting them. They mean what they mean; they are their own meaning. The modern critic reads a poem backwards; he does not want to know whether the vision is achieved or how well; he wants to know what went into the pudding. He wants recipes. And how desperately the critic wants the student to believe what an awesome thing it is to compose a poem.

There is one more bit of private information I want to mention. Off and on for ten years I have been editing literary magazines of poetry and criticism. During this period I have had letters from nearly every living poet of note commending my judgment in the poems I have published. I am not sure what these commendations mean, but I take them at their face value; I weigh them against my distaste for poetry comprehension, and wonder. Can one be a good judge of poetry and a bad comprehender? Precisely. For the act of judgment in reading a poem not only precedes but encompasses comprehension (modern criticism to the contrary). Comprehension is documentation, nothing else. It is the learned appreciation of art and has only as much relation to the poem as the Appendix has to a history book. This is the way poetry is taught and criticized today, by internal documentation, and it is no wonder that the sense of judgment has atrophied. Once in a while, of course, documentation, or what is called analysis, is necessary, as when a painter says to the dealer, "Excuse me, sir, you have hung my picture upside down." This is when the critic pops up and begins to direct the traffic.

Modern Criticism is founded on a premise which I believe to be a profound fallacy. It commits this error consistently: it takes the words of a poem as words found in the dictionary, in the encylopedia, and more likely in *The Encyclopedia of Social Science*. Even if criticism advances some high-sounding concept such as "the auditory imagination," it still tries to keep poetry within the language, even in a literal sense. But poetry cannot be found in any dictionary; it is language in a state of becoming, language trying to escape its condition. Most poetry fails in this high venture.

The relations between the official language, the poetic language of a certain time and place, and the individual poet's language are purely diplomatic. The good poet's language is always at the periphery of the existent languages of his own tongue, from the vulgar dialects to the King's English. Language is his element and he moves through it in every dimension, apart from the dictionary meanings and the semantics of words. The poet uses language plastically, not semantically. The critic will devil you with principles like connotation and association and will even find poems to prove his case. If he can't find them, he will order them from the factory. Ambiguity is one of the favorite principles of the modern critic, but this one has backfired rather badly, killing quite a few graduate students. The critic sees the poem through the dictionary, as if the poet had taken the twenty-three definitions of *green* and used them all at once. But the way the poet uses *green* does not appear in any dictionary. (Incidentally, someone should analyze the dictionary, if analysis is the order of the day. The dictionary is a kind of large bad poem, or rather a fine piece of science fiction. And the card catalogue of the library is surely the most romantic epic of modern man. The greatest books defy classification completely. What is *Thus Spake Zarathustra?* Poetry, prose, philosophy, religion, cosmic science, business administration? Who knows?)

The same word used in a line of prose (and what is *prose?*) and in a line of poetry is two entirely different words, not even similar, except to the eye. Further, the same word used by two different poets becomes two different words. The meaning of the word depends on the poem in which it occurs, not on the dictionary or on *The Golden Bough*. It is in its degenerative phase that poetry moves into lexicography, into meaning that you can look up and find. It then becomes the poetry of verbalization, of wit, of cleverness, of cultural allusion, of metaphysical metaphor, and finally of philosophic abstraction, after which it dies. You will find this well illustrated in the modern anthology. Worse, you can trace this process in the writing of a dozen of the most prominent intellectual poets. A healthy poet uses the dictionary like a phone book; he looks up a number and then dials it; and that is only the beginning. The intellectual poet takes the number down, forgets that it leads somewhere, and begins to do the numerology of the Second Coming of the Messiah. This is known as the poetry of the Tradition, with a capital T.

"She utters senseless sounds, through fever of her love," says a Hindu poem describing the love of Krishna and Radha. It is these senseless sounds which are the "words" of poetry.

Ah, Sun-flower! weary of time,
Who countest the steps of the Sun, . . .

cries Blake in one of the most beautiful lyrics ever written. (I use the word *beautiful* although it is forbidden by modern criticism.) It is hard to explain to the critic that one of the key words of this poem is *Ah*! The letter *O* is the first letter of the poetic alphabet; *Ah* may well be the last. What sounds does Radha make? What is the meaning of *Ah*! If we knew we would not need poetry at all, for the poet does not use words in any sense already known. He uses words in spite of their meaning. Criticism always and necessarily talks about poetry in retrospect, in the language of recollection. But poetry itself projects into the unknown of language and of all experience.

Literature is always at a greater disadvantage than the other arts when it comes to criticism; it is simple for the critic to pretend that the poet's words are also his. In school all but the very brightest students are taken in by this shell game. A real test of critical ability is to have a critic criticize a work of music or a painting. Even Grove's *Dictionary* doesn't contain the musical equivalent for ambiguity. Eventually of course the critic would invent the terminology he wants, even if he had to hire Mortimer Adler to write a whole new *Syntopicon*.

Insofar as criticism is a branch of philosophy we should leave it alone. The poet and the poet-in-us-all have no business hanging around philosophy. But where criticism touches literature we must be on our guard. A criticism of concepts is the more pernicious because it atrophies the judgment and prevents the free play of opinion. Opinion is a mass prerogative, not a matter of personal fiat by some *soi-disant* Dr. Johnson. I admire endlessly the patience of the twentieth-century audience, considering what it has had to put up with in poetry and criticism. The intellectual critic considers its audience stupid and says so. I consider the audience polite to the exploding point. But the audience has contented itself with the quietest type of revenge known to literary man: it has refused to buy the books. The critic has retaliated by cramming the textbook with unreadable and dishonest prose and factory-made poetry and shoving it into the curriculum under the title of Contemporary Literature. The modern anthology is even worse, being only a sugar-coated textbook with photographs of the poets, all taken in 1935. In profile.

Perhaps philosophy would do well to take criticism back. Let us leave the esthetician in quiet to do whatever it is the esthetician does. As for the critic, let him get back to the lost art of judgment, if indeed it is an art and not just an instinct. The business of criticism is discrimination, pure and simple. Analysis belongs to science and to psychology, which is practically a science. It has nothing to do with literature, nothing to do with literary discrimination, nothing to do with the use of poetry. I am exaggerating a little but not much. An honest nonconceptual critic will sometimes analyze a poem, as certain professors used to do in Spain when the peasants came to have a poem of Lorca's interpreted. But this was an act of kindness, not a philosophical *tour de force*. The professional critic depends heavily on the kind of poem which is said to have various "levels" of meaning. Of course there are such poems and some fine ones, but they are in no wise a touchstone of art. The true critic, it seems to me, has an obligation to affirmative judgment; I would go so far as to say that we cannot get a true work of criticism which has a coil of negative emotion lying at the bottom of it. A work of criticism may become a work of art only when the critic is in love with his subject and is carried away by it, exactly as the poet is carried away by his. Think of poor A. E. Housman, who spent his critical life gnawing away at the dreary Latin poet Manilius, whom Housman himself looked down upon. To what end? Housman admired Propertius, not Manilius; what perversion of intellect drove him to spend thirty years on a poet who meant nothing to him?

The chances of relegating criticism to its proper place in the scale of things, as the most tentative and least tried of the arts, are small at the moment. There is already a generation of critics in America and in England (the Anglo-Saxon countries) trained in the special highfalutin of analytical criticism. If they were only a literary faction it would do no harm, but a large number of them are teachers of literature who spread the gospel of impersonality, depersonalization, objectivity, and so forth. They write criticism themselves and even teach classes called "creative." They are the backbone of the big literary quarterlies, the liberal weeklies and even the commercialized book review of the Sunday papers. In short, they are in office. Judgment, the total and immediate perception of a work of art, is ruled out of court. Taste is unknown. An artificial demand has been created for criticism but the natural demand for poetry is nowhere encouraged, except where the poet meets the critic on the critic's terms. Criticism has set up a soundproof wall between poetry and the audience. It keeps poetry incommunicado and talks to its audience only through the *gobble-gobble* of critical prose. And it invents reasons for acting as interpreter. We seem to have forgotten that the reader in Dante's age knew what Dante was referring to; the poetry of Dante was in the language of the newspaper of his time—had there been one. Homer's audience didn't have to consult Bulfinch's *Age of Fable* to find out what Homer meant. We in the twentieth century seem to think that those Greek and Italian audiences must have been almost as learned as Sir James Frazer; we seem to accept the fact that we cannot understand the poet unless someone tells us what he means. Thus has poetry become a part of criticism and a phase of pedagogy.

The critic begins with the premise that the audience does not understand. This is the premise that keeps him in business. But the concept of understanding does not apply in the first place; and secondly, the audience "receptivity" is the only valid receptivity there is. There is indeed a kind of poetry that needs rehearsal with the audience before it can be performed, but this is by no means the best poetry. In any case, poetry is for the audience to judge. The word *audience* is anathema to the modern critic and signifies in his mind popular art and a menacing mob or rabble. The critic prefers his own hand-picked audience of critical trainees and a few students who are on the road to criticism. How puzzled all those critics were when hundreds and thousands of completely uninformed students and even just ordinary people with two ears flocked to hear Dylan Thomas. What had happened!

But the critics had their inning, too. The largest gathering so far recorded to come to hear a poet-critic came to hear T. S. Eliot in Minneapolis. Of course he was not reading poetry; he was talking about the "Frontiers of Criticism." Right on the frontier. So where

Thomas had his thousands, Eliot had his ten thousands. Minnesota has changed since the days of Sinclair Lewis, if it can muster a criticism audience the size of a regiment. Eliot ended the lecture with the nervous remark that maybe criticism has become "too brilliant" in our time, but the speaker left no one in doubt as to the role of the critic, to elucidate poems and to *correct* taste.

Culture poetry, which is what modern poetry is, can be precisely described in every way. We know its forms, its psychology, its subject matter, and even its aims. It has a definite and limited number of themes, a prescribed method of composition, as well as a set formula for comprehension. Under the bad and obscurantist writing of criticism and its textbooks, under the weird confusion of the anthology, we find everything laid out neatly. The atmosphere of modern poetry is that of the hospital, of criticism that of the dissecting room. The patient is never expected to recover.

If we posit two types of poetry, culture poetry and just *poetry*, the first type is that which attempts to explain culture. It can do this in the manner of the Metaphysical poets, who were troubled by scientific knowledge and who wished to compete with science; by rewriting history according to a plan; by tracing the rise and fall of a particular belief, and so forth. Culture poetry is always didactic, as indeed most modern poetry is. It is a means to an end, not an end, like art. Culture poetry is poetry in reverse; it dives back into the historical situation, into culture, instead of flowering from it. And there it remains to enrich the ground for criticism.

It is true that anything can be turned into poetry, even Culture (horrid word). But who has written the poetry of "culture"? Certainly no one in our time, unless Rimbaud. There are passages in Ezra Pound which come close to the "poetry" of money and also the poetry of Mandarin civilization; but on the whole the *Cantos* form a dreary epic of history which never gets off the ground. Sometimes I begin a course in modern poetry with the poem called *"Une Charogne"* by Baudelaire, one of the most vicious of "modern" poems and a true culture poem. Baudelaire attacks the Romantic conception of love (for the culture poet is forever on the attack). He takes his girl to view a female corpse, a carrion lying in a lascivious position and being eaten by maggots. "And that is what is in store for you," observes the poet to his beloved.

> *Et pourtant vous serez semblable à cette ordure,*
>   *A cette horrible infection,*
> *Etoile de mes yeux,* . . .
> And you too shall be like this filthy excrement,
>   This horrible infection,
> Star of my eyes, . . .

The word *ordure* is particularly juicy. In the preface to his poems Baudelaire announces that Paris is a center radiating "universal stupidity." Stupidity is one of the favorite words of culture poets, for modern poetry prides itself on its intelligence, if nothing else. How intelligent this poetry really is, is another question.

Baudelaire's poem and Yeats' "The Second Coming" seem to me two of the best examples of modern cultural or criticism poetry. In his poem Yeats predicts the coming of the Antichrist and even dates it.

> Surely the Second Coming is at hand.
> The Second Coming! Hardly are those words out
> When a vast image out of *Spiritus Mundi*
> Troubles my sight: . . .

It is one of the stagiest of Yeats' poems, about a third of which are culture poetry. But "The Second Coming" is one of the favorites of the age, as far as *correct* taste goes, and it is fine to *elucidate* in a classroom. Yeats was a poet of genius who wandered into the culture camp and never got out. People who have not been indoctrinated with modern criticism have no difficulty discriminating between "The Second Coming" or "Byzantium," famous textbook pieces, and something like "Easter 1916," in which Yeats finds the poetry of modern Ireland. But of course if we used literary discrimination instead of intellectual analysis we would have to lop off quite a few boughs from the sacred oak of culture.

Modern poetry outside English is somehow less pretentious about its use of culture, with the exception of a few poets like Valéry. One can see a simplicity, even in translations, in the works of such poets as

Rilke, Lorca, or Cavafy, who have as much to say about the past and its mythology as Pound, Eliot, and Yeats. Cavafy, the twentieth-century Greek poet, who in some respects is the first poet of our age, has more to say about the past than even the famous Pound-Eliot-Yeats triumvirate, but he never forgets that he is a poet and not a sociologist.

In the religion of modern poetry the Trinity is composed of Pound, Eliot, and Yeats. All three men are provincials, the two Americans being Europeans by adoption. Cultural expatriation is a deeper thing than taking up residence abroad. The most salient act of literary sabotage committed by Pound and Eliot has been their immolation of Walt Whitman. Whitman is the only American poet we have ever produced who deserves the name of greatness, if we must use such an undiscriminating word as great. The shameful and dishonest denigration of Whitman alone should reduce the critical authority of Eliot and Pound to zero, and eventually will. The "Song of Myself" is known throughout the world, but not in the United States, as one of the chief poems of world literature. It is more than that; it is one of the most inspired works of art of man. But modern criticism looks the other way, just as it is inclined to do with Shakespeare. The only nice thing Pound can find to say about Whitman's poetry is that it is not in iambic pentameter. Eliot cannot even say that. Whitman does not fit into the culture program and must be ruled out. One of the reasons why Eliot calls D. H. Lawrence *ignorant* must be Lawrence's honest love and admiration for Whitman. A really cultured poet can't see anything in Whitman but an embarrassing use of grade-school French.

What we call modern poetry is in reality a brief moment in twentieth-century literature, buttressed by a few godfatherly names like Baudelaire and John Donne. The ruling intellectuals themselves are wary of the word *modern* and put it in quotation marks. They do not want to be left behind when the century is over. But modern poetry, with or without quotes, is an actual thing, a small body of poetry and criticism written circa 1915–25. This was the decade that saw the publication of "Prufrock," Valéry's *La Jeune Parque*, Eliot's *The Sacred Wood*, *The Waste Land*, Pound's *Mauberley*, Fenollosa's essay on the Chinese written character, Yeats' *The Tower*, Laforgue's *Derniers Vers*,

THE CRITIC IN SPITE OF HIMSELF

Stevens' *Harmonium*, Cummings' *Tulips and Chimneys*, Marianne Moore's *Observations*, Hulme's *Speculations*, Joyce's *Ulysses*, Richards' *The Meaning of Meaning*, Ernest Jones' *Essays in Applied Psycho-Analysis*, and Pound's *A Draft of XVI Cantos*. Herein lies the whole canon of modern poetry or a fine glimpse of it, and these are the works that dominate literary thinking even today. Yet during the same period were published such works as the poems of Hopkins, William Carlos Williams, D. H. Lawrence, A. E. Housman, Rilke's *Duino Elegies* and *The Sonnets to Orpheus*, Wilfred Owen, and Thomas Hardy. The intellectuals are heavier in criticism; the non-intellectuals, however, produced such prose as Williams' *In the American Grain* and Lawrence's *Studies in Classic American Literature*, which will probably be read long after the *Speculations* of T. E. Hulme, and *The Sacred Wood*, or so I hope.

This is not to say that there were two camps or teams of poetry circa 1915–25 such as Classicists and Romantics, although the intellectual faction calls itself "classical," with characteristic immodesty. But in the first list there is a definite factionalism, the formation of schools, manifestoes, programs of action, and the eventual election to all the cultural boards and committees which reach down through literary society from the royal academies to the Midwestern college town. We cannot imagine D. H. Lawrence at an international culture meet, nor the shy proud Rilke. When Rilke finally became famous in Paris, the French were very disappointed in his salon behavior. He didn't act in the least like the Messiah of intellect or what the sociologist calls in his unbeautiful patois, a "culture hero."

Changes of taste are brought about by critics. The history of art is brought about by critics, while art itself goes on at an entirely different tangent from criticism. It is not the public that changes taste; the public is the victim of it, as much in literature as in millinery. A healthy literary audience comes into view when criticism is removed. Painting is flourishing today because of the relative absence of art criticism and the healthy exercise of judgment. There is a huge population of amateur painters, people who do not aspire to become famous artists but who love to paint. This is the true audience for the dedicated painter. The same is true of contemporary music. But there is no comparable audience of poets, only a grim little army of poet-critics grinding out mean little stanzas under the gooseneck lamp. And for every poem there are ten critics poised over their typewriters, waiting.

What is the remedy against criticism? There isn't any except the creation of new poems which will divert attention away from intellectualism and toward the work of art itself. Nonparticipation is the only rule; no criticism against criticism will do much good, even the kind I am presenting here. We must create a stoppage of meaningless critical work, simply by ignoring it. And we must not force new poems. If poetry is again to grow it must choose its own time. The condition of poetry in America today is similar to that in Russia; the creative spirit is not free; it is dictated to from above. Russia has government control of poetry; we have official criticism at the helm which determines the standards of work, directs the organs of expression, controls the fellowship foundations, and even reaches into the curricula of schools. The only opposition to this state of affairs comes from a self-styled literary Underground. But this Underground plays directly into the hands of the critical police of letters, being itself only a negative version of culture poetry. It is mostly the form of small life found under stones. But at least it is alive. Elsewhere, whatever real poetic talent is available is probably unaffiliated and hides in stunned silence writing its books.

It is necessary to demolish the great empty Bastille of criticism, if only as a symbol of rebellion against it. Our whole conception of literature is by now so overgrown with notions of society, history, religion, and government that we are in a fair way to smother our writers. I do not want to go into the grisly recitation of the lives and deaths of our modern poets, the suicides, alcoholics, and mental cases, except to say that there is a connection between these tragedies and intellectualism. The textbook explanation will give you an equation of poet-versus-society, poet-in-the-industrial-world, poet-and-Original-Sin, or some such thing. I do not agree, but think rather the equation should be poet-versus-criticism, poet-versus-intellectualism. The intellectual tries and sometimes succeeds in converting his own sociological hysteria into what he is pleased to call a mask. He "depersonalizes" so completely that he escapes even himself. The honest poet has no such defenses and is made a prey to the bombardment of ideas from all sides. Unless he has a strong psychic constitution he will sooner or later crumple under the pressures of Criticism. The intellectual will fortify himself behind the barricades of Tradition and Orthodoxy; the honest poet will find no asylum. The intellectual considers his "exile" at an end when he has established himself in society, at the top. The honest poet knows that he is a member of no society, past, present, or future. It is a sad thing to see poets dissipating their talents in culture criticism and city planning. With what a sublime disgust Rimbaud turned his back on all that and marched off into Abyssinia. Rather a slave trader than an intellectual; that was his message. It was not society he spat on; it was modern poetry.

It has taken me twenty years to break away completely from modern poetry and modern criticism, which I consider to be one and the same thing. Being a teacher has helped me immeasurably to see how pernicious this poetry and criticism really are and how destructive they have been to poetry and the faculty of judging poetry. Being an editor has helped me see what has happened to the craft of writing in our time, to witness the essential dishonesty of the modern critic, the dearth of taste, the misuse of understanding as a criterion of appreciation, the shameful muzzling of the audience, and the seizure of poetry by culture theorists. If this sounds like a new evangelism, I apologize, but I look at it that way. Actually, I wrote down all these views as long ago as fifteen years. That was before I had read criticism seriously or become involved in criticism myself. In the interim, my taste has been "corrected" by the intellectuals several times, and indeed they have done their best to educate me. During the notorious Bollingen Prize incident in which a jury of poets and critics gave this famous award to the *Pisan Cantos*, I was almost nudged into voting for Pound myself. Giving that honor to Pound was an act of intellectual arrogance which has no parallel in literary history. Several of the poet-critics in the group made it quite clear to me that they had no use for Pound or the *Cantos* but that they were honoring the *skill* of his controversial book. Eliot had popularized the term *autotelic*, which made it possible for critics to ignore the views of the poet, however unsavory, while commending the technique. Thus, the intellectual critic has it both ways: he can dictate to society about its ills and he can regard a poem as a pure exercise of language, at his convenience. It is another major paradox in modern criticism, bridged in this case by flimsy concepts having to do with change of "sensibility," etc. No scholar has been able to reconcile the fundamental contradictions in Eliot's criticism, any more than one can reconcile Pound's Confucianism with his Fascism.

The practice of criticism is today universal. Taking Western literature as a whole in the twentieth century, the dominant poetry is English; it is not French or German or anything else. Even in those parts of the Orient where there is a contemporary literature of any kind, the dominant poetry is English. Extraordinary as it sounds, this is true in India and in Japan. I have been told by Japanese poets that the most influential poet in Japan today is—T. S. Eliot! This dominant English poetry, however, is at bottom American, or rather the poetry of certain Americans of the little moment of 1915–25: Pound, Eliot, Cummings, Stevens, Tate, and others. The combined poetry and criticism of these men, of this brief period, constitute what we know as Modern Poetry and Modern Criticism. The approach of this poetry is cultural, even sociological, and embodies one or another world-view of art, of esthetics, of politics, of history, and of the ethical bases of human society—all the mistaken approaches to the art of poetry, in other words.

In taking control of the cultural situation the poet-critic has had to accomplish two almost insuperable aims. The first was the neutralization of judgment. By relegating the natural faculty of judgment to the lowest rung of the critical scale of things, he has been able to usurp judgment and arrogate it to himself. The "correction of taste" has superseded the normal, free exercise of taste by the public. Normal opposition to works like *The Waste Land* and the *Cantos* of Pound was defeated as long ago as a generation; and constant reinforcement of the so-called "classical" position has prevented any new voicing of opinion. The disappearance of the poetry audience is a direct consequence of this maneuver. In place of a poetry audience we have today a criticism audience. The actual poetry audience, which is potentially as large as the population itself, has had to betake itself to cellars where it can listen to poetry of some kind in an atmosphere of desperate spontaneity.

Criticism is always the latest and least reliable of the literary arts, the renegade and the spoiled brat of letters. Criticism has an almost congenital tendency to degenerate into something else, anything it can think of—psychology, esthetics, anthropology, politics, or theology. It is the true black sheep of the literary family. The modern phase of criticism encompasses all the "sciences" of culture, but there is virtually no *art* of literary criticism in the twentieth century. In espousing theory and divorcing judgment or discrimination, criticism has set itself a task which has nothing to do with poetry or the arts and everything to do with the misuse of art as an instrument of social value.

What then is the role of criticism? The answer is that *a good work of criticism is a work of art about another work of art*. Anything short of that is failure. I have made no reference to scholarship. I revere scholarship, but no scholar I ever heard of has made the claim that scholarship is art. We need good literary scholarship more than ever today, scholarship based upon honest judgment and not mere intellectual exercise. We may even need good estheticians, but this I cannot vouch for. But the critic who considers himself a man of letters should humble himself before literature and compose his essays in the same spirit of happy dedication as the poet or the novelist. Only the other day I received a new anthology textbook on the essay, half of which was devoted to chapters called "Mass Culture" and "High Culture." This is the way we are training our students—to be culture scientists, not writers.

The absence of good criticism today is a simple indication of the absence of the audience. The war waged against what modern criticism calls popular art has deprived literature of its only soil. There can be no refined art without popular art, even bad popular art. In the absence of popular and folk art and primitive art we get only an artificial hieratic art, art in the laboratory. Modern painting is a healthy art because it has brought into it all the elements of the folk, the primitive, and the popular. A good bit of the calligraphy of modern painting is based on the comic strip and the commercial poster. Modern poetry is a sickly and desiccated poetry because it has cut itself off from elements of daily life and has relied on sociological texts and specially approved classics. "Popular" in the minds of Pound, Eliot, and Yeats signifies debased, when it should signify the raw material for poetry.

In these remarks I have used the word "modern" in a sense which I hope will clarify it at long last. It is a synonym for "ideological" or "cultural" and it applies more to poetry, and the poetry circa 1915–25, than to painting or music or even fiction. It was during this period that Eliot and the "classicists" captured poetry through criticism and even tried to do the same with fiction! For in 1921 Eliot, as chief strategist, announced that the novel was over and done with. The novel, we were told, "ended with Flaubert and James." Of course he was using the word "novel" in some special intellectual sense and as a maneuver to establish James Joyce as the prototype of a new kind of novelist. Fortunately the maneuver failed and the novel was not killed off. It is only recently that criticism has moved in with all its forces to deal with fiction as it has dealt successfully with poetry. But it is too late. Poetry remains the only casualty of modern literature, but it is the most crucial casualty.

Having said all this, I might be expected to conclude with some words of advice to the poet and to the critic of good will, but I have said enough already. Quite obviously, poet and critic must draw apart, and beyond this I have no message. For poets to band together in groups is always fatal; history has a tendency to bury poets in threes. Poets venturesome enough to set up a "school" of their own only offer a large target for critical gunnery practice. Even the individual poet who commits himself to prose must have a care; the critic will always tackle the prose as an excuse to avoid committing himself about the poetry. Coleridge, who deserted poetry to become the father of modern criticism, is the ideal of a dozen or more modern poets of talent who abandoned poetry for criticism. It is one of the literary tragedies of our time.

There is little hope of rescuing the critic who is already mired in ideology and culture. But it is the poet I have in mind when I point to the saurian prose of Eliot, the vulgarity of Pound's essays, and the narcissistic rhetoric of Yeats.

I think the poet will find, once he has turned his back on criticism, that his quarrel with "society" will evaporate. Imagine not having to write poems about the Just City or to make definitions of Culture or to fret like poor Baudelaire about reducing the traces of Original Sin. No more theology, no more economic systems, no more psychology of the depths, not even myth-making or the decline of the West! What a vacation for poetry! "But what else is there to write about?" cries the modern poet, dropping his *Explicator*. "You don't expect me to write about the birds and the bees, or flowers, or *people*! That's all been done, ages ago!"

Yeats speaks somewhere of the fascination of what's difficult, and we all agree, but add: the difficult isn't the only thing that's fascinating. We do not find the difficulties of modern poetry and modern criticism particularly *intelligent* difficulties. Why make a fetish of difficulty-for-difficulty's-sake? Is there no fascination for what's beautiful, or what's unknown, or what's innocent? Or are these things only the province of the "ignorant"?

TO ABOLISH CHILDREN

ᵀₕᵉ BETRAYAL IS an act of vengeance, obviously. But in an age of betrayal, when men of authority traduce their office and violate the trust placed in their hands, betrayal becomes the official morality. "Official morality" shortly becomes "public immorality"; whereupon the fabric of a society rots before one's eyes. In the years since the end of the Second World War, announced by the drop of the first Ultimate Weapon, the world has been stunned, horrified, and ultimately cajoled and won over to the official morality of America and its corollary of public immorality and anarchy. Hardly a leader, whether president, general, public relations man, professor, publisher, or poet, can be held to be honorable in his intentions. Everywhere lies the hidden premise and the calculated betrayal, the secret and chauvinistic lie.

To what end? Who is the betrayer, and why? Who are the betrayed? In a pyramidal society, a hierarchy, one would know the answers. But in a jungle there are no answers, only cries of victory or death. In the modern American jungle there are no answers.

Must America give birth to fascism? Or can it survive its pristine Constitution? Both issues seem doubtful. Can the economic motive live with the mass monster it has created? Can the poor white who has sacrificed his brain to television, or the poor Negro who loots a TV set from the store, ever again cross the line from somnambulism to wakeful joy? Can only the modern artist discover beauty in the twentieth century?

The entire world has become aware of the pervasiveness of American violence. The Americans were the last to discover it. This is as it should be. A betrayed husband is the last to know his situation. America is shocked at itself; someone has handed it a mirror. Instead of the young and handsome heir of all the ages, with his bathing-beauty consort, winners of Olympic Games, we see the soft and rotten killer (almost Hemingway style) with his call-girl WASP girl-friend, wearing a tiny crucifix between her scientifically measured bosoms. Wars are staged and televised on the battlefield; all sports are openly and avowedly big business; all books sell according to the amount of money deposited for advertising; countries are bought and sold in the stock market like cattle. Not that any of this is particularly new. What is new is that it is all now *public* knowledge. And what is awesome is that nobody cares. Everyone wants a share of the rot, the *faisandage*. Ours is a gamy culture from top to bottom. Books about the gaminess are best-sellers.

The goal of any writer or professor nowadays is to defend his—there is an old-fashioned word—honor. Can a writer write what he wants and in his manner? Can a teacher teach what he was hired to teach, in his own manner? Or must he give way to some form of blackmail from above or below, some Big Brother, who reinterprets his role for him. But we have heard enough of this structural mechanism from the time of Aldous Huxley, Orwell, McLuhan, and so forth.

At the bottom of the spectrum of betrayal are the "Movements," the pseudo-revolutionary insurrections without goals. The purest of these aim at simple theft and sabotage, such as occur during and after hurricanes. The more complicated are identified with civil rights and sex, freedom of drugs and pills of various forms, the right to unlimited travel vouchers and hospitalization. These are the heirs to the kingdom of Wall Street—the latest generation of betrayers and destroyers. This is the generation that uses the word Love as a synonym for Hate, that practices infantilism on a scale which has never been seen.

In between are the always duped Bourgeoisie, playing both ends against the middle. The bourgeois pays his children off to stay away, horrified at his mistake of educating these free-wheeling organisms equipped with electric guitars.

Possibly because the economic structure has reached the saturation point, the old order of social development is defunct. The pattern roughly used to be: immigrant (or settler), bourgeois, professional man, and artist (or patron). The child enacts the pattern in reverse: the young man or woman aspires to be artist *first*, deplor-

ing professionalism and education itself, condemning the standards
of safety of the bourgeois (while exploiting the material wealth of the
bourgeois exchequer), and eventually achieving the role of pseudo-
immigrant or "native." The Beats and Hippies are products of the
American aesthetic which has always preached disaffiliation and single combat with the forces of nature and of society. All American dissident movements tend to fall apart as soon as they are organized.
Each artist and pseudo-artist is his own Huckleberry Finn, a moral
expatriate. All of our best artists have been recluses of one kind or another, Melville, Faulkner, Hemingway, Cummings. The American
artist who does not shun the Center is suspect. The dissident, however, misunderstands the commitment of the artist and thinks of this
commitment only in terms of rebellion. The failure of the masses of
dissidents to evolve a politic is inherent in the national aesthetic of
individualism. And because the dissidents offer no organized threat to
the existing order, the existing order continues to consolidate its
gains and to ignore the threat of blackmail. The dissidents simply
supply additional dry rot to the cultural fabric. The burning and looting of slums signify the abysmal failure of imagination of the would-
be revolutionaries, who in fact have no goals. Their only goals are
pillage and revenge. The intellectual infantilism of the American radical makes him a figure of fun or of affection (or disaffection, as the
case may be). The most one can say of an Allen Ginsberg or a Timo-
thy Leary or a LeRoi Jones is that they are sincere. Children are always sincere.

Dissidence spread to the professoriat with the installation of
artists and writers on the campuses of the nation. (I am one of the
writer-professors who encouraged the moral-intellectual drop-out
philosophy for about a decade.) It was easy and sometimes necessary
to equate the mass university with other forms of the bureaucratic organism, but the vagueness of the issues involved and the failure to
clarify them simply added up to an abstract dissent. That a university
can be a democracy is patently absurd. The prattle about Free Speech
at Berkeley which thrilled the sophomores of all ages served simply to
debase whatever issues were at hand. Professors such as myself had
already fought this issue in the courts, and won. The campus rioters

were betraying these gains and taking a little private revenge on the side.

Vietnam itself is a falsified issue in the dissident "revolutions." The war is one of the most evil adventures in our history and its evil effects on the American character are incalculable, but the dissent is largely hypocritical. The "Underground" did not raise its voice against the Russian suppression of Hungary; it pursues a hands-off policy vis-à-vis Castro, even to the endorsement of antique Marxist slogans; it does not agitate for the overthrow of the last big brother of the Axis, Francisco Franco. On the contrary, the dissidents are to be found disporting themselves as frequently in Spain as in other exotic places, pursuing their careers and brushing up on the guitar. If it is laudable to avoid a draft, it is despicable to moralize about it.

The importation of mysticism and pseudo-mysticism into the West was an early stratagem of withdrawal from the known modes of communication. Mysticism is simultaneously an insult and a threat to communal behavior. Mystical evidence is by definition hearsay and inhibits communication. The conveniences of Zen and the Sutras to the dissidents (who were rarely if ever "believers") were that they opened the door to a counter-culture, one in which consciousness was superseded by unconsciousness, and provisioned their minds with a counter-literature. The literature of the Orient has never been and cannot be naturalized in the West, but the stratagem of the haiku, for instance, is supposed to put the quietus on Western poetry.

But neither poetry nor any of the other arts are essential to the existence and furtherance of the "Movement," as its members refer to it with typical mystification. The Beat poets were the only dissidents who maintained even diplomatic relations with poetry, but their poetry was openly propaganda for the Movement. The planks of the primitive dissident platform were simple and narcissistic: pot, homosexuality, and doom-prophecy, a tame and almost Baptist program. The poetry lacked ambition to rise above these themes.

Because poetry was meaningless as a vehicle or an aesthetic to the Movement, the early Beat poetry took to the drum and trumpet (nineteenth-century symbols of slave revolt). The mixture of jazz and verse laid the groundwork for the dissident aesthetic: volume of noise, mass hypnotism, pure size, all canceled out the possibility of dialogue or even thought. Nor did hatred of the electronic world preclude the utmost exploitation of the amplifier. Herewith began the invasion of parks.

The deliberate and mischievous inversion of modes (anything "adult" was proscribed) opened a Pandora's box for the child mentality which would have driven Lewis Carroll to suicide. The wave of male and female hysterics with guitars and brotherhood lyrics turned into a mass industry, on the one hand, and, on the other, a generation of *révoltés* without goals. The dissident music is verbal—both the music and the language descend to levels of callousness and insensitivity heretofore unknown—but the contents are those of the infant banging its fists on the highchair. It is an amazing phenomenon that this art, pitched directly to the level of the five- or six-year-old, should also be the level of the college student. (Dissidence appears to taper off thereafter.) Dissident sartorial fashion also abolishes distinctions between the sexes; the not very subtle transvestism of the dissident costume situates the Movement in the years prior to puberty. The burlesque Edwardianism of the Beatles expresses a nostalgia for the age of aristocracy and unlimited wealth.

Throughout human history the fine arts have provided the nexus between intuitional insight and civilized hindsight. That is what the arts have been for. But at times when intuition usurps the more wakeful states of mind, the arts plunge into the playpen and the cry of "immediacy" fills the air. Immediacy (as in D. H. Lawrence's "immediate present" or the Zen Now!) cripples hindsight and deliberation and prevents criteria from coming into existence. The failure of the Beat community to create poetry or any of the other arts is the most significant fact about the Movement. The hidden aesthetic premise of the Movement is that art is evil and must be hamstrung. Only states of unconsciousness are valid: drug-states, violence in bed and on the street, secret languages, political nihilism. These are the lingua franca of the Movement.

The drug agitprop of the Movement is widely misinterpreted. The Movement does not want drugs to be legalized for their own use; it wants to convert others to drugs. The drug propaganda is entirely evangelistic: take acid and you will be saved is the same message as Jesus Saves. The counter-violence of the police and the drug authorities is not so much opposed by the drug propagandists as it is courted. Legalization of the drugs would remove the thrill; without the official opposition and the melodrama of rebellion, LSD would be about as attractive as ice cream. But the uses of hallucinogenic materials also provide the necessary escape from creativity, from the action of writing a poem or painting a picture. If you have been to the artificial paradise, why write about it? There all the poems and paintings and music are readymade. There everyone is a Michelangelo, a Mozart, and a Shakespeare. The Movement maintains its puritanical aversion to alcohol ("Scotch is for fathers"), for alcohol confers only a temporary nonactivity upon the psyche. Hallucinogens show you the Promised Land.

As the students of medieval and Oriental mysticism know, only about one in a hundred thousand mystics has ever recorded his or her "trip" in even mildly impressive prose or poetry. The jottings of drug-takers are even less engaging. The taker of drugs may be trying to force the gates of the imagination, as perhaps was the case with Coleridge, but the mass movement for freedom of unconsciousness is clearly an aesthetic draft-dodge. The aesthetic arrogance of the drug user in any case lacks the substantiation of visible works. Pot-head, show me your book!

The nihilistic mind is a runaway horse. The Movement blots out literature without ever having cracked a book. Or rather, it burns all literature to the ground. The Movement cultivates cultural brainwashing; even advanced university students pretend to be ignorant of what they know. The fear of cultural infection and the demand for "immediacy" immunize their minds to any responses except to the latest fad or artifact. Their speech and writing degenerate into code (at the moment it is the underworld argot of the slum Negro, a genuine proletarian dialect for him which is, however, awkward and inapplicable to well-wishers and fellow-travelers). The Movement's adulation of the Negro slum-dweller as hero-victim leads it with characteristic naiveté to adopt his sublanguage as a generalized medium of communication. The very mystery of this language gives it credence: the terminology and metaphors of jazz, sex, drugs, double-speak, and revenge supply the necessary circuits of sympathy to the adolescent of the upper worlds. You dig?

The jazz put-on is a major form of cultural blackmail by the Movement. Anyone not "with" the jazz is a marked man. The hagiography of jazz is as immense as the Vatican Library. It is all phony, a conglomeration of the Music Corporation of America and the masses of delayed and permanent adolescents. Jazz is only a minor facet of modern folk music. What is beatified about jazz is that it is Negro. The Negro, as the most obvious victim of society since the latest massacre of the Jews, is thought to be universalizing about the human condition in jazz. Nothing could be further from reality. Negro jazz is—Negro jazz: charming, entertaining, hot, cool, abstract, evangelistic, white, black, blue, but never revolutionary. Negro jazz is masochistic, and that is precisely its failure and its appeal to the adolescent. What it lacks in content it makes up for in sentimentality, sexuality, and volume.

The blotting-out of language in jazz lyrics, the accommodation by skillful musical improvisers to cranked-out dollar-making stanzas, many of them half a century old, attests to the deliberate destruction of language as a medium. The nostalgia of the horn takes over; there is a vague reminiscence of language, unbelievably debased to begin with, whether it came from Tin Pan Alley or from Hollywood. The insistence on jazz, as taken over by the Movement, is the insistence on hysteria as a Way of Life. As such it appeals to the American joy in violence.

The Movement nominates Bob Dylan as great poet. The whining puerilities of this phenomenon are not to be taken lightly in the stock market or in the hearts of millions of children bursting with vitamins and cash. Is he the Leader?

The open release of violence is always a surprise to intellectuals. Rebellion without goals is the most fascinating spectacle of all. The Media intone with relentless stupidity: Why? Why? Congresses mourn. Whole cities are put to the torch while children dance and scream as at a jazz festival or an ice capade. Yet violence is inculcated by the elders and is exactly predictable. Violence is the answer to the question, Why?

It is quite natural and expectable in psycho-politics that Negro looters should espouse white genocide and Nazi anti-semitism. It is quite natural that WASP children in posh suburbs should play Nazi, instead of Cowboy and Indian. In a child society the only authentic emotion is hate. In Hippy language Hate is spelled Love; any four-letter word will suffice.

America is the child society *par excellence*, and possibly the only one ever politically arrived at. It is the society of all rights and no obligations, the society of deliberate wreckage and waste, the only society that ever raised gangsterism to the status of myth, and murder to the status of tragedy or politics. The American adulation of the child mentality leads to an industrialized hedonism, on the one hand, and a chauvinistic psychology of greed, on the other. In advertising, anyone over the age of twenty-one or twenty-five is portrayed as an idiot who has got behind in the science and commerce of rejuvenation. This "adult" is appealed to by an almost invisible Big Brother (Mad-Ave or the Executive in the White House) because the "adult" has made the mistake of legal and contractual obligation. Therefore he is an idiot. The costuming of the so-called radical population is a form of jeering: the beard is not only a red flag with certain flickering political messages; it is also the ultimate taunt at the man in the suit. Arson, looting, and murder are also gentle reminders to the fathers that the tumbrils are rolling. (In many of my creative writing classes the students sit in judgment on their parents and make specific judgments about which of the elders will be allowed to live. Confronted with the fact that the elders and the state are paying their way through education, the students snort and sneer at the stupidity of authorities.)

Humanities departments, notoriously the most deprived segment of the American university system, have been powerless to halt the invasion of the child psychosis in higher education. The effeminate backstairs aggressiveness of the Humanities gives way to the Creative Writing Gestalt. "Creative Writing" is to the Humanities as strychnine is to the horse. Any symptom of guilt discerned by the undergraduate on the part of its elders is parlayed into immediate sabotage—a sabotage which stops short of the curtailment of personal benefits, however. The gangsterism of the American youth mind makes it as easy a prey to the Marine recruiter as it does to the

Creative Writing instructor. The goals are not education but theft, generally theft of scholarships and undeserved preferment. As American literature heroizes the outlaw, so the outlaw student gains advantage over his more serious companions; the style of contempt, the "cool," determines to a large extent the amount of loot acquired and the length of absolution from the institutions which threaten his freedom of operation.

The cultivation of Youth with a capital Y has kept the growth of the American mind off balance since perhaps the early nineteenth century. The trashy frontier mythology, hand-to-hand combat, Horatio Alger, Alger Hiss, spy-psychology, advertising, Hell's Angels, Beats, Hippies, Beatles, dropouts, assassins, amnesiac mass murderers, pseudo-mystics lately from Kyoto or Benares, CIA, Black Muslims and Black Nazis, these are all part and parcel of the American dream of Youth. The dream was dreamed by the fathers, now on the proscribed list.

As Negro anti-semitism is Christian (the only political training the Negro was ever given was the flaming cross), so anti-adultism is American flag-waving in reverse. For this state of affairs there would seem to be no remedy. And indeed there is not. Should one suggest a program to slow down or stop the strangulation of American life by children, it might read:

1. Cut off all sources of economic supply to Youth except what they earn by physical or observable mental labor.

2. Deny all higher education except on absolute proof of ability. No student should be admitted to a college or university unless he or she has earned a scholarship or has otherwise demonstrated unusual ability. Public universities should be more stringent in this respect than private, rich universities (the private school is unsupervisable).

3. Deny free travel privileges to children. For instance, raise the age minimum of drivers' licenses to thirty or forty. Deny foreign travel except to those who have been granted the privilege from their school.

4. Set aside a large land area for all dissidents to reside in, with ingress but no egress. As children think the world is their personal property, give them their acre of personal property. Keep them there.

5. Discourage the cowardice and intimidation of parents and "authorities" by re-educating them to the nature of the Yahoo. Encourage construction of housing, especially suburban housing, to delimit or exclude the child, and to suit the needs and requirements of adults.

6. Disenfranchise those who reject military service, male and female. Why does conscription legislation apply only to male Youth?

7. Abolish the child. Deliberate the intelligent society in which the infant is loved and cared for and controlled until he is ready to be shipped to a place of education, should he be worthy. Consider two types of human beings: the infant and the adult. Destroy all concepts of the adolescent.

Whereupon his "literature" will wither away, his "music," his drugs, his revolutions and murders, his terrorism of everything he lacks the understanding and knowledge to comprehend.

The power-shift lies in this direction. Man is an aesthetic animal. His greatest works are slashed to ribbons by "youth" and will continue to be until Grown Man relinquishes his image of the advertised profile of Youth. As long as Grown Man apes Youth, he will remain the victim of his seed.

The American adult must battle "youth" to the death. "Youth" is a figment of the American imagination which is destroying America itself.

TO REVIVE ANARCHISM

℟ BEFORE A presidential election, a gentleman from the Fund for the Republic asked me for an interview. He was gathering opinions about the coming presidential contest and wanted the reaction of a poet or two. My first thought was to beg off. My second was to tell a white lie and give him the name of one of the two candidates. My third thought was to tell him the truth. So we made a date for the interview.

It is not easy to express your honest views to a stranger, especially if your political ideas happen to be of an unknown or unpopular variety. I wanted very much not to be set down in my visitor's mind as a crackpot or a "fool poet." He had been a Washington correspondent and was a man of quick perception, charm, and great knowledge of politics (compared with mine, certainly). I mumbled and bumbled a good bit before I got out what I wanted to say. What I told him finally was that I had no choice of candidates, that I do not vote (except on local matters), that I am opposed to voting under the "two"-party system, and that I even attempt to spread a no-voting propaganda among my friends and students. After which I tried to make some joke, such as "Pass the hemlock."

I had a distinct impression that my position, or lack of it, was quite familiar to my visitor. The word *anarchism* did not come up in the conversation, but we managed to discuss it without naming it. There were quotes from me out of Thoreau and mentions of the *Catholic Worker*, which I have read for many years. It was a fairly tame, academic talk, and we parted satisfied and friendly.

As a teacher and writer, I have become increasingly aware in recent years of the spread of anarchist thought among the rising generation. They do not call it by that name or any names; they do not philosophize about the State of Nonviolence or Disaffiliation, but the interest is unmistakably there. The Beat movement symbolizes one extreme of youthful anger against the failure of modern society and government to keep peace among men. The Negro equality movement symbolizes a more dramatic failure of society and government to give the citizen his due. Throughout the world, the human right of insubordination against industrial society, colonialism, and militarism and against the entire cult of the Western Tradition (religious, sexual, aesthetic) is making itself felt in a thousand ways. The governments are losing their young. The lifeblood of history is flowing away from the centers of force. Patriotism is having its long-awaited nervous breakdown.

And not only the young. The generation of the total war is also abandoning the conventional political thinking of the past, Left, Right, and Liberal, and is returning to the example of individual moral force, as the world has so far known it through Thoreau, Whitman, Tolstoy, Kropotkin, and Gandhi.

At present we are going through the stage of withdrawal from the old political psychologies of organized governments. And we are witnessing the beginnings of successful passive resistance movements in America and abroad. But no appeal has yet been made to the vast American middle class, the majority class, to detach itself from our competitive industrial insanity. It is indeed our industrial way of life that lends sanction to militarism and colonialism, Preparedness and suppression of human rights. Our enemy, strange as it may sound to American ears, is the Standard of Living. We worship at the altar of the White Rhinoceros, the American kitchen. Standard of Living is the holy of holies in whose name every other evil is committed. To lower this standard or to equalize it among the peoples of the world is our greatest need. And the first step is to disassociate ourselves from the industrial-scientific madness which rules our lives twenty-four hours a day.

The best government, the anarchists tell us, is the least governing. The worst government is the highly organized and centralized state, such as Franco's Spain or the USSR. The present tendency of the United States toward greater organization and centralization is a peril to every democratic freedom we know. We are drifting toward a

totally organized state which is eventually cemented by a secret police, a standing army, an industrial-scientific aristocracy, and a propaganda and communications machine which lies at the very heart of
government. The present competitive mania between Russia and the
United States in "science" opens the way in our country for every
breed of political opportunism. Whether the Eisenhower "diplomatic" Cold War changes into Kennedy's "cultural" Cold War will
make little difference to the basic sense of hostility to which the
central government is committed. The American people have lost
the choice of a peaceful alternative. The switchboard will tell us what
to do.

My central point of reference is Gandhi, perhaps the most extraordinary man our age has produced. We are today experiencing
the effects of Oriental ideas on our lives to an unprecedented degree.
In Gandhi, for instance, we are presented with a new political psychology which is quite foreign to our practical Western minds, as
when he says: "It is against my nature to prearrange." Or more striking, when he says of the law of nonviolent resistance "that it is possible for a single individual to defy the whole might of an unjust empire
to save his honor, his religion, his soul, and lay the foundation for
that empire's fall or regeneration. . . . " Gandhi's belief in the power
of right action (Truth) to prevent violence was demonstrated in his
lifetime a thousand times over; this is a form of political behavior
which is only now beginning to make its way in the West.

Gandhi, of course, was not a provincial Hindu but one who drew
on the entire tradition of the literature of peaceful action, mystical
and secular. One of his earliest works was a translation of Plato's *Apology* into Gujarati, a bitter irony when we remember Gandhi's own
death. He also translated John Ruskin's *Unto This Last*, essays in what
Ruskin called First Principles of Political Economy, and of course he
was deeply influenced by Thoreau and Tolstoy. The expression "the
moral equivalent of war" he took from William James. But the fundamentals of nonviolence, noncooperation, and nonresistance are native to the Hindu world. *Dharma*, for instance, is the concept of
moral pressure applied to an offending party through sufferings to
yourself. To sit *dharma* is to sit mourning. Gandhi's application of

dharma against British military and legal force constituted a one-man revolution against authority and resulted in the greatest awakening of a nation in modern history. His results range from the abolition of the worst superstitions of his religion, such as untouchability, to the equalization of the rights of Hindus and other dark peoples of South Africa and to national independence itself, a fantastic series of accomplishments almost incomprehensible to the Western mind. The West has so far produced no peaceful revolutionaries of the stature of Gandhi, even including Tolstoy, Godwin, or Kropotkin. The gropings of William James toward such a solution as Gandhi's illustrate the dilemma of the American mind with its predominant images of military force.

James published his pamphlet *The Moral Equivalent of War* in 1910. The work makes rather horrifying apologies to the military and to scientific progress; yet the general drift is impressive. "Pacifists ought to enter more deeply into the aesthetical and ethical point of view of their opponents," says James. "So long as anti-militarists propose no substitute for war's disciplinary function, no *moral equivalent* of war . . . they fail to realize the full inwardness of the situation. The duties, penalties, and sanctions pictured in the utopias they paint are all too weak and tame to touch the military-minded." James assumes that Western pacifism has no language of communication with our society at large, which is aggressive and ultimately militaristic. In rather quaint psychology he seeks for some motive for human action which is as "thrilling" (to use his word) as bloodshed. Puritanically, he objects to a mere peace economy on the ground that it may become no more than a "pleasure-economy." "Martial discipline" in peace is therefore a necessity. He would have young men "make war" upon nature—the typical Western fallacy that we know so well from our scientists; he would send youth to the "coal and iron mines, to freight trains, to fishing fleets in December, to dish-washing, clothes-washing, and window-washing," and so forth. Here we see the cautious New Englander of the upper crust to whom dish-washing is almost as much of an epic experience as the charge of the Light Brigade. But at bottom he is right. "The martial type of character can be bred without war," says James. And he ends his essay with the pathetic statement that Fear is indeed great but Fear is not "the only stimulus known for awakening the higher ranges of man's spiritual energy.

James probably supplied no more for Gandhi than the wonderful catchphrase "the moral equivalent of war." It was in an obscure work of Ruskin's that Gandhi found the outline of a practical philosophy. He reduced Ruskin's message in *Unto This Last* to three principles:

(1) that the good of the individual is contained in the good of all;

(2) that a lawyer's work has the same value as the barber's inasmuch as all have the same right of earning their livelihood from their work; and

(3) that a life of labor, i.e., the life of the tiller of the soil and the handicraftsman, is the life worth living.

Gandhi says: "The first of these I knew. The second I had dimly realized. The third had never occurred to me. *Unto This Last* made it as clear as day to me that the second and the third were contained in the first. I arose with the dawn, ready to reduce these principles to practice."

The usual objection to Gandhi's ideas is that they are "Oriental" and do not apply to life in the West, that the conditions under which Gandhi operated in the Transvaal and in India cannot possibly apply to civilized Europe and America. The West has a good deal of fear and loathing for this black little Hindu fakir, as Winston Churchill so elegantly called him. And the more aristocratic Hindus themselves, for instance Tagore the Bengali poet, fought Gandhi at many crucial points. Tagore opposed the reintroduction of the spinning wheel, the key to a national economy; he opposed the burning of foreign cloth, which Gandhi advocated as a method of breaking European economic slavery. Gandhi plunged to the heart of the matter when he told Tagore, "I do not draw a . . . distinction between economics and ethics. Economics that hurt the moral well-being of an individual or a nation are immoral. . . . " Tagore eventually understood and surrendered the knighthood which the Crown had bestowed upon him.

There is a great deal of extremism in Gandhi's philosophy which the West will probably never be able to swallow. His asceticism, his puritanism, his almost violent hatred for the gains of science, extending even to the science of medicine, are things we cannot appreciate. "A multiplicity of hospitals is no test of civilization; it is rather a symptom of decay," said Gandhi, sounding much like a modern poet. Gandhi's covering his belly with a band of raw earth as a cure for dysentery or constipation seems wholly irrational to us. And yet we cannot dismiss his principle of the nexus between science, government, and morality. In the West we are only beginning to examine the irresponsibility of Science, the loading of young minds with scientific and technological nonsense, the consequences of which we learn only when it is too late.

In rearing an unarmed army to disengage India from European rule, Gandhi developed a program of discipline in which the participant took these vows: Truthfulness (which is difficult to explain in Western psychology, though it closely resembles our Know Thyself); Nonviolence (which is a synonym for Soul-Force); Celibacy; Control of the Palate; Non-Thieving; Nonpossession; Fearlessness; and *Swadeshi* (encouragement of Home Industry). Most of these vows fall within the scope of our own traditional religions in one form or another. The one that is foreign to us and that may be of the utmost importance in the West is *Swadeshi*, the encouragement of home industries. *Swadeshi*, in fact, may be the nexus between Gandhism and the West.

The East is especially distinguished from the West in its attitude toward the natural world. The Easterner tends to regard himself as part of nature and of the cosmos. (In our view this is considered Fatalism.) The Westerner tends to regard himself as the enemy of nature. We speak of the *conquest* of space or of new lands; we *subdue* the desert and the frontier; we *wipe out* disease. The Oriental, broadly speaking, does not feel combative with the outer world; rather, he regards himself as part of a flux of life in which he is a single element. The Hebrew-Christian Bible begins with the injunction that man shall have *dominion* over every living thing, an idea quite exotic to the Oriental or to the poet like Walt Whitman who says he thinks he could turn and live with animals.

Swadeshi, home industry, does not have to do with government but with self-sustaining. When Gandhi hit upon the idea of the spin-

ning wheel he had his major revelation. It is staggering to think that
there was no one in India who knew how to spin (European civilization had destroyed the wheel) and that Gandhi had to search the
country from top to bottom to find some old lady who still knew
how. In the same way, an English woman had to search the country
from end to end to discover the Indian temple dances and revive
them. For it is true that mechanization destroys not only the national
economy but the arts of nations. Gandhi favored a break with machine industry, followed by a slow and considered assimilation of the
machine.

Here is a great lesson for the West. To slow down machine
progress, to impede science. To prevent industrialization from becoming the sole way of life. Thoreau says: "Shall we forever resign
the pleasure of construction to the carpenter?" He also says: "We are
in great haste to construct a magnetic telegraph from Maine to Texas;
but Maine and Texas, it may be, have nothing important to communicate." As far as we can tell, Maine and Texas still have nothing
important to communicate. In any event, communication in this
country is private property, as in Russia it is purely state property.
Communication is too valuable to industrial-scientific government to
be passed around indiscriminately. It is always the policeman, the in-
dustrialist, or the diplomat who controls the wires from Maine to
Texas.

True communication is a phenomenon having nothing to do with
newspapers, P.A. systems, universal network control, and radar
bouncing off the moon. The words of Gandhi were communicated
largely by word of mouth throughout India and across the barriers of
about twenty languages. Whereas in America it is virtually impossible
to find out what is going on in Cuba or in the Congo or in any other
place. What is called news in America and probably in Europe as well
is what is left of the truth after Communications has masterminded
the facts. The very term *artist* in the West has come to mean simply a
man who tells the truth. Communications also has the function of
controlling the moods of the people. Disaster is the bread and butter
of the advertiser, newspaper man, broadcaster, and public relations
expert. Little wonder that the Russian ruler visiting the United States
had to have a standing army of bodyguards and Secret Service men to

keep him from being assassinated. How much better off we would be if everyone boycotted the newspaper, television, advertising, radio, and all other self-styled media of communication.

Any gradual and immediate diminution of our involvement with the industrial system, on any level, would have a direct effect on the peace and well-being of our people. To remove ourselves from the world of competition is of paramount importance to the individual and to the nation. Competition is the terrible vice of modern society. Competition is the disease of the West and is the source of our violence. Nonviolence means non-competition. Democracy is a nonviolent form of government which is in peril of destruction by the competition of social and economic violence. *Ahimsa*, nonviolence, is a total force and a way of life. It has the power of Christian humility, upon which it is partly based. It is one of the noblest ideas advanced by modern man, and it is destined to spread throughout the world. It cannot be employed by governments because governments are by definition committed to violence. Nonviolence is not a prerogative of governments but of men, even of one man. One nonviolent man, like Gandhi or Christ, can change history. Governments can only keep history on the march. *Ahimsa* can stop history.

Gandhi went so far as to encourage nonviolence to the venomous snakes of India, which take a terrible toll of life every year. You had to overcome this perfectly natural fear of the reptiles. "The rule of not killing venomous reptiles," says Gandhi, "has been practiced for the most part at Phoenix, Tolstoy Farm, and Sabarmati. At each of these places we had to settle on waste lands. We have had, however, no loss of life occasioned by snakebite . . ." And he adds: "Even if it be a superstition to believe that complete immunity from harm for twenty-five years is not a fortuitous accident but a grace of God, I should still hug that superstition."

Without going into this deep and muddy question, we can learn something from this attitude of non-killing. To destroy the enemy was not an aim of Gandhi's; he must be deposed with dignity, without harm, even with honor. This is another concept foreign to Western thought and almost foreign to Christian practice. Non-humiliation of the enemy means to return him to his humanity after a defeat. Vinoba Bhave, the greatest living disciple of Gandhi, who travels throughout India asking for land for the peasantry from the great landlords and receiving it, says: "I desire to humiliate neither the rich nor the poor . . ." This is the opposite of communist expropriation or of capitalist competition. Without a complete bond of love between the giver and the recipient, there can be no permanent guarantee of peace between the possessor and the dispossessed.

The specific issues for which Gandhi fought are generally accomplished in India, but the deeper meaning of his philosophy and his *Politik* may provide an alternative to the ever-mounting states of crisis which are inherent in statesmanship or what passes under that name. Modern competitive society is incapable of keeping the peace. Modern government, committed to a society of competition, is incapable of keeping the peace. Peace can come about only through the nonviolent action of the people themselves. The present tendency of governments to dissolve their empires provides no guarantee of peace. On the contrary, the formation of new countries modeled upon American or Russian economic systems can do nothing but increase the danger of war. As modern government is contingent for its power upon science and industry, there would appear to be no hope of peace except by the voluntary effort of people to place themselves beyond the lure of science and industry. Standard of Living equals Preparedness. Preparedness is always related to scientific warfare. People must, especially in the scientifically advanced countries, act individually to weaken the power of the industrial-scientific oligarchy over their lives. We must "lower" the Standard of Living. We must learn how to sustain ourselves in peace and happiness beyond the influence of the Switchboard. We must do these things without violence and with the high sense of chivalry which Gandhi inculcated in his followers. Instead of class war and hatred as preached by the communists or industrial-scientific competition as preached by us, to survive we must behave nonviolently and in the spirit of love.

INDEX